AMERICAN ART

IN THE COLUMBUS MUSEUM

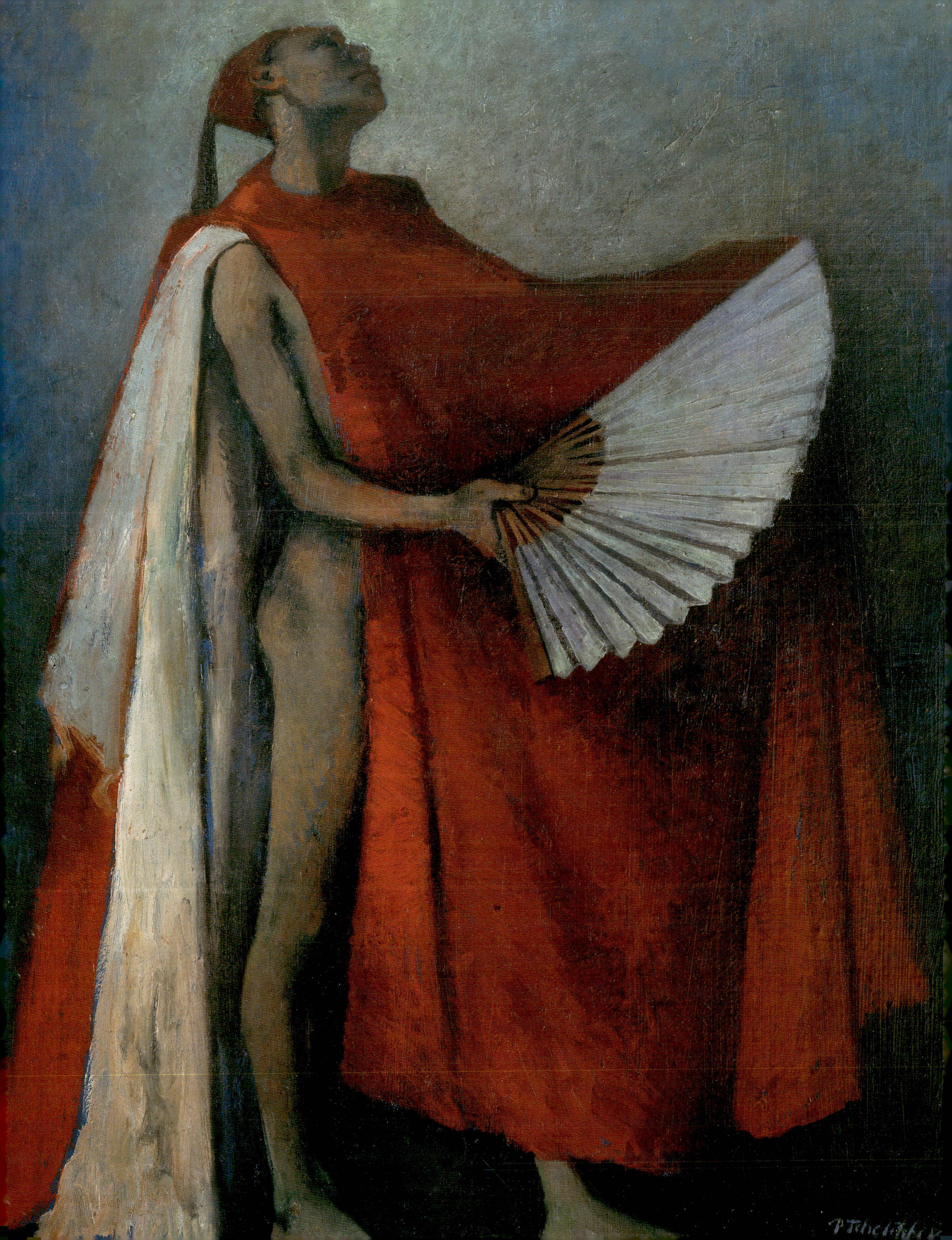

THE COLUMBUS MUSEUM
COLUMBUS, GEORGIA
2003

AMERICAN ART
IN THE COLUMBUS MUSEUM

PAINTING, SCULPTURE, AND DECORATIVE ARTS

Charles T. Butler
GENERAL EDITOR

Philip L. Brewer
Marilyn Laufer
EDITORS

Charles T. Butler
Brigitte Foley
Gail Greenblatt
Marilyn Laufer
Les Reker
Ellie Wheeler
Bitsy Windsor
Philip D. Zimmerman
Kristen Miller Zohn
CONTRIBUTORS

Abbreviations of Exhibitions. (For full references to published materials, please refer to the bibliography.)

Four Seasons
The Four Seasons: American Landscape Paintings, Columbus Museum, 1984.

Select View
A Select View: American Paintings from the Columbus Museum, Knoxville Museum of Art (Tennessee), Madison-Morgan Cultural Center (Madison, Georgia), Paine Art Center and Arboretum (Oshkosh, Wisconsin), R. W. Morton Art Gallery (Shreveport, Louisiana), Louisiana Arts and Science Center (Baton Rouge), Brevard Art Center and Museum (Melbourne, Florida), Columbus Museum, September 4, 1987–October 15, 1989.

Summer Potpourri
A Summer Potpourri: Curators' Selections from the Permanent Collection, Columbus Museum, May 19–July 28, 2002.

Tales from the Easel
Tales from the Easel: Paintings from Southern Art Museums, organized by the Southeastern Art Museum Directors Consortium, Columbus Museum, Tampa Museum of Art, Speed Art Museum (Louisville, Kentucky), El Paso Museum of Art (Texas), February 4, 2004–April 10, 2005.

Towards a New Century
Towards a New Century: Contemporary Art from the Permanent Collection, Columbus Museum, October 31, 1999–January 23, 2000.

Dimensions are in inches, followed by centimeters in parentheses. Height precedes width precedes depth, unless otherwise stated.

Authors:
CTB Charles T. Butler
BF Brigitte Foley
GBG Gail B. Greenblatt
ML Marilyn Laufer
LR Les Reker
EW Ellie Wheeler
BW Bitsy Windsor
PDZ Philip D. Zimmerman
KMZ Kristen Miller Zohn

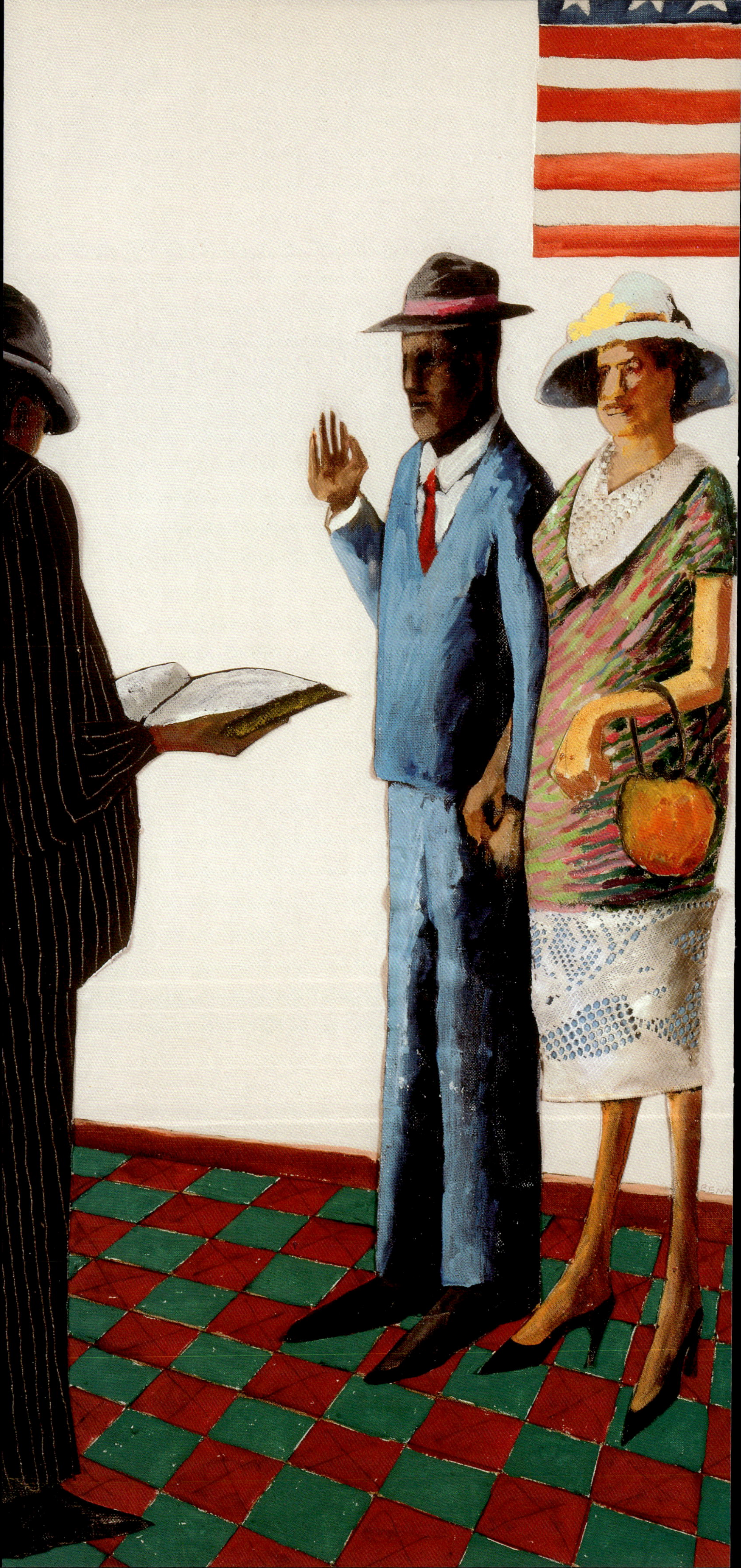

CONTENTS

American Art in the Columbus Museum:
A Brief History
Charles T. Butler
6

Catalogue of the Collection
13

Notes to the Text
216

Bibliography
223

Index of Artists
228

AMERICAN ART IN THE COLUMBUS MUSEUM: A BRIEF HISTORY

The Columbus Museum's permanent collection of fine and decorative art intends to document and represent the changing artistic tastes and aesthetic trends of American culture from colonial times to the present. This publication has allowed us to focus upon an excellent sampling of the holdings that this institution has judiciously acquired over the last fifty years. There are many more examples in our collection than what we are able to include here. Our works-on-paper collection warrants another volume, as does our folk art collection.

The artists that are represented range from such historic notables as Gilbert Stuart, Sanford Gifford, William Merritt Chase, and Stuart Davis to artists that characterize more recent aesthetics, such as Bo Bartlett, William Christenberry, Nancy Grossman, and Robert Motherwell. A concurrent effort has been made to collect the work of artists significant to the South, such as nineteenth-century itinerant portraitists Edward Mooney and C. R. Parker, and Georgia-born contemporary painters Lamar Baker, Alma Thomas, and Benny Andrews.

Similarly, our decorative arts collection is built upon important historic American examples such as a late-seventeenth-century Massachusetts chest; an early-nineteenth-century Hepplewhite-style desk and bookcase attributed to the Boston shop of John Seymour; and an 1810s Philadelphia sideboard attributed to Joseph Barry. Of equal importance are our collections that reflect a specific connection to the Southeast, including an early-nineteenth-century Savannah secretary; an 1830–50 food cupboard made in Stewart County, Georgia; a 1903 Arts and Crafts vase from the Newcomb College pottery; and a 1940s silver set by William Spratling.

The arts have been an integral part of the Columbus community from its earliest beginnings as a frontier town in 1828.[1] The townspeople evidenced a marked interest in all types of art, which included visiting orchestras and vocalists, theatrical groups, circus acts, minstrels, opera singers, magicians, and ventriloquists. In the early years of the city's history, traveling artists who specialized in individual and family portraits often rented studio space in the city and announced their service through the newspapers. Edward Mooney and George Cooke apparently visited Columbus on more than one occasion, leaving behind portraits of many Columbus and Chattahoochee Valley residents.

Though local private collections of art were limited, the early twentieth century did bring about an increased interest in developing a public collection. Charles Frederick Naegele, a portrait painter with residences in New York City and Marietta, Georgia, came to Columbus at the invitation of Mrs. Euphan Collier Stewart, chair of the Art Division of the City Federation of Woman's Clubs. Naegele, in May of 1924, mounted the first of what were to be several Naegele Competitive Art Exhibitions, better known locally as the Penny Art Fund shows.

Naegele arranged for a selection of paintings to come to Columbus, borrowed directly from artists or through New York City galleries. His exhibitions usually featured more than a dozen canvases by such artists as Robert Henri, Guy Wiggins, and Frederick Waugh, and displays of Egyptian scarabs, brasses, and bronzes from China, Tanagra pieces, and other objets d'art. Those who paid the admission charge of ten cents were invited to vote for the painting they liked best. The intent was that at the end of the exhibition, the painting with the most votes would be purchased with the funds raised and placed within a community art collection.

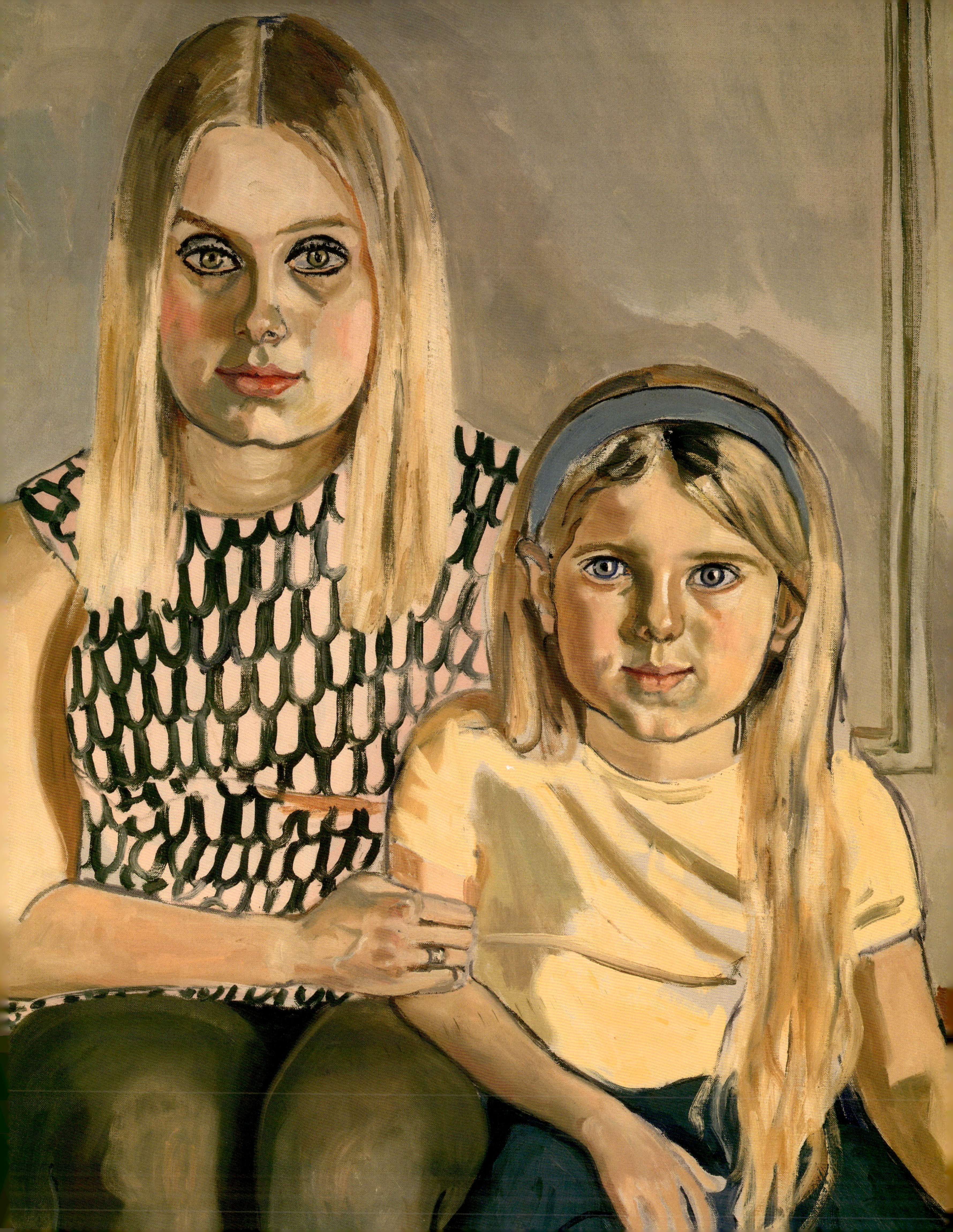

This humble start marks the very beginning of the establishment of a permanent fine arts museum in Columbus. As the years passed, the museum-interest group acquired other paintings for the future museum. Unfortunately, all save one of these artworks were lost in a fire. *Berkshire Mountains (South Egremont, Massachusetts)*, by Hugh Bolton Jones, is the sole surviving painting from the early Penny Art Fund program. Eventually the committee's uphill struggle to create a museum was successful.

Though World War II intercepted initial efforts, perseverance prevailed and on Sunday, March 29, 1953, the association known as the Columbus Museum of Arts and Crafts opened its doors for the first time for a special showing for 400 members, officials of the city and county, and other invited guests. Founding Director Edward Shorter showed the new museum's permanent collection, donated by Mrs. Euphan Collier Stewart. It consisted of many of her father's marine paintings and other assorted objects, including an Emil Carlsen still life that appears in this book.

The museum was handsomely housed in the home of Mr. and Mrs. D. A. Turner, son-in-law and daughter of W. C. Bradley. Through a gift from the Turner family and a local business, this home had been purchased by the City of Columbus, which then turned it over to the Muscogee County School District to be remodeled as a museum. Architect E. Oren Smith undertook the remodeling project, which required that he adapt a forty-year-old Mediterranean Revival family house, built by Columbus attorney Brick Miller in 1912 and acquired by W. C. Bradley in 1925, for use as a modern facility that would provide a safe museum environment. Smith also had to incorporate the nine acres of gardens and grounds, originally designed by the New York City firm of Frederick Law Olmsted, into the museum setting.

The museum's director, Edward Shorter, had not only been part of the original museum planning committee but had worked tirelessly for twelve years at the salary of a dollar a year. In 1965 he decided to retire, and the trustees named him director emeritus. They appointed the museum's second director—Columbus artist Wendell Taylor to the position. Taylor's tenure lasted only two years, as he was happier in a studio teaching environment than in museum administration. In April 1967, after a very short term with Warren P. Brown Jr. as the third director (health problems forced his premature retirement), the museum appointed its fourth director. Clay Aldridge was a career museum professional. He had worked at the Cooper Union Museum for the Arts of Decoration in New York City; the Lowe Art Museum at the University of Miami in Coral Gables, Florida; and the El Paso Museum of Art in Texas.

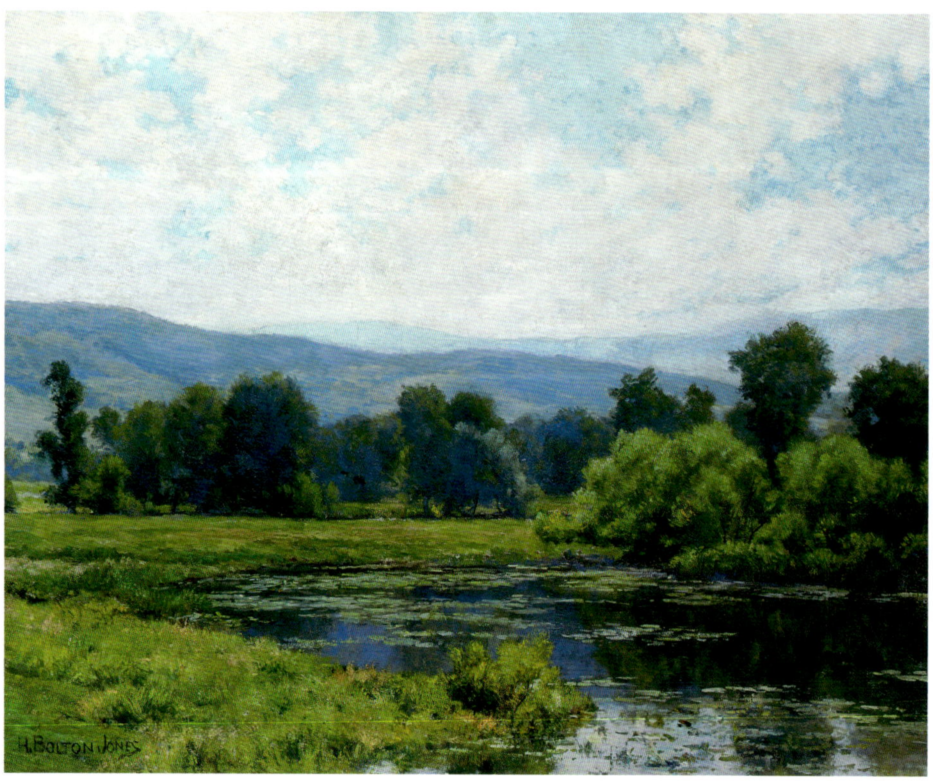

FIGURE 1 Hugh Bolton Jones, *Berkshire Mountains (South Egremont, Massachusetts)*, cat. 26.

As the museum grew so did its permanent collections. By mid-1975, the collection included 251 paintings, 54 watercolors, 10 pastels, 543 graphics, 14 photographs, and 43 sculptures. In April 1976, Aldridge resigned after five years at the helm of the museum. The museum's fifth director, William E. Scheele, was an experienced leader. He had served for twenty-three years as the director of the Cleveland Museum of Natural History, as well as in Miami as director of the Museum of Science. Under Scheele's direction, the museum changed its name to the Columbus Museum of Arts and Sciences.

In 1977 the museum sponsored *Missing Pieces: Georgia Folk Art, 1770–1976,* a statewide Bicentennial project assembled by Columbus native Anna Wadsworth Murray, who had begun collecting Georgia folk art in 1974. Under the sponsorship of the Georgia Council for the Arts and Humanities and the National Endowment for the Arts, the project grew until it became the most comprehensive collection of its kind, eventually consisting of 102 works of folk art produced in Georgia. Objects ranged from traditional pottery, quilts, carvings, and portraits to bizarre environmental constructions by contemporary self-taught artists. The Murray collection was supplemented by two hundred additional pieces of folk art from the Chattahoochee River Valley, most of it assembled by the museum's own folk-life expert, Fred Fussell, who had rejoined the museum in July as folklorist. Fussell scoured the valley and turned up quilts, furniture, primitive paintings (many of which are now part of the collection), and musical instruments, along with folk musicians and performers.[2]

At its meeting in November 1976, the acquisition committee made clear its intention to build on the strength of the museum's American art collection. In time, the museum's fine arts collection would consist only of American works, largely out of necessity. The museum simply could not compete financially in the world art market and believed that concentrating efforts in one area would provide a better opportunity to build a significant collection that represented an important art historical perspective. This decision was announced by the chair of the acquisition committee, Dr. Philip L. Brewer, who had joined the committee in 1975.

Many special acquisition opportunities marked the museum's twenty-fifth anniversary in 1978. A special, board-appointed committee had been established to raise funds to purchase a painting in Edward Shorter's honor. There was an unprecedented flow of donations, ultimately resulting in more than $29,000 in contributions, which were used to purchase a painting, *View of a Garden,* by one of Shorter's favorite artists, Ernest Lawson.

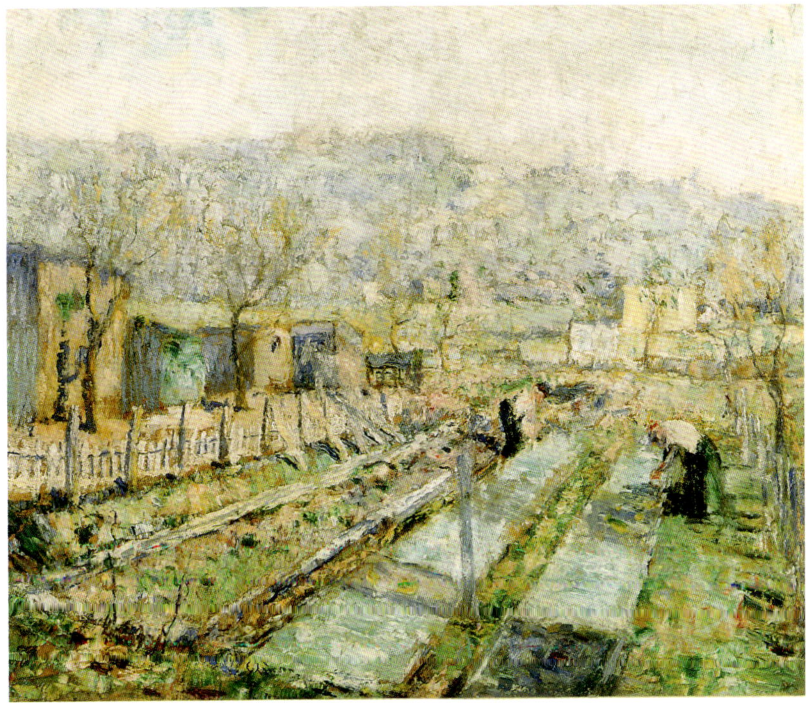

FIGURE 2 Ernest Lawson, *View of a Garden in a Paris Suburb,* ca. 1893. Oil on canvas, 20⅛ × 24⅜ (57.1 × 61.9). Gift of Friends of Mr. Edward S. Shorter, 1978.9.

In March, museum director Scheele announced that the family of the recently deceased artist Alma Thomas was eager to honor her by making it possible for her hometown museum to purchase one of her paintings. As a result, *Air View of a Spring Nursery* was acquired from the artist's estate for the permanent collection. The acquisition committee had also been busy fulfilling a plan to acquire twenty-five new paintings in honor of the museum's twenty-fifth birthday. This project, financed by corporate and individual donations, succeeded beyond anyone's hopes. It resulted in some truly fine acquisitions, including paintings by Lawson, J. Alden Weir, Daniel Garber, Frederick Waugh, and Thomas Hinckley.

In 1979 a room designed by Columbus-born architect Philip Trammell Schutze, designer of Atlanta's famed Swan House and many other important private residences and public buildings, was installed in the museum.[3] This period room made possible the display and collecting of fine decorative arts to fill the space. The museum, that same year, also acquired important works on paper by sixty-eight-year-old, Chinese-born American artist Chen Chi and Walter Anderson, the eccentric Mississippi painter and ceramist who had emerged as an important visionary artist in the United States after a lifetime of near obscurity.

In 1986 the board of trustees voted to change the name of the museum from the Columbus Museum of Arts and Sciences to simply the Columbus Museum, the name by which it is known to this day. With the death of Edward Shorter, the board named an acquisition account in his honor. Anne Timpano became the museum's sixth director. As the museum was planning a significant expansion, the staff chose to tour parts of the permanent collection in *A Select View,* an exhibition consisting of forty-six of the museum's finest nineteenth- and twentieth-century American artworks. The museum published a color-illustrated catalogue to accompany the tour, which reflected the tremendous growth in its American art collection and the vigorous stewardship of the acquisition committee.

Two most important gifts for the collection were received in 1991. A single gift of 312 photographic images from George Dudley Jr. formed the foundation of a twentieth-century photography collection. Artists represented included Sid Avery, Mike Disfarmer, George Hurrell, Robert Mapplethorpe, Arthur Rothstein, Weegee, and F. A. Witzel. Additional acquisitions followed, with images by John Banasiak, Tom Barrow, Paul Caponigro, William Eggleston, Louis Hine, Birmey Imes, Jack Jaffee, Paul Kwilecki, and Patrick Nagatani entering the collection.

The second gift in 1991 was the bequest of Edward Shorter, which brought notable paintings and operating funds to the museum. Works by Lamar Dodd, Edmund Greacen, Carl Holty, Dong Kingman, Max Kuehne, Ernest Lawson, Chauncey Ryder, and Andrew Wyeth, as well as a number of Asian carvings were donated to the museum from Shorter's estate.

Meanwhile, a new museum building was taking shape. Some of the existing rooms of the original museum were retained, as was the original Tuscan architectural style of the Miller-Bradley home. The new 87,000-square-foot museum would include 30,000 square feet of gallery space, 5,000 square feet of collections storage, a 298-seat auditorium, 4,000 square feet for exhibition preparation and an archaeology conservation lab, 1,000 square feet for a 60-seat theater, and 4,000 square feet for an education wing. Included in the gallery space was the 11,000-square-foot Chattahoochee Legacy gallery and 2,000 square feet for the museum's first attempt at a hands-on children's discovery gallery, known as Transformations. The Washington, D.C.–based architectural firm of Kress-Cox incorporated the feel of the museum's old courtyard into impressive interior space by utilizing natural light, fifty-foot-high stone arches, clerestories, and lacquered marble floors. A tall window on the west side offered a commanding view of the museum's gardens.

Soon after the completion of this building, director Timpano requested a nine-month administrative leave, and trustee and retired executive Hugh Landrum stepped in to assume the role of interim director. When Timpano chose to leave the museum rather than return following this sabbatical, Landrum continued his job and actively assisted the trustees in their national search for a new director. Charles Thomas (Tom) Butler was named the seventh director in May 1994.

Acquisitions between 1991 and 2003 reveal that the museum astutely has continued to develop its collections as befitted the new building. Long-term loans from the Metropolitan Museum of Art, Smithsonian American Art Museum, and the New Orleans Museum of Art augmented the museum's own collections when it reopened in 1989, but by 1996 all loans had been returned to make room for new acquisitions. Now sculptures by Leonard Baskin, Jo Davidson, John Flannagan, Gaston Lachaise, Frederick W. MacMonnies, Hiram Powers, William Zorach, and numerous others occupy prominent spaces in the galleries, as do paintings by Roger Brown, William Merritt Chase, Sam Gilliam, William Glackens, Thomas Hovenden, Sarah Miriam Peale, Thomas Sully, and James Guy.

With the opening of the new museum, the works-on-paper collection grew tremendously, with pivotal additions by Thomas Hart Benton, William Christenberry, Winslow Homer, William H. Johnson, Wolf Kahn, Jan Matulka, Frank Stella, and Benjamin West. In May 2003, the collection of American works on paper was greatly improved by the acquisition of the Dr. and Mrs. Philip L. Brewer collection of 126 masterworks spanning three centuries. Aside from the bequest of Edward Shorter, a visionary for the arts in Columbus whose generosity provides significant annual earned income for general support, other important endowment funds have been established by donors, which provide annual earned income to assist the museum's acquisitions, capital needs, conservation, general operations, and publications programs.

Among the most recent gifts were a 1995 bequest from Ella Kirven and a twenty-year charitable lead trust from her estate, which has been designated to assist in the growing acquisitions program. Since 1996 Miss Kirvin's generosity has enabled the museum to acquire significant works by Sanford Gifford, Lee Krasner, Robert Motherwell, Alice Neel, John Sloan, and John Twachtman, among others. At the same

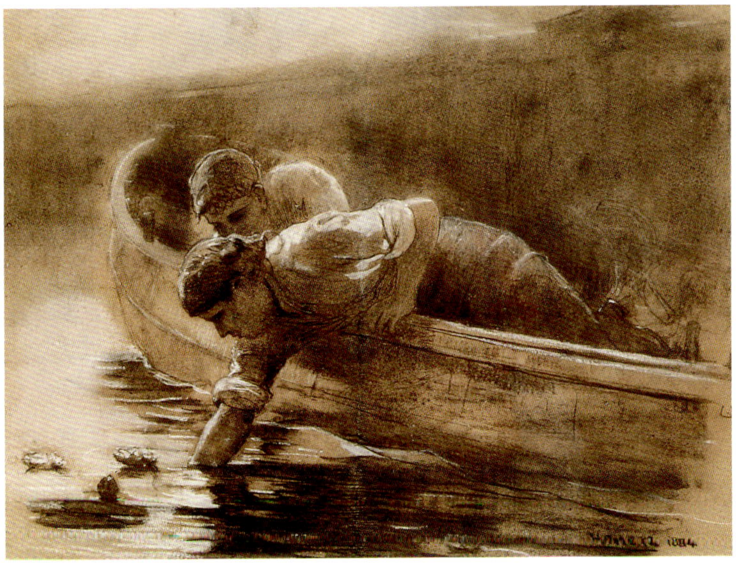

FIGURE 3 Winslow Homer, *Pond Lilies*, 1884. Charcoal, chalk, and gouache on laid paper, 17 × 23 (43.2 × 58.4). Museum purchase made possible by the Endowment Fund in honor of D. A. Turner, the Art and Restoration Fund, and the Edward Swift Shorter Bequest Fund, 1989.2

time, another longtime museum supporter, Norman Rothschild, launched an ambitious acquisitions program in the last two years of his life and made possible the purchase of important works by Joyce Treiman, John Wilde, Leon Kroll, Bo Bartlett, Andrée Ruellan, Richard Mafong, the Art Guys, and Janet Fish. And in 2002 the families of Thornton and C. Dexter Jordan Jr. made possible the acquisition of a major installation by Dale Chihuly to the delight of our wonderful patrons and supportive community.

Today the Columbus Museum is recognized nationally for its serious commitment to American art. Many people have played an important role in this endeavor since an inspired and wise acquisition committee and board of trustees focused the museum's future collection policies. Author William Winn has carefully documented many of these events in the museum's 1996 publication *Building on a Legacy*. I wish to acknowledge Mr. Winn's numerous contributions to our museum and our community over the past few decades. I also wish to thank the scholars who contributed entries for this publication; their research on the artists and objects has made the project possible.

The design of any publication is an integral aspect of the process, and we were fortunate to enjoy the services of the creative team of Marquand Books. Museum registrar Aimee Brooks's coordination of the access to and documentation of more than one hundred objects was handled with grace and skill. Michael McKelvey's photography provides excellent illustrations of some of our most beautiful and important treasures. In addition, I gratefully acknowledge a number of friends of the museum in preparing this manuscript for publication, including Dr. Philip L. Brewer, Dr. Marilyn Laufer, and Dr. Philip D. Zimmerman for their editorial suggestions. In addition, a huge measure of thanks must go to our diligent and patient editor, Norma Roberts.

My final and fullest measure of thanks goes to The John P. and Dorothy S. Illges Foundation, which, in 1999, supported the vision of such a publication and made the funds available to produce this book in a manner that was commensurate with our growing collection. On behalf of all my colleagues who have held the director's chair before me, and the many staff members and trustees past and present who have helped shape this collection, we thank the foundation for their vote of confidence and gracious generosity.

CHARLES T. BUTLER
Director

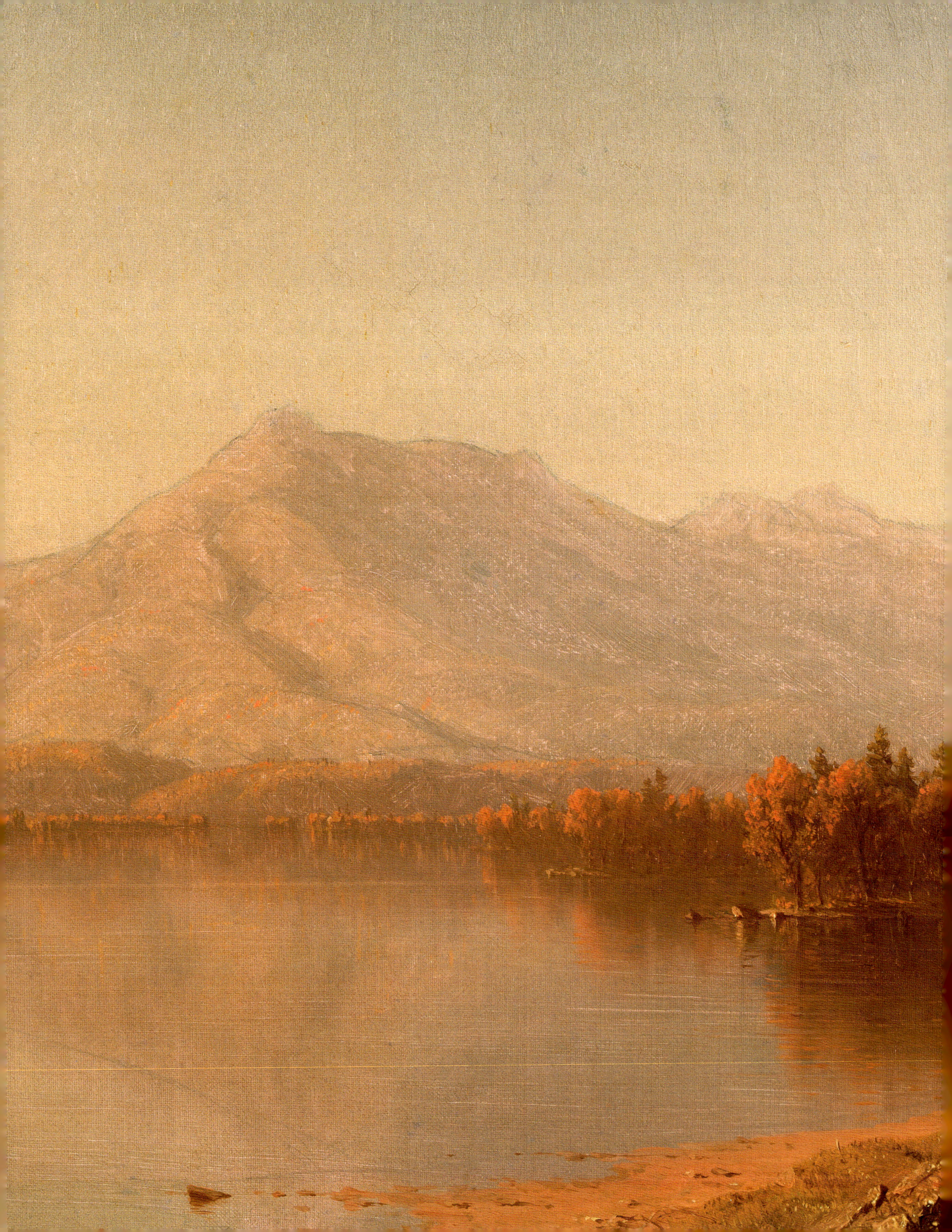

CATALOGUE OF THE COLLECTION

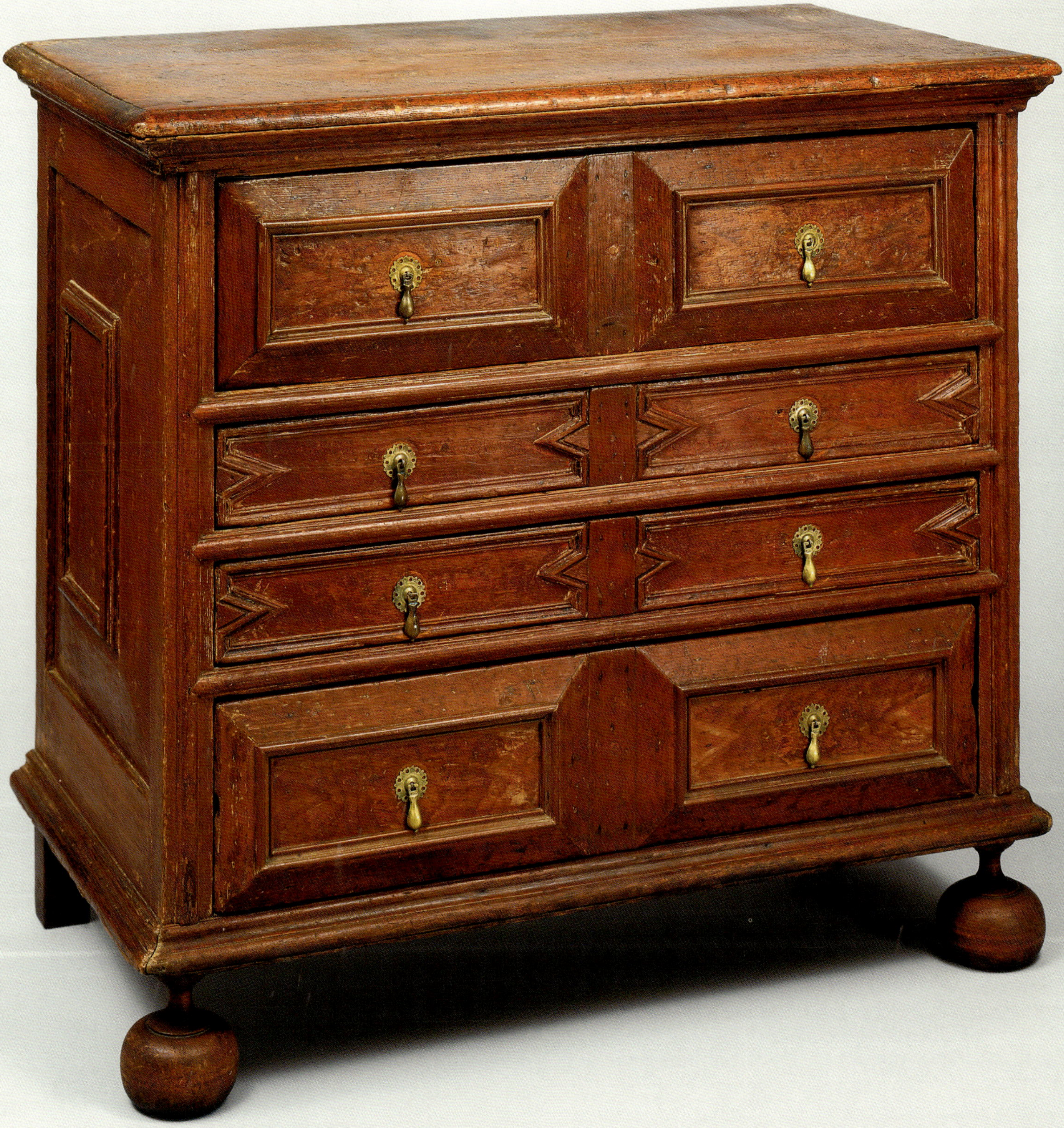

UNKNOWN MAKER

1

Boston, active late seventeenth century–early eighteenth century
Chest of Drawers, 1670–1710
Oak, red cedar, chestnut, cedar, walnut, with secondary wood of eastern white pine; brass, 36¾ × 40 × 21⅝ (92.08 × 101.6 × 54.93)
Museum purchase made possible by the Endowment Fund in Honor of D. A. Turner 2001.14

PROVENANCE: Joe Kindig and Son, York, Pennsylvania.
EXHIBITIONS: *Summer Potpourri.*

There is much discussion concerning when the chest of drawers first appeared. In Europe, this distinct furniture form seems to have come into use by the late sixteenth century in Italy and the early seventeenth century in London.[1] Scattered references to chests of drawers occur in Massachusetts probate inventory records throughout the seventeenth century. Relatively high valuations suggest that they were rare.[2] A consensus among furniture historians holds that American furniture makers working in more urbane communities—in and around Boston, for the most part—began producing chests of drawers by the 1670s. Most of these accomplished artisans, called joyners for their ability to construct furniture and houses with mortise-and-tenon joints, were immigrants from England, who readily transported styles and woodworking techniques from the Old World to the New.

The city of Boston, which was founded in 1630 by John Winthrop (who would become Massachusetts's first governor), Thomas Dudley, and William Blackstone, grew to 7,000 residents by 1690. These people, mostly from England, represented a flourishing marketplace for domestic furnishings. Their houses were very reminiscent of medieval structures, featuring second stories that overhung the first floor and high-pitched roofs that easily shed accumulated snow. Horizontal clapboards, wood roof shingles, and casement windows made of small lead-lined diamonds, or quarrels, of glass kept out much of the weather while huge central fireplaces, low ceilings, and small windows helped to retain warmth. Rooms contained some—but not many—tables, chairs, and lidded chests for storage. Chests of drawers introduced greater convenience by making stored textiles and other belongings more readily accessible.

The museum's chest of drawers is a frame of uprights (called stiles) and crosspieces (called rails) assembled with mortise-and-tenon joints. The sides and back of the case are large boards with tapered edges that fit into channels cut into the rails and stiles. Decorative moldings (forming a vertically oriented rectangle on the sides) are then applied to these panels. Similarly, the drawer fronts have a complex geometric composition of applied moldings that simulate side-by-side drawers. The drawer fronts themselves are nailed to the drawer sides, although in some Boston work of this period they are assembled with large dovetails. These substantially constructed drawers move on runners in deep channels cut into the drawer sides, rather than sliding on the drawer bottoms as occurred after about 1700. Although the rear stiles continue down to the floor, the front stiles probably originally ended in large, turned ball feet, not unlike the present, slightly over-sized feet, which appear to be early replacements. Similarly, the brass drawer pulls are old replacements. There are still traces of the original red paint on the inset wood panels of the two middle drawers.

Although seventeenth-century American chests of drawers are very rare, enough survive to convey a sense of what was made. Two features—the large top and bottom drawers combined with two shallow center drawers and the large vertical side panel—distinguish the group of about a dozen such chests of which the Columbus example is one.[3] Most other American (i.e., New England, since virtually no case furniture survives from other American colonies) chests of drawers, the vast majority of which were made in eastern Massachusetts, have two panels on each side, typically horizontal but sometimes vertical. Moreover, drawer design differs from that of the two shallow center drawers. Some of these other chests of drawers have cases made in two parts, each of which contains two drawers. Such construction may have accommodated moving the chest up and down narrow stairwells, but seventeenth-century owners were probably no different from people today in their reluctance to move this heavy furniture in the first place. PDZ and CTB

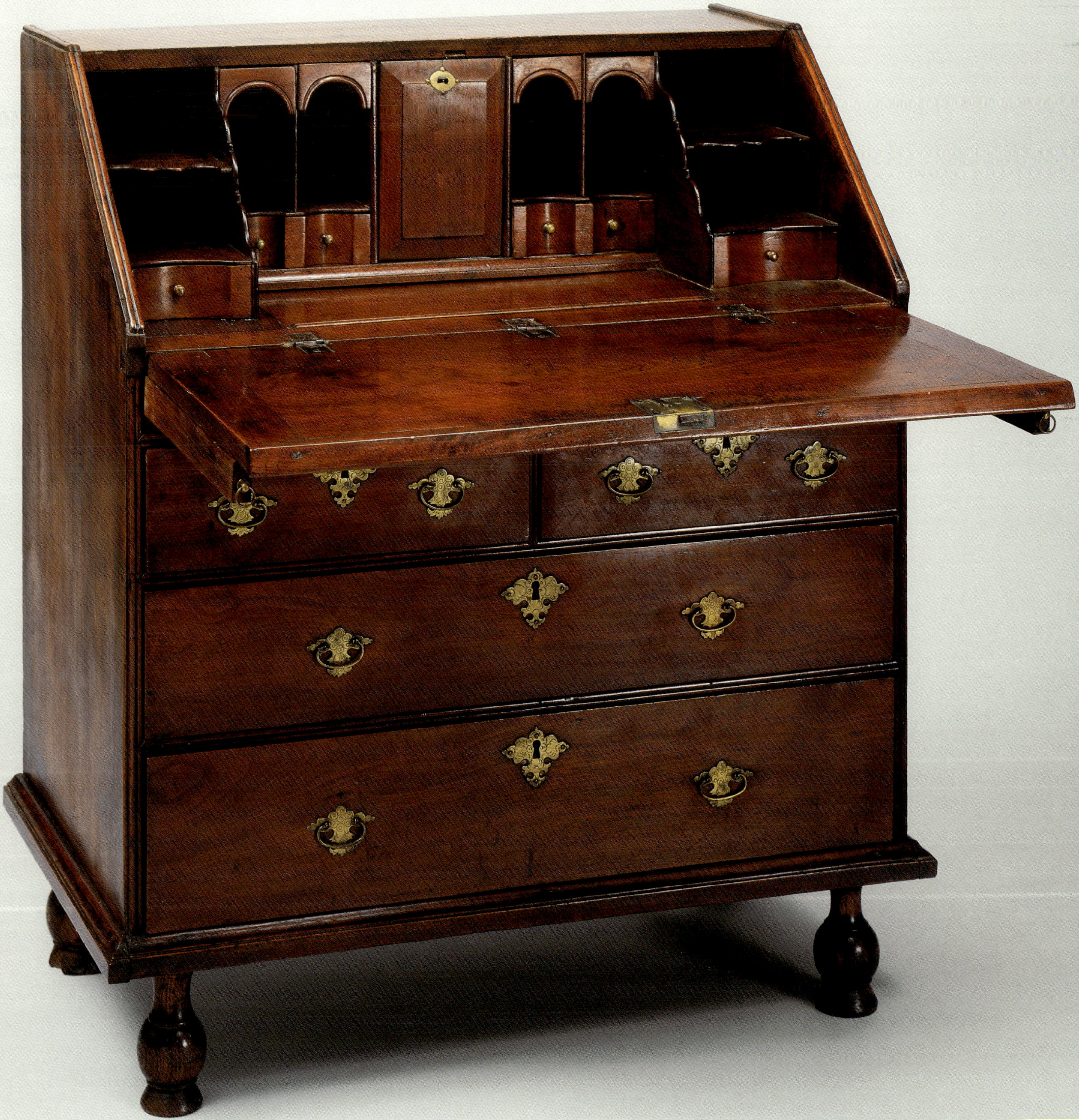

UNKNOWN MAKER

2 Eastern Massachusetts, active early eighteenth century
Desk, 1715–40
Walnut, with secondary woods of white oak and white pine; brass,
36½ × 33½ × 19½ (92.71 × 85.09 × 49.53)
Museum purchase made possible by the Endowment Fund in Honor of D. A. Turner 98.46

PROVENANCE: Howard Joynt, Alexandria, Virginia; Joe Kindig and Son, York, Pennsylvania.

This slant-front desk, probably made in the Boston area, represents a relatively new form in American furniture. Among the earliest references to desks is the 1684 estate inventory of Joseph Wise of Roxbury, Massachusetts, who owned "one desk and old cushion and Carpet."[1] This listing suggests a tablelike desk having the carpet over the desktop with the cushion probably available to support a book. In contrast, eighteenth-century desks (often called scritores or some other version of *escritoire,* from the Latin "to write") had hinged lids supported by pullout slides, or lopers. These lids served as convenient writing surfaces and allowed owners to lock the many small valuables and personal papers stored within the desk away from unauthorized handling by the curious.

The museum's William-and-Mary-style desk is made of walnut panels chosen for their lustrous grain and color and assembled with dovetails rather than set within joined frameworks as was the custom in the seventeenth century. The result was an entirely new aesthetic that was enhanced occasionally with quartered panels of veneer outlined with decorative banding in imitation of English work. The original brass drawer pulls on this desk, held in place by iron cotter pins, have engraved back plates with ornate outlines that accent the front façade. The feet, too, are original. Set off from the rest of the case by a bold base molding, these feet are leaner than many other ball feet of this style, suggesting later preferences for lighter lines and proportion.

Small drawers and cubbyholes make up the desk interior. The rounded arches at the top of each cubby, popularly called valances, are little drawers whose shape echoes the hollowed fronts of the small drawers below. The profiles of the cubby sidewalls and dividers are ogee or S-shaped curves, which became increasingly important elements in eighteenth-century design. The paneled door in the middle of the interior has a lock at the top and lifts off two short pins that secure the bottom. Inside are more small drawers and cubbies. A sliding horizontal board in front of the fitted desk interior allows access to a well for storage of papers immediately above the two side-by-side drawers in the lower part of the desk.

Throughout the seventeenth century and until about 1750, Boston was the dominant urban center in the American colonies. Into this port came immigrant craftsmen with innovative ideas and experience, as well as furniture and printed works that embodied and expressed new designs and styles. Moreover, the thriving Boston economy supported a sophisticated and wealthy clientele that demanded designs that were more stylish. In time, the ports of New York, Philadelphia, and Charleston rivaled and supplanted that of Boston. Yet despite all of the access to European design and practices, colonial artisans developed a distinctively American expression that emphasized lightness, natural materials, and durability—what some consider a degree of practicality that has long characterized American arts. PDZ and CTB

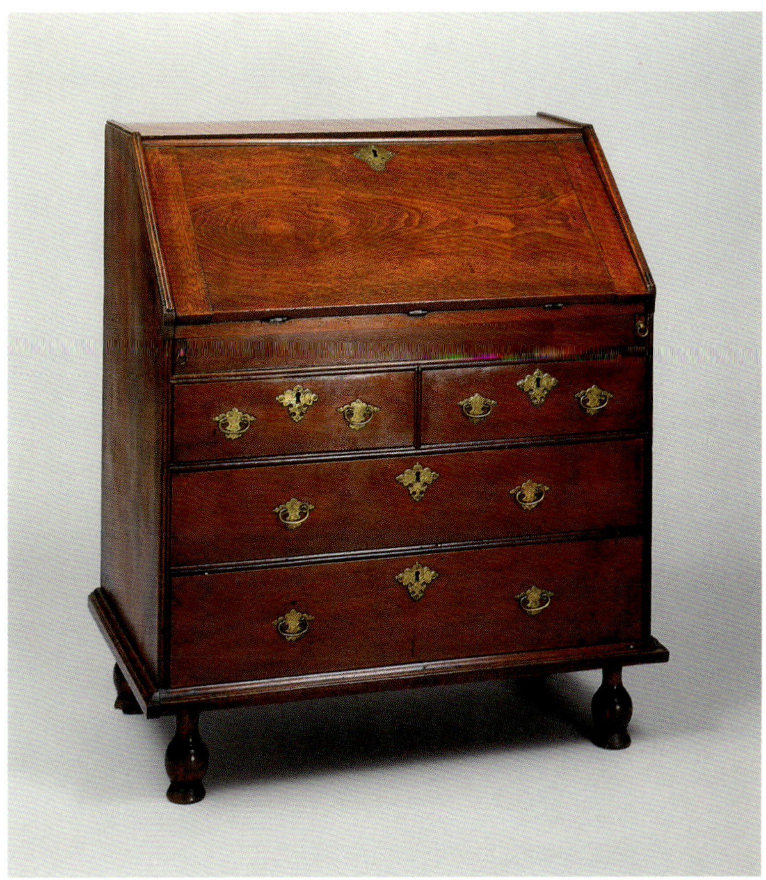

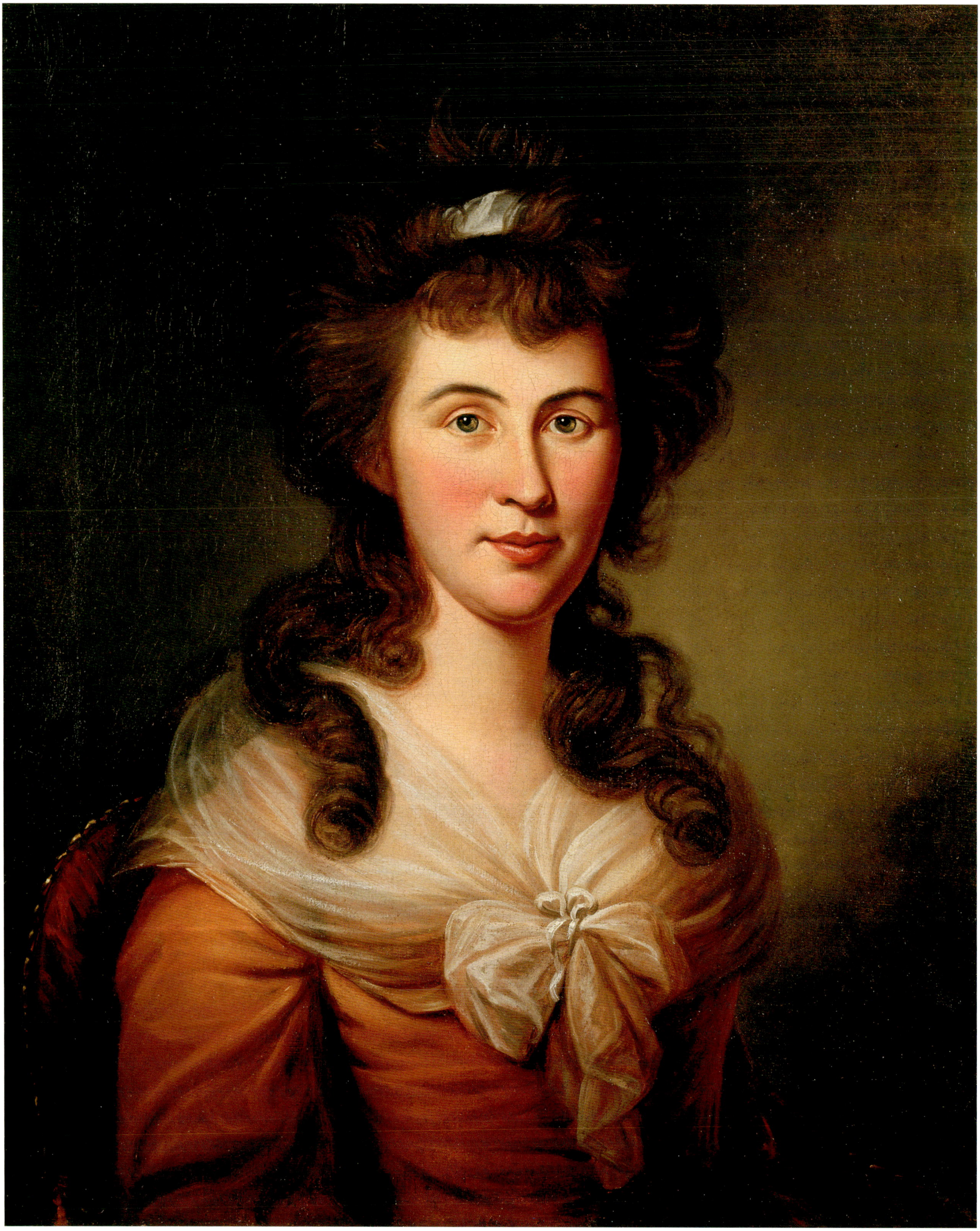

CHARLES WILLSON PEALE

3 b. 1741, Chester, Maryland; d. 1827, Philadelphia
Elizabeth Michael Snyder, ca. 1790
Oil on canvas, 27¼ × 23 (69.22 × 58.42)
Museum purchase 83.37

PROVENANCE: Descendant of the sitter; Sloan's Auction, Washington, D.C.; Frank S. Schwarz and Son, Philadelphia.
EXHIBITIONS: *A Gallery Collects Peales*, Frank S. Schwarz and Son, Philadelphia, July 1987.
PUBLICATIONS: *A Gallery Collects Peales* (Philadelphia: Frank S. Schwarz and Son, 1987), no. 5; Winn, et al., 106.

A student of the paintings of John Hesselius and John Singleton Copley, Charles Willson Peale traveled to London in 1767 and studied with Benjamin West. By 1769 he had returned to America to begin his career as an artist, settling first in Annapolis, not far from his birthplace. After serving in the Continental Army (1775–78), he relocated to Philadelphia, where he established a very successful portrait studio, including among his sitters George Washington, Thomas Jefferson, and Benjamin Franklin.

The patriarch and often teacher of an extended family of artists—brothers, sons, daughters, nieces, and nephews—Peale can also be credited with creating one of the earliest American cultural institutions, the Philadelphia Museum, in 1778. Peale hung his paintings in the gallery and displayed natural history specimens, including a prehistoric mammoth that he unearthed near Newburgh, New York, in 1801. He documented the museum in the 1822 painting *The Artist in His Museum* (Pennsylvania Academy of the Fine Arts).

The Columbus Museum's portrait of Elizabeth Michael Snyder is a good example of Peale's strength as a portraitist. Edgar Richardson describes Peale's portraits of the late eighteenth century in these terms: "A strong outline defines the forms; the light is even and clear; the drawing is exact; color, in broad areas, is almost enameled."[1] Certainly, Peale's technical clarity and deftness as a painter enabled him to define not only the sitter's likeness but also the more subtle aspects of her personality and character.

The subject was the wife of Simon Snyder (1759–1819), who served as one of the original framers of Pennsylvania's constitution and was later elected governor of the state for three consecutive terms beginning in 1808. He married Elizabeth Michael in 1790, the year this portrait was painted. Twenty years later the artist painted Governor Snyder's portrait for his Philadelphia Museum.

Although Elizabeth Snyder was a woman of significant social stature, Peale shunned idealization in favor of a straightforward and frank rendering. Unlike the grand portraits of Gilbert Stuart, there is no emphasis on elaborate interiors, velvet, jewelry, brocades, or other embellishments. Instead, American pragmatism, egalitarianism, and moderation are evident in her pose and expression.[2] The young wife personifies the young nation, handsome but not frivolous, determined but not unyielding, strong but not impassive. In her simplicity and directness there is a resilience that no doubt served her well. Peale's strength as a portraitist was his ability to portray the person without idealization or aggrandizement. His work represents early American portraiture in its most honest conception. LR and ML

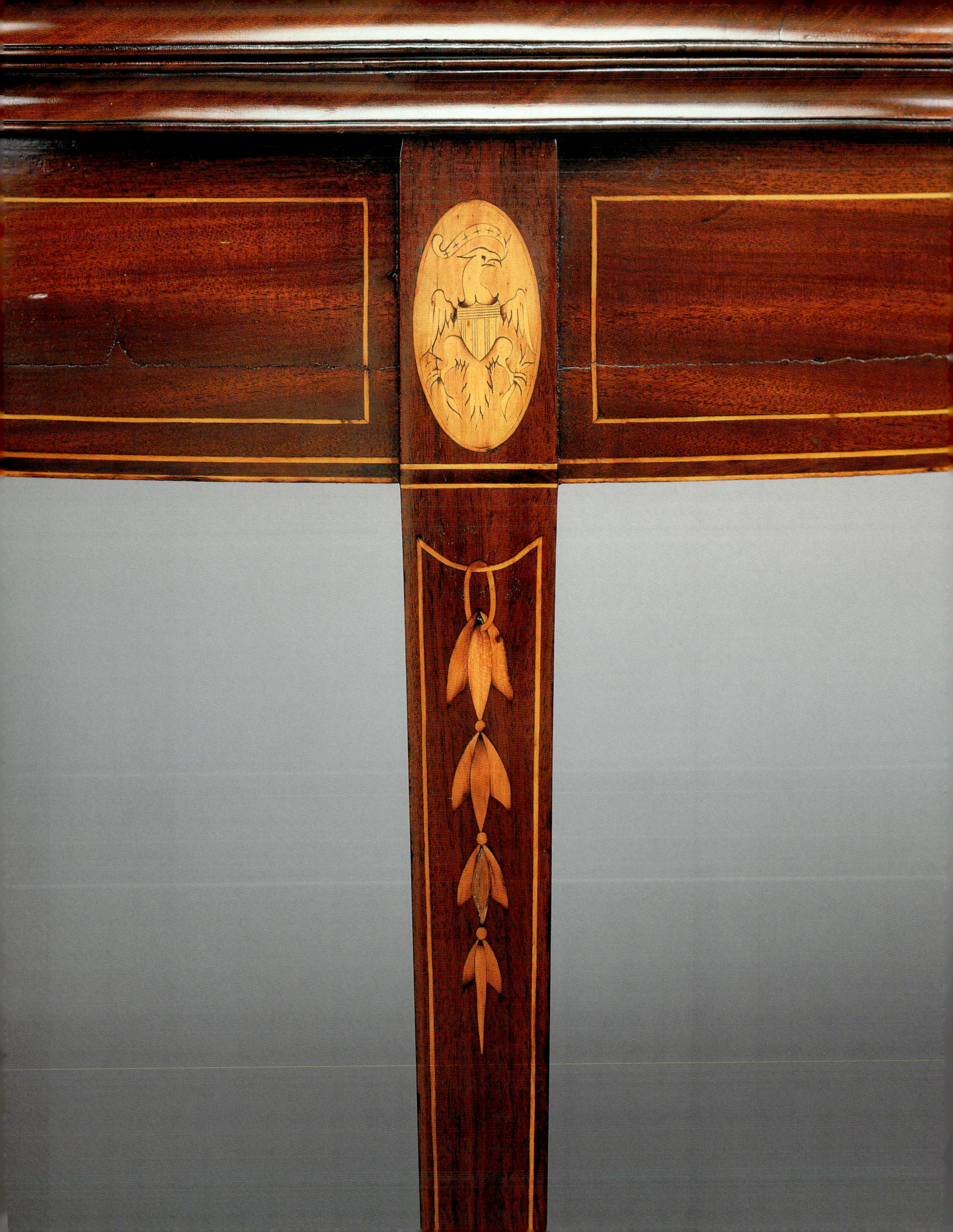

UNKNOWN MAKER

4

Baltimore, active late eighteenth century–early nineteenth century
Card Table, 1790–1810
Mahogany, pine, with secondary wood of oak, 30 × 36 × 18 (76.2 × 91.44 × 45.72)
Museum purchase made possible by generous gifts from The Daniel P. and Shannon L. Amos Foundation, a Friend of the Museum in honor of Mrs. Clarence Butler, and The Watson Fund in memory of Paul C. Watson 2002.13

PROVENANCE: Gardiner Family, Baltimore; Bernard and S. Dean Levy, New York; Joe Kindig and Son, York, Pennsylvania.

In 1750, when Philadelphia, New York, and Boston were flourishing port cities, Baltimore was a hamlet of some two dozen houses, a church, and two taverns.[1] By 1800 the population had expanded to over 25,000 and exports of such things as grain monetarily rivaled those of Philadelphia and New York. Baltimore artisans answered the demand for furnishings commensurate with fashionable townhouses built by newly prosperous citizens. Although the majority of these furniture makers were Maryland-born, British émigrés such as Richard Lawson, Gualter Hornby, John Daugherty, and Thomas Aiton may have helped raise the quality of furniture made there.[2]

The museum's card table represents the very best of Baltimore federal furniture. Card tables were made in the thousands and survive in great numbers, but few achieve the elegant blend of simplicity and refinement of detail embodied in this example. The half-round frame stands on four tapered legs ending in spade feet, which give the table a sense of lift. Each of the legs is decorated with four inlaid bellflowers suspended from a loop, the whole enclosed by stringing. On the frame, above each leg, is a glorious eagle medallion modeled after the great seal of the United States. The eagle has a shield emblazoned on its chest and holds an arrow in one talon and an olive branch in the other. A banner of stars held in its beak floats above.[3] This imagery, which signifies the new nation's identity and independence from Britain, became an important element in designs of this period throughout America. In contrast, the semicircular inlay at the rear center of the tabletop depicts a conch shell, a motif that occurred with regularity in English work. In fact, these large shell inlays were likely imported from English makers. Robert Courtenay of Baltimore advertised in 1793 that he had "just received, from London, per the Ship Republican, . . . Shells for inlaying Mahogany furniture."[4]

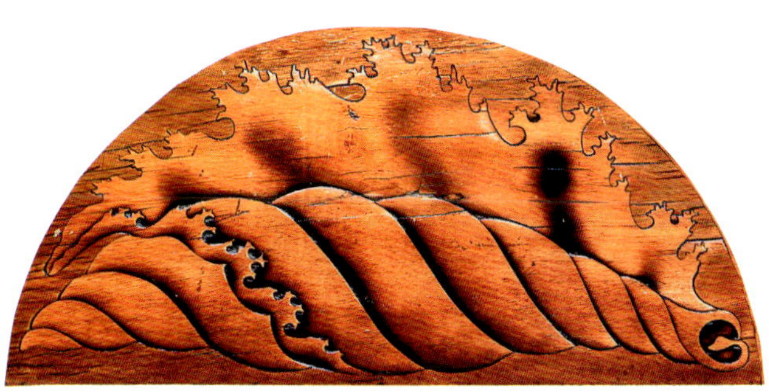

This mahogany card table has construction features that are typical of Baltimore work. Both rear legs are joined to oak rear rails, each of which is attached to the frame with a wooden hinge. The inner fixed frame is of pine. A medial brace running from front to back reinforces the frame. As in almost all card tables of this period, the frame itself is made of laminated boards cut to shape and covered in mahogany veneers. PDZ and CTB

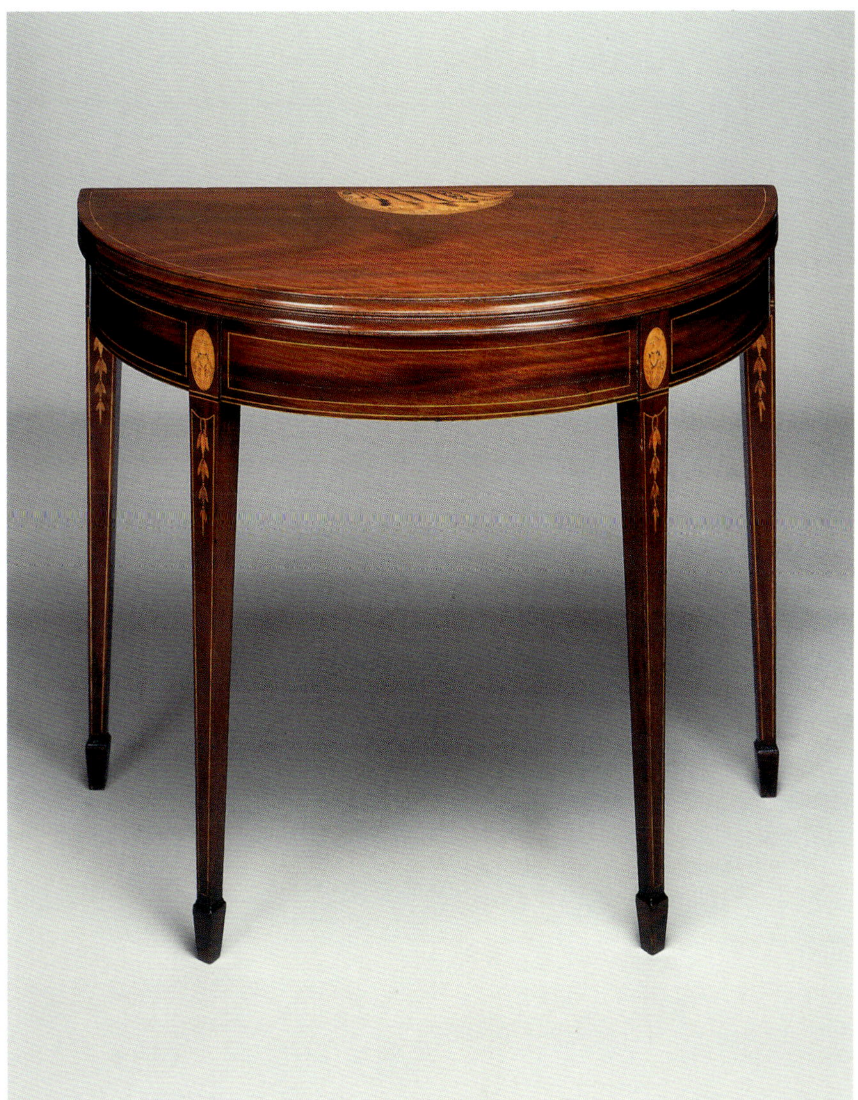

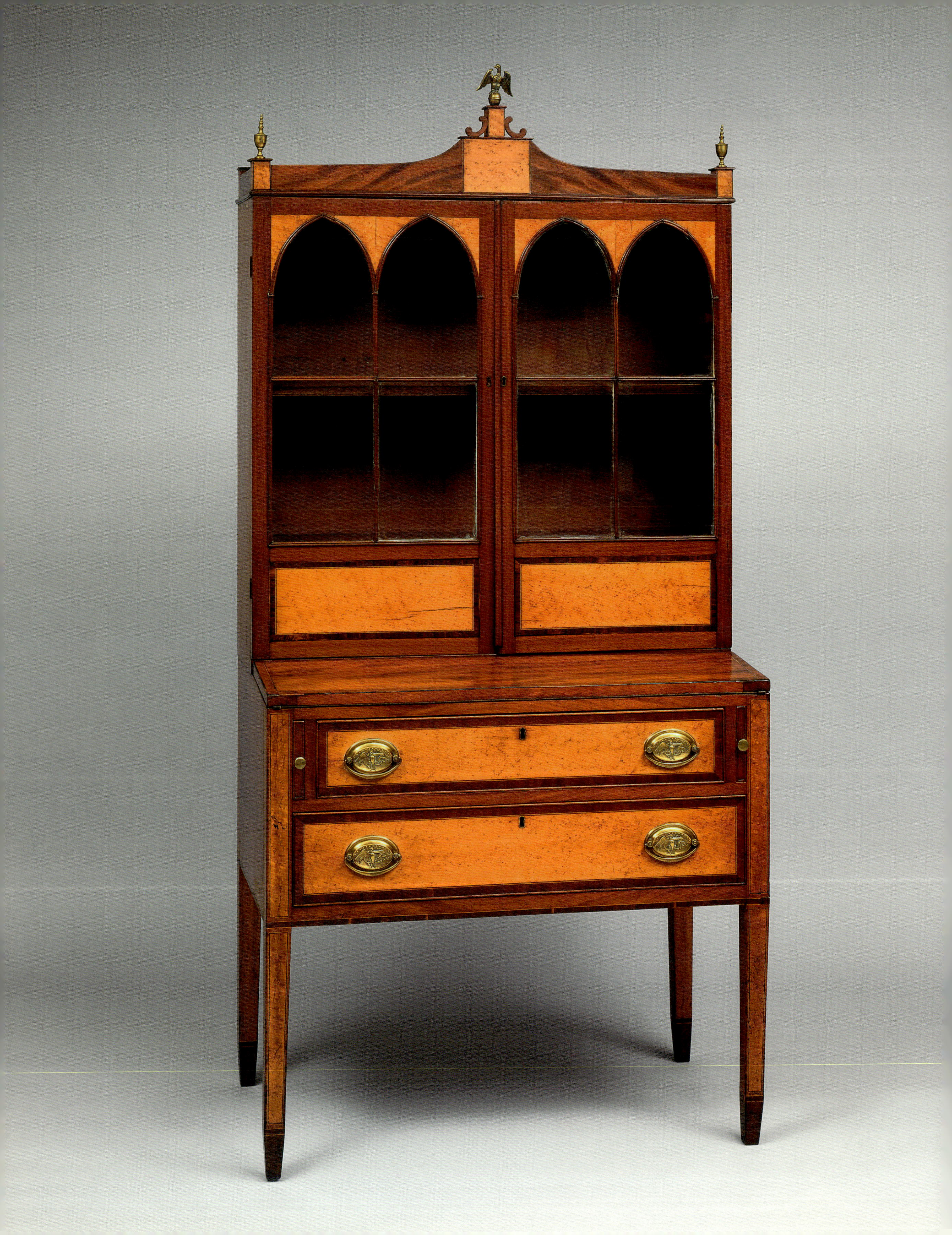

JOHN AND THOMAS SEYMOUR (ATTRIBUTED TO SHOP)

Boston, active 1794–1843

5 **Secretary and Bookcase,** 1800–1810

Mahogany and bird's-eye maple, with secondary wood of pine; brass, 73 × 34¾ × 20 (185.42 × 87.63 × 50.8)

Museum purchase made possible by the Art Acquisition and Restoration Fund 97.21

PROVENANCE: Joe Kindig and Son, York, Pennsylvania.

Contrasting inlays and veneers forming geometric patterns and designs are hallmarks of American federal furniture. Brilliant bird's-eye maple veneers outlined in dark crossbanding (so-called for orientation of the grain across the width) are particularly representative of fine New England cabinetry. The generous and careful use of such colorful veneers and finely wrought inlays, in combination with the overall design of this secretary, suggest that it was made in Boston, perhaps in the shop of John Seymour, the preeminent cabinetmaker.

Seymour, born in Axminister, England, presumably trained there before he immigrated to America in 1785 with his wife, Jane, and eight children. They first settled in Portland, Maine, but relocated to Boston in 1794, where he established a cabinetmaking shop with his son Thomas. Thomas split off from his father in 1804 and carried on business for many years afterward, and John retired in 1813. In Boston, a city with many noted cabinet shops, the Seymours' reputation as exemplary furniture makers was outstanding. John Seymour's selection to the Massachusetts Charitable Mechanics Association—an organization that counted among its members the most successful craftsmen in the city—was a measure of the stature he had attained. A few labeled Seymour examples survive and attest to their high standards.[1] However, other cabinetmakers employed similar details and characteristics making identification of much Seymour work problematic.

The Columbus secretary is often called a lady's desk and bookcase because of its relatively small size and light effect; other massive secretaries had three drawers in the lower case or had four drawers and stood on bracket feet, either design of which imparted a much more substantial appearance. Indeed, period manuscripts assign lower values to ladies' desks than to men's, but little or no confirming evidence connects specific examples, such as this one, to ownership by women. Regardless of its exact use in post–Revolutionary War America, this secretary survives as eloquent testimony of Massachusetts interpretations of neoclassical design.

The secretary is made in two parts. The upper bookcase section has four Gothic arches across the front that open bookshelves to view. Below the arches, broad panels hide smaller compartments and their attendant clutter. The lower section has a folding writing surface that is covered with a green baize (coarsely woven wool) and rests on pullout supports at each side. The entire composition stands on tapered legs, adorned with veneered panels, which end in an additional taper intended to impart further delicacy of form. In addition to obvious color schemes, the maker selected bookmatch veneers for the spandrels of the arches, thereby creating a regular pattern. Similarly, the vibrant grain pattern of the mahogany boards in the pediment is matched to reinforce the bisymmetry of this secretary.[2] PDZ and CTB

SAMUEL ALEXANDER

6 Philadelphia, active 1797–1808
Sugar Urn, ca. 1797
Silver with chasing and engraving, 10½ × 4½ (26.67 × 11.43)
Engraved: Elizabeth Rodman Paul 1797/Laurence Taylor Paul 1897
Stamped under pedestal: S. ALEXANDER
Museum purchase made possible by the Endowment Fund in Honor of D. A. Turner 2000.29

PROVENANCE: S. J. Shrubsole, New York, 1965; Lansdell Christie, 1968; Henry McNeil; S. J. Shrubsole, New York.
EXHIBITIONS: *Summer Potpourri.*

Even after the American colonies separated from Great Britain and established themselves as a new republic in the late eighteenth century, American patrons of fashionable decorative arts continued to favor current trends in English taste. Silversmiths in the newly formed United States quickly adopted the neoclassical or Adamesque style that was all the rage in England at the time. The principal designers of this style replaced the S-shaped, or cyma, curves and naturalistic ornament of the rococo with restrained, symmetrical, and geometric forms enlivened with delicate surface decoration based upon the ideals and design vocabulary of ancient Greece and Rome.[1]

Little is known about the artisan named Samuel Alexander whose stamp appears under the pedestal of this sugar container. Records show that he and Christian Wiltberger Jr., a silversmith who worked in Philadelphia from 1793 to 1817, were business partners between 1797 and 1808.[2] Alexander's relatively short recorded career as a silversmith was typical of a number of young men of his time who often plied a variety of trades.[3]

This sugar container, shaped like a Grecian urn, is engraved with a family crest, set within a neoclassical cartouche, and positioned below an ornately decorated band. The body and foot have twelve concave panels that introduce vertical rhythm. The long-necked cover echoes the base. Beaded and engraved edges punctuate the form and make it quite a remarkable example of a neoclassical silver sugar urn, most of which are usually rather plain.[4] The urn is inscribed with the name Elizabeth Rodman Paul, who married James Paul a member of a prominent Philadelphia family. Since they were married in 1797 (the date inscribed with her name), this presumably was a wedding gift. Mr. Paul was a merchant trader to China and the East Indies. The name of their grandson, Lawrence Taylor Paul, who possibly inherited this piece, is also inscribed, with the date 1897. LR

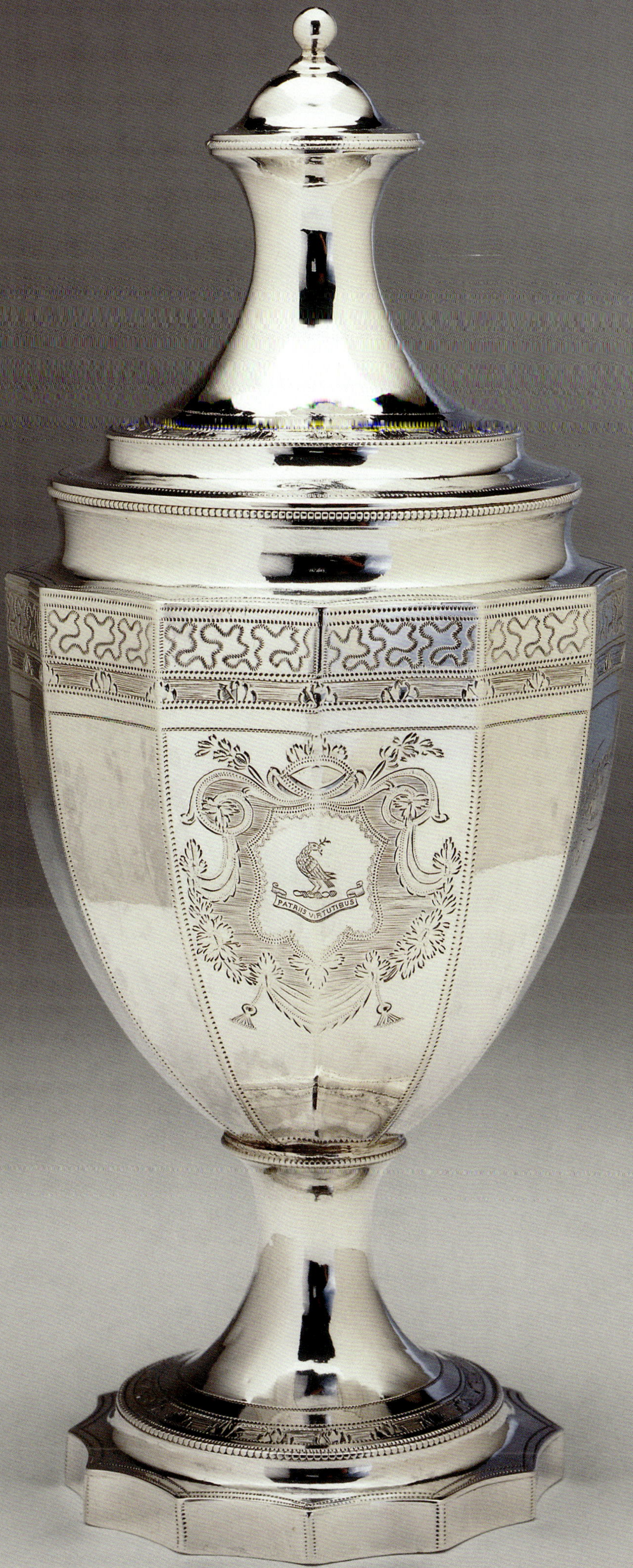
PATRIIS VIRTUTIBUS

GILBERT STUART

7

b. 1755, North Kingston, Rhode Island; d. 1828, Boston
Mrs. Edward Stow, 1802–3
Oil on cradled panel, 29¼ × 23½ (74.29 × 59.69)
Signed lower left: G.S.
Museum purchase made possible by the Endowment Fund in Honor of D. A. Turner 2000.1

PROVENANCE: Edward Stow, Philadelphia; by descent to Louisa Matilda Stow, daughter, 1831; by descent to Caroline Stow Hyatt, sister, Ithaca, New York, 1905; American Art Galleries, New York, sale January 17, 1922, lot 26; Scott and Fowles, New York, 1922; private collection, 1930; Newhouse Galleries, New York; Mr. and Mrs. James C. Brady; Virginia Steele Scott Foundation, 1976; Henry Huntington Library, San Marino, California, 1983; Jordan-Volpe Gallery, New York; Vance Jordan Gallery, New York.
EXHIBITIONS: *Portraits Painted by the Late Gilbert Stuart, Esq.,* Museum of Fine Arts, Boston, 1828, no. 124; *19th and 20th Century American Art from Private Collections,* Whitney Museum of American Art, New York, June–September 1972, no. 377.
PUBLICATIONS: Park, 4: 491, no. 794; *The Huntington Art Collections: A Handbook* (San Marino, Calif.: Huntington Library, 1986), 162; Miles, 227, fig. 1.

Gilbert Stuart began his career as a provincial portrait painter in the American colonies and eventually went to London for further training. Under the generous tutelage of expatriate Benjamin West, Stuart quickly mastered the painterly brushwork of the Grand Manner, which was the favored style of Sir Joshua Reynolds, the leading portraitist of the day. Stuart realized that portrait painting could be a very lucrative business, so he opened what became a successful portrait studio in London. His extravagant tastes however left him with ever-growing debts, which he avoided by fleeing in 1787 to Ireland. Again, in 1793, Stuart was unable to live within his means, and he escaped to New York to avoid debtors' prison.

Stuart painted directly on the canvas, and without benefit of a preliminary drawing completed the work in a couple of brief sittings. In this manner Stuart produced a prodigious number of portraits.[1] He is perhaps known best for his idealized, solemn, and dignified portraits of George Washington, which have come to represent the personification of Washington as the "father of his country." Stuart's unfinished portrait, made at Germantown in 1796 and known as the Atheneum portrait (owned jointly by the Museum of Fine Arts, Boston, and the National Portrait Gallery, Washington, D.C.), remained in his studio for many years, serving as the model for more than a hundred replicas that he produced during his career.

Anna Stow, the subject of Stuart's painting, and her husband, Edward, were a socially prominent couple living in Philadelphia. Their intimate circle included Dolly Madison as well as Stuart and his wife. Soon after this portrait was painted, Stuart moved to Washington, D.C., leaving Edward Stow to serve as his business representative in Philadelphia. Stow remained in Philadelphia, while his wife and son lived in Bordentown in genteel poverty. Based upon this portrait, it would seem that Anna Stow would have been most unaccustomed to anything other than a luxurious lifestyle. She wears her hair in elaborate curls adorned by a floral ornament. Her delicate pearl earrings and choker correspond to her empire-style, pearl-white dress, which was the height of fashion at the time. The gold brocade wrap over her shoulders and arms further conveys the idea of wealth and offers the artist an opportunity to display his most fluent brushwork, which is similarly apparent in the red drapery that is raised to reveal a dramatic sky. Perhaps Stuart's expedient approach to his work can explain the awkwardness of his rendering of the sitter's right hand. The companion work, *Edward Stow,* painted around 1803, is in the collection of the National Gallery of Art in Washington, D.C. In a comparison of the two portraits, it appears that the artist lavished more attention to the finishing of Anna Stow's portrait.[2] LR

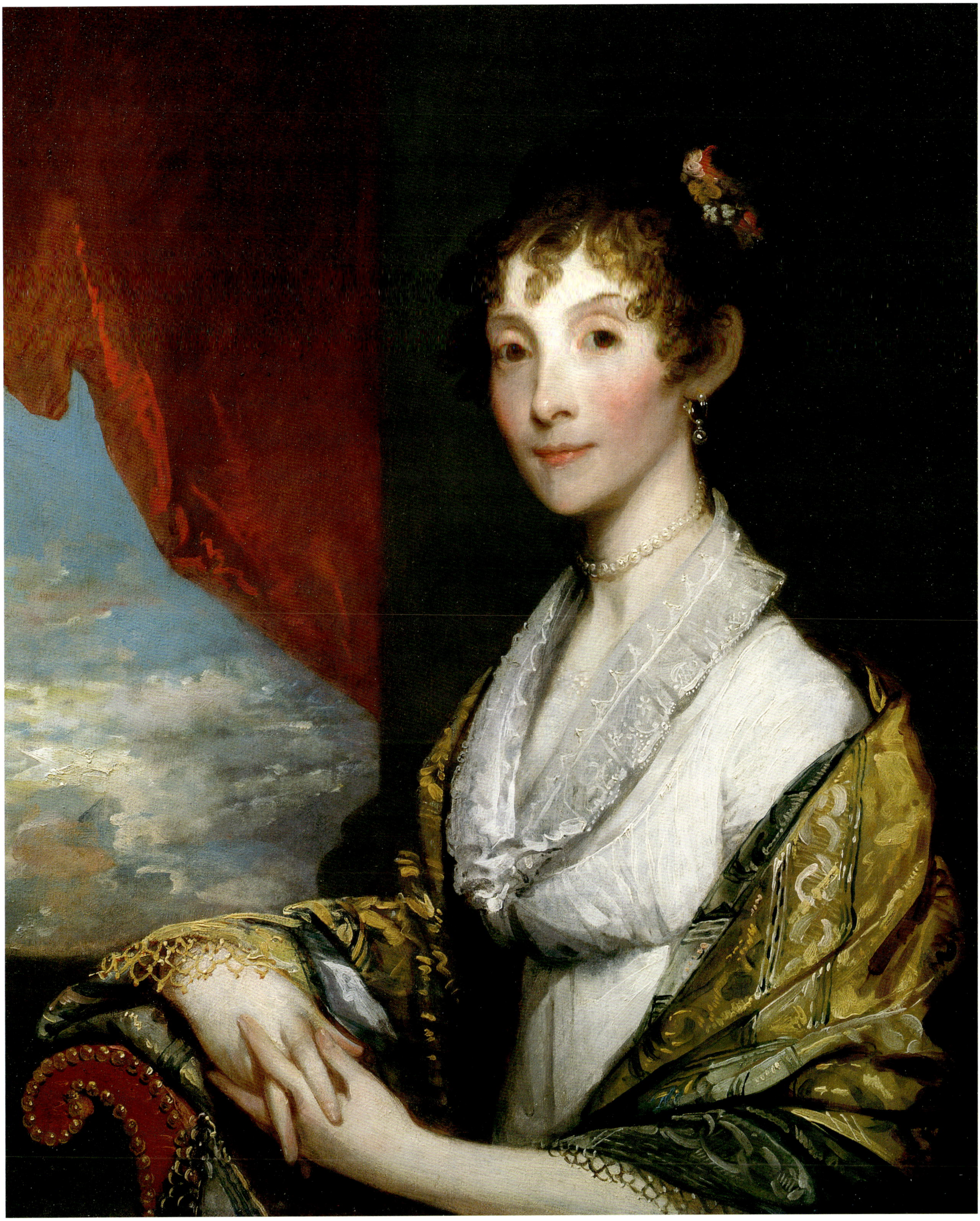

UNKNOWN MAKER

8 Philadelphia (attributed), active nineteenth century
Pair of Card Tables, 1810–20
Mahogany, mahogany veneer, with secondary woods of oak and yellow pine; brass, 20¾ × 35 × 17½ (52.71 × 88.9 × 44.45)
Museum purchase 83.57a–b

PROVENANCE: Dr. Henry J. Berkley, Maryland; Joe Kindig and Son, York, Pennsylvania.
PUBLICATIONS: Burroughs, 80–81, pl. 12.

Card tables were among the most common table forms made in America in the federal period, namely from the late 1780s through about 1820. An acceptable part of an evening's entertainment was to participate in a variety of games such as dice, cards, chess, draughts, or backgammon. When not playing games (or using these tables for a variety of other purposes), homeowners often used them as pier tables or consoles, placing them directly against a wall—a fact that explains the rarity of American pier tables from this time. Pairs of tables could be arranged symmetrically, flanking doorways, windows, or fireplaces.[1]

This pair of card tables represents a specific design that is well described in contemporary references. Price books, which detailed for journeymen and shop owners the prices for making a wide range of furniture, describe such card tables as "pillar and claw," the pillar being the central support and the claw the leg. The 1810 New York price book specified a pillar-and-claw card table with "three claws . . . two of ditto to turn out with the joint rail."[2] That cryptic entry describes a mechanism built into these card tables whereby supports for the folding table leaf are linked to iron rods running through the pillar to the legs. When a user swings out the supports, the side legs swing back to form a more stable tripod base capable of supporting the broader table expanse. Although this mechanism is not specified in the Philadelphia price list of 1811, pillar-and-claw card tables are listed, affirming that such tables were made there as well. This mechanism seems to be uniquely American.[3]

Although Philadelphia and New York pillar-and-claw card tables appear at first glance to be similar, Philadelphia examples differ in the shapes of the tops and legs, molding profiles, and placement and style of carving.[4] Whereas New York makers opted for double- and treble-elliptic curves, namely two or three broad curves, Philadelphia versions had curved or bowed central segments that met the rounded corners in an S-shaped or reversed curve. Tabletops in Philadelphia were typically reeded at the edge, in contrast to veneered edges in New York. Most New York tables had single-curve sweep legs rather than the S-shaped, or cyma-curved, legs evident in this pair of tables. Philadelphia legs were molded on the sides instead of being left plain. Philadelphia acanthus carving, visible on the knees, is less stylized, and it appears abbreviated in length compared to the longer New York acanthus leaves. PDZ and CTB

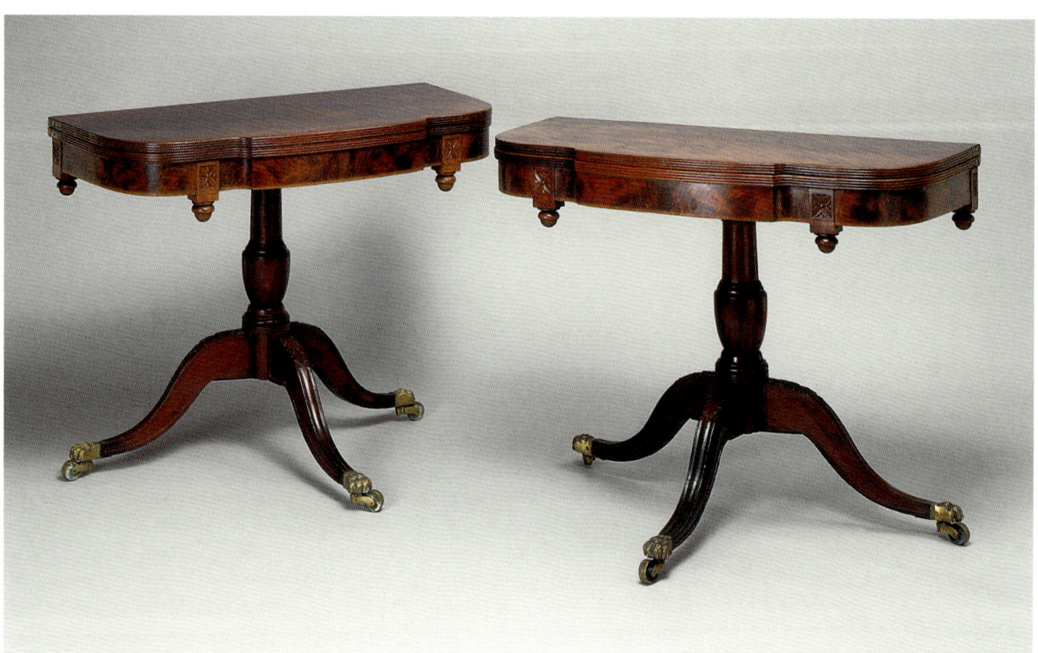

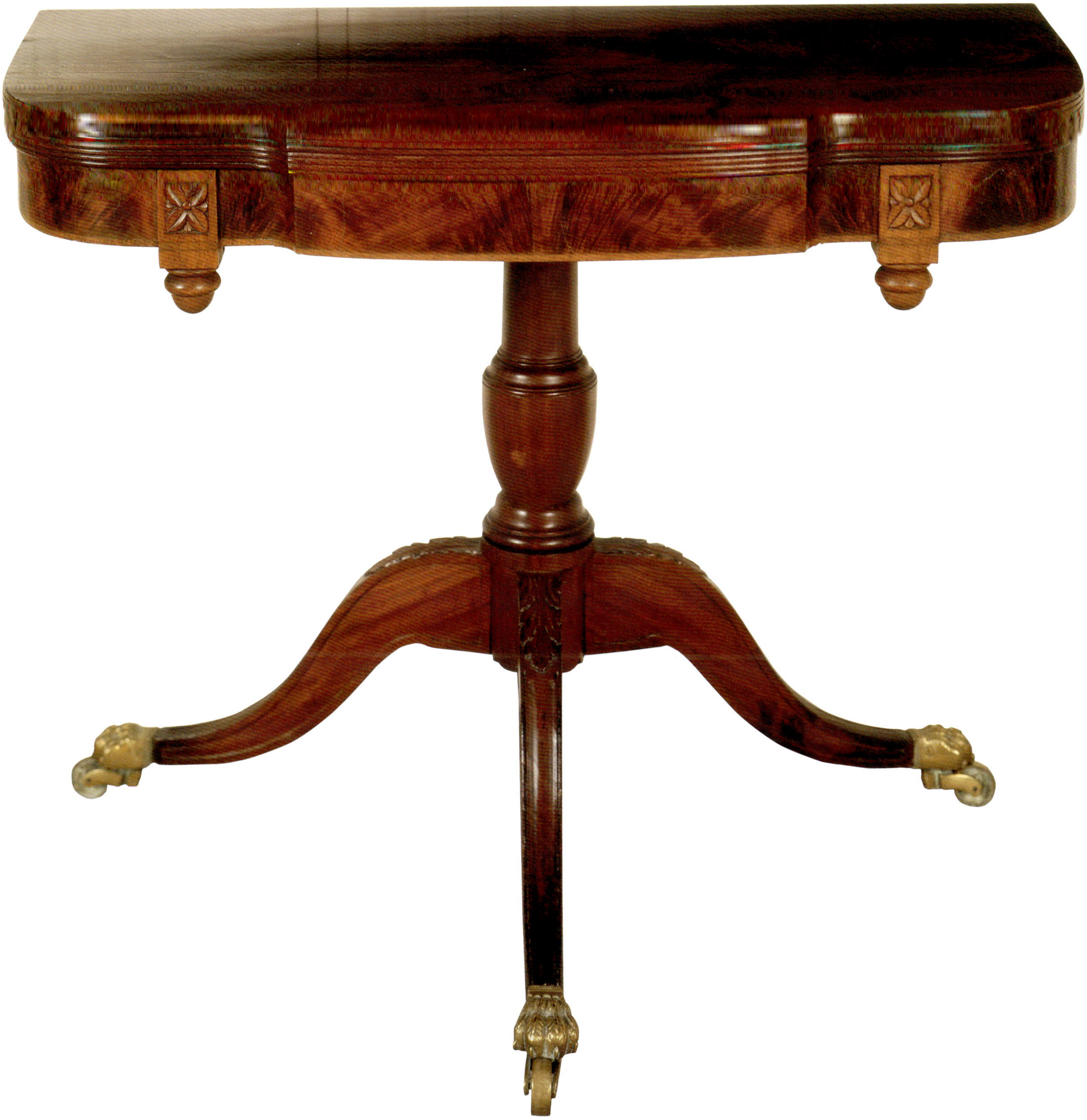

THOMAS SULLY

9

b. 1783, Horncastle, Lincolnshire, England; d. 1872, Philadelphia
Mrs. Caleb Newbold and Her Son Thomas, 1813
Oil on canvas, 35 × 40 (88.90 × 101.60)
Signed and dated lower right: T. S. 1813
Museum purchase made possible by the Edward Swift Shorter Bequest Fund 93.8

PROVENANCE: Elizabeth Ross Newbold, Philadelphia (the sitter); by descent to Charles Newbold, son, Philadelphia; by descent to Newbold Drayton, great-grandson, Philadelphia, by 1922; by descent to Mary Newbold Harding, New York; Christie's, New York.
EXHIBITIONS: *Annual Exhibition,* Pennsylvania Academy of the Fine Arts, Philadelphia, 1814, possibly as *Lady and Child,* no. 186; *Memorial Exhibition of Portraits by Thomas Sully,* Pennsylvania Academy of the Fine Arts, Philadelphia, 1922, no. 49.
PUBLICATIONS: Winn, et al., 121.

Thomas Sully, who was born in England, immigrated to Charleston, South Carolina, in 1792. His earliest art training came from family members, including his brother Lawrence and brother-in-law Jean Belzons, a painter of miniatures. He began his professional career in Virginia, and then settled in Philadelphia in 1808.[1] The next year, carrying a letter of introduction from Charles Willson Peale, Sully went to London to study with expatriate Benjamin West.[2] When he returned to Philadelphia, he quickly established himself as a much-sought-after portrait painter. A prolific worker, he created more than 2,600 works, of which at least 2,000 were portraits.[3] Perhaps his most important commission was to paint Queen Victoria during her coronation festivities in 1838. In preparing for the portrait, Sully produced approximately thirty-five works, including drawings, oil sketches, and paintings, which culminated in the final grand portrait of the beautiful young queen, newly crowned, ascending the steps to her throne (private collection).[4]

In the museum's painting, *Mrs. Caleb Newbold and Her Son Thomas,* Sully depicts a mother and child from a prominent Philadelphia family. Elizabeth Ross married Caleb Newbold in 1808. Her husband was involved in the Pennsylvania Canal Company and ran a business importing goods to the United States from Calcutta. Her son Thomas, the eldest of her four children, became a lawyer, stockbroker, and editor of the *Philadelphia North American.*[5]

The loving intimacy of the moment stands in direct contrast to the formal restraint of most American portraits of this day, suggesting that this painting was probably not intended for a public audience. Instead, it is a glimpse into the private lives of this family. Sully has painted a moment when Newbold's rambunctious three-year-old has playfully captured her comb and is proudly waving it at the intended viewer, his father. While there is no doubt of the wealth of the family, as reflected in the luxurious silks and velvets they wear and the well-appointed furnishings and statuary that is part of their setting, Sully has captured the everyday personal interactions of a young mother and child and made these most elegant and memorable. The graceful nature of the sitter's pose, her luxuriant hair worn down, and her look of reverie were important elements of Sully's developing romanticism and the new painterly style he had mastered while in London.

Sully maintained a register of daily work, noting almost every painting, its size, its beginning and ending dates, its patron, and the price of its commission. He listed this painting as "Newbold, Mrs., and her child," a half-length portrait, 25 × 30 inches, standard size, but in reality the painting is larger. Begun February 4, 1813, it was completed July 25, 1813. The Newbolds paid Sully $200 for the double portrait. Sully's notation omits any mention of the rounded top edges of the canvas, a distinct deviation from the standard portrait form. BF

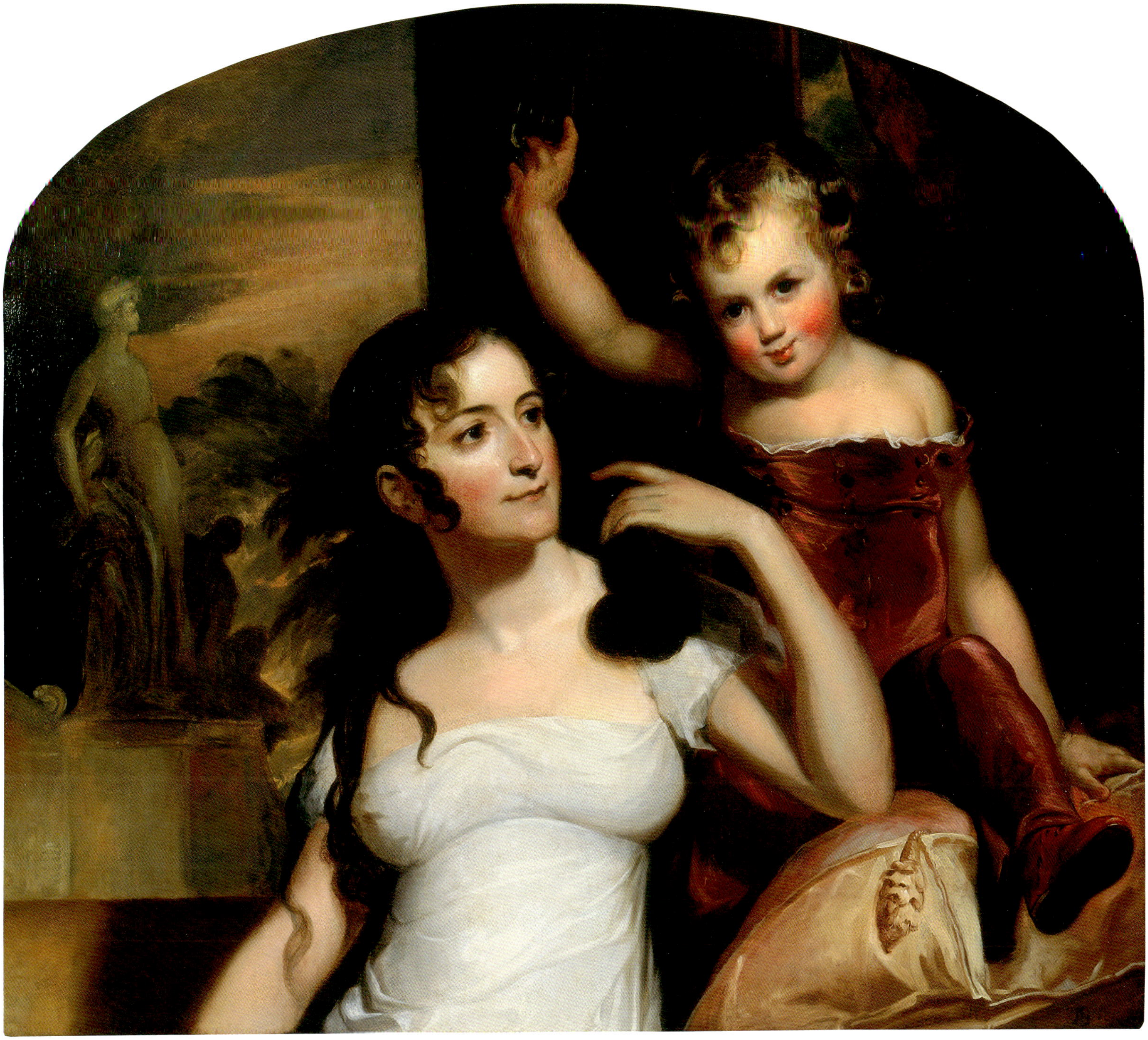

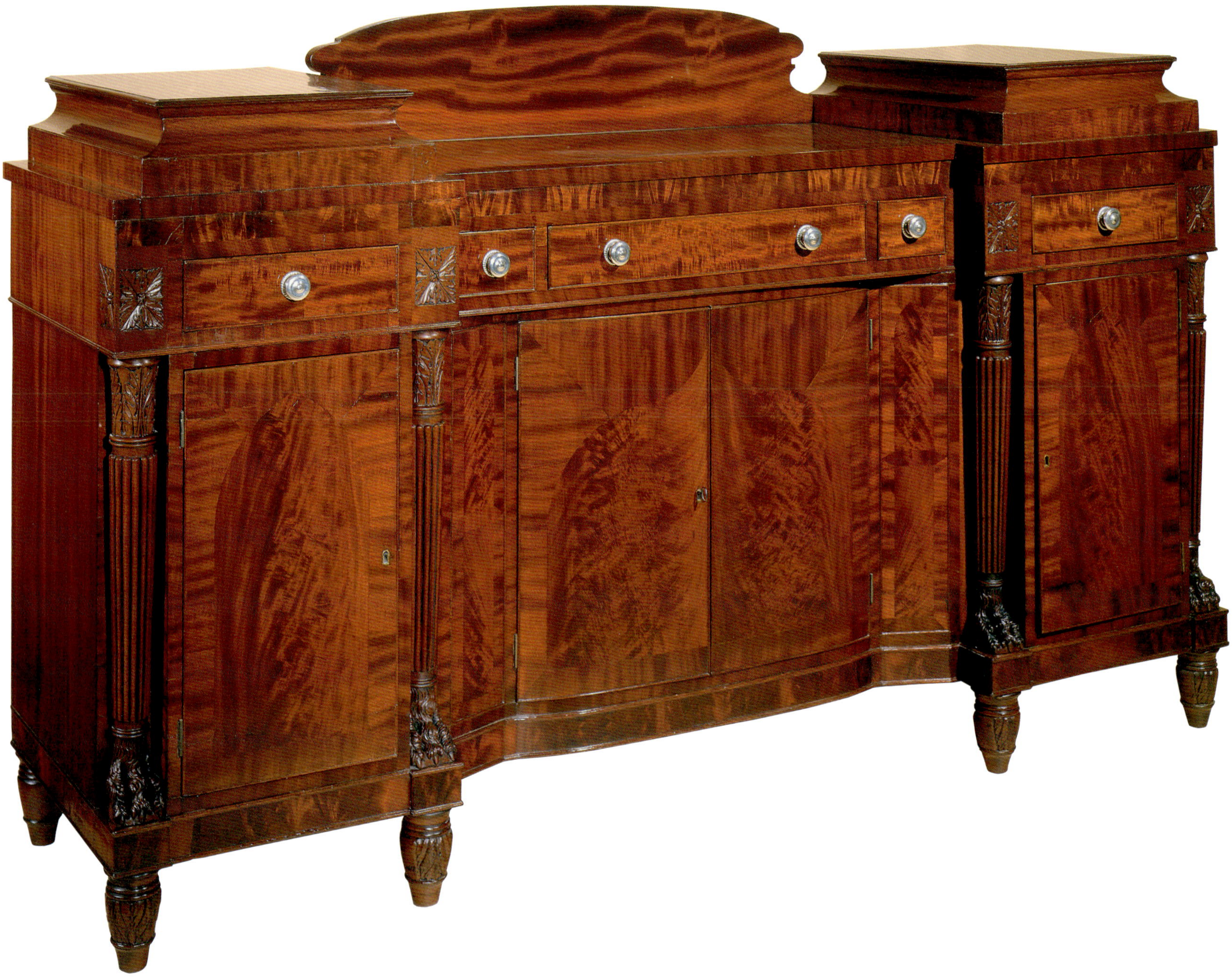

JOSEPH B. BARRY (ATTRIBUTED TO SHOP)

b. ca. 1757 Dublin, Ireland; d. 1838 Philadelphia

10 **Sideboard**, 1810–[illegible]

Mahogany and mahogany veneer, with secondary woods of poplar, pine, maple, silver-plated pulls, 51⅜ × 83¾ × 23¼ (130.49 × 212.72 × 59.01)

Purchase made possible by the Ella E. Kirven Charitable Lead Trust for Acquisitions 2000.12

PROVENANCE: Robert Trump; Hirschl and Adler Galleries, New York.

EXHIBITIONS: *Summer Potpourri.*

Of monumental scale and sober mood, this sideboard realizes in Philadelphia furniture some of the classical antique designs popularized in European design books of the early nineteenth century. Drawing from Egyptian, Greek, and Roman sources, designers such as Pierre de la Mesangere of Paris and Thomas Hope and George Smith of London introduced new ideas based on more archeologically correct interpretations. Several plates from Smith's *Collection of Designs* (1808) illustrate sideboards, legs, and other elements—notably reeded and tapered columns with animal feet and the deep scotia molding at the top of each pedestal—that recall the Columbus sideboard.[1] The gently arched splashboard ending in profiles of bold moldings differs from the usual shallow pitch pediment and lends a softer character to the overall design.

Engaged columns enclosing four cupboard doors describe in part the large, mahogany-veneered, rectangular French-inspired sideboards produced in America as alternatives to colorfully inlaid and veneered sideboards having shallow cases raised on tapered legs and shaped in the front. The mahogany veneers on the Columbus sideboard create a dynamic visual effect. Gothic and ogival (also called Moorish) arches on the cupboard doors display carefully matched figured veneers. Mahogany with exquisite ribbon effects enhances the drawers, splashboard, and flat moldings. The reeded and carved columns, in contrast, are made of mahogany with a uniform grain.

Joseph B. Barry, the probable maker of this sideboard, arrived in Philadelphia about 1794 from London and Dublin. Likely due in part to his energy and breadth of vision, he seems to have assumed a leading role among cabinetmakers in the city and could name Thomas Jefferson among his clients. For two months in 1798, he developed a business in Savannah, followed by another venture in Baltimore, where in 1803 he advertised his "Cabinet furniture of the newest London and French patterns." In 1811 he traveled to Europe, returning to Philadelphia the following year. Barry remained in business until his death in 1838.[2]

Attribution to Barry rests on several factors. Sideboards of this design and quality are rare, hence were likely made by few artisans. The strongest evidence of Barry manufacture, however, lies in the similarities between the Columbus sideboard and another signed by Barry and dated 1813 in a private collection. Another example of this type of sideboard differs in having an open center. Formerly in the collection of Andy Warhol and now at the Winterthur Museum in Delaware, it closely parallels an 1814 auction advertisement in Philadelphia that specified a "Large recess Sideboard, Barry's make, with column and side closets [and] a set of knife cases."[3] Barry's interest in the antique is evident in his announcement in the *Philadelphia Aurora General Advertiser* on January 19, 1810, that he and his son supplied "the newest and most fashionable Cabinet Furniture, superbly finished in the rich Egyptian and Gothic style." PDZ and CTB

HARVEY LEWIS

11

b. 1783, Philadelphia; d. 1835, Philadelphia

Six-Piece Coffee and Tea Service, ca. 1823

Silver with engraving, wood handles; coffee pot, 13¼ × 14 × 7 (33.66 × 35.56 × 17.78); two tea pots, 11¼ × 10½ × 6½ (25.58 × 31.75 × 16.51); sugar bowl, 10 × 9 × 6¾ (25.4 × 22.86 × 17.15); creamer, 7¾ × 6⅞ × 4¾ (19.69 × 17.46 × 12.07); and waste bowl, 6 × 9 × 9 (15.24 × 22.86 × 22.86)

Stamped on each piece except the creamer: HARVEY LEWIS

Museum purchase made possible by the Endowment Fund in Honor of D. A. Turner 2000.4

PROVENANCE: Commissioned by Isaac Cooper and Hannah Firth Jones; Hannah Elizabeth Jones Smith, 1865; Woodruff Jones; Mary Carpenter Jones; Mary Carpenter Emlen; Carswell Rush Berlin, New York.

EXHIBITIONS: *Summer Potpourri.*

At the turn of the nineteenth century, accomplished architects, furniture designers, and painters were fashioning elegant pieces in the neoclassical or federal style. Concurrently, the thirty leading silversmiths who advertised regularly in Philadelphia newspapers were also creating pieces fashioned in the same styles with a skill comparable to that invested in the finest English imports. Silversmiths in both countries manufactured classic, urn-shaped teapots, covered sugar bowls, and creamers in the form of ancient warriors' helmets. Often accompanied by a waste bowl and a larger coffee pot, these pieces comprised a matching set, a popular accoutrement in fashionable homes.

The museum's six-piece silver coffee and tea service by Harvey Lewis is a rounded interpretation of the earlier, more angular forms, and the floral decoration is more naturalistic than that on earlier, more stylized counterparts. The lids on every piece in this silver service are adorned with repoussé decoration and surmounted by a cast acanthus and lotus flower finial.[1] Each of the urn-shaped vessels is mounted with applied decoration, and a circular pedestal base supports the body. The coffee pot and the teapots have carved wooden handles. Each piece bears the engraved initials IC/1823, and, on the opposite side, the initials HEJS/1865. Lewis (and subsequent silversmiths) engraved the names of all the owners dating from 1823 until 1938 under the base of each piece.

Harvey Lewis was apprenticed to Philadelphia silversmith Joseph Lownes.[2] He began business as a silversmith as early as 1804, and took on apprentice Henry Clark in August of that year. Lewis and his colleague Joseph D. Smith borrowed money from the well-known silversmith Joseph Richardson Jr. to set up business as Lewis and Smith Silversmiths, 2 South 2nd Street, Philadelphia, between 1805 and 1810. The partnership was eventually dissolved. In 1823 Lewis married Elizabeth Sellers, a cousin of his longtime friend, Coleman Sellers. Sellers and his wife, Sophonisba (daughter of Charles Willson Peale) named their third son Harvey Lewis Sellers (b. 1813), in honor of Sellers's lasting friendship with Lewis.

Lewis's work is among the finest examples in American neoclassical silver. His most famous work is an inkwell supported by three winged sphinxes (Yale University Art Gallery).[3] Its design emulates an ancient incense burner as interpreted by French goldsmiths of the Napoleonic era and later English ceramists.[4] Another spectacular example is Lewis's ewer (Maryland Historical Society), made for Isaac McKim of the firm John McKim and Son, a Philadelphia-based China trade merchant.[5] LR

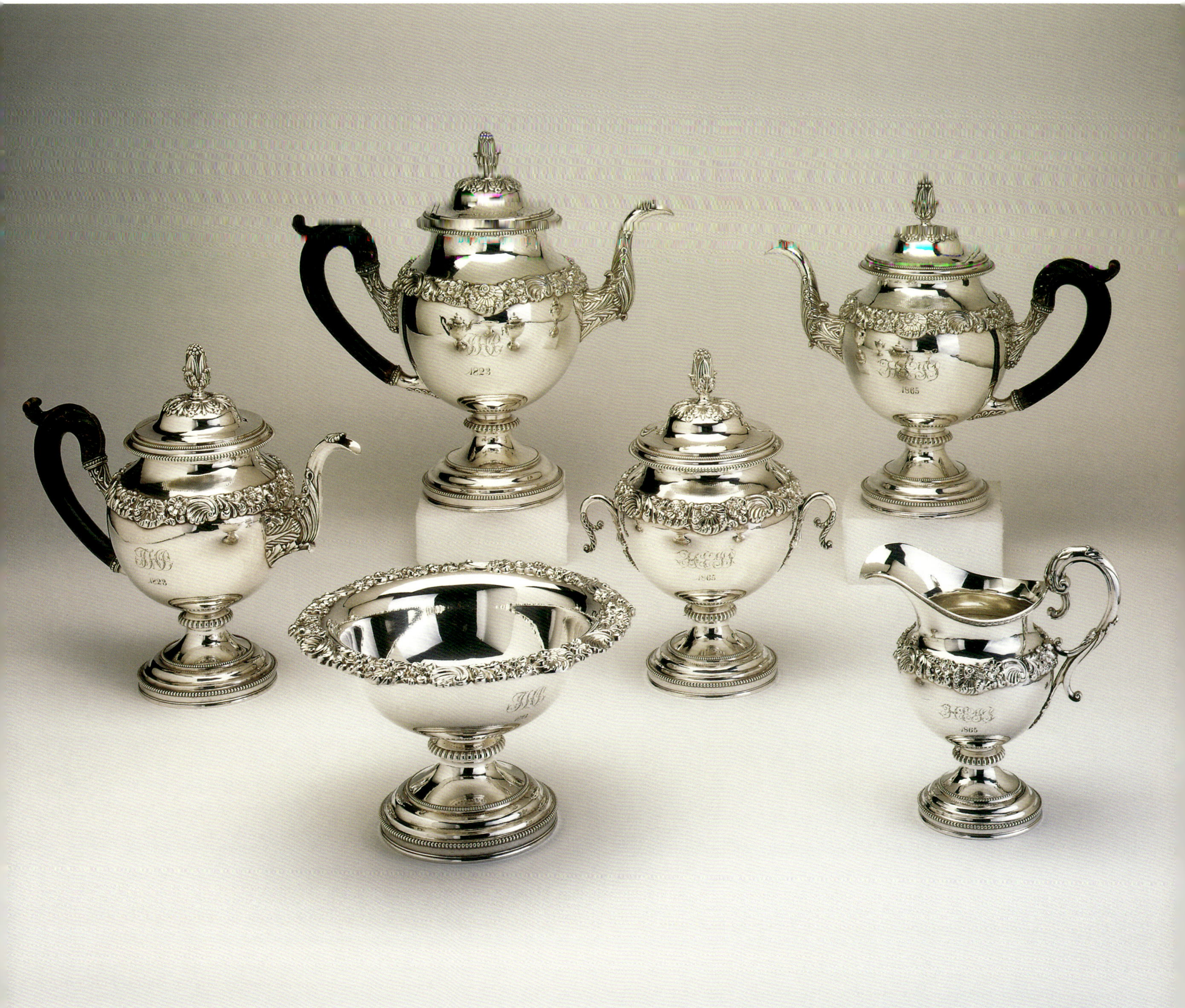

WILLIAM ELLIS TUCKER AND COMPANY

12

Philadelphia, active 1826–38

Vase-shaped Pitcher, ca. 1830

Glazed, mold-cast, soft-paste porcelain with enamel and gilt, h. 9⅜, diam. 3¾ (h. 23.81, diam. 9.53)

Museum purchase made possible by The Endowment Fund in Honor of D. A. Turner 98.5

PROVENANCE: Hirschl and Adler Galleries, New York, 1996.
EXHIBITIONS: *Tucker China 1825–1838*, Philadelphia Museum of Art, May 4–September 9, 1957, no. 353 (lent anonymously).

William Ellis Tucker and Company, the first commercially successful large-scale manufactory of porcelain in the United States, produced a wide variety of table and ornamental wares inspired by early-nineteenth-century French and English porcelain.[1] Tucker was born in Philadelphia on June 11, 1800. His father, Benjamin, was a Quaker schoolmaster and proprietor of a china shop. William too began his professional life as a teacher, and he assisted his father in the family-owned store as well. It was there that he began to decorate the plain pieces received in shipments from abroad. The elder Tucker allowed his son to build a kiln in the backyard of the shop in which to fire and set the applied enamel paints. In 1826 William began to experiment with ceramic production, mixing his own clay and kaolin.[2] His experiments culminated in the formulation of creamware (earthenware with cream-colored glaze) and porcelain. Realizing they would need bigger kilns for this kind of production, the Tuckers leased factory space in the old Philadelphia waterworks.

About 1827 the Tucker factory fired their first kiln loaded with porcelain. By the fall of that year, the factory was producing a wide range of vessels, including pitchers, cups, saucers, and ceramic fruit baskets. In 1827 and 1828 Tucker's porcelains won silver medals at the Franklin Institute's exhibitions.[3] William's younger brother, Thomas, became an apprentice in the factory in 1828 and began painting decorations on production ware.

Due to the high costs of producing porcelain, financial instability dogged the factory throughout its twelve years of operation. Having no other choice, William sought outside investors for his business.[4] In 1831 William undertook his last and most successful partnership, with Judge Joseph Hemphill.[5] The well-traveled Hemphill was familiar with prevailing European styles, and it may have been his influence that resulted in the introduction of the French Sèvres style of decorative painting and a more lavish use of gold in Tucker ware production.

When William Tucker died in 1832, Hemphill assumed legal control of the factory and made Thomas Tucker superintendent. Because of the national financial upheavals of the 1830s, Hemphill also brought in new partners and reorganized the company as the American Porcelain Company in 1835. He had to sell his interest in the factory in 1837. Thomas continued production, renting the factory for a year, but the firm's financial problems were never resolved, and the factory closed in 1838.

Tucker porcelain shapes were generally ovoid, based on classical prototypes, and represented in the current style.[6] Tucker was the first domestic manufacturer to picture native themes and American landscapes on porcelain, such as views of Philadelphia, and patriotic heroes like the Marquis de Lafayette. Given the number of surviving examples, pitchers and jugs were among their most popular pieces. The decorative types and motifs found in Tucker porcelain cannot be separated into precise periods of use. However, it is believed that uncomplicated motifs point to the early years, and elaborate gilt and polychrome decoration indicate the final Tucker and Hemphill period. Festoons and bouquets of flowers, fruit, and birds, all with gilt garlands and bands, were popular motifs during the entire twelve-year period of production.[7]

Although most shapes in the Tucker line were direct copies of French Empire porcelain, the vase-shaped pitcher was uniquely Tucker's design. The museum's piece is a particularly fine example of the type. It features a high-arched handle and a corrugated, molded band around the base. In the production pattern books, the shape was offered with eleven different decorative schemes, from simple gilding and rosebuds to an elaborate design with gilded borders and floral bouquets on front and back, as in the museum's example. Of the known dated examples of the vase shape, most are from 1828, though others date as late as 1834. It is generally accepted that this form was made and sold during the entire existence of the factory. An examination of the clay composition and other technical aspects of the piece indicates that the museum's example is not an early Tucker piece.[8] It was included in the seminal exhibition of Tucker porcelain held at the Philadelphia Museum of Art in 1957.

KMZ and PDZ

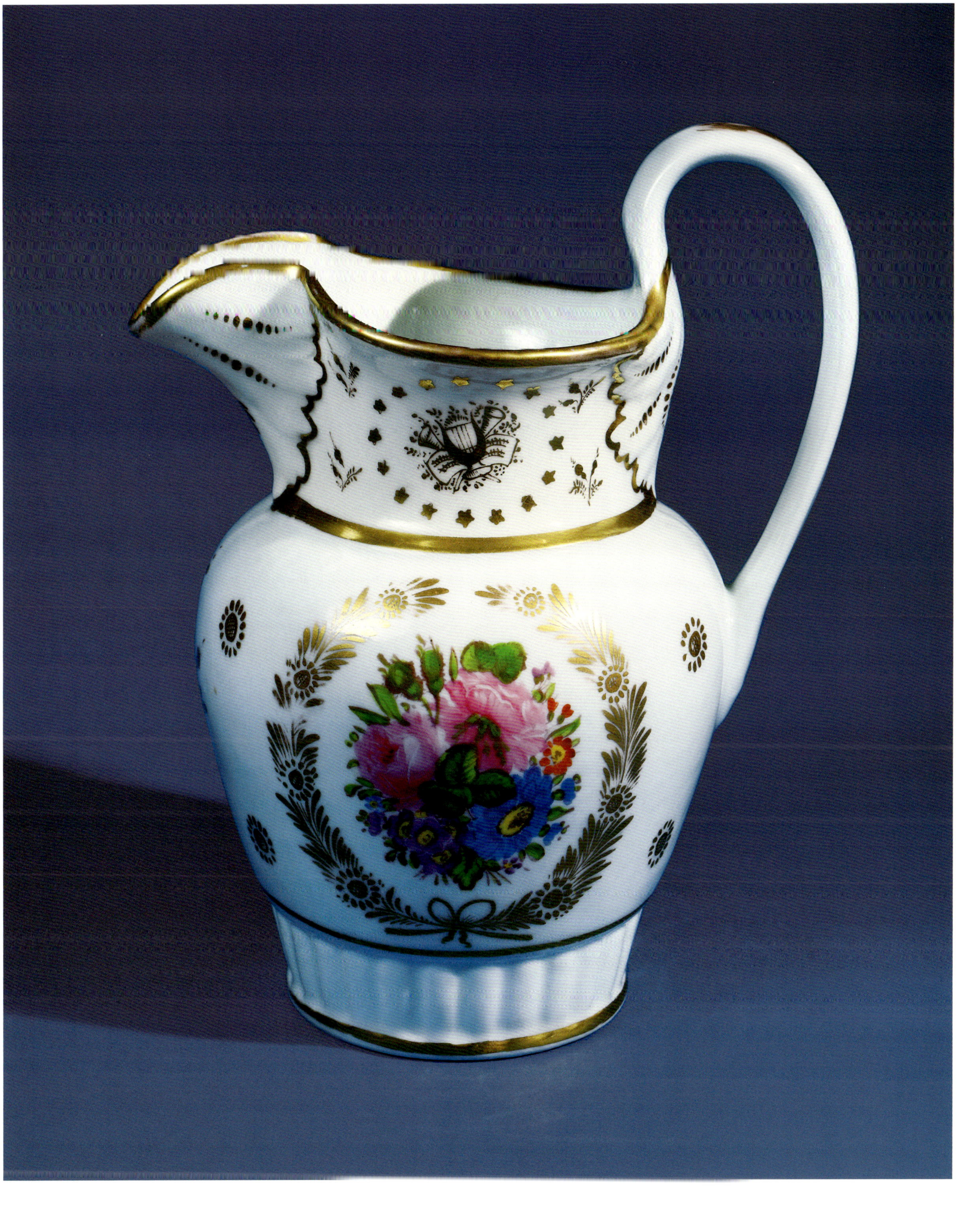

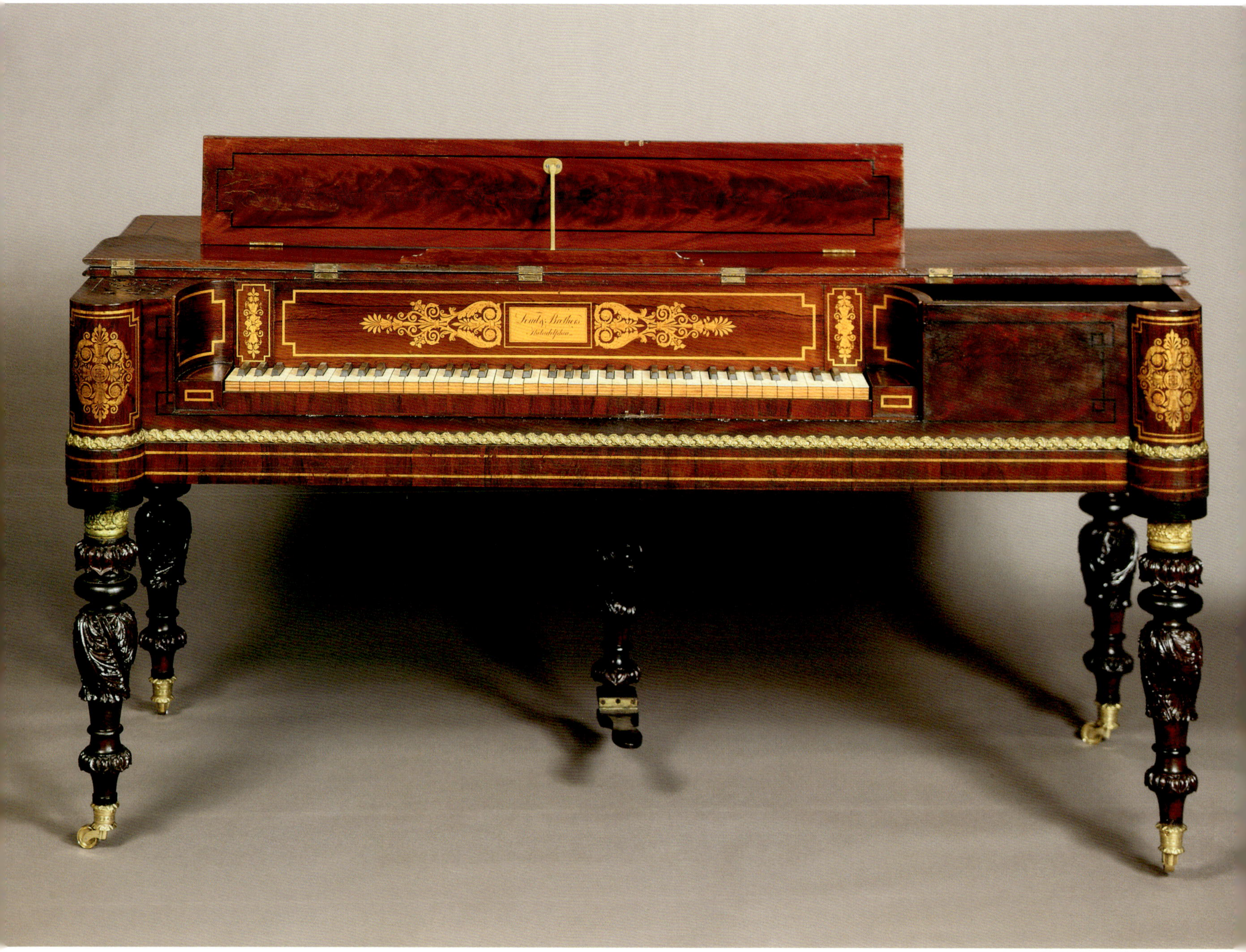

WILLIAM MOORE

Philadelphia, active 1800–1840
Loud and Brothers, Philadelphia, 1822–33

13 **Square Piano,** 1831

Mahogany and rosewood veneers, with secondary wood of pine; embossed brass, metal, and ivory, 32 × 69 × 30 (81.28 × 175.26 × 76.2)

Inscribed on soundboard: Loud & Brothers/Philadelphia/Wm. Moore Phila/June 25, 1831, No. 509/1121. Inscribed on nameboard: L.B. 127

Museum purchase made possible by the Art and Acquisition Fund 96.2

PROVENANCE: David Peebles, Virginia; Lisburne Lane Antiques, Ordinary, Virginia.

This imposing square piano from the Philadelphia firm of Loud and Brothers dominates its surroundings. It reflects a time during the first half of the nineteenth century when music became increasingly important in the life of affluent American families and the piano became the favored musical instrument. Boston and New York supported notable piano-making dynasties, but Philadelphia led the United States in production in the 1830s, with Loud and Brothers accounting for a large share.

Though similar in appearance, pianos differ from harpsichords in that strings are struck with a padded hammer in the former and plucked with a quill in the latter. Bartolommeo Cristofori, a Paduan harpsichord maker, is credited with making the first piano; the dates usually given are 1709 and 1711. Cristofori called his new instrument *gravicembalo col piano e forte,* a harpsichord with soft and loud, referring to the modulation of sound by means of a foot pedal that dampens vibration of the strings. Not only were its tones mellower but it could be played softly so as not to overpower a gentle singing voice.

The museum's square piano is almost identical to examples in the Sewell C. Biggs Museum of American Art (Dover, Delaware) and the Metropolitan Museum of Art.[1] William Moore, a member of the Society of Journeymen Cabinet-Makers in the directories of 1828 to 1836, signed both the Columbus and Metropolitan Museum pianos and likely specialized in this type of cabinetry. Little else is known of him.[2] He used rich mahogany and rosewood veneers and highlighted these by gilt stencil decoration, black-painted bands, and gleaming brass. Ornate and stoutly turned and carved legs with brass casters support the body of the instrument and readily unscrew from the case for ease of movement. With such rich and sumptuous design and unusual size, this piano would certainly be the centerpiece of any grand parlor. CTB and PDZ

SARAH MIRIAM PEALE (ATTRIBUTED TO THE ARTIST OR HER STUDIO)

14 b. 1800; d. 1885, Philadelphia
Bishop William Capers, ca. 1840–45
Oil on canvas, 29½ × 25¼ (74.93 × 64.14)
Stamped on back: From/John C. Simons/Artist Repository/No. 208 King Street/Charleston, S.C.
Museum purchase made possible by the Art Acquisition and Restoration Fund and the Endowment Fund in Honor of D. A. Turner 90.1

PROVENANCE: The Rev. William Capers; Frank Vogan Capers; Ruth Capers Rinfrette; Kay Elizabeth Rinfrette, 1954; Frank S. Schwarz and Son Gallery, Philadelphia.
EXHIBITIONS: *Philadelphia XL,* Frank S. Schwarz and Son Gallery, Philadelphia, no. 17.
PUBLICATIONS: *Philadelphia XL,* Frank S. Schwarz and Son Gallery, Philadelphia; Winn, et al., 12.

Sarah Miriam Peale was the youngest of six children.[1] Her father, James Peale, was the brother of Charles Willson Peale and a painter in his own right. Her mother, Mary Claypoole Peale, was the sister of the artist James Claypoole. Sarah began her studies as a studio assistant to her father, and sometimes painted vivid and elaborate fabrics into his works. In 1824 she and her sister, Anna Claypoole Peale, became the first women members of the Pennsylvania Academy of the Fine Arts.

Sarah Peale left Philadelphia in 1825 to study with her cousin, Rembrandt Peale, in Baltimore. She later opened a studio there and became a popular portrait painter, with commissions that exceeded the number received by celebrated male painters Thomas Sully, Jacob Eichholtz, and John Vanderlyn Thomas. From 1841 to 1843, she made several trips to Washington, D.C., where she painted distinguished public officials, including Millard Fillmore, General George Armstrong Custer, and the Marquis de Lafayette. In 1847 Peale moved to St. Louis, where she continued to paint for thirty-two years. Although in later years she still advertised as a portraitist, she concentrated on still-life painting and won numerous awards for these works. In 1878 she returned to Philadelphia and spent her last years with two older, widowed sisters.

More than a hundred portraits and still-life paintings are attributed to Peale. Her style reflects the work of Charles Willson Peale, her uncle, in its clarity of line and restrained brushwork, and the work of Rembrandt Peale, her cousin, in its rich color and accurate detailing. Most of her portraits focus on the single figure, but a few are double portraits. All are distinctive in the precise rendering of textures such as furs, laces, and textiles.

The museum's portrait of William Capers is attributed to Peale or her studio.[2] Capers was born in 1790 and was raised near Charleston, South Carolina.[3] In 1821, after his ordination as a Methodist minister, he was appointed missionary to the Creek Indians in western Georgia, the area in which the city of Columbus was established in 1828. He made regular trips to the Chattahoochee River Valley, and in 1822 in the frontier village of Coweta he established the first regional school for Creek youths. He kept a detailed diary that included accounts of Indian life in Georgia during this period. In 1825 Capers became editor of the *Wesleyan Journal;* later he was named Bishop of the Methodist Episcopal Church, South. He died in 1855 and is buried in Columbia, South Carolina.[4]

In this portrait, the bishop wears a ministerial white collar and black jacket. The back of the red brocade chair in which he is seated is visible over his left shoulder. The portrait is believed to date from 1840 to 1845 based on the stamp at the back of the canvas alluding to the John C. Simons art shop located on King Street in Charleston during that time. However, there is no evidence that Peale ever visited that city. The attribution to Peale, made by Frank Schwarz and Son Gallery, is based on the following factors. From the mid-1830s on, Peale used a 30 × 25-inch canvas and favored similar half-length compositions and poses. She was never consistent in signing her works, and after the mid-1830s her signature rarely appears on any of her work. In addition, it was at this time that she moved from the boldness and high color of her early works to a more sober style as befitted her upper-middle-class patrons. The portraits from this period often display a strong well-lit silhouette of the figure against an unadorned dark background, as in the Capers portrait. KMZ

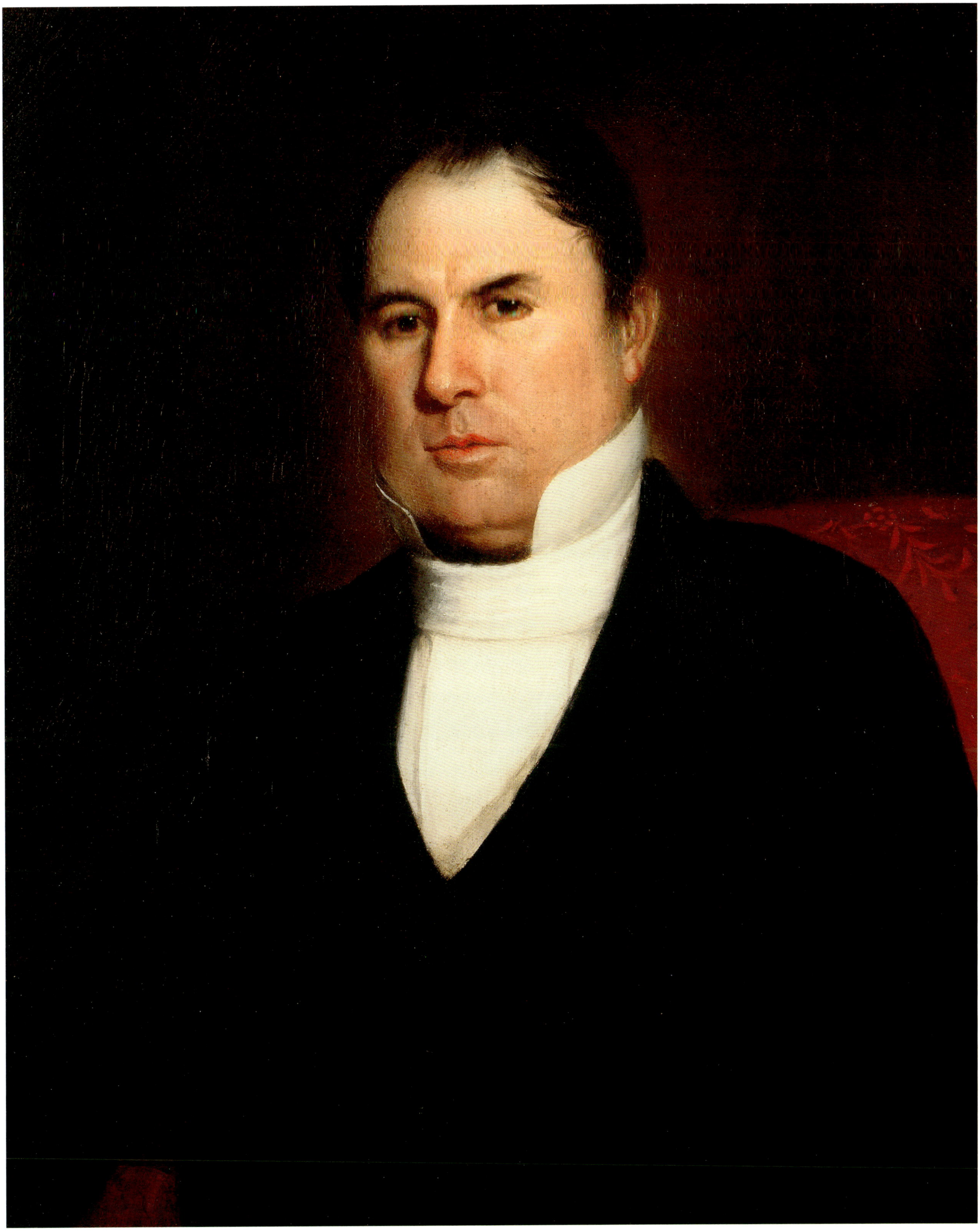

HIRAM POWERS

15 b. 1805, Woodstock, Vermont; d. 1873, Florence, Italy
Proserpine, ca. 1844
Carved marble, 20½ × 16 × 8½ (52.07 × 40.64 × 21.59)
Signed: H. Powers
Museum purchase made possible by the Crowley Foundation Art Acquisition Fund 91.9

PROVENANCE: Estate of Richard G. Carrott; Christie's Auction House, New York.
PUBLICATIONS: Winn, et al., 117.

While working at a Cincinnati grocery store, the youthful Hiram Powers was said to have sculpted animals and monsters in butter in his spare time. His first formal art training, however, began in Cincinnati in 1823–24, when Powers studied clay modeling and plaster casting with the Prussian artist Frederick Eckstein. One of his earliest efforts was repairing and mechanizing wax figures for the Western Museum in Cincinnati. In 1834 a patron, Nicholas Longworth, provided funds to enable Powers to move to Washington, D.C., and later to Europe. In 1845 Powers established his international reputation with *The Greek Slave,* which made him incontestably the most famous American sculptor of his day.[1]

Up to this time, America, with its puritanical sensibilities, disapproved of nude figures. *The Greek Slave* endured because critics thought it to be not about sexuality but about morality. Powers depicted the slave girl cruelly divested of her garments by her captors. Her unwilling nakedness therefore becomes the purest form of the human ideal. The artist, a confirmed Swedenborgian, felt that the nude statue should represent an unveiled soul.[2] An attitude such as this made the virginal nudes of Gilded Age paintings and sculpture more acceptable.

Before moving to Paris in 1836, Powers enjoyed a strong reputation in Washington, D.C., for his portrait busts. His commissions included Andrew Jackson, Daniel Webster, and John Quincy Adams. The overwhelming success of work made after his move to Europe overshadowed these earlier portrait pieces. By 1837 Powers and his family had settled in Florence, where there was an abundance of marble and cheap skilled laborers to assist him, and artists were free to model nudes without suffering the social criticism prevalent in America.

Powers originally produced a full-figure carving of Proserpine (or Persephone) for Philadelphia collector Edward Carey in 1843 for about $500. The intricacies of this first version proved too time-consuming, and so subsequent replicas were simplified. The museum's sculpture dates to around 1844, and represents the personification of spring. According to Ovid, one of Cupid's arrows struck Pluto, causing him to become smitten with the beautiful Proserpine, whom he saw picking flowers in a meadow. Shamelessly, he abducted her, taking her to his underworld kingdom. Her mother, Ceres, goddess of earth and agriculture, searched for her, and finding her with Pluto negotiated Proserpine's return each year to earth to visit her. Proserpine was thereafter associated with the coming of spring and plants that return to life every year. She wears a wreath of wheat in bloom on her head, and her bare breasts rise out of a ring of acanthus leaves symbolizing nature's regeneration and immortality. The ancient myth was a perfect theme for the neoclassical style of this era. Even the whiteness of the Italian marble seems to evoke spiritual idealism. The smoothness of the stone, the delicate turn of the figure's head, and her downcast eyes convey a sense of eternal calm and repose. It is estimated that Powers made approximately one hundred fifty copies of this sculpture, making it one of the most frequently reproduced works by an American artist. EW and CTB

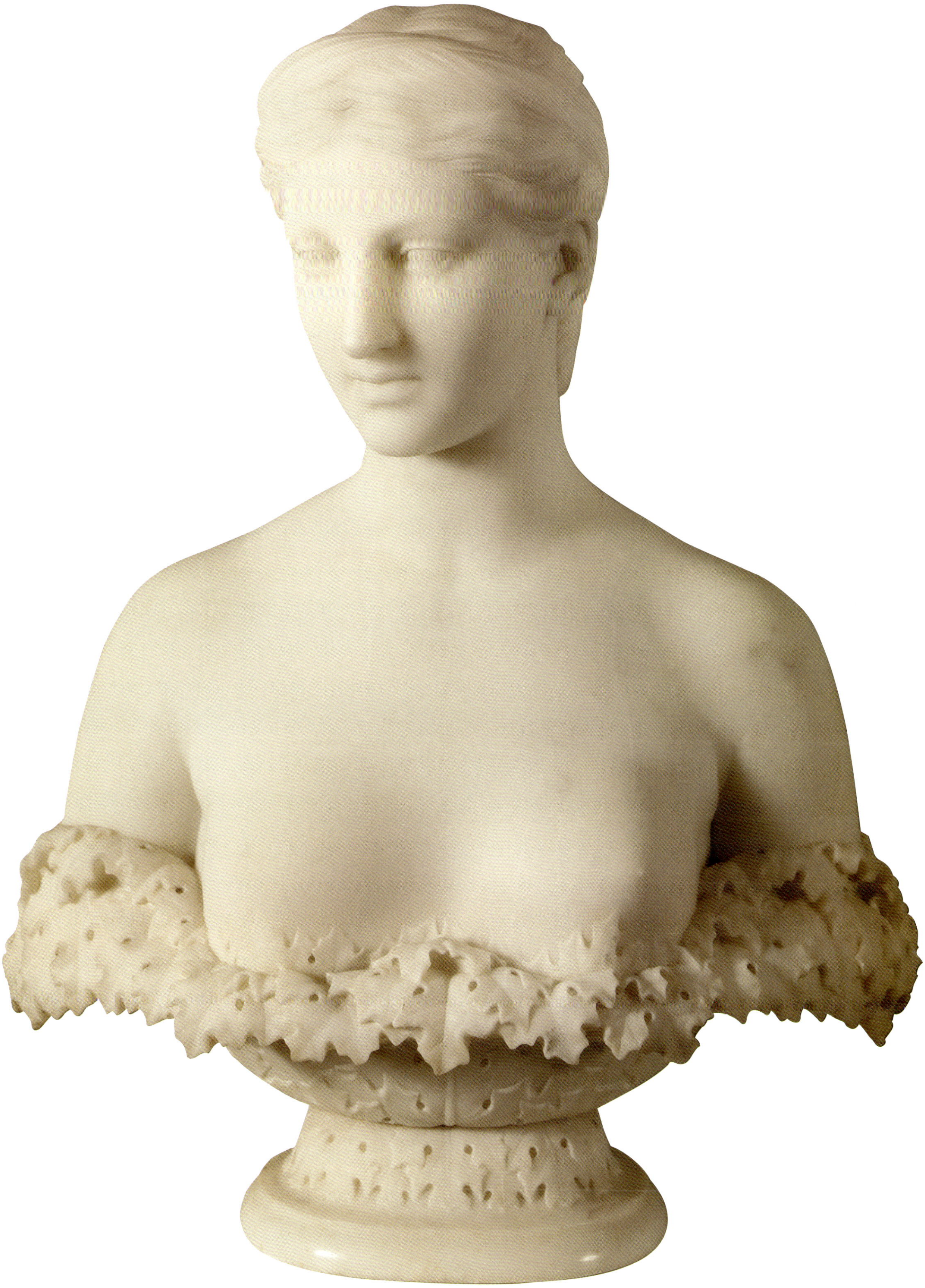

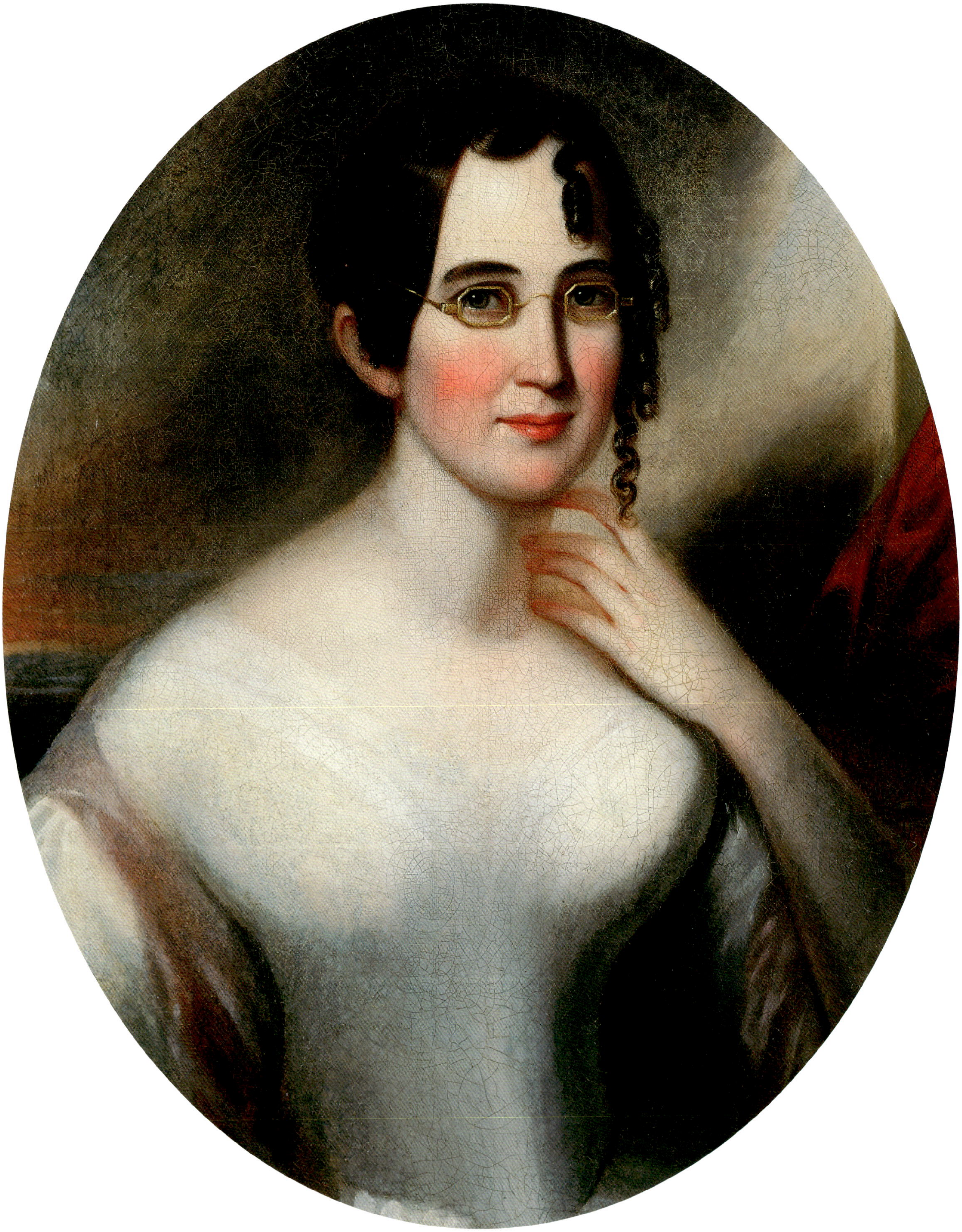

16 b. 1793, St. Mary's County, Maryland; d. 1849, Athens, Georgia
Mrs. Philip A. Clayton, 1843
Oil on canvas, 29½ × 24 (81.28 × 92.71)
Gift of Mrs. Mary Beall Fuller 60.62

PROVENANCE: By descent to Mrs. Philip A. Clayton's family.
EXHIBITIONS: *George Cooke 1793–1849*, Georgia Museum of Art, University of Georgia (Athens), Montgomery Museum of Art (Alabama), Gibbes Art Gallery (Charleston, South Carolina), Bayly Museum of Art (now University of Virginia Art Museum, Charlottesville, Virginia), February 2, 1991–March 15, 1992.
PUBLICATIONS: Keyes, *George Cook*, cat. 13.

George Cooke aspired to become an artist and had been accepted as a student of Rembrandt Peale, but the steep price of instruction ($2,000 for two years) deterred him. Instead, he worked in the mercantile trade until a decline in business led him to pick up his paintbrush again. His earliest artistic forays included portrait commissions, which he received through the intercession of family members and business contacts. In 1824 he went to study with the noted artist Charles Bird King in Washington, D.C.[1] Several years later, Cooke was able to further his studies in Europe. On a journey of five years, he visited museums in Paris, Milan, Florence, and Rome, making copies of masterworks, principally history paintings in the grand manner. While he may have wished to become a history painter, his commissions limited him to more modest paintings such as portraits and landscapes.[2] In 1831 he returned to America and spent the next nine years traveling back and forth between New York and North Carolina.

Cooke arrived in Georgia in 1840. Between 1842 and 1843, he traveled throughout Georgia, finding patrons in Augusta, Athens, Columbus, Dahlonega, Milledgeville, and Macon. "Cooke lingered in Georgia, always comparing the hospitality to that of 'old Virginia in her balmy days.'"[3] Eventually he settled in New Orleans, where, with the financial assistance of a patron, he established his own National Gallery of Painting featuring his own work. It was a financial venture that gained him little success.[4]

Local newspapers of 1838–54 indicate that ten or more painters set up temporary quarters in Columbus, Georgia, to sell paintings or accept commissions.[5] The Columbus Museum is fortunate to have acquired the work of some of these itinerant artists, who exposed smaller communities like early Columbus to prevailing artistic trends. Portraits by C. R. Parker and George Cooke are significant historical artifacts showing a variety of artistic sophistication in this region of the South in the early nineteenth century.

At first the identity of the sitter in this portrait was disputed. Cooke had painted portraits of two very different women, both of whom the artist identified as Mrs. Philip A. Clayton. Because this appeared to be in error, the conclusion was drawn that the museum's portrait was not Mrs. Philip A. Clayton.[6] However, a search of genealogical records showed that indeed there were two women named Mrs. Philip A. Clayton, and their husbands were first cousins. The museum's subject is Elizabeth Ann Williamson, who married Philip Augustin Clayton in Milledgeville in 1828; by 1835 the couple were living in Columbus, where the husband served in the Columbus Guards.[7] The subject of the other portrait was from Athens. Cooke had been a guest in the Clayton home in Athens, which led to an introduction to the Columbus Claytons and, eventually, the two portraits.

Cooke closely followed a traditional portrait pattern in this composition. He focused all of his attention on the sitter's head, painting her porcelain skin tinged with a rosy hue as she manages a small shy smile. But for the cascade of curls that tumble at her left brow, her hair has been arranged smoothly about her face. Her eyes are bright and focused and stand out behind her glasses, a rare and unusual detail for a mid-nineteenth-century female portrait. In addition, he painted the delicate fingers of her left hand raised toward her face to reinforce the central focus of the composition. In contrast, Cooke avoided any detailed visual description of her costume. She wears a simple garment with little indication of the quality or type of fabric, and she is without adornment or jewelry. According to a popular custom of the time, Cooke placed the figure in front of a reddish sunset, which is balanced by a swag of red drapery. The oval presentation was also a tradition of the mid-nineteenth century. BF

ALBERT BIERSTADT

17 b. 1830, Solingen, Germany; d. 1902, New York City
Hunting in the White Mountains, New Hampshire,
ca. 1857–58
Oil on paper mounted on board, 19 × 14½ (48.26 × 36.83)
Signed lower right: Abierstadt
Gift of Dr. and Mrs. Louis Hazouri 80.49.2

PROVENANCE: Dr. and Mrs. Louis Hazouri, Columbus, Georgia.
EXHIBITIONS: *Four Seasons; Select View.*
PUBLICATIONS: *Four Seasons,* n.p.; Timpano, cat. 2; Winn, et al., 153.

Albert Bierstadt's family emigrated from Germany to New Bedford, Massachusetts, when he was an infant. Little is known about his earliest artistic training. As a young man he went to Düsseldorf, Germany, to begin formal art instruction. While in Europe he forged lasting friendships with other American artists like Emanuel Leutze, Sanford Gifford, Worthington Whittredge, and William Stanley Haseltine.[1] After several years, he returned to America and established a studio in New York. In 1859 he began traveling throughout the American West. It was through his large-scale paintings of the expansive and undeniably beautiful landscape of the Rocky Mountains that his fame was firmly established.

Bierstadt, who had grown up in New England, equally loved the landscape of the northeastern United States. As early as 1852 he began exploring the White Mountains, the highest peaks in the northeast and part of the Appalachian Mountains range. After his return from Germany, he made subsequent painting trips to the region. These mountains were a popular retreat for artists such as Thomas Cole, Jasper Cropsey, Frederick Kensett, and Asher Durand.[2]

Bierstadt frequently made his studies in situ, using oil paint on paper as his primary medium. *Hunting in the White Mountains, New Hampshire* may have been one such oil study, although the unusual detail and level of finish elevates it above Bierstadt's standard sketches.[3] The artist transformed this diminutive subject into a grand mountain scene without sacrificing the intimacy of its scale. Bierstadt's early work coincides with the later years of the Hudson River school, a truly American interpretation of landscape painting that often included moralistic and religious messages. Bierstadt, however, seemed to relish nature for its own sake, without overt commentary.

In *Hunting in the White Mountains,* the artist describes some thick foliage he encountered on a walk in the mountains. Nature is his primary subject, even though he includes an almost obscured hunter in the lower central portion of the composition. The viewer's eye is drawn instead to the painstakingly painted details of tree leaves and undergrowth, especially the reddish orange leaves of the tree in the center. In the distance the cool greens of the forest recede into the pale blues of the mist-covered mountains, evoking the serenity of an early autumn day. BF

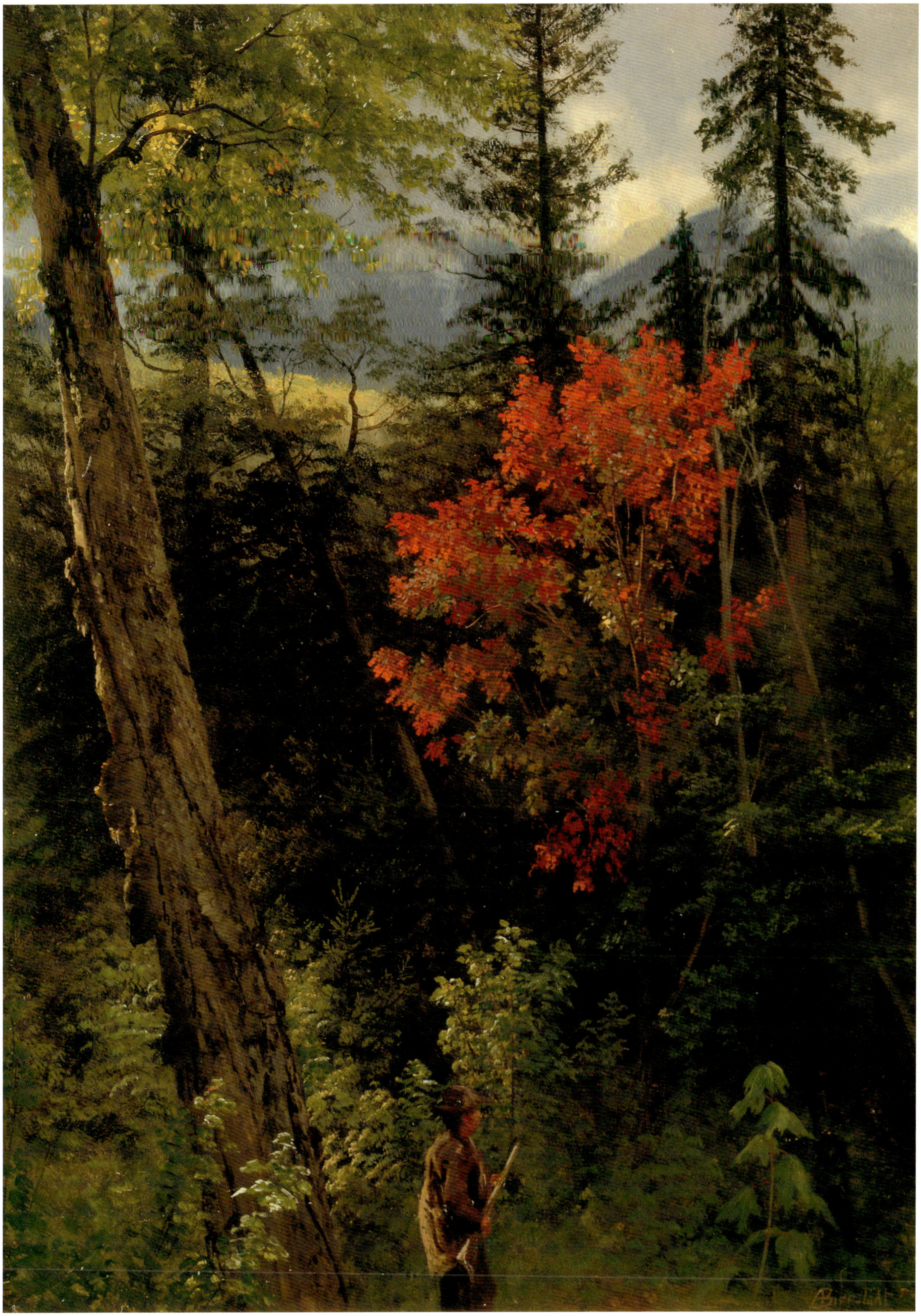

DAVID GILMOUR BLYTHE

18

b. 1815, East Liverpool, Ohio; d. 1865, Pittsburgh
Land of Liberty, ca. 1858–60
Oil on canvas, 24 × 20 (60.96 × 50.8)
Signed lower left: Blythe
Museum purchase made possible by the Endowment Fund
in Honor of D. A. Turner 96.25

PROVENANCE: J. J. Gillespie and Company, Pittsburgh (artist's dealer and friend); Christian H. Wolff, Pittsburgh, 1860; Paul C. Wolff; George David Thompson Sr., Pittsburgh, 1936; George David Thompson Jr., Pittsburgh, by 1950; Coe Kerr Gallery, New York, by 1980; Macbeth Gallery, New York; Paul Peralta-Ramos; Hirschl and Adler Galleries, New York; Christie's, New York, 1996.
EXHIBITIONS: *An Exhibition of American Genre Paintings,* Carnegie Institute, Pittsburgh, 1936; *The World of David Gilmour Blythe,* National Collection of Fine Arts (now the Smithsonian American Art Museum), Washington, D.C., 1980–81; *Tales from the Easel.*
PUBLICATIONS: Chambers, *World of David Gilmour Blythe,* 69, fig. 45; Eldredge, Eiland, and Butler, cat. 8.

David Gilmour Blythe was born to Irish immigrants who settled in East Liverpool, Ohio. His early life included a strict moral upbringing and an education that focused on the Bible and the literary and poetic writings of British and Scottish authors. Blythe's first artistic inclinations focused on the practical arts of wood carving and cabinetmaking, in which he apprenticed before enlisting in the navy. Following his military service, his interest in art reemerged. Although he was primarily self-taught, Blythe received several commissions for portraits. After the sudden death of his wife in 1850 and the financial strain incurred when a traveling show of a panoramic landscape he painted did not produce its expected revenue, Blythe's career foundered.[1]

In 1856 Blythe moved to Pittsburgh, where he shifted from portraits to genre subjects. Satire and wit were dominant features of his interpretations of everyday life in America. The artist poked fun at many groups and commented broadly on social issues in contemporary society. He often emulated the types and figures he saw in caricatures and cartoons in current newspapers and journals.

Blythe's *Land of Liberty,* which initially sold for $35, is an excellent example of his social satire. An entry in the art ledger of Christian Wolff (the first owner) claims, "a characteristic picture—bad in drawing and colors; but full of point and humor."[2] The two central figures in the painting are a Native American, represented by a cigar-store Indian that apparently has come to life, and a recent Irish immigrant. Beyond them is a ship docked in the harbor, signifying that the Irishman may have just set foot on American shores. The figures are easily recognized through their exaggerated features, stereotypical clothing, and symbolic accoutrements. As the two confront each other, the Indian seems to offer the Irishman a peace pipe. The painting's title, *Land of Liberty,* suggests an immigrant being welcomed to America by one of the first Americans. However, it is evident through gestures and expressions that this welcome is not a particularly warm one. The Indian regards the Irishman with disdain, reluctantly extending the long pipe to yet another newcomer. The Irishman, in tattered clothes, teeth clamped down on a stubbed pipe, and wielding a shillelagh symbolic of his ancestral belligerence, is portrayed with simian-like features—a common disparagement used by political cartoonists in the nineteenth century.

The tobacco leaf hanging in the doorway of the store, and phrases such as "Native Leaf" printed on the storefront refer to the political notions of the Know Nothings (also known as the American Party), with which the artist aligned himself. Activists of this organization sought to prevent recent immigrants from voting or holding office. After the 1850 federal census, the term "native" was used to describe anyone born in America. Hence, Blythe's use of the storefront Indian was more a symbolic representation of the American people than a racial reference. His intended message was that those who were foreign-born were antipathetic to American culture.[3] Blythe's *Land of Liberty* is a reminder that intolerance and prejudice are integral parts of American history. BF and ML

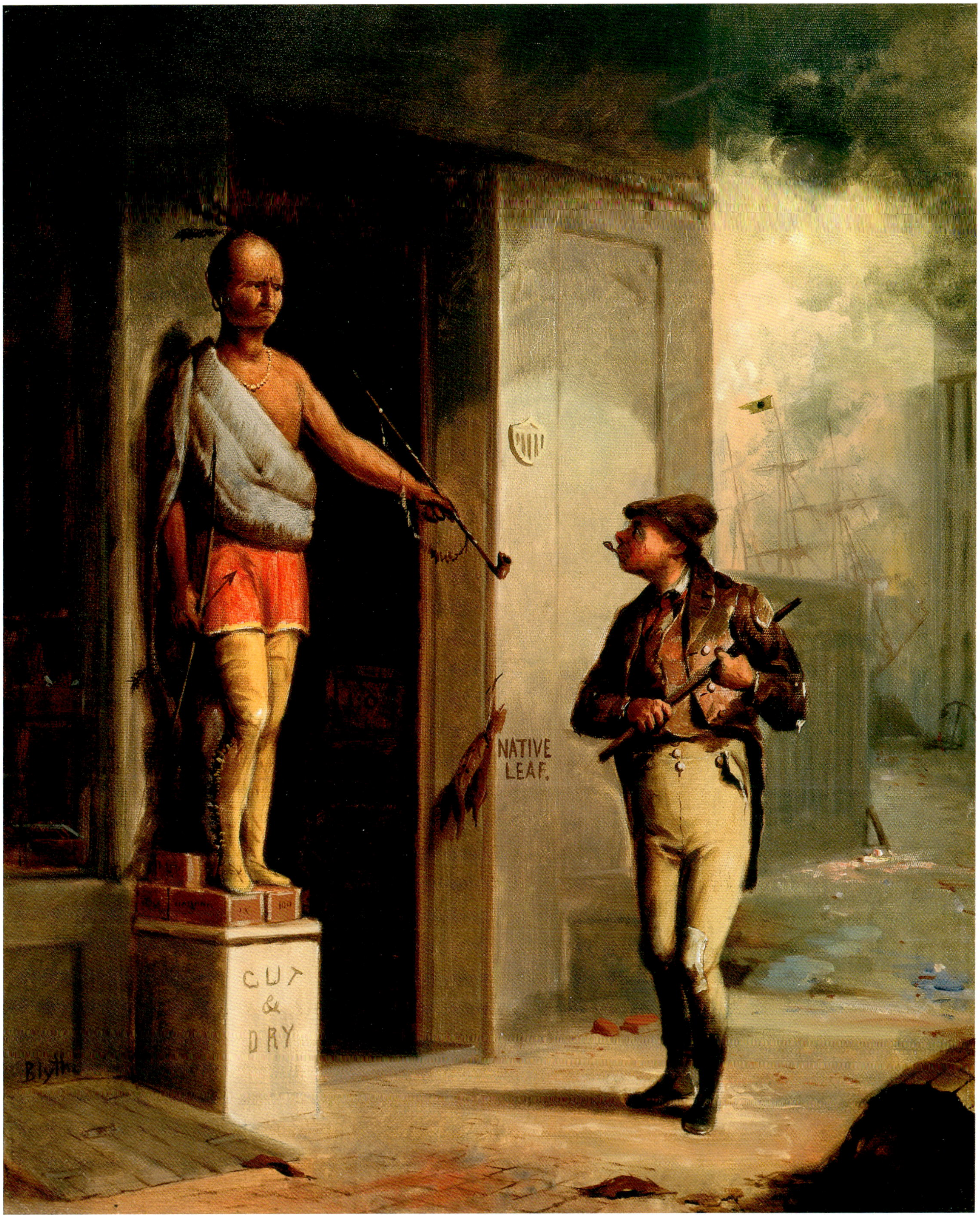
NATIVE LEAF.
CUT & DRY
Blythe

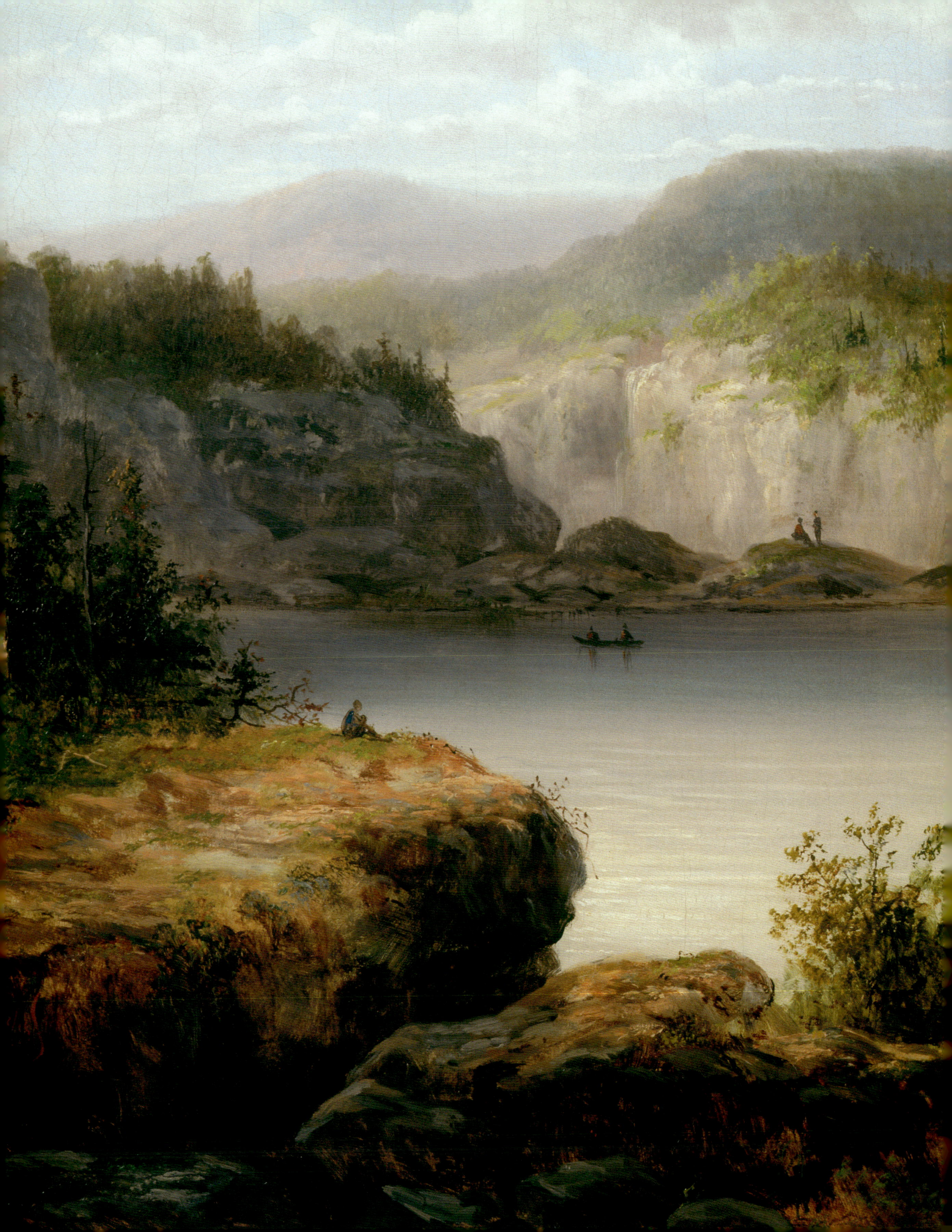

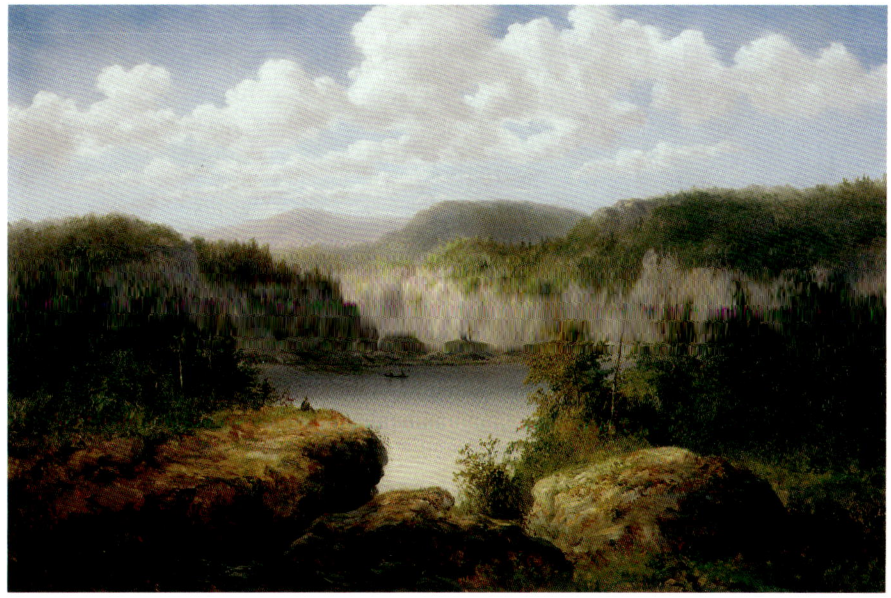

WILLIAM FRERICHS

b. 1829, Ghent, Belgium; d. 1905, Tottenville, Staten Island, New York

19 ***Mt. Toxaway from Lodge at High Hampton, N.C.,*** ca. 1863
Oil on canvas, 30¼ × 46 (76.83 × 116.84)
Signed lower left: W. Frerichs
Gift of Dr. and Mrs. Louis A. Hazouri 80.57

PROVENANCE: Private collection; Mr. and Mrs. Louis Hazouri, Columbus, Georgia.
EXHIBITIONS: *Select View.*
PUBLICATIONS: Timpano, 22, pl. 11; Winn, et al., 180.

William Charles Anthony Frerichs was born in Ghent, then a part of the Netherlands.[1] He entered the Academie van Beeldende Kunsten at the age of six, studying under the tutelage of landscape painters Andreas Schelfhout and Bartholomeus J. van Hove, who were both important figures in mid-nineteenth-century Dutch art. Schelfhout had a particular interest in the light-reflective qualities of snow and water, a concern that was to have a lasting effect on his pupil. In 1850 Frerichs immigrated to America and settled in the Greenwich Village section of New York City.

Little is known of his early years in New York except that he exhibited at the National Academy of Design in 1852, and that same year became a member of the New York Sketch Club. In late 1854 he accepted a teaching position as professor of drawing, painting, and French at the Greensboro Female College in North Carolina. Following his relocation to the South, Frerichs often sketched on his rambles through the Blue Ridge, the Great Smoky, and the Appalachian Mountains. He would derive inspiration from his sketches for full-size canvases the rest of his career. After the Civil War, Frerichs returned to the New York area, settling in Staten Island in 1868. He lived there until his death in 1905.

That the artist chose to depict a bucolic scene of rustic peace and beauty around 1863, the most terrible year of the Civil War, is curious, especially since in the same year Greensboro College was destroyed by fire and along with it Frerichs's studio and all the work stored there. At the time, the artist was working under appointment or conscription to the Confederate Corps of Engineers in the Sauratown Mountains region. In 1862 or 1863 he probably visited the remote locale of Lake Toxaway, a popular tourist destination. The painting is a composite of several views of the highland lake based on the artist's field sketches and notes. Included here are tourists enjoying the quiet setting—an indirect reference to the famous lodge that would later host Henry Ford and John D. Rockefeller. The image heralds a general connection between art and tourism that would greatly increase after the Civil War. Frerichs's early training is evident in the shimmering lake surface and the distant rocky chasm defined only by the light reflecting off its stone walls. Today a nondescript dam and numerous vacation homes exclude most sightseers from the now-private lake. CTB

XANTHUS SMITH

20 b. 1839, Philadelphia; d. 1929, Edgehill, Pennsylvania
Soldiers' Quarters at Hilton Head, South Carolina, 1865
Oil on panel, 9 × 12¾ (22.86 × 32.26)
Signed and dated: Xanthus Russell Smith, 1865
Gift of Dr. and Mrs. Louis Hazouri 80.51.1

PROVENANCE: Dr. and Mrs. Louis A. Hazouri, Columbus, Georgia.
EXHIBITIONS: *Select View.*
PUBLICATIONS: Timpano, 31.

Xanthus Russell Smith was born into a family of Philadelphia painters. His parents taught him drawing until he began his studies at the Pennsylvania Academy of the Fine Arts. With the Civil War at hand, Smith enlisted in the navy and received a favorable commission as a captain's clerk through the intercession of a family friend.[1]

Smith's naval career offered the young artist new subject matter—ships and distant places. While serving on Rear Admiral Samuel Francis du Pont's flagship, the *Wabash,* and then the steamer *Augusta,* Smith studied the vessels and meticulously articulated their details in his drawings. The small scale of his illustrations shows his personal penchant for undersized, compact, and neat, compositions. He often found patrons for these drawings among the men with whom he served. Writing to his parents during his tour of duty in 1863, Smith noted, "I have only done one sketch on my large paper yet, it is a careful pencil sketch, tinted with the crayons of the machine shop. But it has given such satisfaction to the few that have seen it, that two of the officers are determined to have copies of it and I am engaged on one of the copies now. I am to get seven dollars each for them."[2]

After Smith's naval service ended, he made a career of producing accurate and detailed depictions of ships and battles at sea. His compositions brought him critical praise and many patrons.

Scholars have found that the subject of Hilton Head Island and the coast of South Carolina appears in at least two canvases by Smith painted in 1864, and in one canvas and three panel paintings produced in 1865. Each of the six paintings was priced at $25. The museum's panel painting, *Soldier's Quarters at Hilton Head, South Carolina,* depicts a group of ramshackle huts at the water's edge with figures, only two of which appear to be in military dress. Its dimensions closely correspond to those of the three panel paintings made that year, but its current title does not. Thus it is possible that the original title for the museum's painting may have been one of the following assigned to the panel paintings: *Shore Scene, Hilton Head, S.C.; Group of Contraband Huts, Hilton Head, S.C.;* or *U.S. Signal Station, Hilton Head, S.C.*[3]

Smith did not often paint people, but for this narrative, he included nine figures, male and female, black and white. Most gather in small groups: two women at the door of a hut, two uniformed soldiers standing on the beach near two seated people, and two men readying boats that have been pulled ashore. In the distance at left is a ship at full sail. This quiet genre picture belies the usual commotion one might expect of an army encampment, leaving the viewer to wonder about the activity at hand.

Smith thinned his oil paint to create delicate, opaque layers in this diminutive composition. His tight, meticulous brushwork captures every detail of the scene. No arbitrary or unnecessary strokes of paint exist, not even in the foliage or cumulus clouds above. With this painstaking technique and popular subject matter, Smith's renderings of historical narratives found a faithful audience. BF

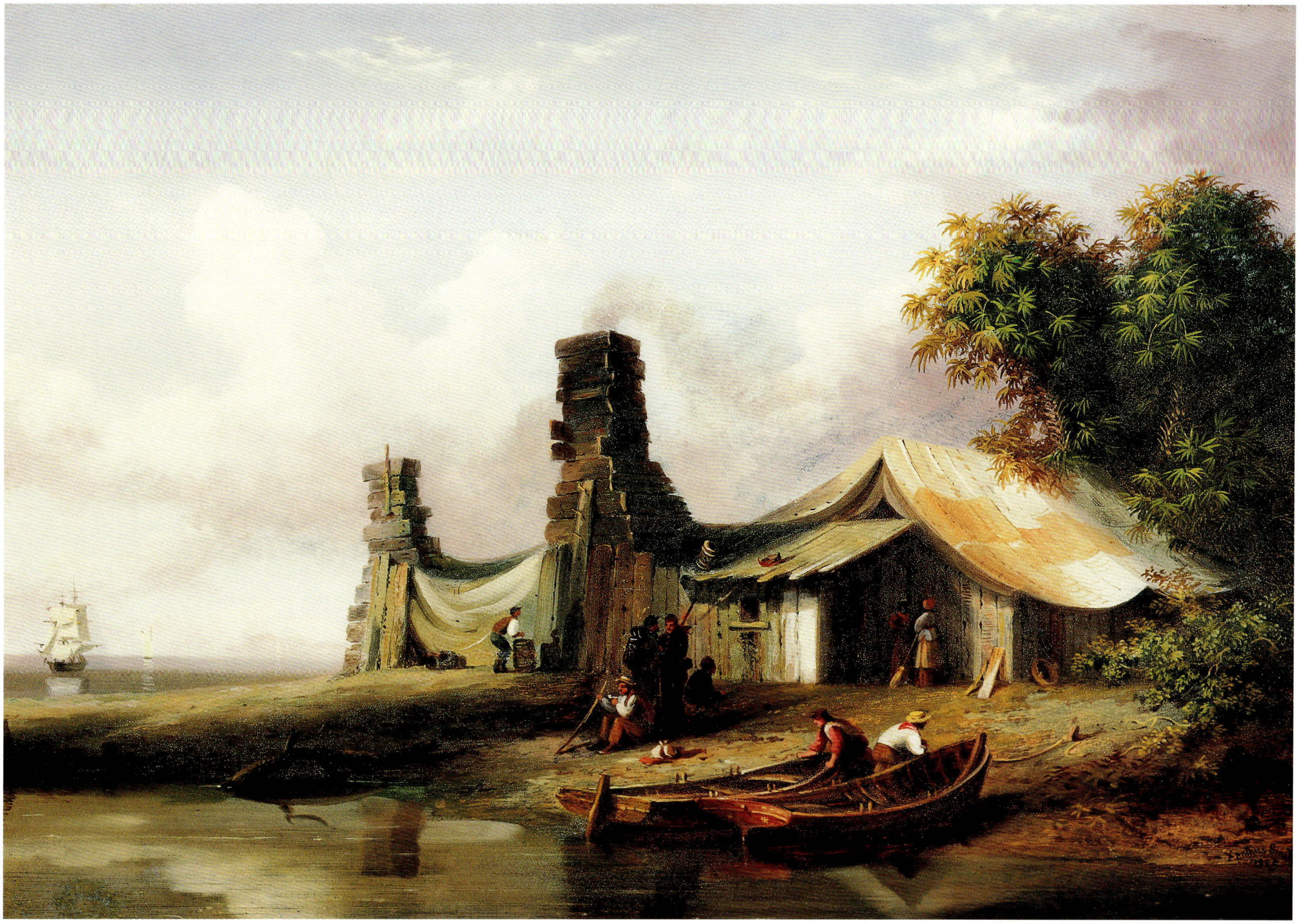

SANFORD GIFFORD

21 b. 1823, Greenfield, New York; d. 1880, New York City
A Home in the Woods, 1868
Oil on canvas, 18¼ × 34½ (45.72 × 87.63)
Signed and dated lower right: S R Gifford 68
Museum purchase in honor of Dr. Philip L. Brewer for his extended years of service to the Museum and made possible by The Art Acquisition and Restoration Fund, The Endowment Fund in Honor of D. A. Turner, The Crowley Foundation Acquisition Fund, The Daniel P. and Shannon L. Amos Foundation, Inc., Mr. and Mrs. Donald M. Leebern, Dr. and Mrs. Philip L. Brewer, Mr. and Mrs. Donald F. Broda Jr., Mrs. Frank D. Foley Jr., Mr. and Mrs. Ben H. Hardaway III, Mr. and Mrs. Christopher D. Hohlstein, Mr. and Mrs. W. Michael Ogie, Mr. and Mrs. Richard M. Olnick, Dr. and Mrs. D. Ronald Watson, the Estate of Lamar Baker, and the Museum's general acquisitions funds, and partial gift of Mr. Richard Manoogian 99.6

PROVENANCE: Collection of the artist; by descent to the Gifford family; Alex Acevedo; Richard Manoogian, Detroit; Babcock Galleries, New York.

Sanford Robinson Gifford attended Brown University before abandoning academic studies for the life of an artist in New York City. He attended classes at the National Academy of Design, painting mostly portraits during his student years. By the late 1840s his sketchbooks included his initial explorations of the New England landscape. In the 1850s Gifford traveled through Europe for two years, studying the landscapes of England, France, Germany, Italy, the Netherlands, and Scotland. His grand tour also involved museum visits and meeting European and American artists such as Emanuel Leutze, Albert Bierstadt, and Worthington Whittredge, and even the renowned British theoretician John Ruskin.[1]

Painting at the time when Thomas Cole and the Hudson River school artists had become known for their moralizing American landscapes, Gifford and others introduced a new style, infusing their images with an atmosphere of pure light. That style has become known as luminism. Although the definition and parameters of this art movement vary, Barbara Novak notes some of its predominant characteristics:

> In a luminist landscape, nature is presented on a smooth, mirror-like surface that shows barely a trace of the artistic hand. In removing his presence from the painting, the artist acts as a clarifying lens, allowing the spectator to confront the image more directly and immediately. Perhaps because of the absence of stroke, time stops, and the moment is locked in place—locked even more by a strong horizontal organization, by an almost mathematical ordering of planes in space parallel to the picture surface, and by deliberately aligned vertical and occasional diagonal accents.[2]

Novak's description applies well to *A Home in the Woods.* In this painting Gifford employed traditional compositional elements: a detailed foreground, a middle ground with reflective water, and a background of mountains. To enhance the viewer's experience, he modified the pattern by emphasizing the effects of color and light as filtered through the atmosphere. He further manipulated the scene by eliminating the hills in front of the distant mountain—probably Mount Chocorua—thus presenting a more dramatic staging of the water and its reflections.[3] By incorporating a thinly drawn line to delineate the mountain against the horizon, the artist also emphasized its mirror image in the lake. The mountains serve to contain the light-filled atmosphere within a controlled space. This is a scene that glows with radiance, lending it an aspect of spiritual contemplation. Fellow landscape painters and contemporary American writers also celebrated nature as transcendent and sublime.

Gifford used the theme of the pioneers' presence in the American wilderness in several paintings. *A Home in the Woods* is one of the last in the series, and dates prior to his 1868 trip to Europe.[4] In this painting, the evidence of a human presence remained relatively insignificant in the context of nature's grandeur. The tree stumps in the foreground are one reminder of that presence, however, and might suggest that this wilderness will slowly vanish in the event of continuing encroachment. On the other hand, it also suggests the richness of the land that provided a wealth of natural resources and sustenance for early settlers. Gifford advocated the concept of Manifest Destiny, which declared that the settlement of America and the utilization of its resources was providential, but he also foresaw that the sanctity of the virgin land would someday be lost to those who would make it their home. BF

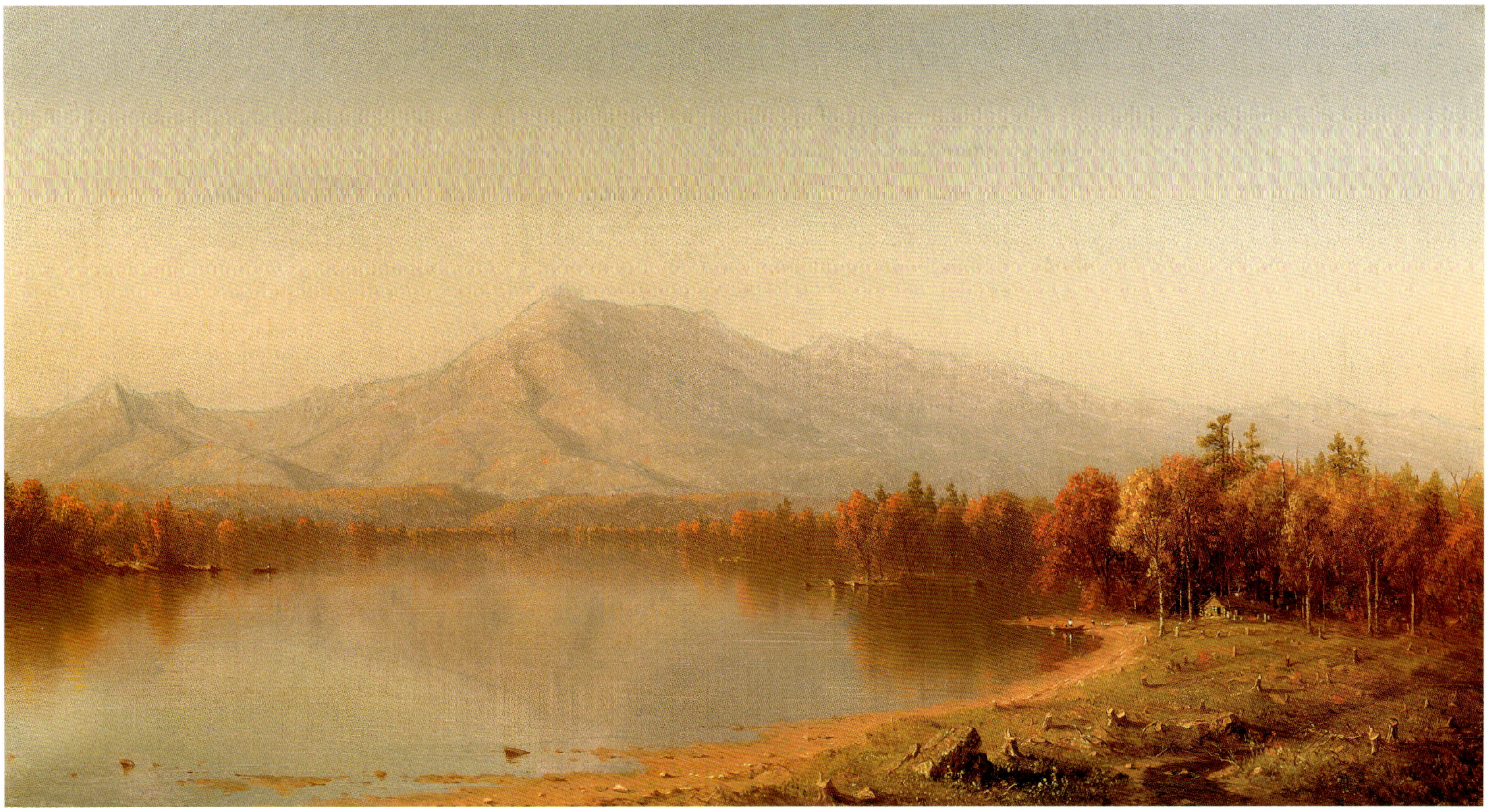

THOMAS W. MARSHALL

22 b. 1850, Brooklyn, New York; d. 1874, New York City
Catskill Mountain House, Twin Lakes, Autumn, 1869
Oil on canvas, 18 × 36 (45.72 × 91.44)
Signed lower left and dated: T. W. Marshall '69
Museum purchase made possible by The Art Acquisition and Restoration Fund and The Endowment Fund in honor of D. A. Turner 84.11

PROVENANCE: David David, Philadelphia.
PUBLICATIONS: Winn, et al., 152.

Little is known about this talented artist who died at the age of twenty-four. Thomas W. Marshall showed a decided talent for oil painting at an early age but received no formal training. Nevertheless, he gained a lasting reputation and critical acclaim for his landscape paintings. During his brief career, he studied nature in the mountains of upstate New York, and in 1872 traveled to Brittany and Switzerland in the company of fellow artist A. Wordsworth Thompson.[1]

In New York, he exhibited his paintings of the Catskill and Adirondack Mountains, scenes of which are typically associated with Thomas Cole and artists of the Hudson River school. He was a member of the American Society of Painters in Watercolor, and he exhibited several pictures at the National Academy of Design in the summer of 1871, according to an obituary notice in the *New York Times,* December 12, 1874.

This autumn landscape, painted before the artist left for Europe, is a bucolic view of a grand hotel perched above two mountain lakes. This spectacular panorama is a view from the same vantage point where in 1855 Jasper Cropsey painted a similar scene (*Catskill Mountain House,* 1855, Minneapolis Institute of Arts).[2] Marshall, like Cropsey and Thomas Cole before him (*A View of Two Lakes and the Mountain House, Catskill Mountains,* 1844; Brooklyn Museum), did not make the famous hotel the focal point of the work. Instead, it is a foil against the vast expanse of wilderness. One marvels at Marshall's ability to convey the unbounded space of the Catskills. The sky takes up nearly half of the painting, stressing the horizontal expanse of the land. The elevated viewpoint is typical of most Hudson River school paintings, and autumn, with its red and golden foliage, was a favorite season for these painters. In his composition, Marshall contrasts the broken and aged branches scattered about the flat rock observatory with the lush living vegetation that spreads in all its vastness before him. Only the glistening dome of the hotel indicates any evidence of a human presence in this vista.

The Catskill Mountain House was a popular nineteenth-century resort hotel and a frequent and favorite subject of Hudson River school artists. Built in 1823, it rested on a steep mass of rock 2,200 feet above sea level. People from around the world visited this white neoclassical hotel, acclaimed for its fabulous views of the sunrise. To reach the hotel from New York, guests traveled by steamboat up the Hudson River and then rode a stagecoach for another four hours. Once at the hotel, they enjoyed the beauty of the wilderness with all the conveniences of home. Visitors knew the Catskill Mountain House as the Grand Hotel, but local residents called it Yankee Palace. The hotel was demolished in 1963. GBG and CTB

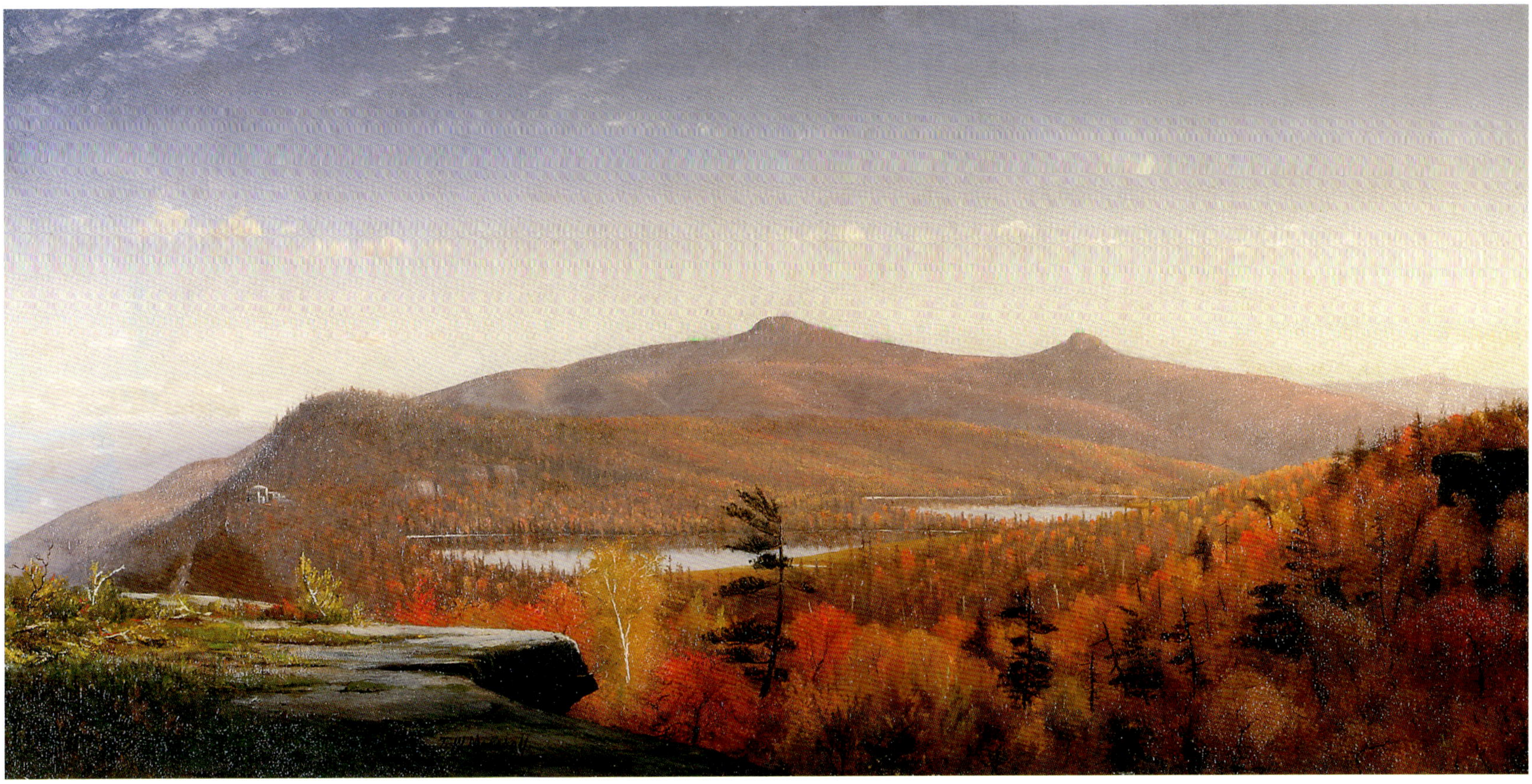

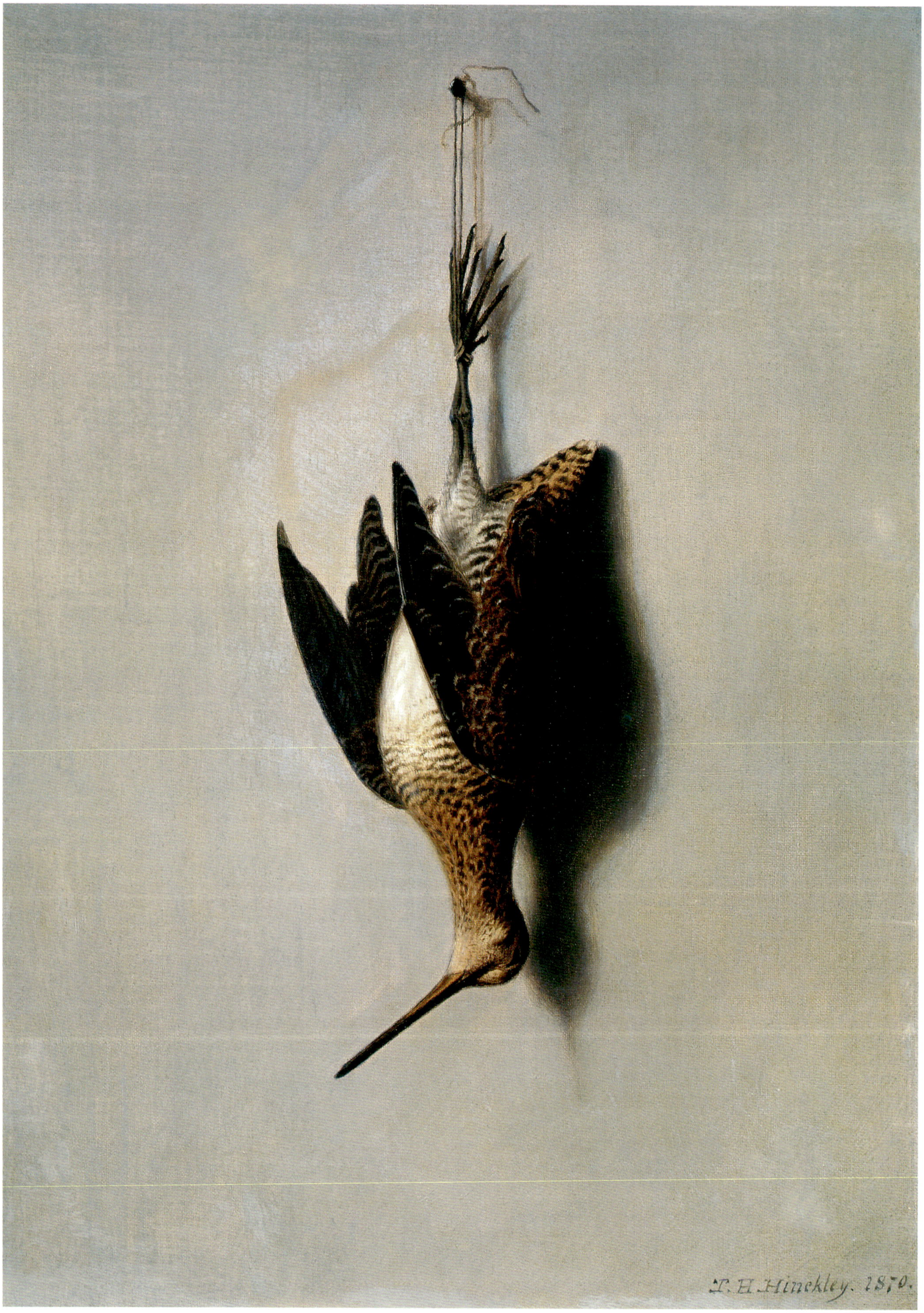
T. H. Hinckley. 1870.

THOMAS HEWES HINCKLEY

23 b. 1813; d. 1896, Milton, Massachusetts

Hanging Jack Snipe, 1870

Oil on canvas, 24¾ × 19¾ (62.87 cm × 50.17)

Signed: T. H. Hinckley 1870

Gift of Mr. and Mrs. Ben H. Hardaway III 77.42

PROVENANCE. [illegible] Gallery, New York; Vose Galleries, Boston; James Cochran, Ocala, Florida.
EXHIBITIONS. [illegible] *from The Columbus Museum*, Madison Morgan Cultural Center, Madison, Georgia, June 12–September 23, 2001.
PUBLICATIONS. Timpano, 24.

Thomas Hewes Hinckley toured widely, from California to Europe, always returning to the house in Milton, Massachusetts, where he lived his entire life.[1] His desire to travel was probably inspired by his father, Robert Hinckley, the captain of a ship that sailed from Boston to England. Although Thomas expressed an early interest in becoming an artist, his father strongly disapproved and arranged for him to apprentice with a Philadelphia merchant in 1829. Unknown to his father, however, Hinckley also took drawing classes at night from William Mason. Determined to be an artist, he returned to Milton in 1833 and began painting signs and portraits. He soon turned his attention to painting animals, a subject for which he would gain much acclaim. By 1845 his animal paintings were selling well, and he established a studio. He was most noted for his cattle paintings, commissioned by farmers who were proud of their prize-winning livestock.

In 1851 Hinckley visited Europe, and there he admired the work of British animal painter William Landseer, as well as that of Dutch and Flemish masters. In 1858 he exhibited two of his hunting scenes at the Royal Academy in London. He also exhibited at the Pennsylvania Academy of the Fine Arts and the National Academy of Design. In the 1870s he traveled to California to paint deer, antelope, and elk in their natural habitats. Hinckley remained active in his studio to the end of his life.

The still-life painting *Hanging Jack Snipe* is an unusual subject for Hinckley, whose fame derived from portraits and paintings of animals in lush landscape settings. Hinckley made twenty to twenty-five such paintings a year. At the end of his life, scholars accounted for an estimated 478 paintings that were signed by him. According to his biographer, Hinckley painted only one other bird picture, *The Hawk and the Chicken,* of 1871. However, the Smithsonian American Art Museum inventory lists two other bird pictures by Hinkley: *Hanging Grouse* and *Snipe Shooting,* both in private collections.

The museum's still life is sometimes referred to as a dead game picture or a hunting trophy. Still lifes such as this first appeared in fresco on the walls of Roman villas, where they were known as xenia, images that represent a bountiful and generous household. Hinckley would have become familiar with the subject through his studies of seventeenth-century Dutch and Flemish artists such as Frans Snyders, Jan Fyt, and William van Aelst when he traveled in Europe in 1851. Eighteenth- and nineteenth-century American painters Charles Willson Peale, James Peale, and Raphaelle Peale were celebrated for their still-life compositions showing arranged objects on a table or hanging on a wall. Hinckley could have seen these works when he was an apprentice in Philadelphia.

Here, in a precise tromp l'oeil manner, Hinckley depicts a Jack Snipe (a bird of the sandpiper family) tied to a string suspended from a nail. The bird is seen in three-quarter view against a plain background of beautifully modulated gray-green. Elegant lines flow throughout the composition: in the long beak, the delicate claws, and the curve of the thin string holding the bird to the nail. The palette is uniform, with subtle variations of brown, cream, green, and gray. The enamel-like surface shows no brushstrokes. The bird casts an elegant shadow that blends into the background and fades out at the tip of the beak. The work assumes the monumental importance of a memento mori (symbol of mortality) as much as it implies a hunting trophy. KMZ

JOHN FREDERICK KENSETT

24

b. 1816, Cheshire, Connecticut; d. 1872, New York City
The Sea, Long Island Sound from Fish Island, 1872
Oil on board, 15¼ × 29⅞ (38.73 × 75.88)
Museum purchase made possible by the Endowment Fund in Honor of D. A. Turner 82.23

PROVENANCE: Estate of the artist; Thomas Kensett, the artist's brother; Metropolitan Museum of Art, New York, 1874, acc. no. 74.35; George Gerry, New York; David Lawall, Charlottesville, Virginia; Richard York Gallery, New York.
EXHIBITIONS: *Select View; Paintings of Light: 19th Century Landscapes by Americans,* Richard York Gallery, New York, 1991; *Images of Contentment: John Frederick Kensett and the Connecticut Shore,* Mattatuck Museum, Waterbury, Vermont, September 15–November 18, 2001.
PUBLICATIONS: Driscoll and Howat, 149, fig. 81; Timpano, no. 24, fig. 1; Winn, et al., 178; Simon, pl. 10.

The son of an engraver-publisher, John Frederick Kensett worked in various shops learning engraving in the 1830s. During these years, he met and corresponded with artist John W. Casilear, who encouraged him to become a painter.[1] Beginning in 1840, he and Casilear traveled and sketched for seven years in Europe, where Kensett met J. M. W. Turner and Asher B. Durand. He worked extensively in Paris making copies of the atmospheric landscape paintings by French baroque artist Claude Lorraine. After returning to the United States in 1848, he joined the National Academy of Design.

In the early 1850s Kensett painted throughout New England before taking his second trip abroad to paint in the British Isles. In 1858 he traveled by train through the Midwest sketching with Durand and Sanford Gifford. After another trip to Europe, he traveled down the Mississippi River and to Colorado. He established the Artist's Fund Society in 1865, and in 1870 became a founding trustee of the Metropolitan Museum of Art. In 1872, after attempting to save the drowning wife of the painter Vincent Colyer at Darien, Connecticut, Kensett became ill with pneumonia. He never fully recovered and died of heart failure at his New York studio on December 14, 1872.[2]

Kensett belonged to the second generation of Hudson River school painters. Influenced by the poetry of William Wordsworth, he too contemplated the wonder, majesty, and power of nature, and, inspired by the writings of William Cullen Bryant, he sensed the embodiment of the divine spirit in trees, flowers, meadows, and mountains. In such as these Kensett found his calling as an artist.

The Sea, Long Island Sound from Fish Island is from a group of thirty-eight paintings found in Kensett's studio at his death by his brother, Thomas. Referred to as "The Last Summer's Work," these paintings were donated by the artist's family to the Metropolitan Museum of Art in 1874.[3] The subject of many of his later paintings was the Long Island shore. In the museum's coastal scene, wide expanses of sea and sky glow and sparkle in a symphony of nature. Warm hues infuse the tonalities to give a luminous quality to the atmosphere. Like most of the landscape paintings of his later years, this work reveals the artist's expertise with the compositional placement of large masses and shapes. Here, an expanse of beach in the foreground is balanced by a rocky headland in the middle distance, and everything is surrounded by a large sweep of shimmering sky. The sketchlike quality of the work, the delicate colors, and the transparency of the pigmentation suggest that the artist most likely made the painting on location at the water's edge. CTB

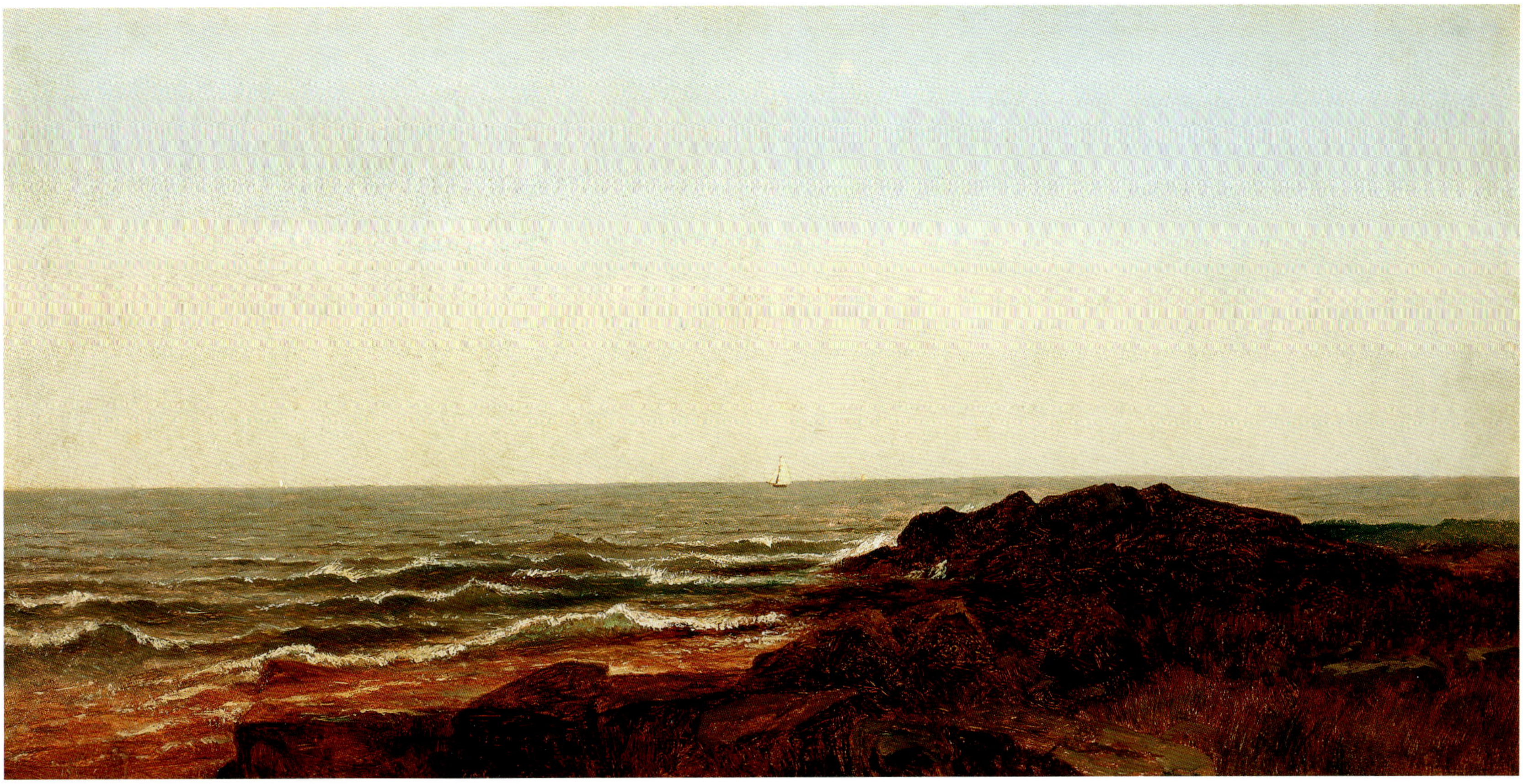

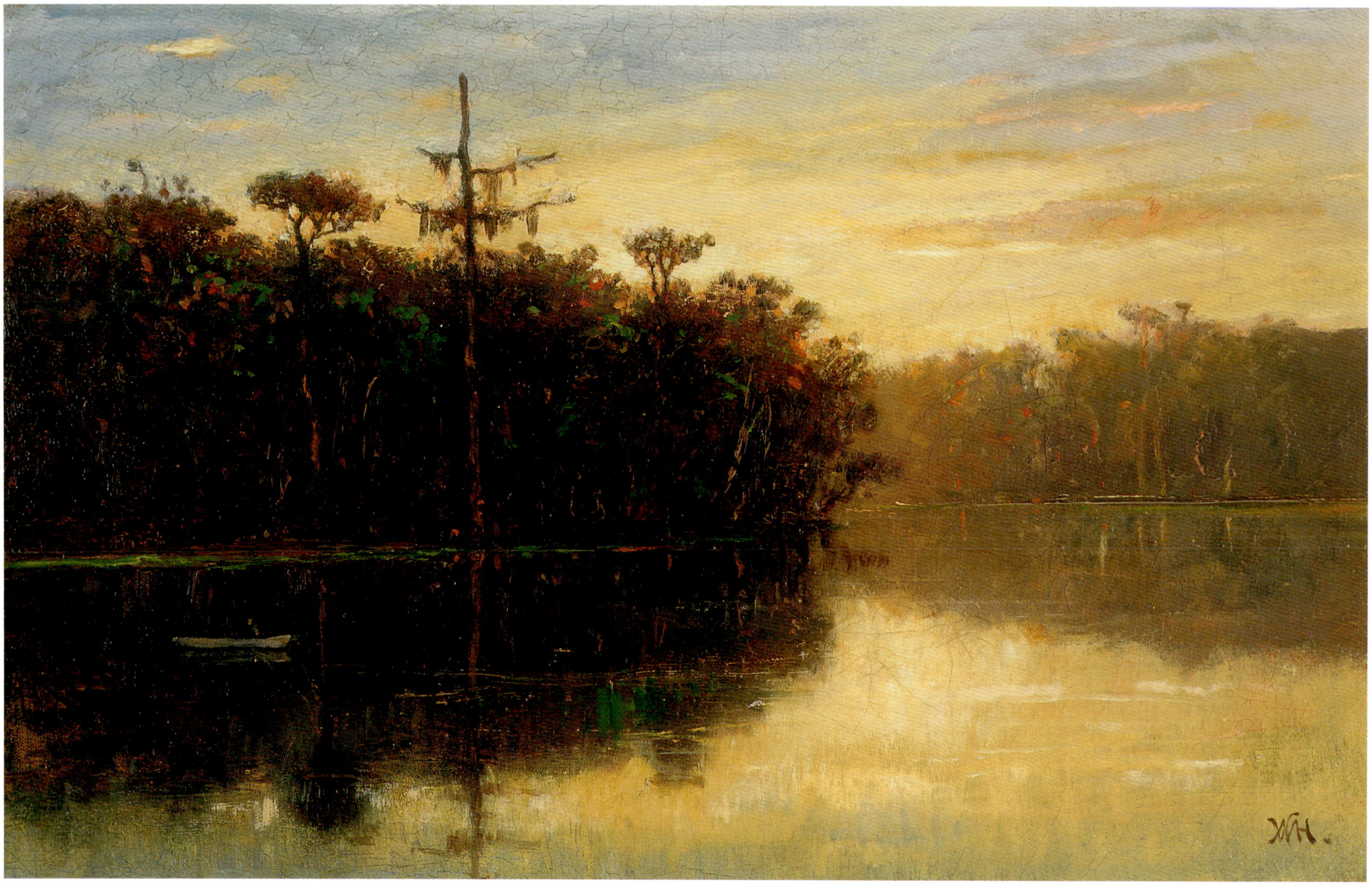

WILLIAM MORRIS HUNT

b. 1824, Brattleboro, Vermont; d. 1879, Appledere Island, New Hampshire

25 ***Governor's Creek, Florida,*** ca. 1873–74
Oil on canvas, 10 × 16 (25.4 × 40.64)
Signed lower right: WH
Museum purchase 83.4

PROVENANCE: J. Malcolm Forbes, 1879; Mrs. J. Malcolm Forbes, 1924; Henry S. Forbes, Milton, Massachusetts, 1976; Robert Skinner, Boston.

EXHIBITIONS: *Exhibition of the Works of William Morris Hunt,* Museum of Fine Arts, Boston, December 20, 1879–January 31, 1880; *Memorial Exhibition of the Works of William Morris Hunt,* Museum of Fine Arts, Boston, March 8–31, 1921; *William Morris Hunt 1824–1879,* Cushing Memorial Gallery, Newport, Rhode Island, 1960, *The Late Landscapes of William Morris Hunt,* University of Maryland Art Gallery (College Park, Maryland), Albany Institute of History and Art (Albany, New York), January 15–April 25, 1976; *Select View; Before 1948: American Paintings in Georgia Collections,* Georgia Museum of Art at University of Georgia, Athens, January 15–March 14, 1999; *Subdued Hues: Mood and Scene in Southern Landscape Painting, 1865–1925,* Morris Museum of Art, Augusta, Georgia, November 18, 1999–January 16, 2000.

PUBLICATIONS: *Late Landscapes,* fig. 24, no. 9; Timpano, no. 22, pl. 1; Winn, et al., 176; Keyes and Domescik, no. 23; Pennington, *Subdued Hues,* 45.

Born to an aristocratic New England family, William Morris Hunt had many opportunities to pursue a variety of activities, including studies at Harvard, but it soon became evident that his primary interest was in painting and sculpture. He went to Boston to study painting with John Crookshank King. Later, he made the grand tour of European arts capitals, including Düsseldorf and Paris. He made the decision to become a professional artist when he was studying with Henry Kirk Browne in Rome. Another major influence was Emanuel Leutze, whom he met in Rome in 1844–45.[1] In France, he followed strong examples set by Thomas Couture and Jean-François Millet of the Barbizon school. He returned to America in 1856 and by 1862 had established a studio in Boston. Hunt was a champion of the Barbizon style and a highly regarded teacher, whose straightforward and honest approach was appreciated by his students. In 1872, after a fire destroyed much of his work, he decided to paint landscapes, subject matter that for him was relatively unexplored.

Governor's Creek, Florida evolved from sketches made during a trip to Florida in the spring of 1873. As the guest of a close friend, John Murray Forbes, Hunt explored northeastern Florida around St. John's River. Governor's Creek, a tributary of the river, flows through Green Cove Springs, in Clay County, the home of a fashionable spa during the 1870s and 1880s.[2] Hunt seldom painted panoramic views, confining himself to a more intimate engagement with his subject. Done in muted colors, many of these unpopulated views convey a vague melancholy and sense of loneliness, characteristics that may reflect Hunt's depressed psychological state. Yet he found beauty in the lonely landscape. As he wrote to a friend,

> We are having real summer weather here. Thermometer sometimes as high as 82°, or even higher. Alligators sunning themselves in the creeks, and the foliage now so dense that the novelty of it is passed; also that lovely contrast of the brown masses of trees with the bright, tender green. All this, with an occasional gigantic cypress reflected in the perfectly still water of the creeks, make pictures to wonder at if not to paint.[3]

During this trip, Hunt made charcoal drawings of the river, then painted *Governor's Creek, Florida* as well as other Florida landscapes upon his return to the studio.[4] The water scenes, with reflections and encroaching foliage, captivated Hunt and inspired him to further explore the natural world. That he placed a solitary figure in a boat here is almost overlooked, yet its presence seems only to reinforce the isolation of this place. The artist evenly divided the canvas in half horizontally, at the edge of the river, but by placing asymmetrical masses of vertical trees at both right and left he has defined and activated the space. The darker half of the composition at left carries more visual weight, creating a slight dynamism in an otherwise static landscape. Hunt's evocation of Florida's unsullied wilderness also resonates in the stark solitude of the scene, and in elements of nostalgia and melancholy. BF

HUGH BOLTON JONES

26

b. 1848, Baltimore, Maryland; d. 1927, New York City

Berkshire Mountains (South Egremont, Massachusetts),
ca. 1875

Oil on canvas, 24½ × 35½ (74.93 × 90.17)

Signed lower left: H. Bolton Jones

Gift of the Bradley Library and the Children of Columbus Public Schools 54.96

PROVENANCE: Children of the Columbus, Georgia, Public Schools; W. C. Bradley Library, Columbus, Georgia.
EXHIBITIONS: *Naegele Competitive Art Exhibition,* organized by Charles Frederick Naegele, Muscogee Club, Columbus, Georgia, 1925–26; *Select View.*
PUBLICATIONS: Timpano, no. 23.

Hugh Bolton Jones rose to prominence as a landscape painter in the late nineteenth century. He began his career as a student at the Maryland Institute (now the Maryland Institute College of Art). Subsequently, he moved to New York City, where he saw the work of many prominent Hudson River school painters. In 1865 he studied with Horace Wolcott Robbins Jr., who had just returned from a year of travel with Frederic Edwin Church in Jamaica and the Caribbean. Two years later, Jones exhibited his paintings at the National Academy of Design. As he traveled from Maryland to West Virginia and north to the Berkshire Mountains of western Massachusetts between 1865 and 1876, Jones painted many of the traditional landscape motifs that the Hudson River school artists had painted.[1]

In 1876 Jones and his brother Francis Coates began a four-year sojourn in Europe, where Jones studied traditional French and German landscape paintings. He joined an artist colony in Pont-Aven, Brittany, for a time, as did other post–Civil War painters, including his acquaintance Thomas Hovenden, a genre painter. Upon Jones's return to the United States, he settled in New York and spent summers at a cottage he purchased in South Egremont, Massachusetts.

Jones probably painted *Berkshire Mountains (South Egremont, Massachusetts)* in the years preceding his European travels. The composition shows the influence of the Hudson River school in the brilliant midday light and natural, botanical details. Moreover, there is a Barbizon-like depiction of soft light and shadow, which is executed with energetic brushstrokes. Despite the fact that this populated area was rapidly developing, Jones seems intent on capturing the spectacle of a poetically conceived landscape devoid of human intrusion.

The acquisition of *Berkshire Mountains (South Egremont, Massachusetts)* has a special place in the museum's history, which involves Charles Frederick Naegele, an esteemed New York portraitist. Naegele had befriended members of the community when he was commissioned to do a number of portraits in Columbus. Beginning in 1924, he organized a series of exhibitions—at first called the Naegele Competitive Art Exhibitions, then Penny Art Fund shows—to introduce local schoolchildren to the fine arts. Naegele would borrow the paintings directly from the artists or through New York galleries and install the exhibitions in the Muscogee Club in downtown Columbus. For the admission fee of a dime, visitors could vote for their favorite painting, and at the end the painting with the most votes was purchased with the money collected. However, the funding often fell short of the actual price, and artists were encouraged to take what had been offered.[2] Jones's painting, which originally hung in the W. C. Bradley Library in Columbus, was acquired in this way between 1925 and 1926. It became part of the museum's permanent collection in 1954, one year after the museum opened to the public. LR

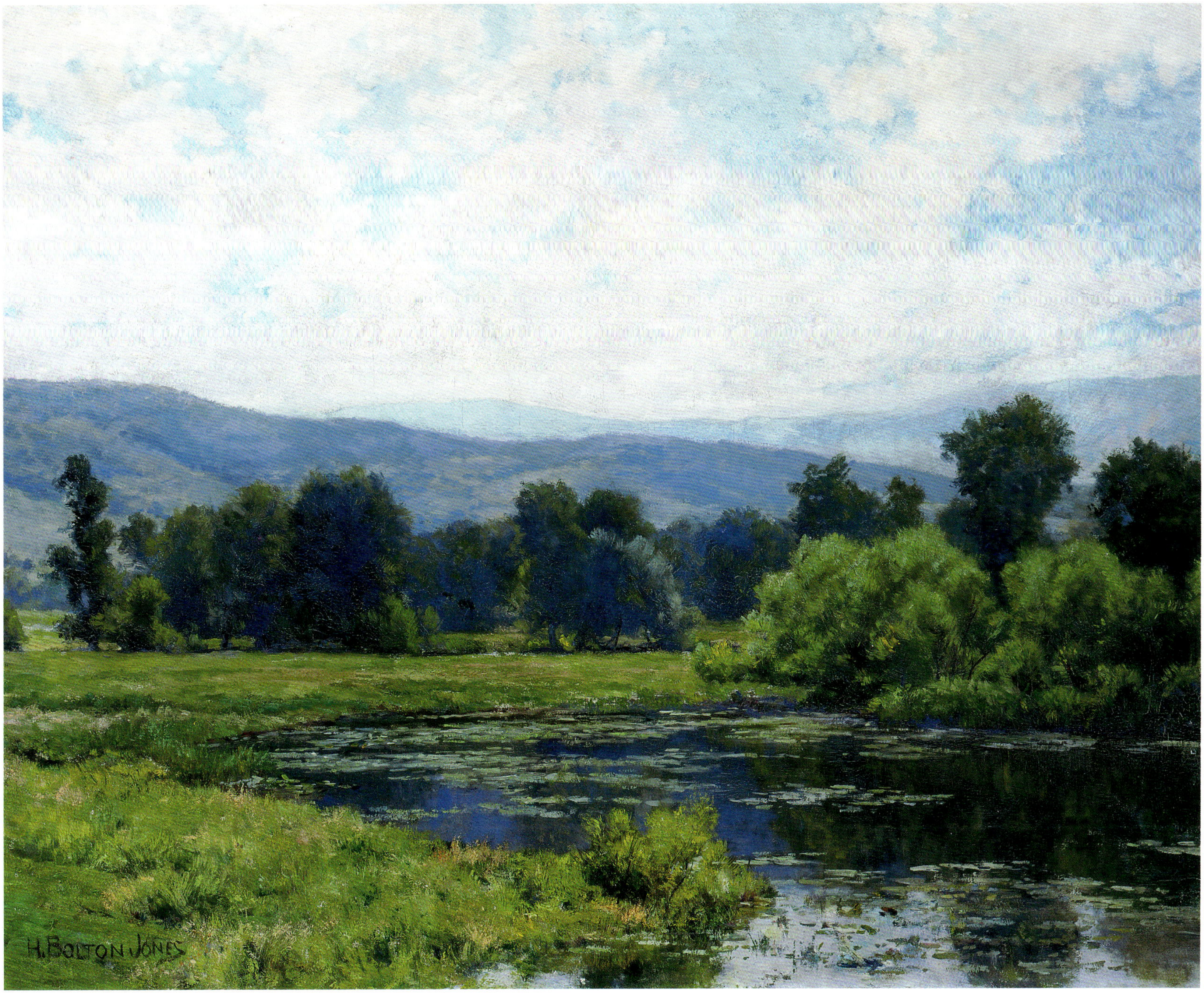
H. BOLTON JONES

THOMAS HOVENDEN

27

b. 1840, Dunmanway, Ireland; d. 1895, Plymouth Meeting, Pennsylvania

Contentment, 1881

Oil on canvas, 21½ × 26½ (54.61 × 67.31)

Signed and dated lower right: Hovenden 1881

Gift of Dr. Philip L. Brewer in honor of Dr. Delmar Edwards 93.23

PROVENANCE: Unidentified Boston art gallery, until 1910; by descent from her mother to Mrs. Marion McCarthy, Fort Lauderdale, Florida, 1946; Vose Galleries, Boston, until 1977; Dr. Philip L. Brewer, Columbus, Georgia, 1977.

EXHIBITIONS: *Georgia Collects,* High Museum of Art (Atlanta), Telfair Museum of Art (Savannah), January 24–June 11, 1989; *Local Wonders: Treasures of American Art from Columbus Collections,* Columbus Museum, February 6–May 29, 1994; Reynolda House Museum of American Art, Winston-Salem, North Carolina (by exchange), October 1998–January 10, 1999; *Tales from the Easel.*

PUBLICATIONS: *Georgia Collects* (Atlanta: High Museum of Art, 1989), 77; Winn, et al., 125; Eldredge, Eiland, and Butler, cat. 34.

Thomas Hovenden began his career in County Cork, Ireland, where he served as an apprentice to a frame maker and wood carver who paid for his earliest art instruction.[1] In 1863 he immigrated to New York, where he made a living as a gilder and frame maker while attending evening classes at the National Academy of Design. The young artist later moved to France, where he initially sought instruction from Jules Breton, but soon transferred to Alexandre Cabanel's studio. Hovenden later joined the art colony at Pont-Aven in Brittany, remaining there for most of the six years he lived in France. Like so many other American expatriate artists, Hovenden found the French peasantry to be ample subject matter.

After returning to the United States in 1880, Hovenden began to paint genre subjects that reflect his American surroundings and include subtle references to the sociopolitical tone of the time. Having extolled the virtues of the French peasantry, he now focused on the tranquility and intrinsic worth of domestic life among working-class Americans, infusing his canvases with easily recognizable narratives according to the academic realism he had mastered in the ateliers of France.

After marrying Helen Corson (a painter of animal images and fellow Pont-Aven art colony member), Hovenden settled on her family's property at Plymouth Meeting, Pennsylvania. He was greatly impressed by his wife's Quaker family, their role as abolitionists, and the part they played in the Underground Railroad. The personal risks and sentiments of his new family certainly influenced his sympathetic renderings of African Americans at a time when they were caricatured in popular prints such as the Dark Town series produced by Currier and Ives. Much earlier, in the 1830s, William Sidney Mount had pioneered the use of African American subjects in his narrative compositions.

Traditionally, American genre painting reflected a sense of optimism and nationalism—that is, until after the Civil War, when such images offered a sense of comfort and sanctuary.[2] During the 1880s Hovenden sought African Americans to serve as models for his scenes of home and family, as in *Contentment.*[3] A rich example of Hovenden's pictorial narrative, the painting is an intimate view of a humble but tidy home. The artist has used shadow and light to de-emphasize the surroundings and focus attention on the figures and their interaction. Here, in this pleasing environment, they have found refuge and can relax and converse in an intimate and comfortable manner. Hovenden has avoided using the racial stereotypes so prevalent at the time, and instead lends his subjects the dignity and honor they merit. His audience would be familiar with just such a moment, when a couple quietly talks about the day's activities as the dinner dishes are cleared away. Portraying this everyday occurrence as a Black experience no doubt was intended to prompt his predominantly white audience to reconsider their expectations and perceptions of race and class.

Hovenden exhibited his work widely, and his patrons were a steady source of income. In 1886 he replaced his friend Thomas Eakins as professor of painting and drawing at the Pennsylvania Academy of the Fine Arts. Among his students were Robert Henri and Henry Ossawa Tanner. Unfortunately, his life ended in tragedy; he was killed trying to save a little girl from an oncoming train. BF

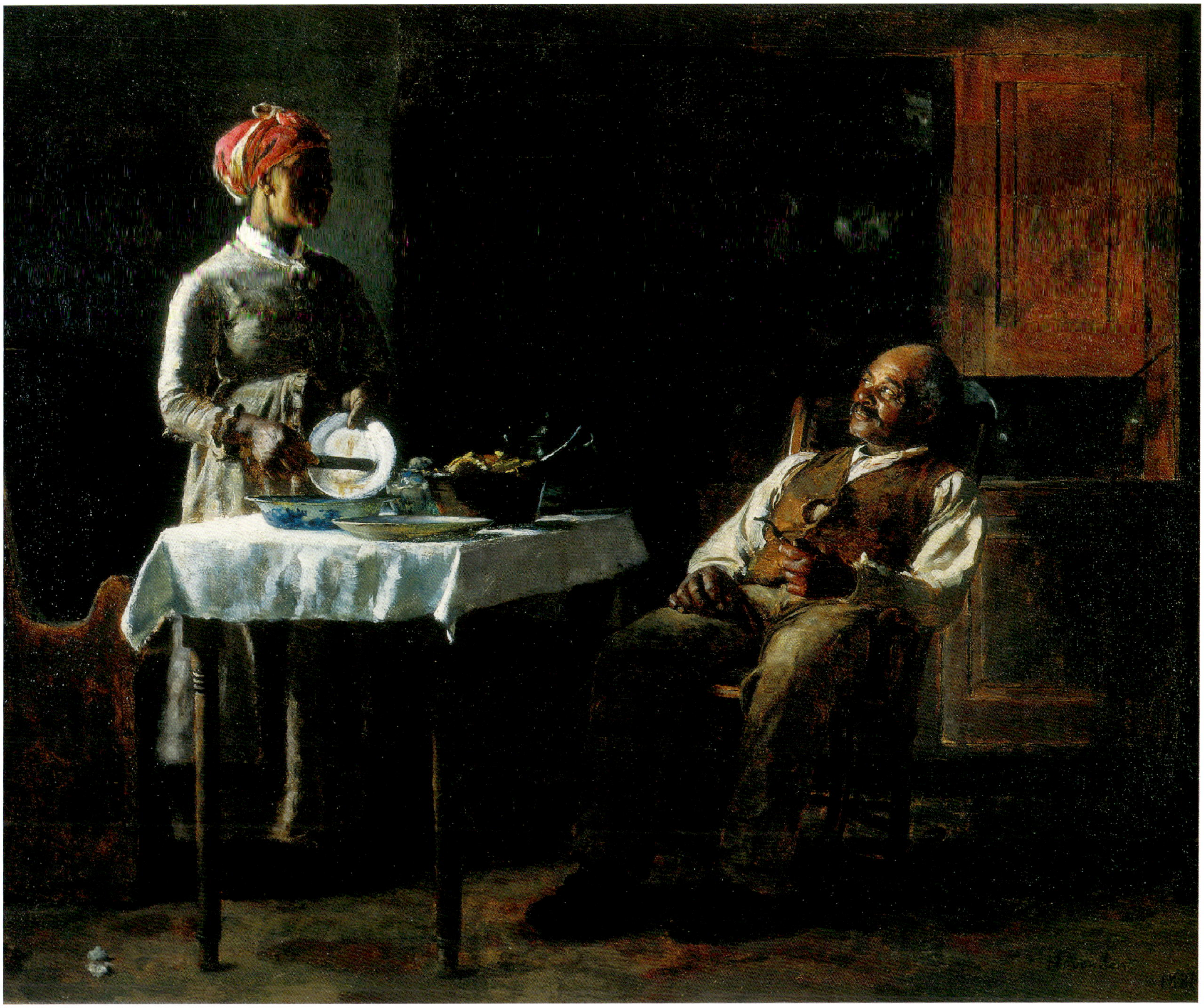

EASTMAN JOHNSON

28 b. 1824, Lowell, Maine; d. 1906, New York City
The Earnest Pupil (also known as *The Fifers*), 1881
Oil on panel, 26¼ × 22¼ (66.68 × 56.52)
Signed and dated lower right: E. Johnson 1881
Museum purchase made possible by an anonymous donor 98.26

PROVENANCE: Macbeth Gallery, New York; Dalzell Hatfield Galleries, New York; John Graham, New York; private collection, 1982–95; Spanierman Gallery, New York, 1995–98.
EXHIBITIONS: *Exhibition of Americana,* Macbeth Gallery, New York, November 1939; *An American Genre Painter: Eastman Johnson (1824–1906),* Brooklyn Museum, 1940; *Tales from the Easel.*
PUBLICATIONS: William Waltman, "Eastman Johnson, Painter," *Scribner's Magazine* 40 (1906), illus. opp. 270; *Exhibition of Americana,* Macbeth Gallery (New York, 1939), as *The Fifers*; Baur, *An American Genre Painter,* no. 96, pl. 33; Eldredge, Eiland, and Butler, cat. 36.

Eastman Johnson began his art career as a lithographer's apprentice in Boston when he was sixteen. Because he had exceptional artistic ability and socially connected friends, the young artist enjoyed success drawing portraits of prominent citizens in Washington, D.C. (Dolly Madison and John Quincy Adams), and Boston (Nathaniel Hawthorne and Ralph Waldo Emerson).

In 1849 Johnson decided to further his education in Germany at the Düsseldorf Academy, where he studied for two years and befriended other American students including Emanuel Leutze and Albert Bierstadt. In Holland, Johnson discovered the work of the seventeenth-century masters Rembrandt and Van Dyck, which inspired him to develop a freer handling of paint, a richer palette and a penchant for picturesque subjects.[1] Johnson went on to study briefly with Thomas Couture in Paris. While there, he gained his deep appreciation for the genre paintings of Jules Breton and Jean-François Millet, who depicted working people with dignity and honor.

Johnson returned to America in 1855. His first major work, *Negro Life in the South* (New York Historical Society, now called *Life in the Old South*), depicted the backyard of his father's home in Washington, D.C.[2] The painting was included in the 1859 exhibition *Life in the South,* held at the National Academy of Design, where it received equal praise from both sides debating the issue of slavery.

For the next twenty years, Johnson's subject matter ranged from images in which he considered the plight of runaway slaves (making clear his abolitionist point of view) to bucolic scenes of young women and children in rural settings, the latter being happy themes with gentle human appeal.[3] In the 1870s his work became ever more somber, as he increasingly used light and deep shadow to suggest the introspective nature of his subjects.

Of the few genre scenes that Johnson created during his later years, *The Earnest Pupil* has been singled out as one of his best.[4] Art historian Patricia Hills calls it a "first rate genre painting of 1881."[5] Writing about Johnson, Hills reflected, "In his late genre paintings he often chose themes that suggested such traditional values as the benefits of communal work, the passing of knowledge from an older to a younger generation, and the camaraderie of the older generation."[6] In this painting, an older man dressed in a coat and cap reminiscent of a Civil War uniform teaches a young boy how to play the flute. The youth watches and listens intently as the man demonstrates his own expertise with the instrument.

Hills noted that the man's coat and cap are brown, rather than the blue or gray of a Union or Confederate uniform, suggesting, perhaps, that instead of taking sides it was time to come together as a nation.[7] The old soldier no longer practices the art of war; instead he instructs the future generation in the art of music. Johnson's painting recalls the war's devastation even as it invokes the restorative powers of art and human interaction to heal the rupture of that awful struggle. LR and ML

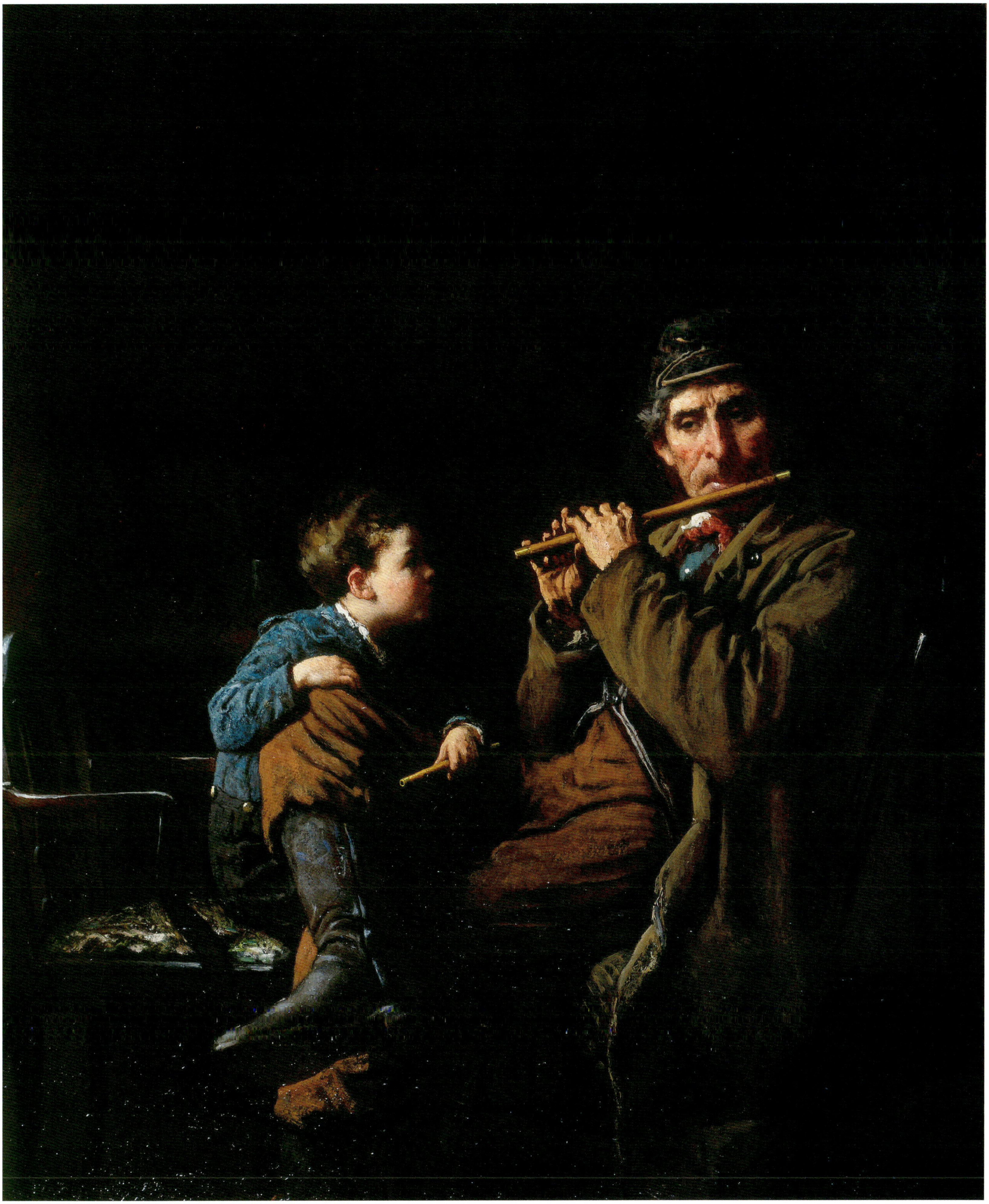

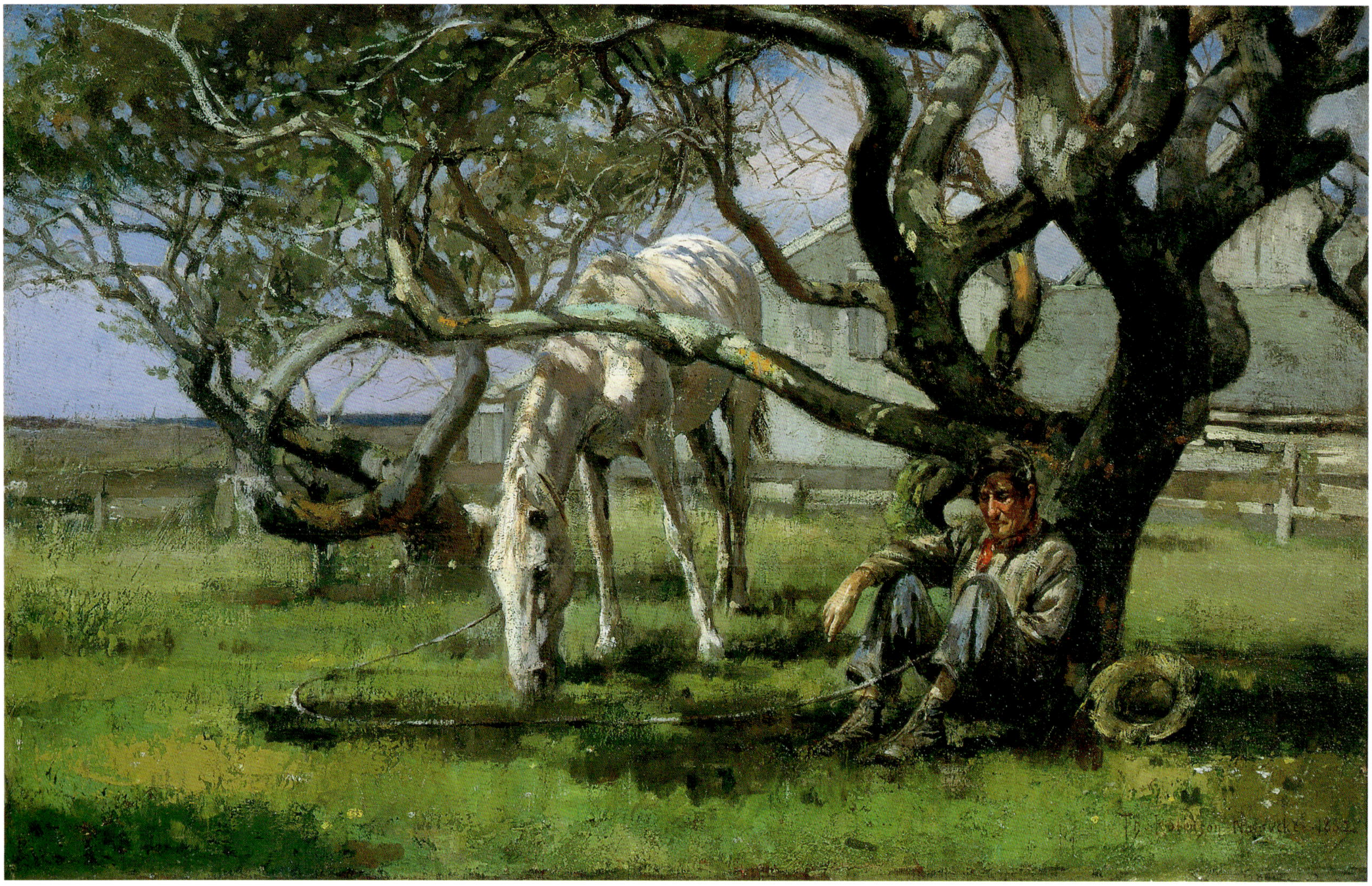

THEODORE ROBINSON

29 b. 1852, Irasburg, Vermont; d. 1896, New York City

Nantucket (formerly *Man and Horse beneath a Tree*), 1882
Oil on canvas, 20¼ × 32¼ (51.44 × 81.92)
Signed and dated lower right: TH Robinson. Nantucket 1882
Museum purchase 63.03

PROVENANCE: Ralph N. Crawford, 1895; Harry Shaw Newman Gallery, New York, by 1946; Joseph Katz, Baltimore, by 1951; Hirschl and Adler Galleries, New York.
EXHIBITIONS: *Theodore Robinson, 1852–1896*, Brooklyn Museum, 1946; *Select View; The Beauty in the Beast: American Artists Observe the Horse*, Columbus Museum, October 16, 1994–January 8, 1995.
PUBLICATIONS: *Panorama* (February 1947), n.p.; Timpano, 30; Winn, et al., 149.

Theodore Robinson had a rich but short artistic career. He studied in Chicago and at the National Academy of Design in New York. In 1876 he traveled to France where he became a student of such realist painters as Carolus-Duran, Jean-Léon Gérôme, and Benjamin Constant. In Paris he shared a studio with Will H. Low, Birge Harrison, Carroll Beckwith, and John Singer Sargent.[1] Returning to the United States in 1879, he stayed in Boston, where, under the guidance of artist John La Farge, he taught and painted murals. Later, Robinson moved to New York. Eventually, he returned to Europe, working in Paris until his important meeting with Claude Monet in 1888.

Robinson followed Monet to Giverny, where he began a relationship with the older artist and his work. He subsequently rejected his academic realist training in favor of more spontaneous and colorful impressionist techniques. Monet enjoyed his privacy at Giverny and avoided most of the artists who ventured there, but Robinson was a rare exception. He wrote to his friends about visiting with Monet and looking at his paintings of Rouen Cathedral:

> Never, I believe, has architecture been painted so before, the most astonishing impression of the thing, a feeling of size, grandeur and decay, an avoidance of the banal side of the subject. . . . Isn't it curious, a man taking such material and making such magnificent use of it. . . . Monet was cordiality, itself—It's very pleasant to think I have a place in his affection.[2]

Monet and Giverny inspired Robinson the rest of his life, even in the American subjects he painted after returning to the United States in 1892. In 1895 gallery owner William Macbeth gave Robinson his first solo show in New York, which received a lukewarm critical response and resulted in few sales. With such a meager income from painting, Robinson was compelled to teach at several art schools to make ends meet. For years he trekked through the eastern seaboard searching for American subjects and landscapes that he might portray in his personal adaptation of impressionism. He was not alone in his pursuit of impressionist methods; he and comrades J. Alden Weir and John Henry Twachtman became known as the foremost American impressionists in the 1890s. Robinson's hard-earned reputation, however, was short-lived, for he succumbed to asthma at the age of forty-four.

Nantucket dates from 1882, several years before Robinson met Monet. He was living in New York at this time, having recently returned from his student years in Europe. Robinson and other artists, including Abbott Thayer and Joe Evans, summered in Nantucket and produced a number of paintings based on local scenes.[3] But for all the greenery, the distant marsh meadow at left, and the barely discernible sliver of the ocean beyond it, this subject of horse and rider resting under a tree with barn and fence in the distance could be mistaken for Colorado or Texas rather than an island off the coast of Massachusetts. Though he had found a subject that seemed decidedly American, its location could be anywhere.

The composition reveals the artist's fascination with light, which is especially evident in the dappled effects on the tree branch, rider, and horse. Robinson's brushwork here is controlled in comparison to his later impressionist technique of building surfaces with layers of impasto. Here he mixed colors on his palette; later he would rely on optical mixing. *Nantucket* is an image of serenity and peacefulness, a projection of his interest in landscape and light before he explored such subjects with an impressionist approach. BF

CHARLES C. CURRAN

30 b. 1861, Hartford, Kentucky; d. 1942, New York City
Self-Portrait, 1892
Oil on canvas, 20 × 12¼ (50.8 × 31.12)
Inscribed lower left: To My Beloved Mother, May 15, 1892, Charles C. Curran
Gift of Mr. and Mrs. Ben Hardaway III 97.11

PROVENANCE: Gift of the artist to his mother, Elizabeth Thompson Curran, 1892; gift to the artist from his father, Ulysses Thompson Curran, 1912; Emily Curran Liang, the artist's daughter, 1942; Kaycee Benton, 1973; Kennedy Galleries, New York, 1980; Mr. and Mrs. Benjamin Hardaway III, Columbus, Georgia.

Charles Courtney Curran was raised in Sandusky, Ohio.[1] He studied briefly at the Cincinnati Academy of Design before moving to New York, where he became a student of Walter Satterlee at the National Academy of Design in 1881. That same year, at the age of twenty-three, Curran was given his first public exhibition at the academy. In Paris in 1889 Curran studied at the Académie Julian with Benjamin Constant and Jules Lefebvre. He was awarded prizes for his paintings at the Paris Salon of 1890, the Columbian Exposition of 1893 in Chicago, the Paris Exposition of 1900, and the Pan-American Exposition of 1901 in Buffalo. He was assistant director of the latter.

In 1903 fellow artist Frederick Dellenbaugh invited Curran to visit him at the art colony in Cragsmoor, New York, in the Hudson River Valley.[2] Curran was so taken with the place that by 1910 he had established a studio there. During the next thirty years of his career he divided his time between Cragsmoor and New York City.

Curran is known best for his paintings of women posed before picturesque vistas of the Cragsmoor landscape, usually rendered in an impressionist style. He also painted genre scenes, portraits, and landscapes, as well as a series of views of the imperial temples of Peking. Curran died in New York City on November 9, 1942.

Curran painted this unusual portrait as a gift for his mother.[3] The artist is situated in three-quarter view in the foreground, while his wife, Grace Wickham Curran, is seen just beyond his left shoulder holding their month-old son, Stanley. This unusually composed painting of the family was intended as an homage to the artist's deceased brother, for whom the child was named. The dark tonalities used in the background and in the artist's dark three-piece suit may reflect the artist's mixed emotions as he experiences contentment with his new family and grief at the reminder of his loss. The controlled brushwork and warm tones used to define the faces are in sharp contrast to the dark surroundings. On the back wall, the artist included the bottom left corner of a gilt frame and an unframed portrait of a man, perhaps Curran's deceased brother. KMZ

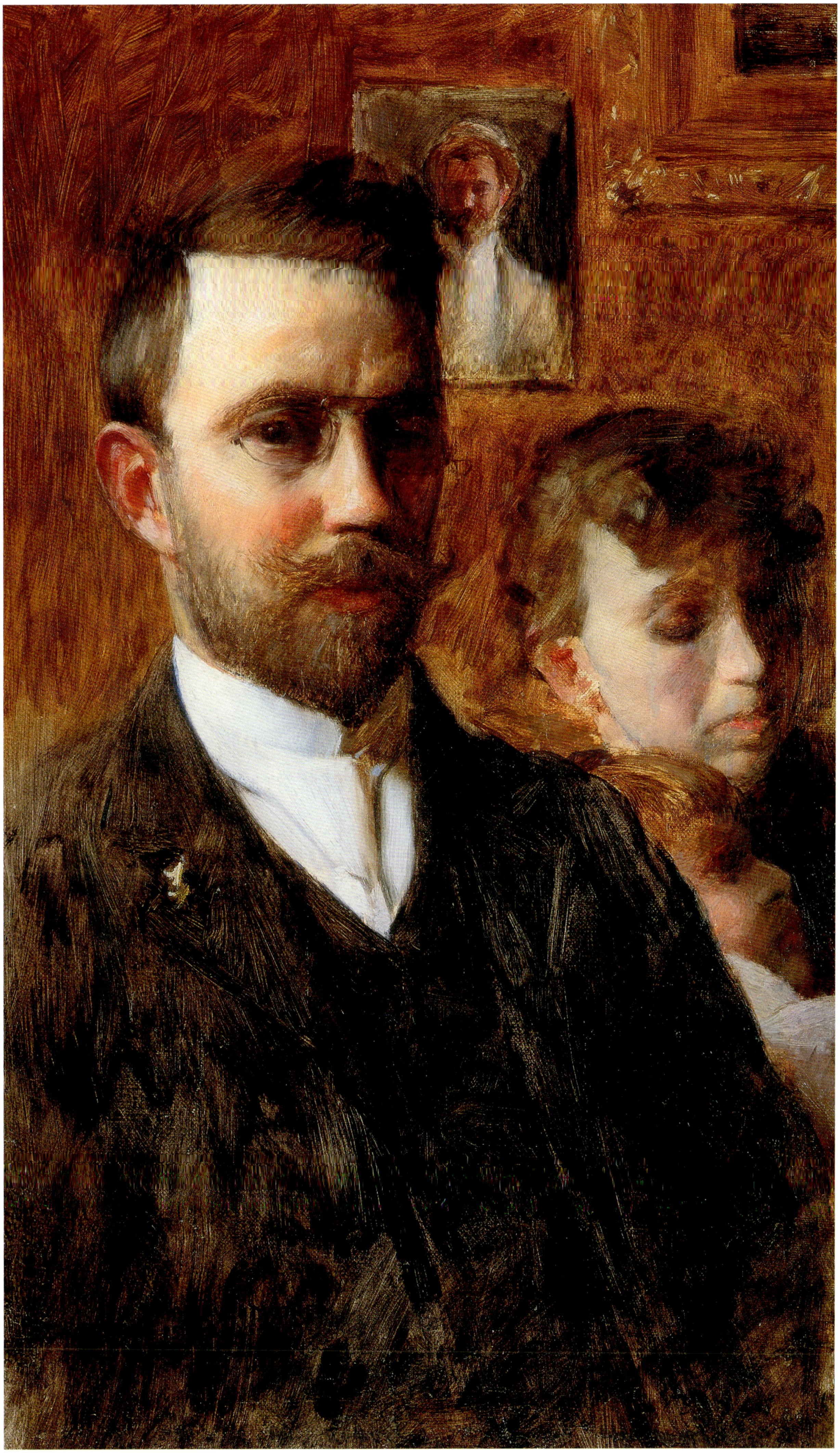

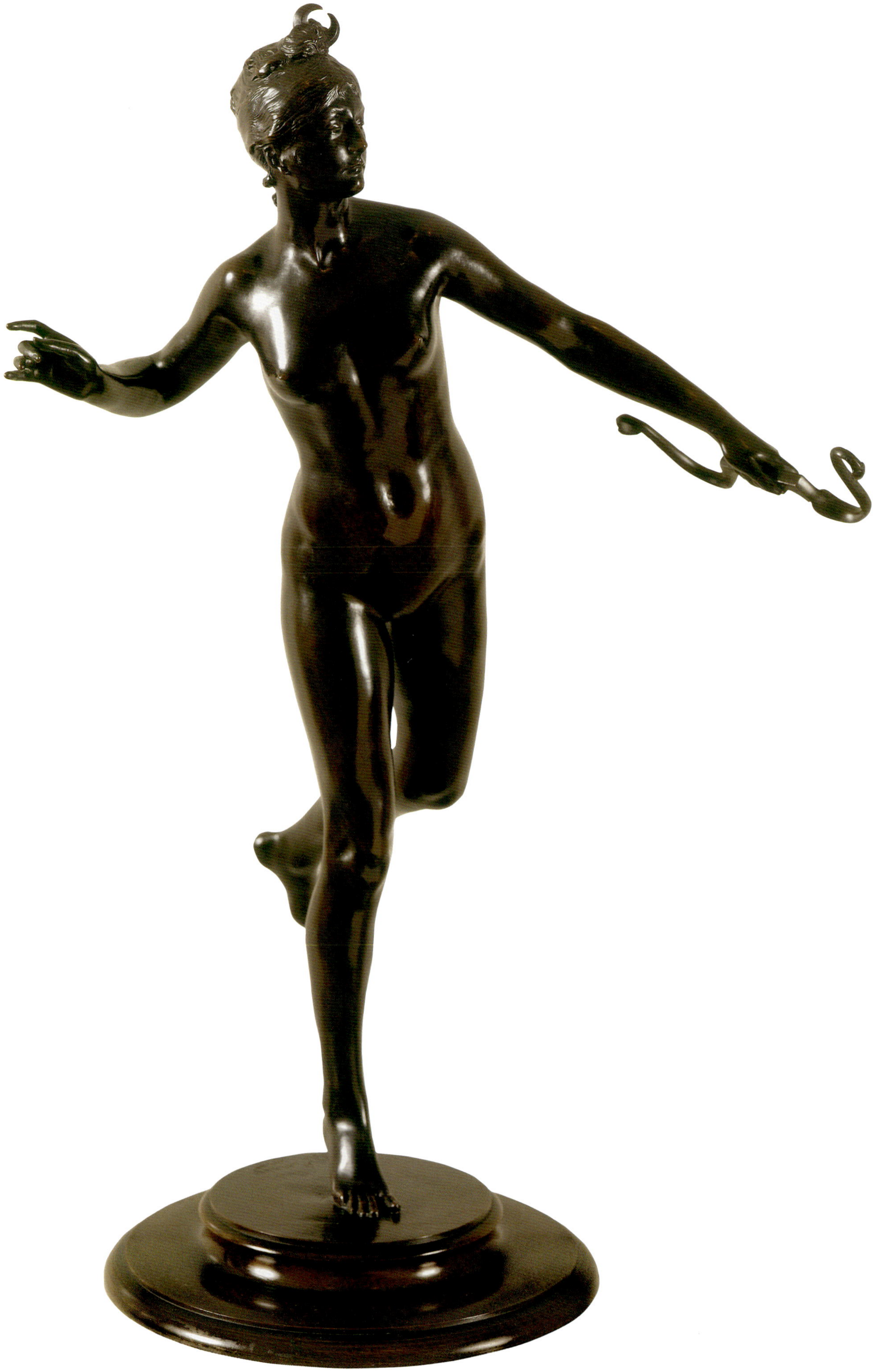

FREDERICK MACMONNIES

31 b. 1863, Brooklyn; d. 1937, New York City
Diana, 1890 (cast after 1894)
Cast bronze, 30 × 16 × 20½ (76.2 × 40.64 × 52.07)
Signed at rear of base: F. MacMonnies 1890, copyright 1894
Museum purchase made possible by the Simon Schwob Acquisition Fund 92.4

PROVENANCE: Private collection, 1925; Sotheby's Auction House, New York, 1990; Conner Rosenkranz, New York City.
PUBLICATIONS: Wink, et al., [illegible]; Conner and Rosenkranz, 124–25.

As a boy, Frederick William MacMonnies modeled small figures and animals in white wax.[1] Though his parents recognized that he was gifted, they lacked the financial resources to send him to art school. MacMonnies found work doing odd jobs in the New York studio of sculptor Augustus Saint-Gaudens, who soon became aware of the young man's innate artistic ability and made him his assistant. In the evenings, MacMonnies studied at the National Academy of Design and the Art Students League.

In 1884 he went to Paris and entered Jean Alexandre Falquière's sculpture class at the École des Beaux-Arts. In two successive years, he won the highest prize available to a foreign student at the school—the Prix d'Atelier, which was second only to the Prix de Rome. At the Salon of 1889, MacMonnies received an honorable mention for the original plaster of *Diana*. The museum's bronze casting of *Diana* dates to after 1894 but probably before 1910.[2]

Diana was a deity of antiquity, known primarily as the virgin huntress. As the twin of Apollo, god of the sun, she was also goddess of the moon. To the Greeks she was Artemis. According to art historian Wayne Craven, MacMonnies's *Diana* may have been derived from classical mythology, but the artist chose not to make this sculpture in the neoclassical tradition.[3] Instead, he portrayed the goddess as svelte and delicate, following the beaux-arts style and rejecting the heavier classical proportions of ancient times. The goddess's usual attributes—the crescent moon entwined in her hair and the bow clasped in her left hand—remain.

Following his success with *Diana* at the Paris Salon, MacMonnies's fame increased, and he received many commissions on both sides of the Atlantic. With this sudden prominence also came criticism, especially with his 1893 statue of *Bacchante* (Metropolitan Museum of Art), which was seen as condoning amorality.[4] Today, MacMonnies, who was regularly commissioned to create public statues, is considered to be one of America's elite sculptors of the Gilded Age, which dated from the mid-1870s to the early 1900s. Within this thirty-year period, sculptors, architects, and painters sought to create art that would refine the public's artistic taste. Using as inspiration the images of ancient Greece and Rome and the Italian Renaissance, these artists revised mythological subjects and heroic allegories to create works that were often buoyant, decorative, and highly expressive. MacMonnies's *Barge of State,* completed for the Chicago World's Fair (1892–93) was all of this and more, measuring sixty feet in length and containing thirty-eight figures.[5]

In 1896 MacMonnies received the Order of the Chevalier of the Legion of Honor from the French government. By 1905 he had opened a studio school in Giverny, France, where he lived with his wife, Mary Louise Fairchild of St. Louis. MacMonnies returned home in 1915 because of the First World War. Despite changing aesthetic tastes in postwar America, he never strayed from his beaux-arts approach to sculpture. Over one hundred years after its making, *Diana* still speaks eloquently of a time in the nation's history when elegance was embraced. BW

GEORGE OHR

32 b. 1857, Biloxi, Mississippi; d. 1918, Biloxi, Mississippi
Teapot, ca. 1895–1900
Glazed ceramic, 7½ × 7 (19.05 × 17.78)
Stamped: Geo. E. Ohr/Biloxi, Miss
Purchased with funds provided by the Edward Swift Shorter Bequest Fund 2002.24

PROVENANCE: Estate of the artist; James Carpenter, New Jersey, 1972; Jean Bragg Gallery, New Orleans, 2002.

In the late 1870s Joseph Meyer, a family friend, invited George E. Ohr to join him in New Orleans to learn pottery as a trade. Meyer was nine years older than Ohr and already well established as a ceramist.[1]

Ohr took to the work naturally and immediately set about mastering the craft. As part of his training he decided to make a two-year tour of ceramics studios in the United States.[2] Upon completing this tour he returned to his hometown of Biloxi and set up his own pottery shop using scavenged materials.[3] Following the lead of his mentor and teacher, Ohr dug clay from the banks of the Tchoutacabouffa River. In 1883 he opened his own business in Biloxi and over the next two years produced more than six hundred ceramic pieces.

Not long after opening his shop, Ohr met and married Josephine Gehring, and they began to raise a family.[4] In 1889, because of increased family responsibilities, Ohr accepted Meyer's offer to return to New Orleans and assist him at H. Sophie Newcomb Memorial College.[5] However, the pull of Biloxi proved stronger, and the artist soon returned to his gulf port hometown.

Upon his return, Ohr increased production and developed a very personal style of glazing. A travel editor at the *Daily Picayune* wrote that Ohr's pink-painted shop at this time had more than ten thousand ceramic objects to chose from—which was probably an exaggeration, but not by much. By 1893 his shop was overflowing with ceramic pieces, as seen in a photograph of that year showing Ohr, the art potter, as he now referred to himself, standing beside his shop with hundreds of pots lining exterior shelves in the courtyard.[6]

Ohr created his forms by manipulating, pleating, crinkling, twisting, and folding the clay. Sometimes he incorporated accidents into the overall design, recognizing them as part of the finished product. Most of his pieces were less than six inches tall, small enough that Ohr could alter them from top to bottom in one or two continuous, controlled motions on the wheel. Larger pieces and those with handles and extreme body manipulations are less common. The best of these, with one or a combination of Ohr's trademark glazes, are extremely rare. The museum's lidded teapot is seven and a half inches tall and features the artist's gunmetal and red glazes and a serpent-headed spout.

Ohr's earliest glazes were tobacco browns, dark greens, and occasionally gunmetal, used as an accent by most traditional potters of the day. Eventually he developed brilliant pinks and reds, vibrant greens, scintillating metallic-lustered blacks and blues, and combinations of orange and yellow with splotches of violet. Ohr marked most of his pieces, and all but a few bear one kind of designation or another. The type of symbol serves to date his pieces, as he periodically changed his marks. Earlier pieces bear the simple block stamp designation, "Geo. E. Ohr/Biloxi, Miss," which is on the bottom of the museum's vessel; later pieces were incised with Ohr's script signature.[7]

Although his inexpensive functional pots sold well, Ohr was still unable to find an appreciative audience for his art vessels, which were priced higher. Indeed, the artist's pricing of these works indicated that he saw them as quality art objects.[8] Over the years, Ohr became increasingly eccentric. He grew a two-foot handlebar moustache and made wild proclamations that he was the "unequaled, unrivaled, undisputed greatest art pot-Ohr on earth."[9] Locally he became known as the Mad Potter of Biloxi. In 1917 he was diagnosed with cancer of the throat; he died several months later at the age of sixty-one.

Shortly before the end of his life, Ohr stored his "mud babies" in crates in the attic of his son's auto repair shop, leaving instructions that the trove was not to be opened for fifty years, when the world would be ready for his visionary works. In 1968 James Carpenter, an antiques dealer from New Jersey, discovered more than seven thousand Ohr pots and forms, and acquired them four years later. Today Ohr's works are collected by individuals and museums around the world.[10] CTB

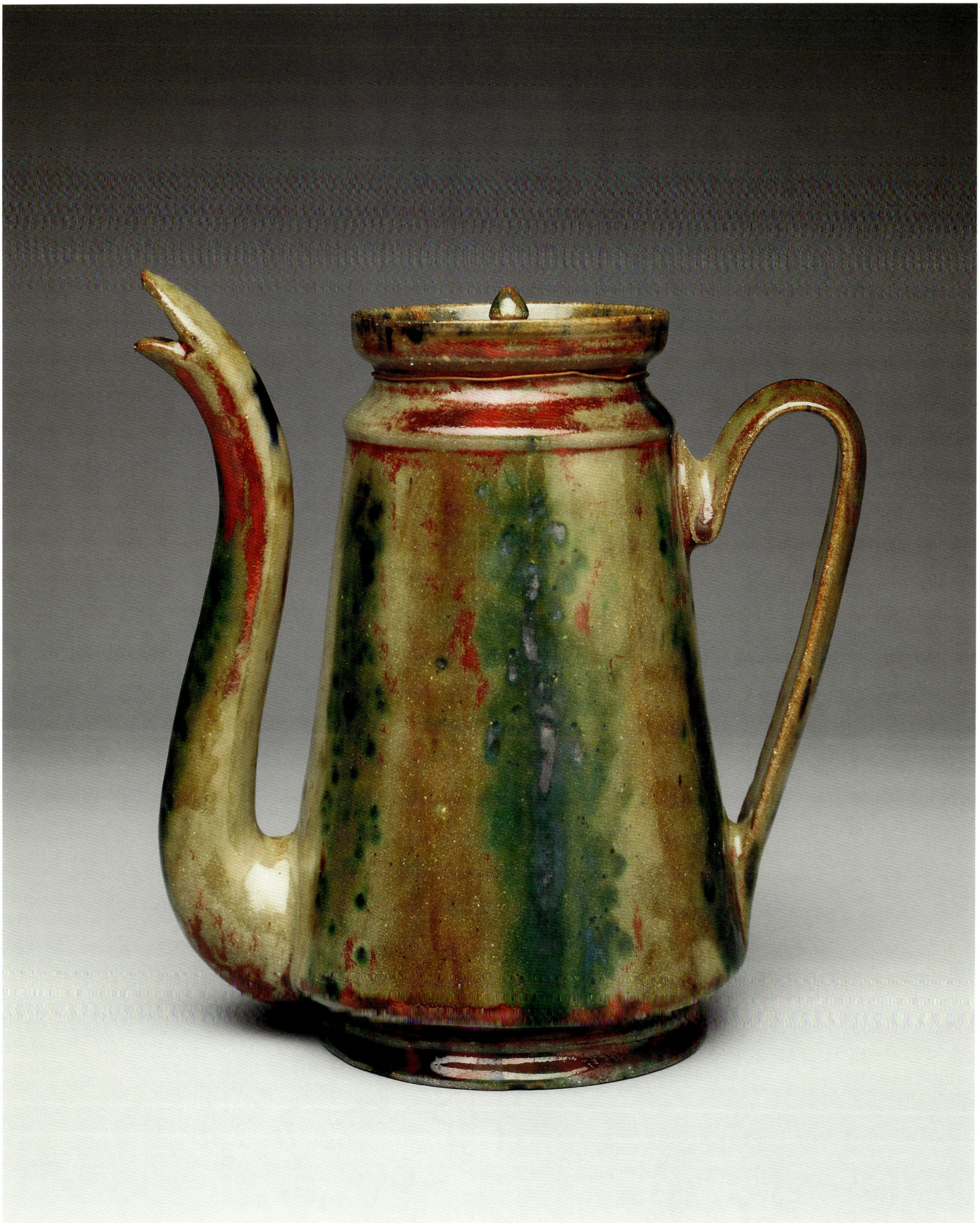

WILLIAM MERRITT CHASE

33 b. 1849, Franklin, Indiana; d. 1916, New York City
My Daughter, Alice, ca. 1898–99
Oil on canvas, 24⅛ × 18¼ (54.15 × 46.36)
Signed upper left: Wm. M. Chase
Museum purchase made possible by Friends of the Museum; a gift in memory of Mrs. Elizabeth B. Turner; the Daniel P. and Shannon L. Amos Foundation; Mr. and Mrs. Donald F. Broda Jr.; Mr. and Mrs. Ray E. Crowley; Mrs. Frank D. Foley Jr., in honor of Sally Foley Hughston, Frank D. Foley IV, Jack Mayo Hughston, George Woodruff Foley, William Coleman Foley and Jack Ross Foley; Mr. and Mrs. William T. Heard Jr.; Mrs. Howell Hollis; Dr. and Mrs. Jack Hughston; Mrs. E. Buford King Jr.; Mr. and Mrs. David G. Lewis Jr.; Mr. George W. Mathews Jr.; Helen Jordan Olnick; Mrs. Alan C. Ramsay Jr., in honor of Sarah Turner Butler; and Dr. and Mrs. Davis R. Watson 2000.2

PROVENANCE: Private collection, Cold Spring Harbor, New York, 1979; Newhouse Galleries, New York, 1979–82; Mr. and Mrs. Louis Silver, New York, 1983; private collection; Spanierman Gallery, New York.
EXHIBITIONS: *A Leading Spirit in American Art: William Merritt Chase (1849–1916),* Henry Art Gallery at University of Washington (Seattle), Metropolitan Museum of Art (New York), October 2, 1983–June 3, 1984.
PUBLICATIONS: Pisano, 111; Pisano and Longwell, 110.

Born in Johnson County, Indiana, William Merritt Chase first studied art in nearby Indianapolis with B. F. Hayes. He continued his studies at the National Academy of Design in New York, then went to Europe and entered the Royal Academy in Munich in 1872. While traveling in Europe, Chase stayed in Venice with fellow artists Frank Duveneck and John Henry Twachtman. In 1887 he returned to New York, where he was elected to membership in both the National Academy of Design and the National Institute of Arts and Letters. Later, he founded the Society of American Artists.

Throughout his career, Chase taught art—at the Brooklyn Academy of Art, the New York School of Art, and privately at his home and abroad. Most important was his twenty-three-year affiliation with the Art Students League, where he became a very popular instructor whose students included Kenneth Hayes Miller, Marsden Hartley, Rockwell Kent, Charles Sheeler, Georgia O'Keeffe, and Edward Hopper.

The dark, rich palette and painterly brushwork of Franz Hals and Diego Velásquez inspired the young Chase. Later, under the influence of French impressionists, his palette lightened considerably. Combined with other turn-of-the-century influences, notably those of James McNeill Whistler and Alfred Stevens, Chase developed what Ronald Pisano referred to as the International Style.[1] In 1902 he joined a group known as the Ten American Artists, who regularly exhibited together and came to be regarded as the elite of American impressionism.

Chase painted portraits, interior views, and depictions of parks, beaches, and the landscape around his summer home at Shinnecock, Long Island. Perhaps his most endearing paintings are those of his immediate family. His wife, Alice, and his daughter, Alice Dieudonnée (her middle name means gift of God), were favorite models. The warmth and affection evident in these works accounts in part for their enduring charm.

This painting of the artist's eleven-year-old daughter shows Chase at the height of his skills as a portraitist. *My Daughter, Alice* reflects his fatherly adoration as much as his skill at visual rendering. Also known to the family as Cosy, young Alice posed for her father in his New York studio wearing an oversized, dull-colored smock, in contrast to the bright flowers in her hair. The red blossoms, the red scarf at her neck, and the red fullness of her lips direct the viewer's attention to her face and her doelike eyes, which are attentive and thoughtful. Chase's bravura brushwork energizes the otherwise subdued subject, suggesting that he knew of the enthusiasm and delight that lay just beneath the surface of his beloved child. LR and ML

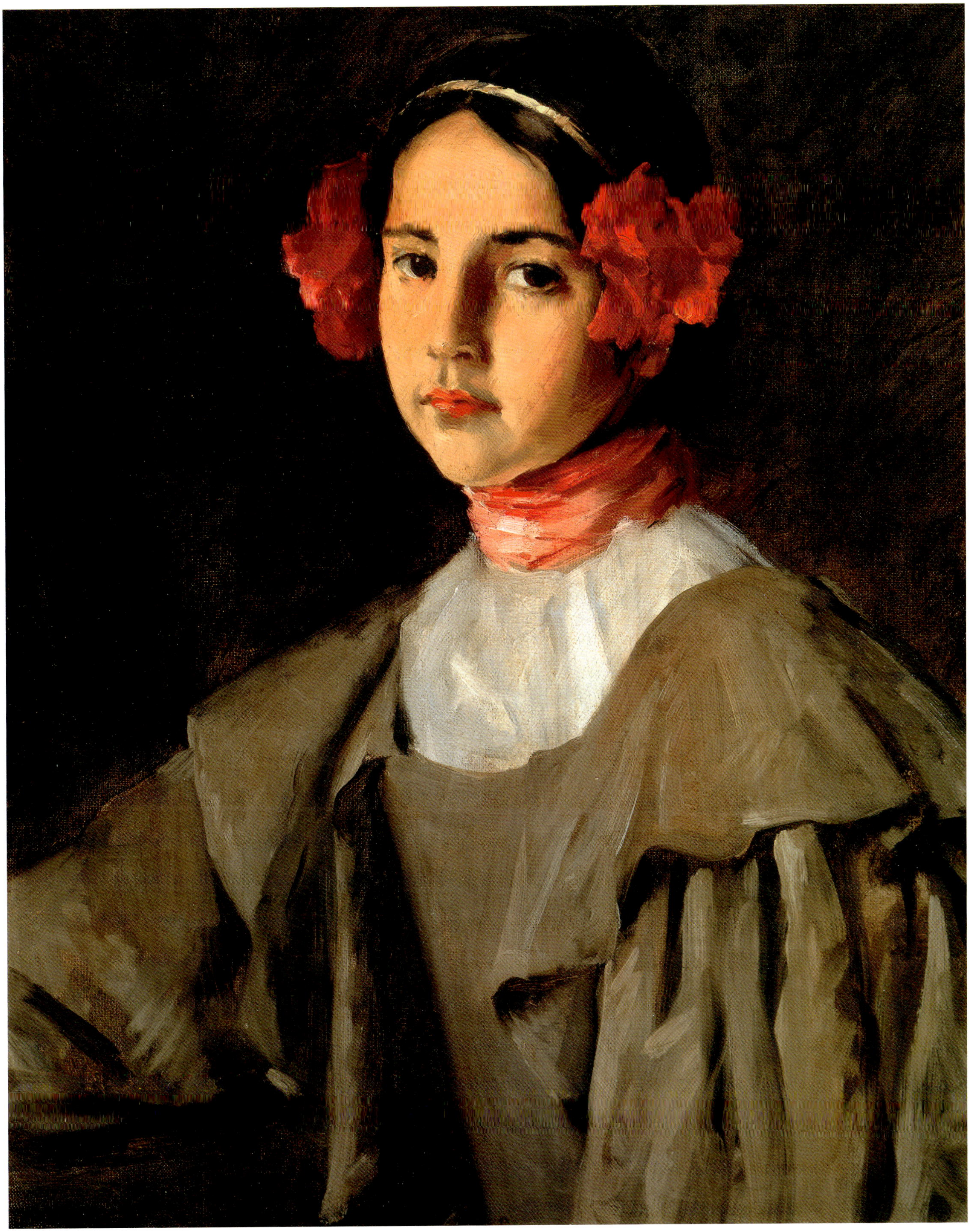

JOHN PETO

34

b. 1854, Philadelphia; d. 1907, Island Heights, New Jersey
Table with a Whale Oil Lamp, ca. 1899
Oil on canvas, 13½ × 11¾ (34.29 × 29.85)
Museum purchase through the Endowment Fund in Honor of D. A. Turner 82.28

PROVENANCE: Private collection; Christie's, New York; Meredith Long and Co., Houston.
EXHIBITIONS: *Select View.*
PUBLICATIONS: Timpano, no. 36, fig. 3; Winn, et al., 124.

John Frederick Peto probably first saw original paintings in his father's picture frame shop.[1] Surviving sketchbooks suggest that he was producing watercolor paintings and drawings at a very early age. Though he listed himself as a painter in the Philadelphia city directory of the mid-1870s, Peto did not begin his formal art training until 1877–78, when he studied at the Pennsylvania Academy of the Fine Arts. He could have met fellow student William Michael Harnett at that time. Harnett and Peto are considered to be among America's greatest trompe l'oeil still-life painters, for each had the ability to render objects with such authenticity that they often made viewers think they were looking at the real thing. The style, which first gained popularity in seventeenth-century Holland, was often dismissed by critics as little more than a show of technical expertise, but the general public was truly fascinated.

During his extensive research on Harnett, Alfred Frankenstein discovered that Peto actually painted twenty still lifes previously credited to Harnett. Apparently, an unscrupulous dealer obtained Peto's work illegally in 1905, and forged Harnett's signature on them. This discovery of the 1940s led to a renewed interest in American trompe l'oeil works. Frankenstein, in his 1969 preface to the revised version of *After the Hunt: William Harnett and Other American Still-Life Painters,* suggested that Peto's work differed from Harnett's in "its Baroque restlessness."[2] He went on to note that in Peto the presence of motion is evident, "Everything slides, falls, dangles, or balances in the most precarious and alarming fashion."[3] Moreover, Peto's arrangement of objects is frontal while Harnett relied on a receding pyramidal design.

Peto completed *Table with a Whale Oil Lamp* after he and his wife relocated to the New Jersey coastal community of Island Heights in their later years. Here is the artist's preferred frontal arrangement of objects as well as his interest in imminent motion. The red book cover hangs precariously while the pipe and matchsticks rest at the table's edge. To challenge his technical proficiency, Peto took pleasure in assembling items of various textures, such as the ceramic stein and inkwell, the pewter oil lamp, the tattered book, the wooden table, and the meerschaum pipe. His strong sense of color is seen in the red book cover against the deep blue cloth on the table. LR and CTB

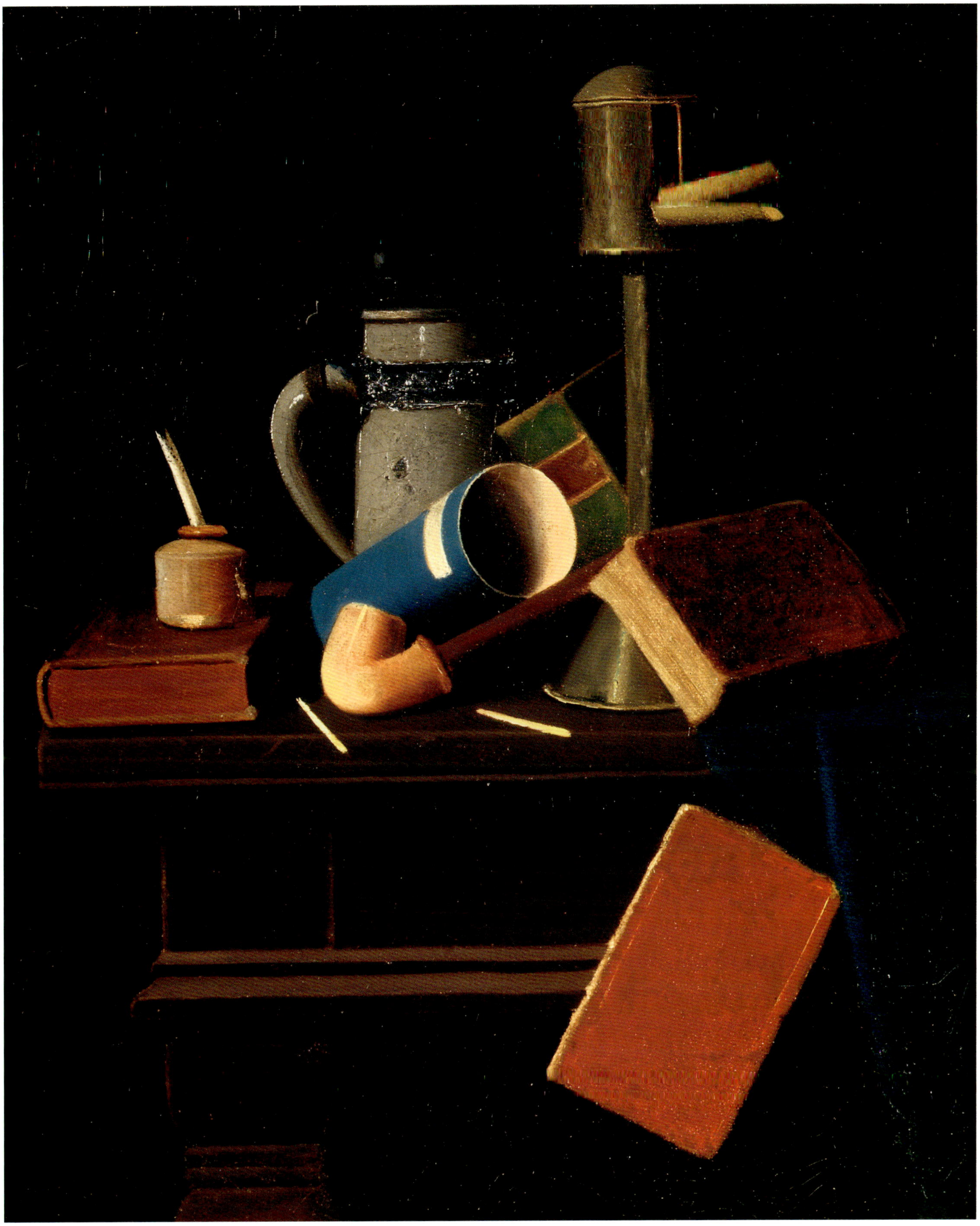

FREDERICK JUDD WAUGH

35

b. 1861, Bordertown, New York; d. 1940, Provincetown, Massachusetts

The Silver Sea, after 1900

Oil on canvas, 30¼ × 40¼ (76.84 × 102.24)

Signed lower left: Waugh

Gift of Virginia C. Courts 82.2

PROVENANCE: Virginia Courts, Atlanta.

EXHIBITIONS: *Select View.*

PUBLICATIONS: Timpano, 31; Winn, et al., 179.

Frederick Judd Waugh was born into an artist's family. His first teachers were his father, Samuel B. Waugh, a respected Philadelphia portrait painter, and his mother, Mary Eliza Young Waugh, a miniaturist. With encouragement from his parents, he attended the Pennsylvania Academy of the Fine Arts, where he studied with Thomas Eakins and Thomas Anshutz. After three years he left for Paris, where he entered the Académie Julian and studied under Adolphe William Bouguereau and Tony Robert-Fleury. In 1883, while he was still a student, his work was accepted for the Paris Salon. His father's death in 1885 brought him back to the United States, where he spent the next seven years doing commercial work and painting some portraits. In 1892 he returned to Paris.

Although Waugh was very versatile and accomplished in depicting a variety of subjects, it was his marine paintings that brought him critical attention. Visiting Sark Island in the English Channel in 1893, he began to study water, rocks, and sky, often battling the elements to paint out-of-doors.[1] By 1895 Waugh had set up his studio in the English coastal town of Saint Ives, Cornwall, where J. M. W. Turner had painted eighty years earlier. A large window in the studio provided an intimate view of the ocean, and he could continue his intensive study of waves in greater comfort. His wave paintings have been referred to as majesty in motion.[2]

Waugh remained in England for twelve years, working as an illustrator for various newspapers and magazines in London, and returning to Saint Ives to paint when time allowed. The museum's painting dates to his years in England and could very well describe the view from his studio in Cornwall.[3] In *The Silver Sea,* Waugh painted the light as it reflected off the water's surface. Viewing the painting, one can almost hear the sound of the waves rolling in and crashing against the rocks, or taste and smell the spray of seawater. Waugh often applied color directly out of the tube, building a heavy impasto on the canvas. His use of unmixed color added to the freshness of this painting, making the waves look bright and wet and suggesting the unrelenting power of the pounding surf.[4] In *The Silver Sea,* Waugh did not feel compelled to provide a narrative by including a figure or boat. Instead, it is his depiction of the implacable beauty of the sea that captivates and piques the viewer's imagination.

In 1907 Waugh returned to the United States, eventually settling in Provincetown, Massachusetts. He was elected a member of the National Academy of Design in 1911. For five consecutive years he was voted the favorite artist of the prestigious Carnegie International Exhibition in Pittsburgh. Waugh was known to have painted up to ten canvases a month to keep up with the demand for his work. The United States government called on him to help camouflage the naval fleet in World War I. Fittingly, upon his death, he was buried on the New England coast within sound and sight of the sea. EW

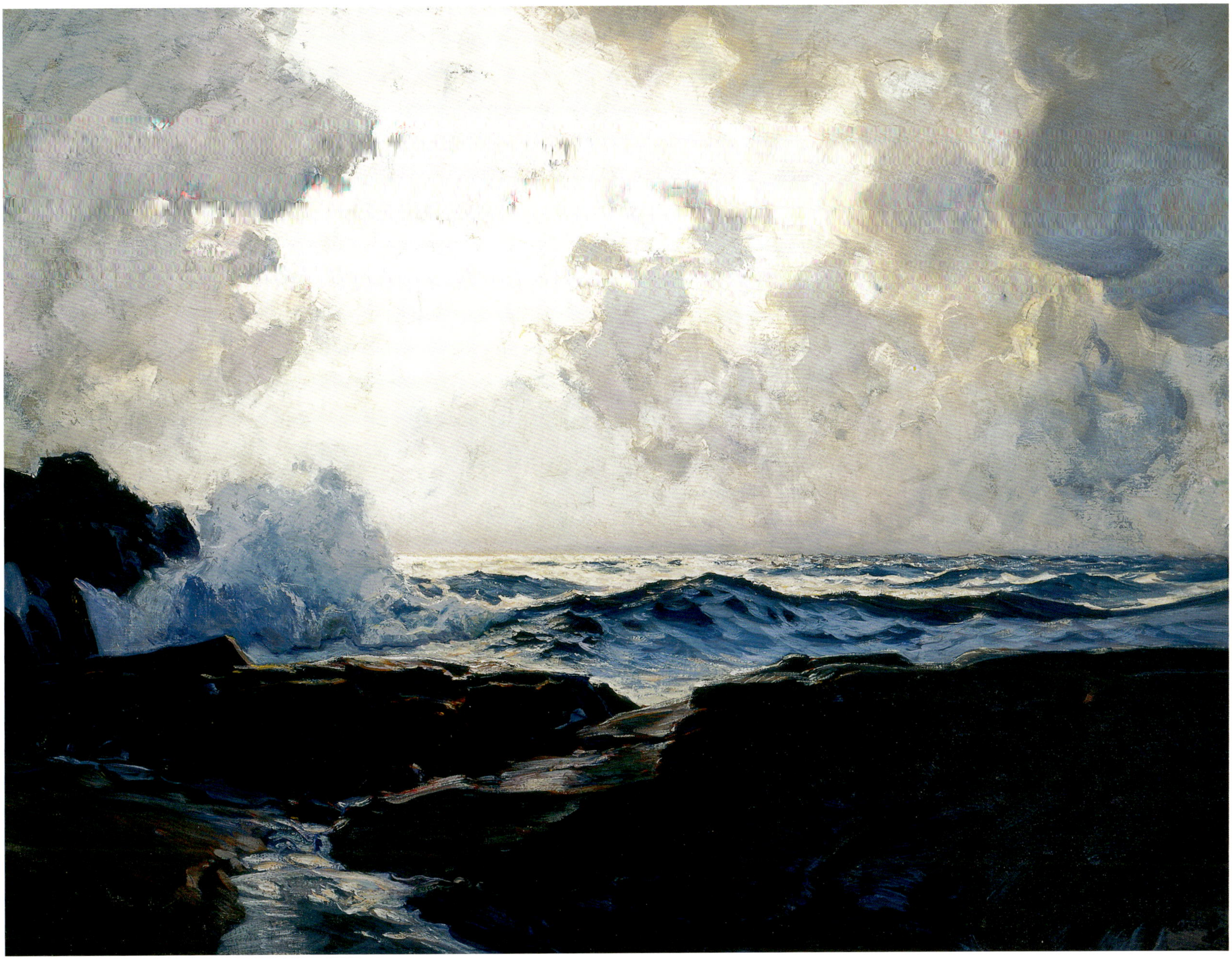

JOHN HENRY TWACHTMAN

36 b. 1853, Cincinnati; d. 1902, Gloucester, Massachusetts
Horseneck Falls, ca. 1900
Oil on canvas, 30 × 25 (76.2 × 63.5)
Museum purchase made possible by the Ella E. Kirven Charitable Lead Trust for Acquisitions 97.4

PROVENANCE: Twachtman family; Macbeth Gallery, New York, 1918; Theodore T. Ellis, Worcester, Massachusetts, 1918; James Graham and Sons, New York, 1965–ca. late 1960s; private collection; Spanierman Gallery, New York, 1997.
EXHIBITIONS: Joslyn Art Museum, Omaha, long-term loan, 1987–92.

John Henry Twachtman's first contact with art was very likely through his father, an immigrant from Germany in the 1840s who for a while painted still lifes and landscapes on window shades.[1] By 1874 Twachtman was studying with Frank Duveneck, who encouraged his students to paint people they met on the streets of Cincinnati. When Duveneck returned to Munich in 1875, he took Twachtman with him. The young artist enrolled in the Royal Academy of Munich and studied with Wilhelm Leibl, who encouraged his students to paint their first-hand experience of the world.[2] Twachtman and Duveneck also traveled throughout Europe at this time.[3]

During the following decade, Twachtman traveled back and forth between Europe and Cincinnati and New York, exhibiting his works and teaching. In New York he forged friendships with contemporary American artists such as William Merritt Chase, J. Alden Weir, John Weir, Theodore Robinson, and Childe Hassam. Perhaps influenced by these new contacts, he moved to Paris, where he enrolled at the Académie Julian in 1883.

Twachtman at this point had begun to focus on landscape painting. He was equally interested in capturing the atmospheric conditions of a scene in the tradition of English artist John Constable, and in interpreting natural elements through expressive painterly techniques as seen in the work of J. M. W. Turner. Twachtman expanded the visual design elements of color, line, and perspective to create a certain perceptible mood in his paintings. In 1897 he became a founding member of Ten American Painters, a group of artists who were influenced by French impressionism and disassociated themselves from the Society of American Artists and their exhibitions. As the first generation of American impressionists, members of the group brought the French movement to the forefront of the American art scene.

In 1890 Twachtman purchased a seventeen-acre farm in Connecticut and set up a studio. When he first walked the land he discovered Horseneck Brook, a humble stream that fed a small waterfall. Upon seeing this watercourse, it is said he exclaimed, "This is it!"[4] It was a scene that he would paint repeatedly. The farm was the inspiration for much of his later paintings, providing subjects that ranged from the waterfall to his gardens, arbors, woodlands, and even a footbridge he had constructed. Visible in all of these compositions is the inspiration he found in the work of Claude Monet.

Horseneck Falls was painted late in the artist's life. Lisa Peters noted,

> In scenes of the waterfall on his Greenwich property, he sought to capture the character of his subject. Leaving backgrounds undifferentiated, he brought the falls into the foreground, drawing our attention to the changing rhythms of the water, which he expressed by varying the force and energy of his brushstrokes and the thickness of his paint. Without a sense of scale or context, the images focus on the falling water itself rather than on the symbolic associations evoked by the subject or on its scenic appeal.[5]

Twachtman's capricious colors and his lavish impasto lend spontaneous and vibrant beauty to the rushing cascade, which hovers on the verge of abstraction. The effervescence of light gleaming off the water as it tumbles over rocks and across fissures is as much about nature as it is about the act of painting. The artist's exuberance is also visible in this fully realized work by a master in complete control of his process. BF

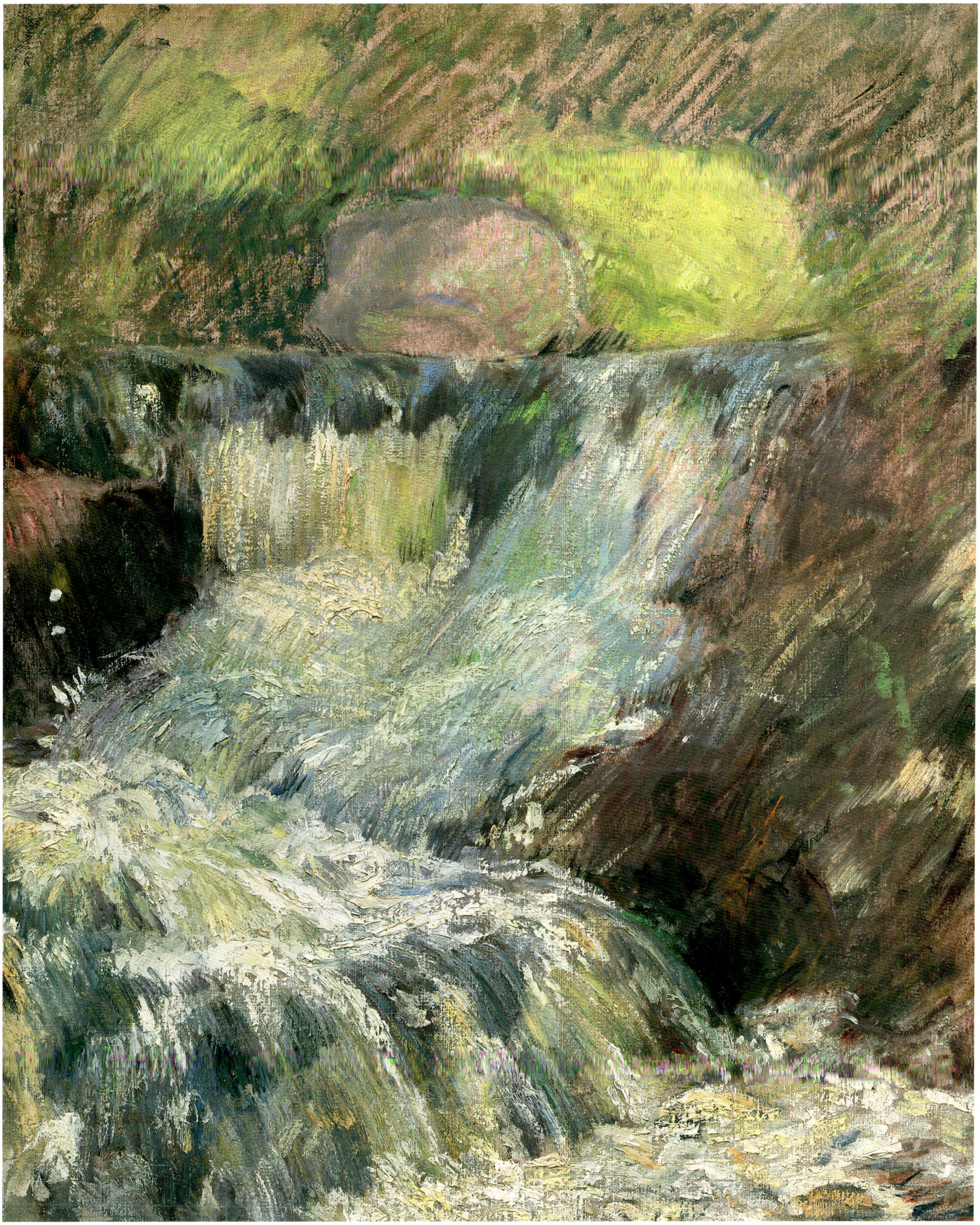

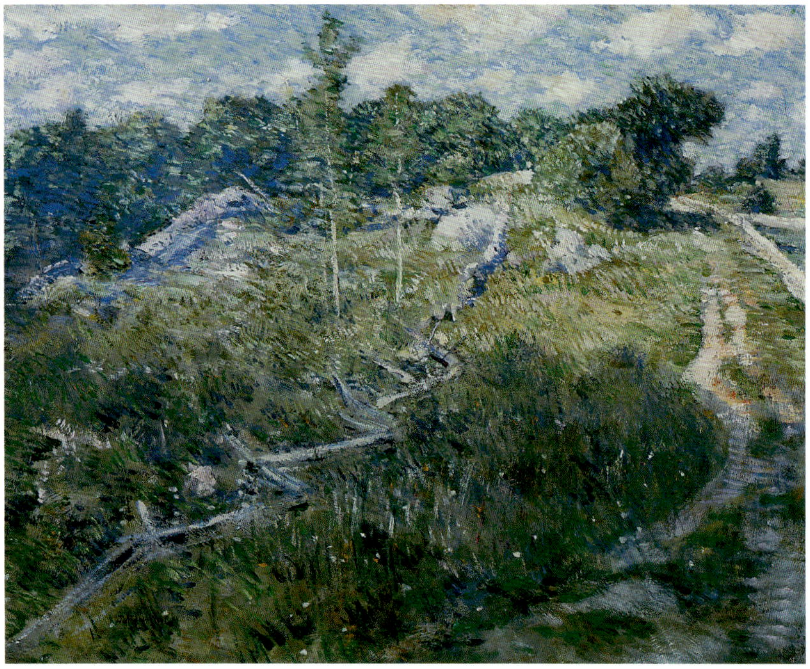

J. ALDEN WEIR

37

b. 1852, West Point, New York; d. 1919, New York City

Pelham Lane, ca. 1902

Oil on canvas, 20⅛ × 25⅛ (51.12 × 63.82)

Signed lower left: J. Alden Weir

Gift of the A. and M. L. Illges Memorial Foundation, Inc. 77.35

PROVENANCE: Henry Smith, New York, after 1908 and until 1920; Milch Gallery, New York; Levy Galleries, New York.
EXHIBITIONS: *Exhibition by Ten American Painters,* Pennsylvania Academy of the Fine Arts, Philadelphia, April 11–May 3, 1908, no. 90, as *Pelham's Lane;* National Academy of Design, New York; Century Club, Boston (and other locations unknown), before 1920; *Select View; French and American Impressionism,* Albany Museum of Art, Georgia, September 12–November 3, 1996; *A Connecticut Place: Weir Farm, An American Painter's Rural Retreat,* Parrish Art Museum (Southampton, New York), Bruce Museum (Greenwich, Connecticut), April 15–September 17, 2000.
PUBLICATIONS: Timpano, pl. 2; Close, 40; Winn, et al., 151; *A Connecticut Place,* 93, fig. 87.

Art, family, and home played key roles in the early childhood of Julian Alden Weir, who was one of sixteen children. His first art teacher was his father, who taught drawing at West Point Military Academy. As a young man, Weir traveled to Paris and studied at the École des Beaux-Arts with Jean-Léon Gérôme. Four years later, he returned to the United States and began teaching at the Art Students League in New York.

Weir's art reflected his academic training until the 1880s, when he was drawn to the influence of impressionism. His landscapes, which earlier revealed his admiration for the Barbizon school, had become distinctly impressionistic by the 1890s. Initially, Weir's reaction to impressionist paintings was far from enthusiastic. After attending an exhibition, he wrote,

> I never in my life saw more horrible things. . . . They do not observe drawing or form but give you an impression of what they call nature. It was worse than the Chamber of Horrors. I was there about a quarter of an hour and left with a head ache.[1]

His late conversion to impressionism was encouraged by his friends John Henry Twachtman and Theodore Robinson. Weir became one of the founding members of Ten American Painters, a group that developed in 1898 in reaction against the restrictive exhibition practices of the Society of American Artists.

In 1882 Weir purchased a large farm in Branchville, Connecticut, where he built his studio. The farm and its environs served as the artist's primary subject matter for the next thirty years, and it became a favorite gathering place for his circle of friends, which then included Twachtman, Robinson, Albert Pinkham Ryder, Childe Hassam, John Singer Sargent, and others.[2]

Pelham Lane, the subject of the painting, marked the southern edge of Weir's farm before he purchased the adjacent property.[3] Weir wrote in a letter of November 30, 1902, to his friend Col. C. E. S. Wood,[4]

> I have two canvases in the city, 20 by 24, one of an oak in sunlight and the other a lane with old fences and a fine sky. . . . I have not changed in any way not even in the subjects chosen, but it is my hope and desire to get close to Nature, to know her character more intimately, but I will be old, old, old before I can do even the little I do without her assistance.[5]

In *Pelham Lane,* Weir incorporated impressionist color and brushwork with design elements of Japonisme, seen here in the high horizon line, use of diagonals, irregular cropping, and asymmetry. Both the dusty road at right and the sharp switchback of the rail fencing lead the viewer's eye across the expanse of wildflowers and green meadow to the trees and sky beyond. The subtle delineation of shadow in the foreground and bright sunlight beyond define the expansive space and the sun-drenched atmosphere of this particular place on that day. Weir's work characterizes the best of American impressionism. BF

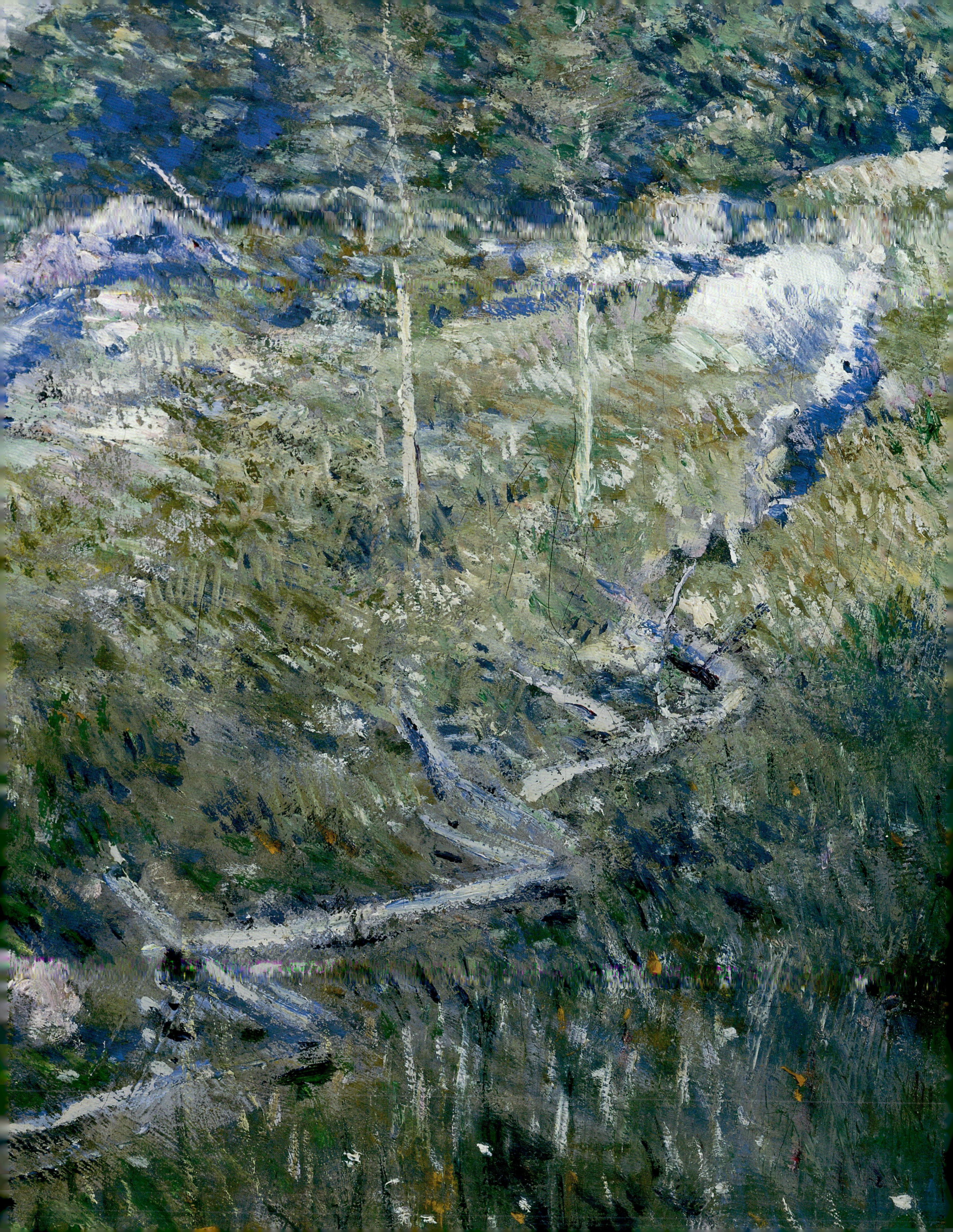

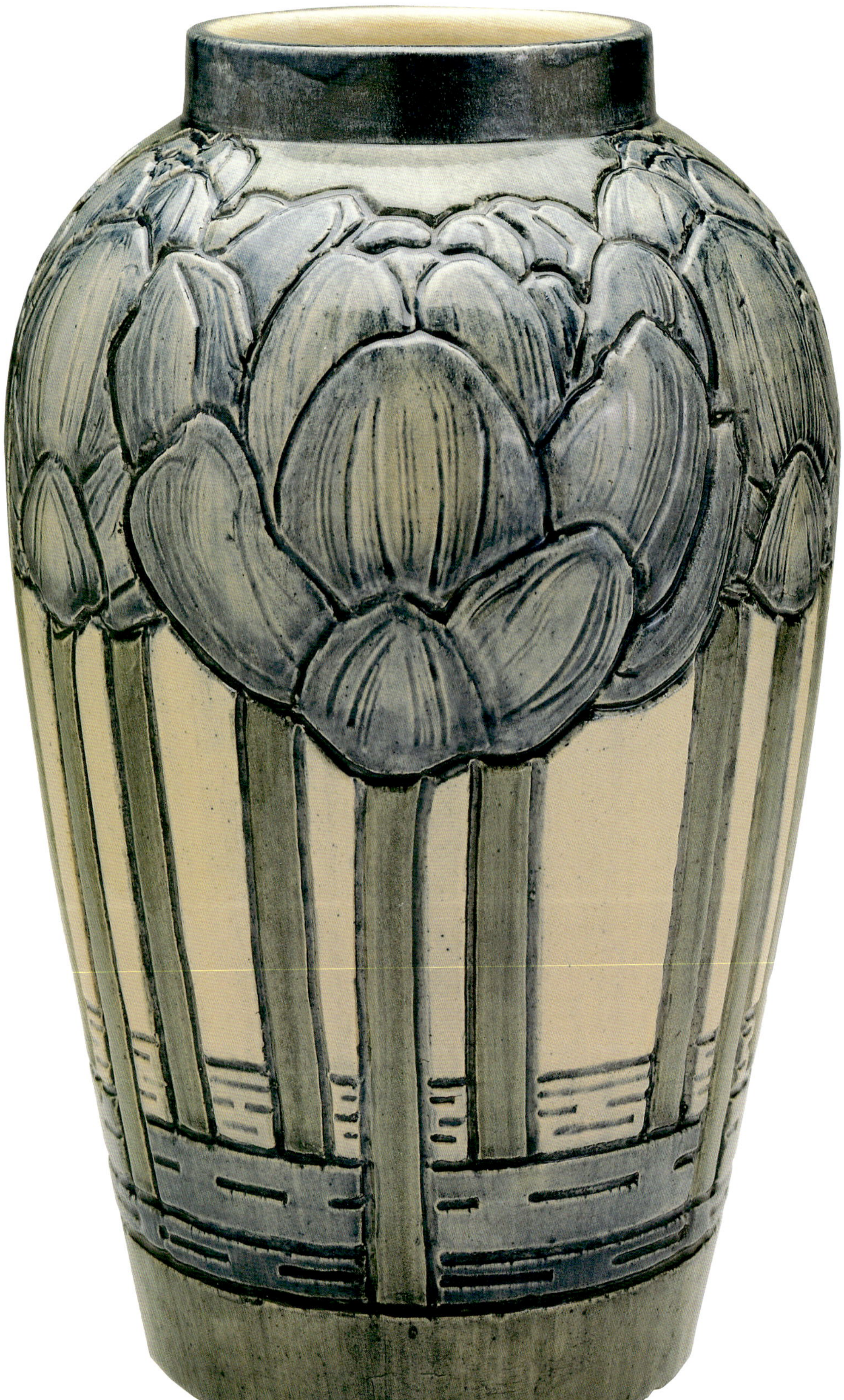

SABINA WELLS

b. 1876; d. 1943, Charleston, South Carolina

JOSEPH MEYER

b. 1848, Buthiers, France; d. 1931, New Orleans

38 **Vase,** 1903

Wheel-thrown and incised earthenware, with underglaze and high-gloss glaze, h. 12, diam. 8 (h. 30.48, diam. 19.2)

Stamped on bottom: SE Wells/SS100. Also stamped "Q" and with an emblem "U" inside the letter "N," for Newcomb College

Museum purchase made possible by The Endowment Fund in Honor of D. A. Turner 98.35

PROVENANCE: Private estate, New Orleans; Jean Bragg Gallery, New Orleans.

PUBLICATIONS: Eleanor H. Gustafson, "Museum Accessions," *Magazine Antiques* (March 1999): 366.

In 1894 faculty from H. Sophie Newcomb Memorial College, the women's coordinate unit of Tulane University in New Orleans, created an innovative program of vocational training in the arts for women.[1] This program provided job opportunities for its graduates at a time when employment for women was limited. Students who completed their undergraduate work could enter a two-year graduate program and submit their work for jury selection and sale. In this way, students gained professional status before working on their own. The college held the first public exhibition and sale in June 1896 in a salesroom maintained by the art department.

The idea behind the Newcomb pottery project was inspired by the Arts and Crafts movement, which began in Britain in the nineteenth century and sought to revive the production of hand-made decorative objects. The movement quickly spread to the United States, where it thrived well into the twentieth century. Many American pottery centers were established at the time. Newcomb was unusual, however, because it was connected to the educational program of a college. Over a forty-five-year period the Newcomb studio produced approximately seventy thousand pieces designed by ninety women artists.

Newcomb production was not entirely from the hands of women. Male potters were hired by the school to mix clay, throw the basic shapes, and run the kilns. French-born Joseph Fortune Meyer was one of these. He joined the project as a potter in 1896, and continued to work at Newcomb until his retirement some thirty years later. Having learned his craft from his father, a potter who sold utilitarian pottery in the New Orleans French Market, Meyer was acclaimed for the experimental glazes he formulated. In 1904 he received a bronze medal at the Paris International Exposition and was also honored at the Louisiana Purchase Exposition in St. Louis.[2]

Each Newcomb piece was distinct, and many were glazed with a distinguishing range of cobalt blues and sage greens. The simple forms were made from local clay gathered from the banks of the Tchoutacabouffa River. The decoration, often based on natural forms found in the South, was painted or incised on the vessel.[3] Incised lines indicate that the decorator was involved earlier in the process while the clay was still wet. Deeply carved designs were particularly characteristic of Newcomb wares produced between 1903 and 1907, many of which were the work of the gifted designer Sabina Elliott Wells.

Wells went to New Orleans from Charleston, South Carolina, to study at Newcomb. In 1902–3, she was ranked as a Special Art Student, and in 1903–4, she was a student in the pottery design class. After that her name disappeared from the Newcomb rosters. Her patterns are characterized by accurate rendering of natural forms, a strong sense of design, and the use of bold color combinations.

The museum's vase, with its vigorous overall decoration, is a masterpiece of Newcomb pottery. Meyer's construction of this form is technically flawless. It is incised with a complex pattern of stylized flower buds, possibly meant to be swamp lilies. Their vertical stems grow out of the still water, suggested by linear patterns at the foot of the vase. An article in the *Harlequin,* a New Orleans weekly, praised Wells, saying, "For originality, and bold well-constructed designs, Miss Sabina Elliot Wells is most conspicuous. Her sureness of touch, her sense of fitness and proportion, and her knowledge of 'what to leave out' . . . make her work admirable."[4] Three of her works were included in Newcomb's exhibits at the St. Louis Louisiana Purchase Exposition in 1904. She eventually left New Orleans to work for a Baltimore firm. In 1915, long after Wells's departure, Newcomb College exhibited works by her at the Panama-Pacific International Exposition in San Francisco. KMZ

EMIL CARLSEN

39

b. 1853, Copenhagen; d. 1932, New York City
Still Life, 1904
Oil on canvas, 34¼ × 39½ (87 × 100.33)
Signed and dated lower right: Emil Carlsen, 1904
Bequest of Georgie Collier Comer 54.79

PROVENANCE: Georgie Collier Comer.
EXHIBITIONS: *Select View*; *Quiet Magic: The Still-Life Paintings of Emil Carlsen,* Vance Jordan Fine Art, New York, October 28–December 10, 1999.
PUBLICATIONS: Timpano, pl. 5, no. 5; Hiesinger, 76, pl. 23.

In 1872, at the age of nineteen, Søren Emil Carlsen emigrated from Denmark and settled in Chicago. Though his formal art education was minimal, his expertise landed him a teaching position in what later became the School of the Art Institute of Chicago. After a trip to Paris in 1875, Carlsen moved to Boston, where, it is thought, he began to study the work of eighteenth-century French artist Jean-Baptiste-Siméon Chardin, whose assimilation of the seventeenth-century Dutch still-life tradition he greatly admired.[1] By the mid-1880s Carlsen's work was regularly included in exhibitions. This recognition led to a commission from a New York dealer to paint floral still lifes. After two years, Carlsen took a teaching position in San Francisco. He returned to New York in 1891.

Although Carlsen also painted impressionistic landscapes and academic portraits, his still-life paintings were his greatest success. According to one critic, "Emil Carlsen is unquestionably the most accomplished master of still-life painting in America today. . . . It is evident that Carlsen has lifted his art to a height it has never reached before."[2] The artist himself postulated on the status of still-life painting in an article he published in 1908:

> Still-life painting is considered of small importance in the Art schools, both here and abroad, the usual course being drawn from the antique, the nude, and painting from the draped figure and from the nude. . . . Then why should the earnest student overlook the simplest and most thorough way of acquiring all the knowledge of the craft of painting and drawing, the study of inanimate objects, still life painting, the very surest road to absolute mastery over all technical difficulties.[3]

As early as the 1880s Carlsen's preference for the "kitchen still lifes" of Chardin had aligned him with painters such as William Merritt Chase, who also favored depicting ordinary everyday objects in a painterly style—as opposed to the tromp l'oeil style of John Frederick Peto that was very popular at this time.[4] By the 1900s Carlsen had begun to simplify his still-life arrangements, repeating shapes and contrasting textures by means of dramatic lighting. In these paintings, the artist usually focused on an array of unpretentious kitchen items, taking obvious pleasure in their simple beauty.

Such is the case in the museum's *Still Life,* with its collection of plain household objects: a ceramic storage jar glazed in aqua, a large black glass wine or spirit bottle, a copper kettle, garlic and onion bulbs, and brown nuts. The contrast of natural and fabricated materials in bright reflective light and deep shadow alters them from mundane to eloquent.

Carlsen believed that successful still-life painting is the combination of technical mastery and innovative personal expression. In a display of virtuosity, he has captured each object's distinctive texture, offering the viewer a visual experience of the tactile and at the same time challenging his own abilities to explore the light-reflective qualities of texture. Note, for example, the reflection of a high, multipaned window (the picture's light source) on the convex surface of the glass bottle. A less distinct reflection of the window is seen on the shiny glaze of the small blue ceramic vessel. Light also reflects off the inner surface of the copper kettle. The garlic and onion bulbs in subtle tones of white were often repeated in his compositions of this time. *Still Life* amply demonstrates the artist's technical mastery as well as his personal sense of the implicit beauty in familiar objects. BF

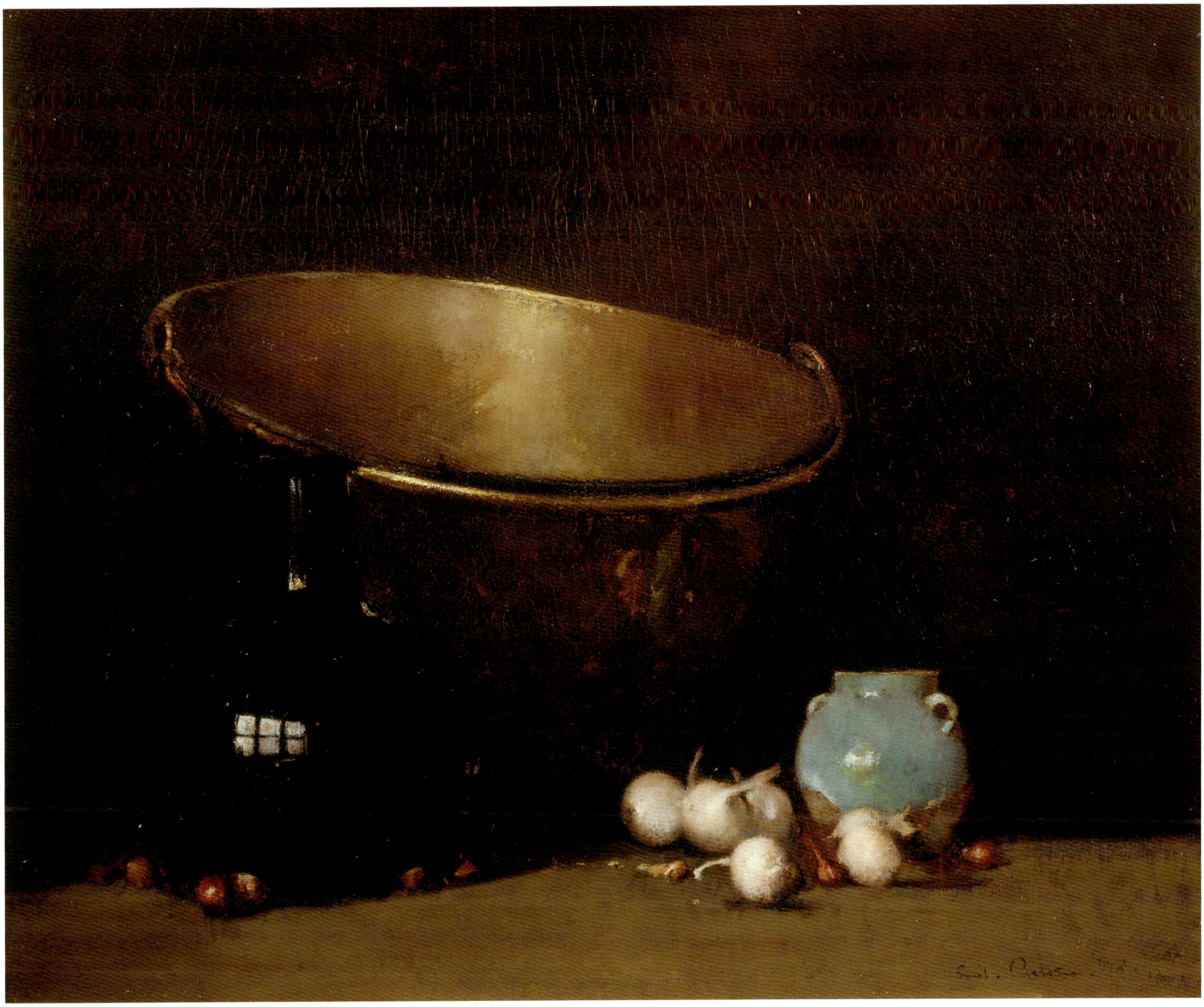

ERNEST LAWSON

40

b. 1873, Halifax, Nova Scotia; d. 1939, Miami Beach
Trolleys in the Snow, New York, ca. 1906–16
Oil on canvas, 21¾ × 24½ (55.25 × 60.03)
Signed lower left: E. Lawson
Bequest of Edward Swift Shorter 91.7.3

PROVENANCE: Edward Swift Shorter.
EXHIBITIONS: *Georgia Collects,* High Museum of Art (Atlanta), Telfair Museum of Art (Savannah, Georgia), January 24–June 11, 1989.
PUBLICATIONS: Vigtel, ed., 84; Winn, et al., 146.

In 1888 Ernest Lawson, then fifteen, enrolled in classes at the Kansas City Art League School in Kansas City, Missouri, where he studied with Ella Holman.[1] By 1890 he had saved enough money to move to New York and enroll at the Art Students League under John Henry Twachtman. Lawson developed his impressionist style while studying with Twachtman and J. Alden Weir, and like his mentors he became devoted to landscape painting.

In 1893 he went to Paris and enrolled at the Académie Julian to study with Jean-Paul Laurens and Benjamin Constant. While there, he shared a studio with English novelist Somerset Maugham, whose fictional character Frederick Lawson in *Of Human Bondage* is based on the artist. In France, Lawson met Alfred Sisley, who became an important influence on his work. Returning to the United States, Lawson married his one-time art teacher, Ella Holman, in 1894. Subsequently, Lawson accepted a teaching position in Columbus, Georgia, where he and his wife lived for a short time.[2]

By 1898 Lawson and his family had settled in Washington Heights, New York, an area that provided him with charming landscape views for the next several years. When Lawson relocated to Greenwich Village in 1906, he met William Glackens, who introduced him to a like-minded group of American artists including Arthur B. Davies, Maurice Prendergast, Everett Shinn, Robert Henri, John Sloan, and George Luks. Together with Lawson and Glackens, this group, known as the Eight, exhibited together in 1908 at Macbeth Gallery in New York City. In 1910 Lawson was a featured artist and an organizer for the *Exhibition of Independent Artists,* the first show in America to have no jury or prizes. He served on the Committee of Foreign Exhibitions for the 1913 Armory Show, and he participated in the 1915 Panama-Pacific International Exhibition.[3] In 1916 Lawson won a prize from the Corcoran Gallery that allowed him to take his family abroad. When he returned in 1917 the National Academy of Design elected him to full membership.

Despite these prestigious accolades, financial success eluded him. Most of his life he was plagued by alcoholism, economic pressures, and marital problems. Despite his discomfort with teaching, he returned to it later in life, taking a position at the Kansas City Art Institute in 1926, followed by a teaching assignment at the Broadmoor Art Academy in Colorado Springs. By 1936 he had relocated to Coral Gables, a suburb of Miami. In 1939 authorities found Lawson dead on the beach. Recent research suggests that he may have died of a fatal heart attack after a robbery.[4]

A committed landscapist, Lawson worked out-of-doors, painting directly on the canvas.[5] Like the impressionists, he used contrasting colors and short brushstrokes creating an impasto surface on his canvas. After he became associated with the Eight, he painted fewer picturesque rural scenes, and instead concentrated on urban subjects, of which *Trolleys in the Snow, New York* is an excellent example.[6] The artist, presumably working at an elevated window or atop a building, recorded the snowy street scene below, filled with people, street lamps, trolleys, a ticketing station, and buildings, all in diagonal rows across the composition. Contrasting shades of pink and green dominate the background. Lawson repeated the colors in the trolleys and buildings, and even in light reflected off the snowy pavements. With short, staccato brushwork, he applied white mixed with tinges of yellow, blue, pink, and brown, to capture the energy, bustle, and daily life of the city in winter, a theme that he returned to many times. KMZ

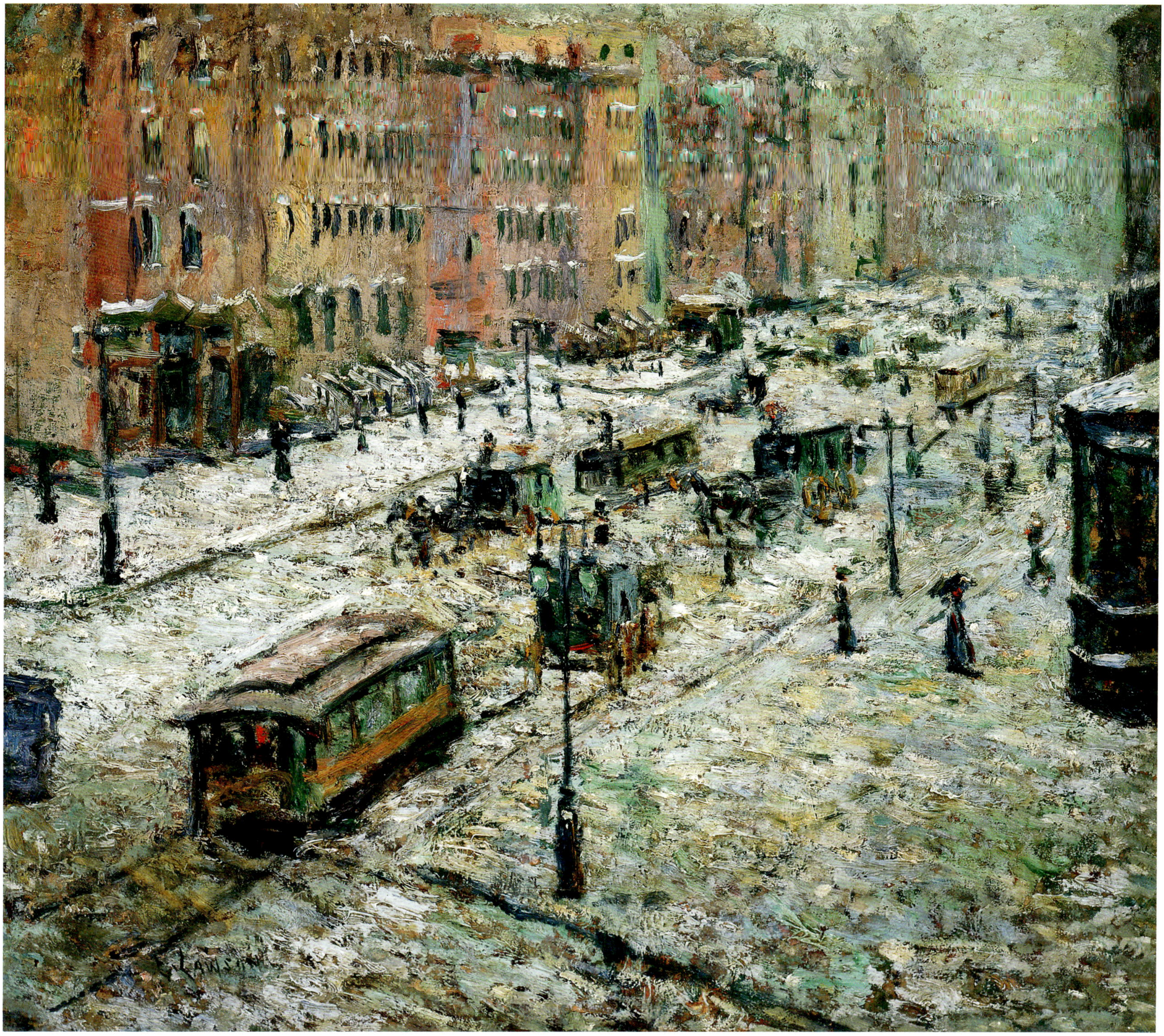

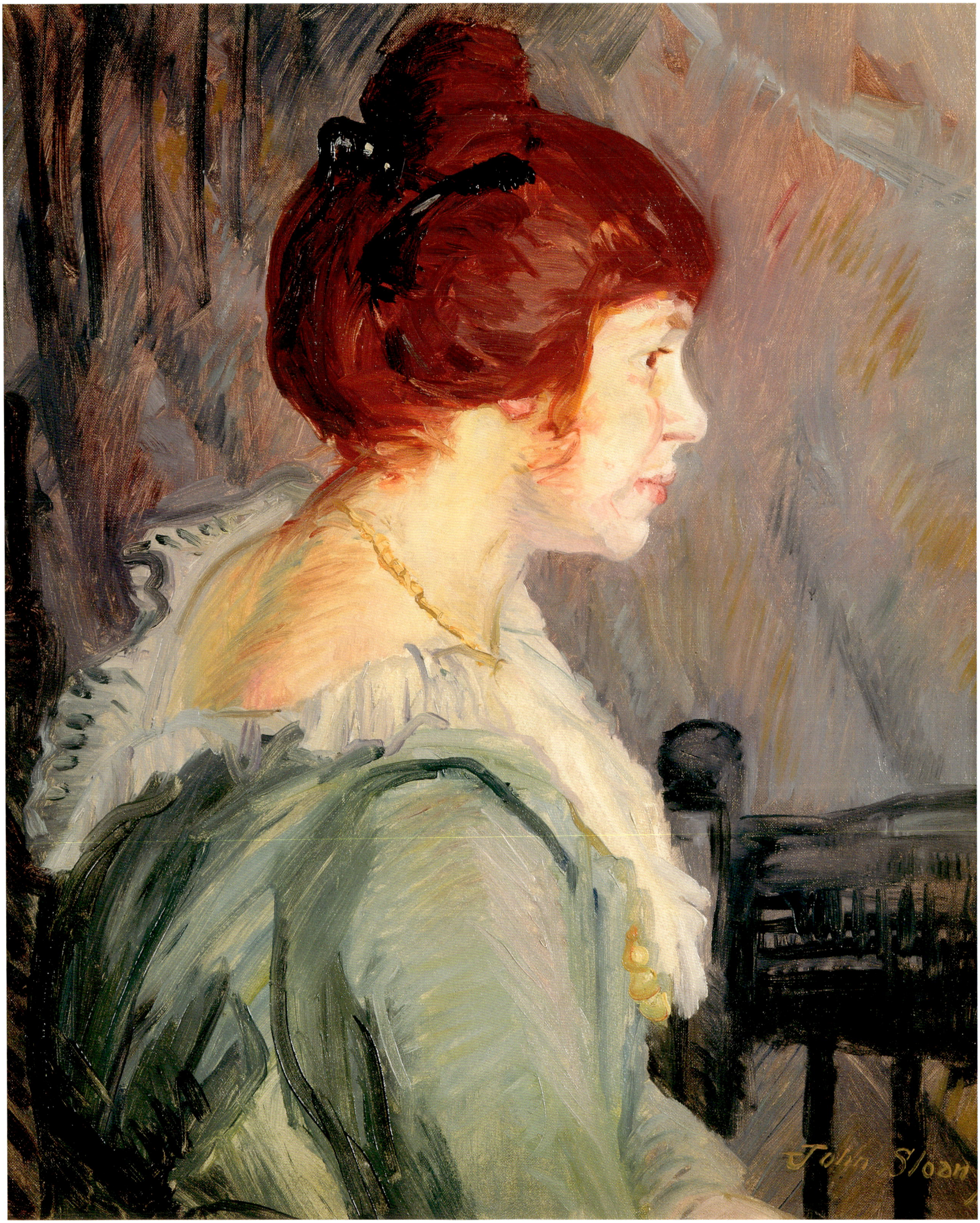
John Sloan

JOHN SLOAN

b. 1871, Lock Haven, Pennsylvania; d. 1951, Hanover, New Hampshire

41 ***Dorothy Hart, Green Dress,*** 1913

Oil [illegible], 24 x 20 (61.6 x 50.8)

Signed and dated lower right, John Sloan/14

M[illegible] purchase made possible by the Art Acquisition and Restoration Fund 96.3

PROVENANCE: Estate of the artist; Kraushaar Galleries, New York.

EXHIBITIONS: *13th Exhibition,* Macdowell Club, New York, February 19–March 2, 1914; *John Sloan, The Gloucester Years,* Kraushaar Galleries, New York, April 26–June 4, 1994; *Making Faces: A Selection of Portraits by John Sloan,* Kraushaar Galleries and Columbus Museum, May 20–October 27, 2001.

PUBLICATIONS: Elzea, part 1, 132, no. 234, pl., n.p.; Kraushaar Galleries, *John Sloan,* no. 2; Winn, et al., 108; Kraushaar Galleries and Columbus Museum, cover (detail), 12.

John Sloan began his career as an illustrator for the *Philadelphia Inquirer* and the *Philadelphia Press.* While employed at the newspapers, he enrolled for one year as a student of Thomas Anshutz at the Pennsylvania Academy of the Fine Arts. Camaraderie with other young newspaper artists soon led to the formation of a group that met at Robert Henri's studio to paint and discuss art theory and criticism.[1] In 1904 Sloan followed Henri and the others to New York City, where he worked as an illustrator for publications such as *Harper's* and *Scribner's.* In his drawings, paintings, and etchings, he captured the life of the city and its people of all social and economic classes. In 1908 he participated in the first exhibition of the Eight at Macbeth Gallery. The artists known as the Eight broke with academic tradition by developing individual styles and choosing unconventional subject matter.

Sloan remained active in the New York art scene throughout his life, serving as the president of the Society of Independent Artists. He also made summer trips to Gloucester, Massachusetts, and Santa Fe, New Mexico, to meet new and interesting people and to explore new landscapes. Portraiture remained an integral part of his work. He wrote, "Students find it hard to create a portrait, because they are so concerned with superficial likeness that they are afraid to use their imagination. You must find something that strikes you about the person; put it down as your point of view."[2]

That may have been the case with the sitter in *Dorothy Hart, Green Dress.* Dorothy Hart was the subject of at least five other paintings done at this time. This one, completed in 1913, according to the artist's own records (though he dated it 14 on the canvas), clearly shows Sloan's response to the artworks he had seen in the Armory Show that same year.[3] Here, Sloan has begun early exploration of modernist techniques. As he himself noted, "After I saw the Van Goghs in the Armory Show, there was a more conscious planning of the palettes for undertones and top drawing colors that could be used like unblended graphic descriptive strokes as though made with pastels."[4] On the importance of color he wrote, "Color is like music. The palette is an instrument that can be orchestrated to build form."[5]

In *Dorothy Hart, Green Dress,* the model is seated in profile. From his angle slightly above her, Sloan chose to emphasize the curve of her upper back and exposed neck. He noted, "A good portrait keeps going right on through the neck and shoulders and the way the folds occur on the sleeves. It is a great plastic gesture that passes through the bulk of the figure and the arms and hands, and culminates in the head."[6] Taking his cue from the postimpressionists in the Armory Show, Sloan enlivened his palette with brilliant color. The sitter's bright red hair juxtaposed with the complementary green of her dress heightens the effect of each hue. Sloan kept his colors pure, placing one on top of another and taking care not to mix them on the canvas. Using intense colors and applying them aggressively, Sloan was able to define objects and textures without heavy outlines and deep shadows. His isolation of the figure in the foreground against a backdrop of soft pinks and lavenders suggests a contemplative mood in spite of the forceful color that dominates this composition. BF

WILLIAM GLACKENS

42

b. 1870, Philadelphia; d. 1938, New York City
Nude with Red Hair, ca. 1915
Oil on canvas, 31¼ × 25¼ (79.38 × 64.14)
Signed lower right: W Glackens
Museum purchase made possible by the Ella E. Kirven Charitable Lead Trust for Acquisitions, and from Katherine and Louis Hazouri, by exchange 2001.11

PROVENANCE: Estate of the artist; Kraushaar Galleries, New York.
EXHIBITIONS: *William Glackens: American Impressionist,* Gerald Peters Gallery, New York, November 20, 2003–January 3, 2004.
PUBLICATIONS: Glackens, cover; Leeds, *William Glackens* (forthcoming).

William Glackens began his professional career as an artist-reporter for the *Philadelphia Record* and the *Philadelphia Press,* where he met Everett Shinn and George Luks. While working for the newspapers, Glackens attended night classes at the Pennsylvania Academy of the Fine Arts with his high school friend John Sloan. Glackens, Sloan, and others soon formed the Charcoal Club, a group that met twice a week to draw from life and have their work critiqued by Robert Henri. Glackens continued his career as an artist-reporter in New York, working for the *New York Herald, New York World, McClure's, Scribner's, Putnam's,* and *Saturday Evening Post* until 1914, when he decided to devote himself full-time to painting.[1]

In 1908 Glackens participated in the Eight exhibition at the Macbeth Gallery. He also played a significant role in organizing the *Exhibition of Independent Artists* in 1910, and in 1913 served on the American art selection committee for the *International Exhibition of Modern Art* (the Armory Show). As an advisor to Albert C. Barnes, he assisted in building one of the most noteworthy collections of European modernist art in the world.

Glackens first traveled to Paris in the company of Henri in 1895. Originally influenced by the rich colors and adept brushwork of the Dutch and Spanish baroque masters, Glackens was soon drawn to the impressionists, whose lighter palette he adopted. As a follower of Henri, he looked to modern life for his subject matter, but his focus became the pleasant world of leisure activity as seen in the work of Édouard Manet, Edgar Degas, and Henri Toulouse-Lautrec rather than his mentor's urban realism. Because his skills of observation had been honed from years as a newspaper artist, he had an intuitive sense of composition as he painted the lively scenes he saw in New York restaurants and parks or at the seashore. Although he tended to avoid portraiture, he delighted in painting solitary figures.

By 1910 Glackens had become enamored with the later paintings of French artist Auguste Renoir, resulting in canvases filled with the more atmospheric elements of impressionism. The museum's painting dates from a period in Glackens's career when he was interested in interior settings. *Nude with Red Hair* is a voyeuristic view of a young woman completely absorbed in dressing. The subject may be somewhat reminiscent of Degas's bathers, but the application of paint echoes the style and technique of Renoir.[2] Glackens's colors are brilliant but softened by his long, sweeping, vertical and curvilinear brushstrokes, which echo the curves of the figure and the overstuffed furniture. Glackens painted the model frequently, and the upholstered furniture appears in other paintings from this period. Though color abounds—from the orange chair to the model's red hair to the red-and-green floral wallpaper and the blue dress piled on the red sofa at the left of the figure—Glackens's skill as a painter is seen in the sensual tactility of the model's flesh. He used undertones of blues and greens in the rose and alabaster shades of her skin, and contrasted this with the dark blue stocking that she is pulling on. Yet, it is in her demure concentration on dressing and her unawareness of the viewer that Glackens projects the girl's innocent charm and youthful beauty. BF

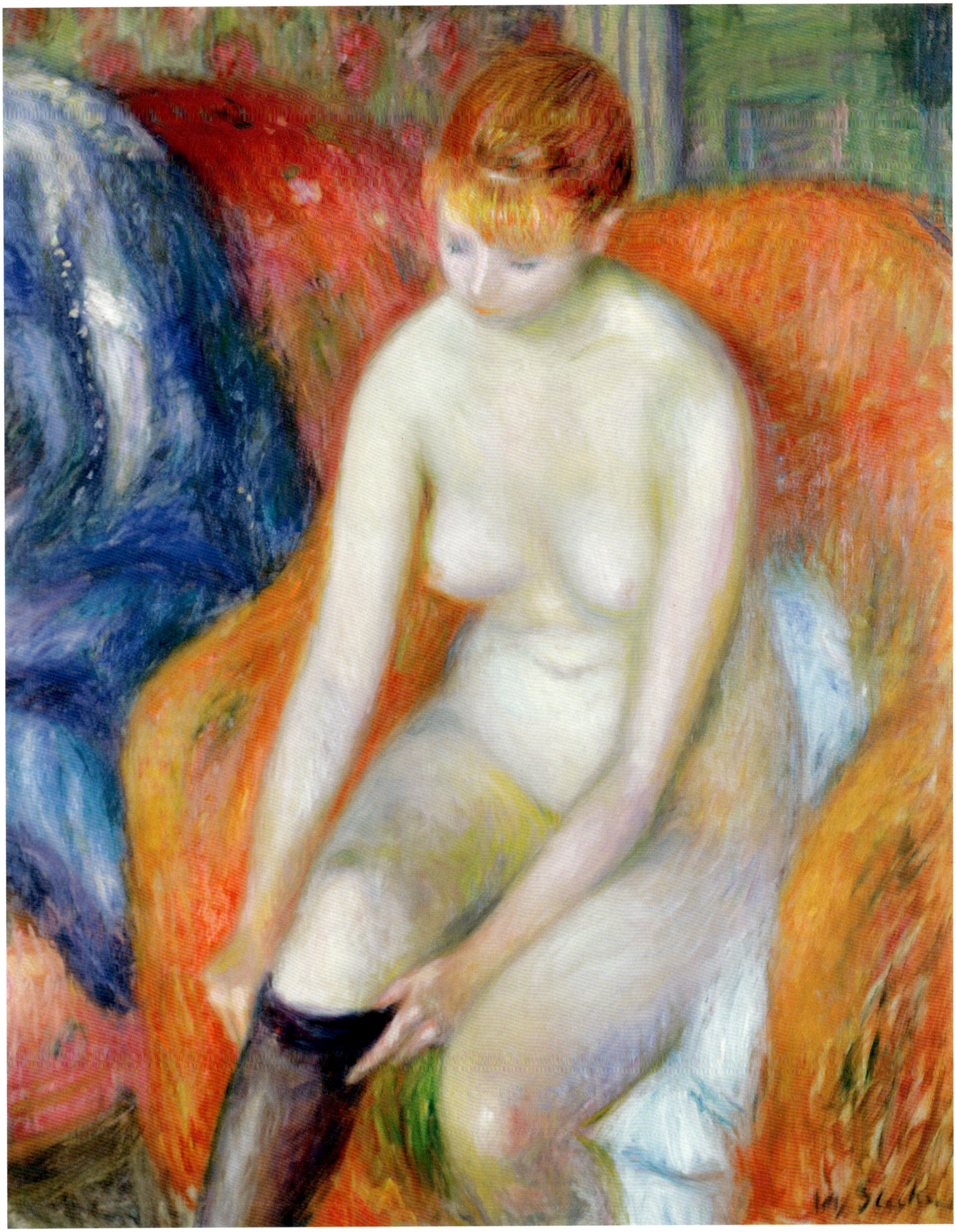

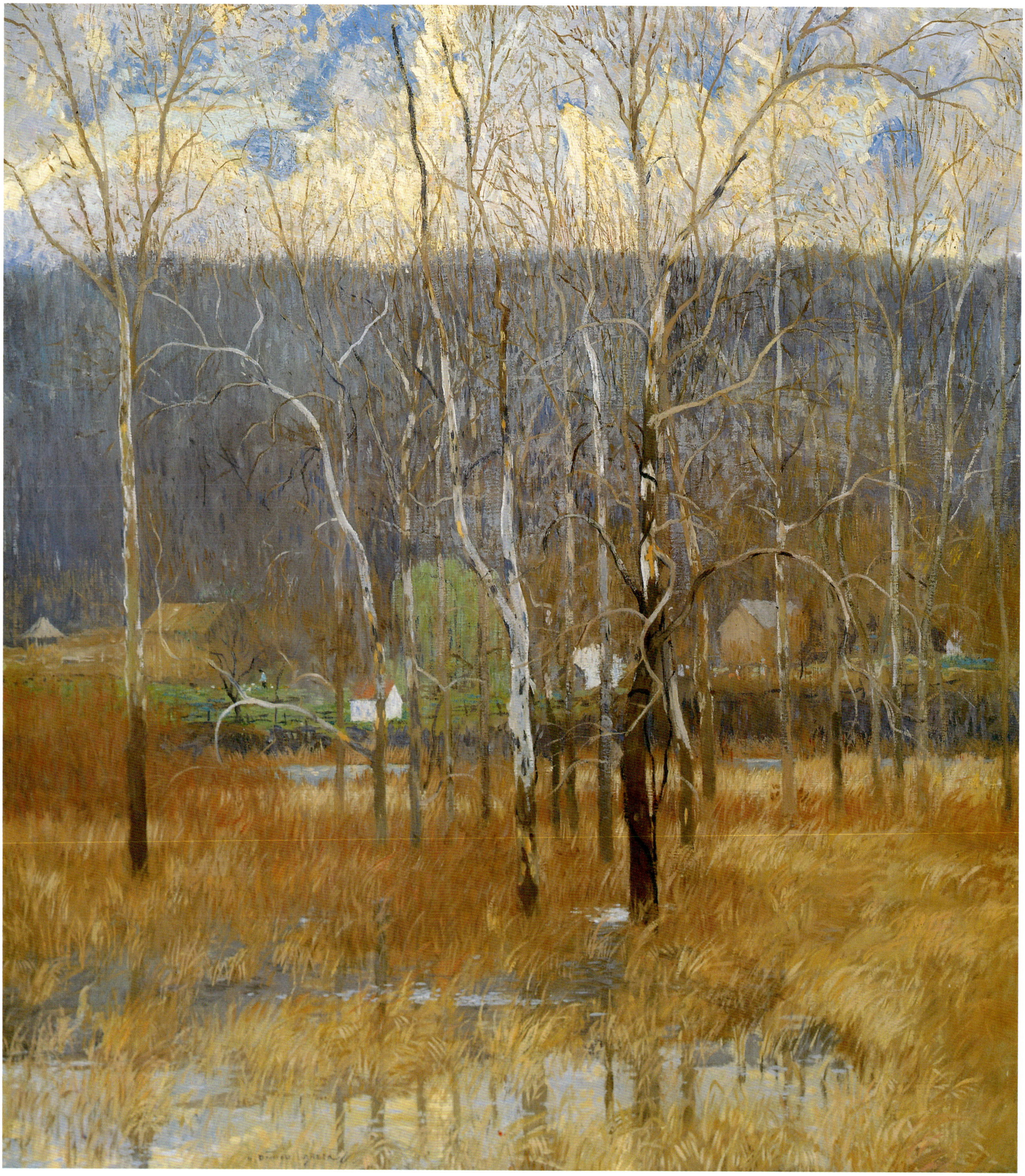

43

b. 1880, Manchester, Indiana; d. 1958, Lumberville, Pennsylvania
Gray Day, March, ca. 1914
Oil on canvas, 50 × 46 (127 × 116.84)
Signed lower left center: Daniel Garber
Museum purchase [illegible]

[illegible] Pittsburgh, 1916; acquired by James Graham at public auction, 1966; Mr. and Mrs. Nathan Seltzer, Philadelphia, 1971; David David, Philadelphia, 1977.

EXHIBITIONS: *Winter Exhibition*, National Academy of Design New York, 1914; Pennsylvania Academy of the Fine Arts, 1915; *Contemporary American Paintings*, Brooklyn Museum, New York, 1915; *Tenth Annual Exhibition of Selected Paintings by American Artists*, Albright College, Reading, Pennsylvania, 1915; *Tenth Annual Exhibition*, Saint Louis Art Museum, 1915; *Twenty-eighth Annual Exhibition of American Oil Paintings and Sculpture*, Art Institute of Chicago, 1915; *French Impressionists Influence American Artists*, Lowe Art Museum, University of Miami, Coral Gables, Florida, 1971; *Four Seasons; Select View.*

PUBLICATIONS: "Studio Talk," *International Studio* 65, no. 267 (June 1915), 65, 68; *Catalogue of the 110th Annual Exhibition*, no. 367; *Tenth Annual Exhibition*, no. 40; *Twenty-eighth Annual Exhibition*, no. 132; *Permanent Collection of Paintings Checklist*, 10; *French Impressionists Influence*, 29, cat. 39; *Four Seasons*, n.p.; Timpano, no. 12; Winn, et al., 150.

Daniel Garber was seventeen when he left home to study at the Art Academy of Cincinnati. Later he enrolled at the Pennsylvania Academy of the Fine Arts in Philadelphia, where he studied with William Merritt Chase, J. Alden Weir, and Cecilia Beaux. In 1905 the academy awarded him a William Emlen Cresson Traveling Scholarship, which he used to study in England, France, and Italy for two years. By 1909 he had joined the faculty of the academy, where he taught painting and drawing for the next forty-one years. Also in 1909 the National Academy of Design awarded Garber the coveted Hallgarten Prize for painting.

Known as one of the most original of the Pennsylvania impressionists, Garber painted large landscapes of the quarries, woods, and river valleys of Bucks County, Pennsylvania, and Hunterdon County, New Jersey.[1] He appears to have simultaneously developed two different approaches. In one, Garber depicted the landscape realistically, including evidence of a human presence. In such paintings, subtle nuances of shape and detail almost glow from the canvas.[2] It is with his other mode, however, that he formed his more distinct style: a highly decorative and somewhat abstract expression that transforms trees and branches into stitchlike patterns that appear to be woven throughout the image. In these paintings, the artist often departed from the traditional, panoramic rectangle of landscape painting, using a square or nearly square format.[3] Art historian William Gerdts has noted that Garber's two painting modes exemplify the primary directions that American postimpressionist painting took in the second decade of the twentieth century.[4]

Gray Day, March is an excellent example of Garber's decorative abstract style. Here the artist used staccato brushstrokes to construct a lyrical and almost mosaic-like pattern of colors. The filtering of light and shadow among the tree branches and plants of this river and meadow view evoke the sense of a chilly, overcast day in early spring. The early blossoming of the willows in the far middle ground offer a respite of green in an otherwise gray scene. The thawing marsh in the foreground reflects the sky and clouds, linking heaven and earth.

Garber received twenty-nine major prizes and medals for his paintings over his lifetime. He was a member of the American Institute of Arts and Letters, the Salmagundi Club, and the National Arts Club. He died at Cuttalossa, his home on the banks of the Delaware River in Lumberville, New Jersey. LR

RANDALL DAVEY

44 b. 1887, East Orange, New Jersey; d. 1964, Santa Fe, New Mexico

Lady Wearing a Hat, ca. 1915

Oil on canvas, 24 × 20 (60.96 × 50.8)

Signed lower right: Randall Davey

Museum purchase 85.47

PROVENANCE: Estate of the artist; Christie, Manson and Woods, New York (as *Lady Wearing Hat*).

EXHIBITIONS: *Randall Davey, Artist/Bon Vivant, A Retrospective Exhibition,* Museum of Fine Arts (Santa Fe), Museum of the Southwest (Midland, Texas), Speed Art Museum (Louisville, Kentucky), December 1984–January 1985; *Select View.*

PUBLICATIONS: Hoopes, *Randall Davey,* no. 3; Christie, Manson and Woods, *Randall Davey: 100 Works, Property of the National Audubon Society* (New York, 1985), lot 100, cover; Timpano, fig. 5, no. 6; Winn, et al., 107.

Randall Davey studied first at Cornell University but left there in 1908 to study under Robert Henri at the New York School of Art.[1] The following year, when Henri founded his own program, Davey became a student of Charles W. Hawthorne, who took over Henri's classes.[2] Hawthorne directed his students to go beyond rendering the mere visage of a subject and to try to express the sitter's psyche or inner workings. The idea remained with Davey even after he left Hawthorne's class to continue his work with Henri.[3] It was in Henri's new class that he met George Bellows and Stuart Davis.

In 1910 Davey was included in the *Exhibition of Independent Artists,* and in 1913 the Armory Show in New York, both of which fostered progressive art in America. In 1915 he won the National Academy of Design's Second Hallgarten Prize and an honorable mention at the Panama-Pacific International Exposition. Davey was a founding member of the Society of Independent Artists. In 1919, at Davey's suggestion, the John Sloans and the Daveys drove to Santa Fe, an arduous journey of six weeks. Davey and his wife were so enamored with the place that they purchased an old mill outside of town and converted it into a studio. It remained their primary residence for more than forty years. Davey was deeply involved in Santa Fe's arts and social scene before a tragic accident ended his life in 1964.

After moving to New Mexico, Davey held several teaching positions, including those at the Broadmoor Art Academy in Colorado Springs, the School of the Art Institute of Chicago, the Kansas City Art Institute, and the University of New Mexico. He received several mural commissions, one of the most successful being the cycle created for the Will Rogers Memorial Shrine in Colorado Springs.

Davey's real strength lay in portraiture. *Lady Wearing a Hat* is a fine example of the work he produced around 1915 at the height of his fame in New York. It was at this same time that Henri, Bellows, Sloan, and Davey worked together toward the development of a fixed color chart, or set palette, derived from the theories of H. G. Maratta around 1909. This system centered on twelve major colors and their fixed modifiers (the same colors but grayed) called hues. Davey came up with a simplified version of this system for his own use, which he called the Randall Davey Color Arrangements.[4] The museum's painting demonstrates his system, with its palette of four principal colors—white, black, pink, and aqua—and the variations created by combining these colors. His sitter, a very fashionable woman shown in three-quarter view, glances at the viewer from under her huge black hat with blue adornment. Davey used the dark hat, which casts the upper portion of her face in shadow, to contrast with the cream and rose tones of her cheeks, chin, and neck and the red of her perfect, heart-shaped lips. Her wraparound dress is also a bold statement in dark purple with black trim. KMZ

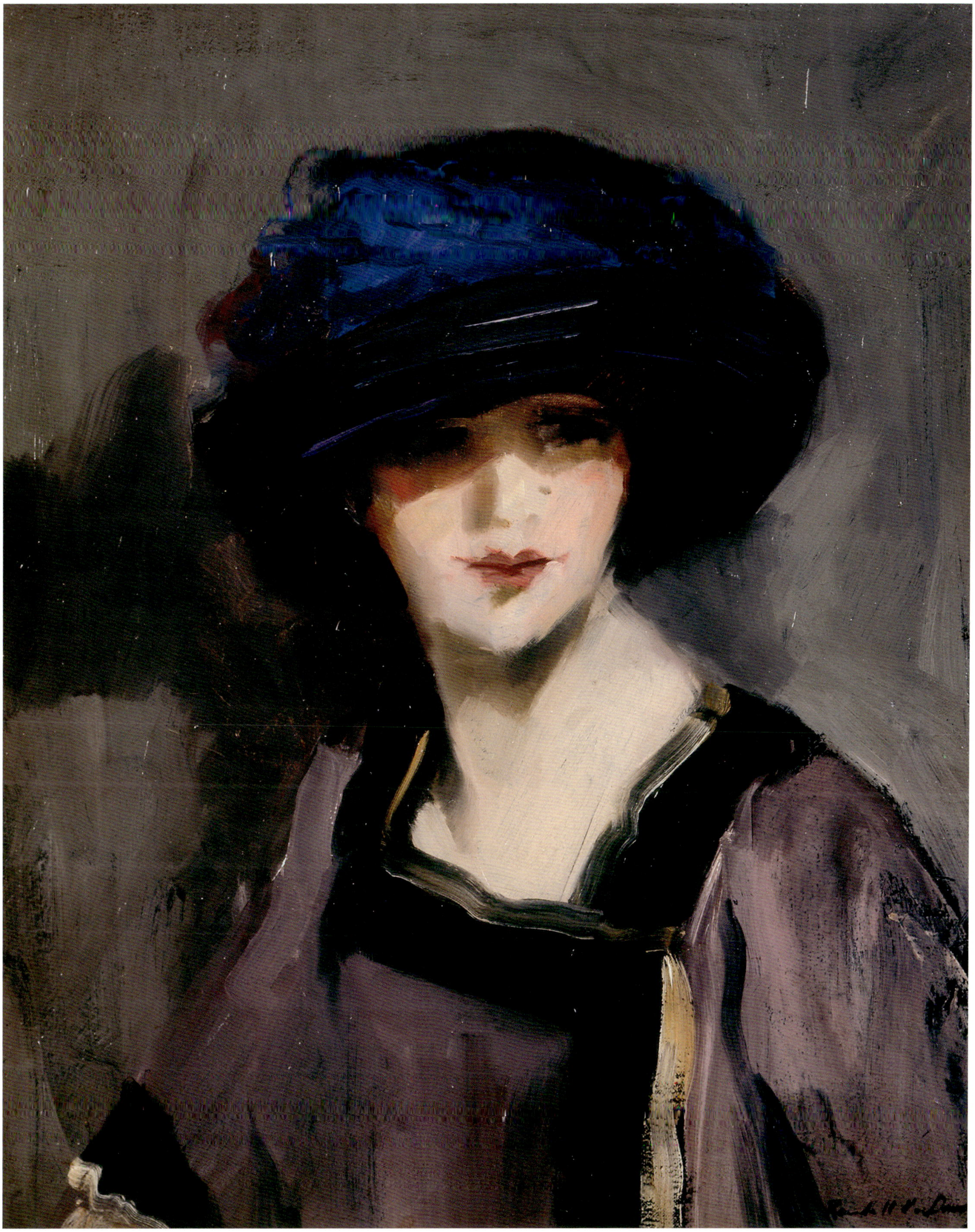

RICHARD MILLER

45

b. 1875, St. Louis; d. 1943, St. Augustine, Florida
La Toilette (or *Morning Sunlight*), ca. 1914
Oil on canvas, 40 × 32½ (101.6 × 82.6)
Signed lower right: Miller
Museum purchase made possible by Mrs. J. B. Knight Sr. in memory of her husband. 55.77

PROVENANCE: Albright Art Gallery, 1914–43; Carlton Palmer, Atlanta.
EXHIBITIONS: *Ninth Annual Exhibition of Selected Paintings by American Artists at the Albright Art Gallery,* Buffalo, May 1914; *Select View; American Impressionism in Georgia Collections,* Georgia Museum of Art at University of Georgia (Athens), Museum of Fine Arts (St. Petersburg, Florida), Mint Museum of Art (Charlotte, North Carolina), September 11, 1993–June 19, 1994; *French and American Impressionism,* Albany Museum of Art, Georgia, September 12–November 3, 1996.
PUBLICATIONS: Timpano, cover; Keyes, *American Impressionism,* pl. 35; Winn, et al., 111; Close, 32.

Richard Emile Miller began his formal training in art in 1891, attending night school at the St. Louis School of Fine Arts. While he was still a student, his work was accepted in the 1895 and 1896 St. Louis Expositions, which featured the paintings of Mary Cassatt, William Merritt Chase, James McNeill Whistler, and Claude Monet.[1] In 1897 Miller worked as an artist for the *St. Louis Post Dispatch*. That year he also joined the Society of Western Artists, a group of midwestern artists who felt excluded from shows in major eastern cities. In 1898 he enrolled in the Académie Julian, in Paris, where he studied with Jean-Joseph Benjamin-Constant and Jean-Paul Laurens. After his studies in Paris, Miller moved away from the academic teachings of his youth and developed a much more colorful and spontaneous approach, possibly inspired by the first fauve exhibition at the Salon d'Automne and Joaquin Sorolla's first solo show in Paris. Also strongly influenced by the French plein air painters of the day, Miller adopted the techniques and color of the impressionists. He believed that "art's mission is not literary, the telling of a story, but decorative, the conveying of a pleasant optical sensation." He wanted his pictures to be hung not in public galleries but in "the modern homes, the urban apartments and the country cottage."[2]

By 1907 Miller, with fellow artists Edmund Greacen, Frederick Carl Frieseke, Guy Rose, and Lawton Parker, was regularly summering in Giverny, the home of Claude Monet. Unlike many impressionists, he was less interested in landscapes than in figures, sometimes in interior settings but always articulated in vigorous brushstrokes and intense color.[3] In 1910 Miller exhibited with Rose, Parker, and Frieseke at the Madison Gallery, New York, and two years later he had his first solo show at Macbeth Gallery, New York.

Critic Clara T. MacChesney felt that Miller had reached his "high water mark" in 1914, the year he painted *La Toilette*.[4] At the outbreak of the First World War in August 1914, Miller returned to the United States. By 1916 he had relocated to Pasadena, California, where he became an instructor at the Stickney Memorial School of Art. In 1919 he received a commission to produce murals for the State Capitol in Jefferson City, Missouri. Miller eventually settled in Provincetown, Massachusetts. He became a founding member of the Provincetown art colony. There he taught art classes and painted models in gardens or sunlit interiors and marinescapes well into the 1930s.

In *La Toilette* a young woman sits at a dressing table, looking at her reflection in a mirror she is holding. A cup and saucer and a glass bottle with stopper comprise an impromptu still life on the table before her. Beyond the glass doors of the room is a sunlit garden, bright with flowers delineated in short brushstrokes. Miller's predominantly cool palette of violets, blues, and greens sharply contrasts with the intense shots of red to the left of the figure's head and reflected in her hand-held mirror. This remarkable painting, with its luxurious colors and an elegant and sensuous figure seemingly lost in reverie, was surely a bright expression of hope in a world that was arming for war. GBG and CTB

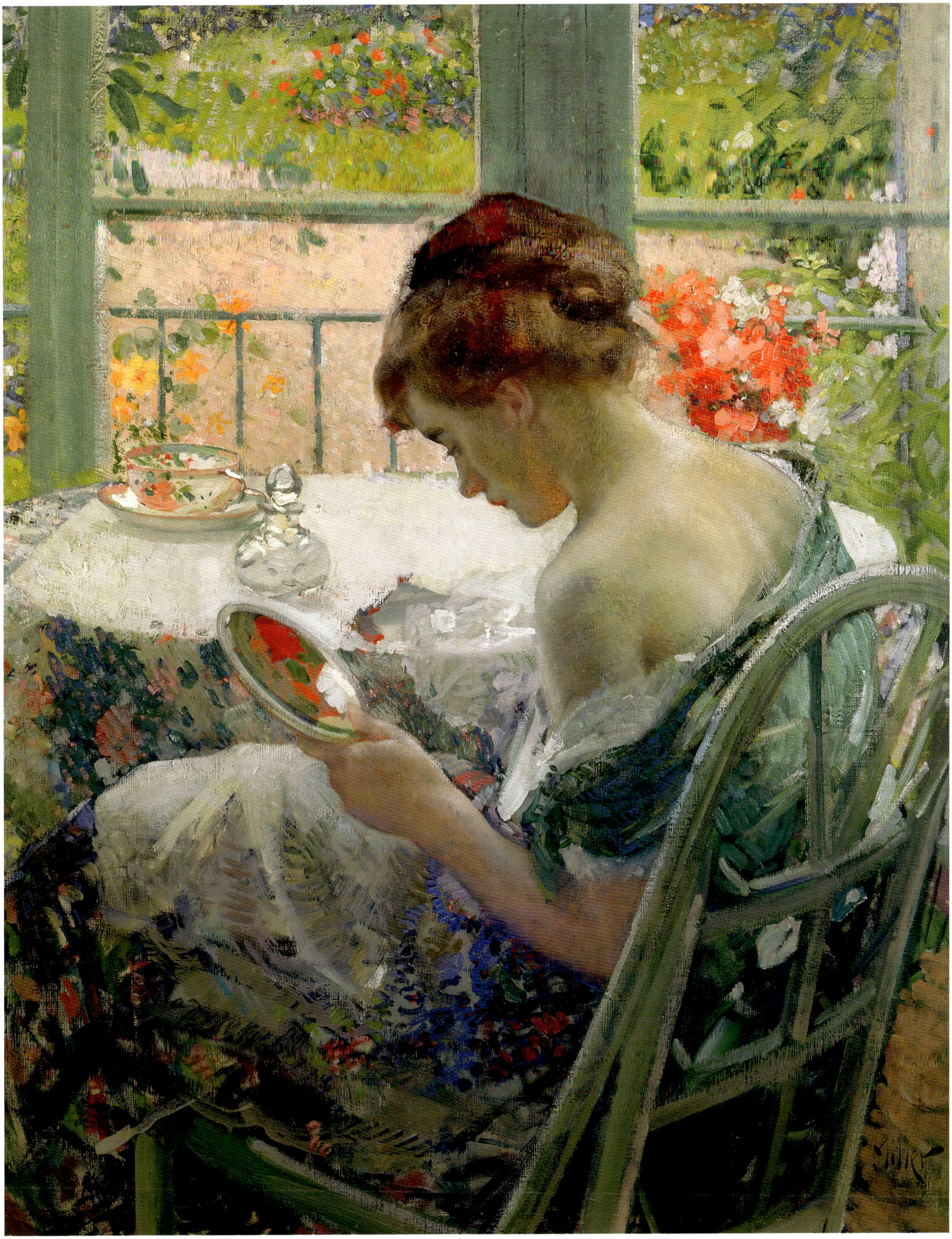

WILLARD METCALF

46

b. 1858, Lowell, Massachusetts; d. 1925, New York City
The Thawing Brook, 1917
Oil on canvas, 36¼ × 36 (92.08 × 91.44)
Signed lower right: W. L. Metcalf. Inscribed on verso: The Thawing Brook, W. L. Metcalf–1917 (Cornish, N.H.)/Important, Do Not Varnish/W. L. M.
Gift of Jack Melchers Passailaigue Sr. in memory of his late devoted wife Mary Flournoy Passailaigue 89.16

PROVENANCE: Macbeth Gallery, New York; Boyd B. Jones, Haverhill, Massachusetts, February 1919; Grand Central Galleries, New York, by 1960s; Mary and Jack Passailaigue, Columbus, Georgia, 1960s.
EXHIBITIONS: Macbeth Gallery, New York, 1918; Rosenbach Gallery, Philadelphia, 1918; Carnegie Institute, Pittsburgh, solo exhibition, 1926, as *Melting Brook*; *Forty Years of American Art,* Macbeth Gallery, New York, January–February 1932; *Georgia Collects,* High Museum of Art, Atlanta, January 24–March 6, 1989; *American Impressionism in Georgia Collections,* Georgia Museum of Art at University of Georgia (Athens), Museum of Fine Arts (St. Petersburg, Florida), Mint Museum of Art (Charlotte, North Carolina), September 11, 1993–June 9, 1994; *Winter's Promise: Willard Metcalf in Cornish, New Hampshire 1909–1920,* Hood Museum of Art, Dartmouth College, Hanover, New Hampshire, January 9–March 14, 1999, no. 14.
PUBLICATIONS: "Willard Metcalf," *Country Life* (June 1920): 36; de Veer and Boyle, figs. 152, 153; Vigtel, ed., 84; Gene Paletta, "Willard Metcalf," *Classical Realism Quarterly* 6 (summer 1992), 1; Keyes, *American Impressionism,* fig. 34; Winn, et al., 147; MacAdam, *Winter's Promise,* fig. 1, cat. 14; MacAdam, "Willard Metcalf," 191.

With the encouragement of his parents, Willard Leroy Metcalf began his formal art studies with George Loring Brown at the Lowell Institute in Boston.[1] He later won a scholarship to the School of the Boston Museum of Fine Arts, where he continued his studies until 1878. With savings and income earned from an 1883 painting exhibition, he was able to travel abroad. In Paris, he enrolled at the Académie Julian. In 1886 he accompanied Theodore Robinson to Giverny, where he met Claude Monet and became one of the first Americans to work there.

Upon his return from Europe, Metcalf settled in New York, teaching at both the Cooper Union and the Art Students League. He penned the statement of secession for the Ten American Painters, who in 1897 broke away from the National Academy of Design to exhibit on their own.[2] In 1904 Metcalf spent part of the year in Clark's Cove, Maine, rediscovering the New England landscape, and he returned to New York with twenty-one landscapes unlike any he had painted before. Metcalf continued traveling and painting throughout New England. In 1909 he joined the art colony in Cornish, New Hampshire.[3]

The Thawing Brook is a snow-covered landscape with a dark running creek that winds through it. Bare tree branches grace the composition in the middle ground, and the deep green pine trees in the background provide a bold contrast with the white snow and the blue-gray of the overcast sky. Though the location of the scene is unknown, the stream resembles Blow-Me-Down Brook, which wanders southwest through the township of Plainfield into Cornish, New Hampshire. Within walking distance of Metcalf's accommodations in that area, the brook was one of his favorite local subjects.[4] A photograph from 1917 shows the artist working on this painting out-of-doors.[5] Winter landscapes were favorite subjects for Metcalf and his colleagues.[6]

When *The Thawing Brook* was exhibited at Macbeth Gallery in 1918, *New York Tribune* critic Royal Cortissoz praised it:

> His [Metcalf's] values are perfect. The large white areas of the scene, the greens of the distant trees, the browns of those growths which fill the intervening space, and the decisive dark tones of the shallow brook are fused into a harmony ruled by the quiet illumination of the hour chosen. *The Thawing Brook* is one of those fortunate works in which an artist rises to the top of his powers.[7]

KMZ

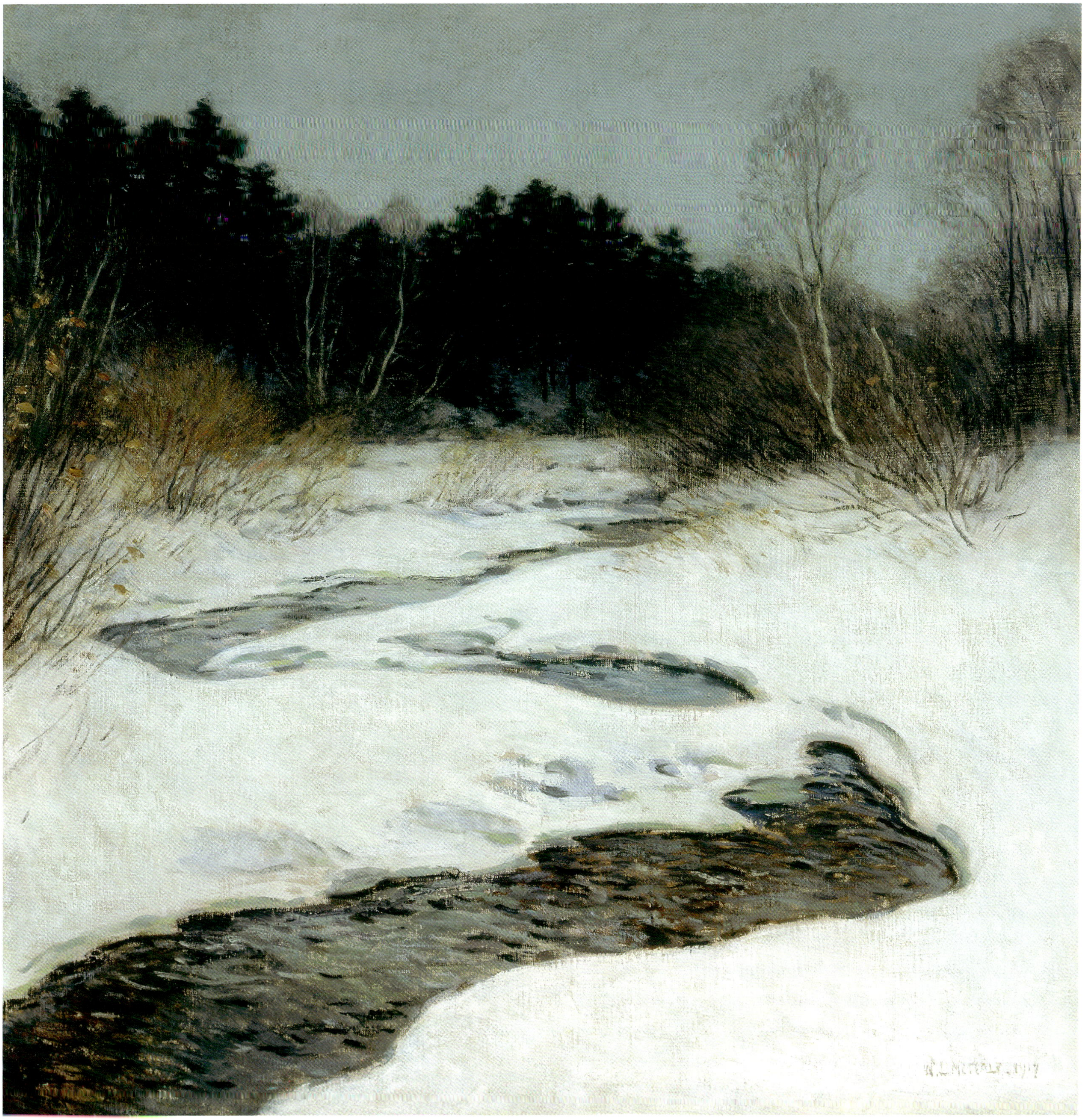

GARI MELCHERS

47

b. 1860, Detroit; d. 1932, Falmouth, Virginia
Kate Kendall (The Scarlet Jacket), 1919
Oil on canvas, 76 × 32 (193.04 × 81.28)
Signed center left: Gari Melchers
Gift of Jack Melchers Passailaigue Sr. 98.38.1

PROVENANCE: Belmont Foundation, Fredericksburg, Virginia; Graham Gallery, New York, by 1978; Jack Melchers Passailaigue, Columbus, Georgia, after 1978.
EXHIBITIONS: *An Exhibition of Paintings by Gari Melchers,* American Academy of Arts and Letters, New York, 1932; *Gari Melchers 1860–1932: American Painter,* Graham Gallery, New York, September 26–October 28, 1978; *Georgia Collects,* High Museum of Art (Atlanta), Telfair Museum of Art (Savannah, Georgia), January 24–June 11, 1989; *Local Wonders: Treasures of American Art in Columbus Collections,* Columbus Museum, February 6–May 29, 1994.
PUBLICATIONS: *An Exhibition of Paintings by Gari Melchers* (New York: American Academy of Arts and Letters, 1932), n.p.; *Gari Melchers, 1860–1932: American Painter* (New York: Graham Gallery, 1978), nos. 27, 29; Vigtel, ed., 3; "Local Wonders: Treasures of American Art in Columbus Collections," exh. bro. (Columbus, Ga.: Columbus Museum, 1994), cover.

Gari Melchers, who was born Julius Garibaldi Melchers, was first taught by his father, an artist who had immigrated to the United States from Germany. When he was seventeen Melchers's family sent him to continue his studies at the Düsseldorf Academy. After a few years in Germany, Melchers moved to Paris, where he enrolled at the Académie Julian and later at the École des Beaux-Arts.[1] Melchers's studies in Paris, as Joseph Dreiss noted, resulted in a "lighter palette and looser quasi-Impressionism . . ." due to the influence of Édouard Manet, although his figures remained much more modeled and less flattened.[2]

Melchers remained in Europe after completing his studies, and he received numerous awards for his work. He settled in Holland, making return visits to the United States.[3] He gained an international reputation at the 1889 Paris Universelle Exposition of 1900, where he shared the grand prize for painting with John Singer Sargent, an honor not previously bestowed on an American artist. In 1909 Melchers relocated to Weimar, the cultural center of Germany, to preside over the art academy there. At the onset of World War I, he returned to the United States and settled in Virginia.[4] Well acquainted with the modern French artists and their aggressive use of color and gesture, Melchers began to work with a moderate to heavy impasto, coarse brushwork, and a light palette. In 1916 the National Academy of Design invited him to become a member, and in 1931 the Corcoran Gallery of Art in Washington, D.C., elected him to their board of trustees. Melchers died at Belmont, his Virginia estate, in 1932.

The subject of *Kate Kendall (The Scarlet Jacket)*[5] was Katherine Prescott Kendall, who studied with Melchers in Paris and exhibited at least one portrait at the 1899 salon of the Société Nationale des Beaux-Arts.[6] Melchers painted the full-length figure with wide, bold brushstrokes, laying on a thick impasto. Like the impressionist painters he admired, Melchers avoided the blending of color in the costume and allowed the pigment to remain rich and pure. To balance the expanse of the full-length figure, he added subtle details in the background wallpaper mural and included a small, exquisite still life to the right of the figure.

The date originally ascribed to this painting was the turn of the twentieth century.[7] However, further research revealed that Melchers created the work in 1919 as part of a series of figure paintings in which models posed in interiors with historic wallpapers. In *Kate Kendall,* the backdrop is an 1810 French scenic wall covering called "Bay of Naples" from the series Views of Italy, probably designed by Jean-Gabriel Charvet. This wall covering once hung in historic Gay Mont, a home in Virginia owned by close friends of the Melcherses. Melchers's wife posed before this same wallpaper for a painting completed around 1920. The similarities in the palette of the two portraits, as well as the lighting and the strongly modeled qualities of the figures support the dating of the painting to around 1919. In addition, the same glass vase of nasturtiums can be seen in other works dating from around this time.[8] EW and BF

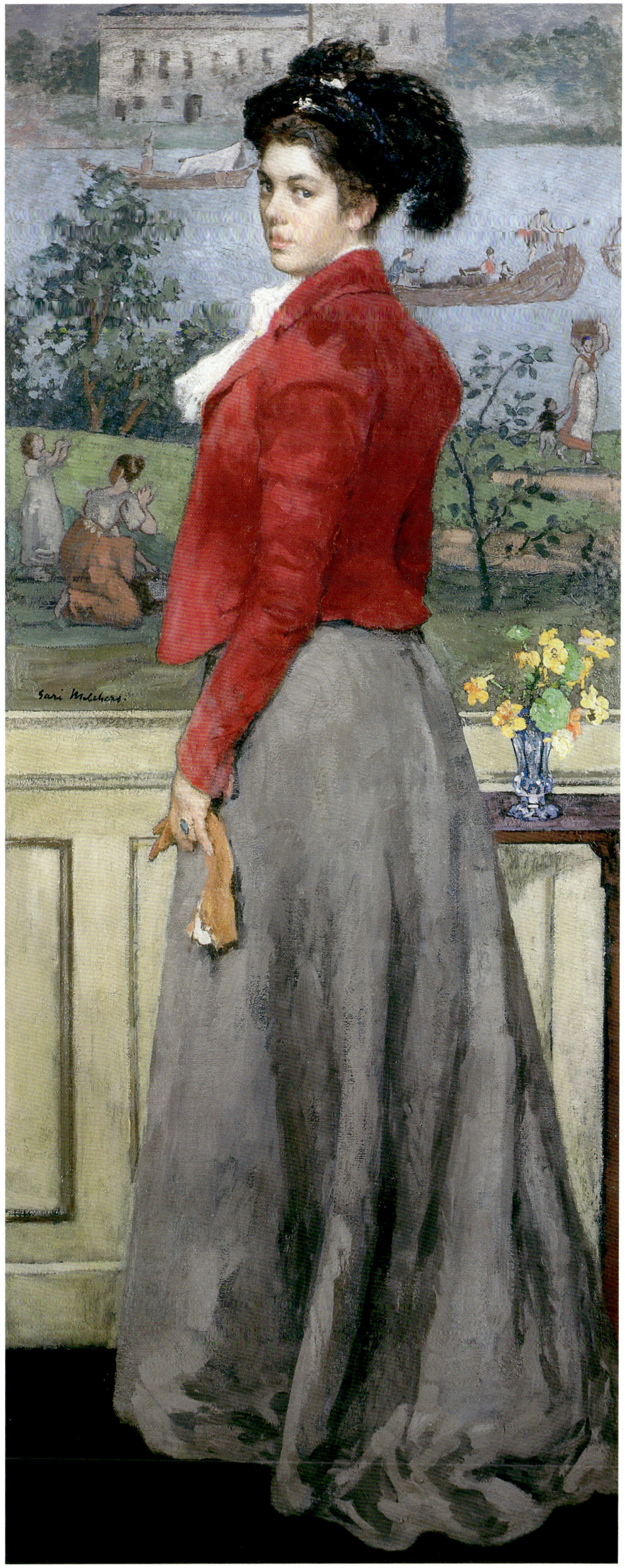
Gari Melchers.

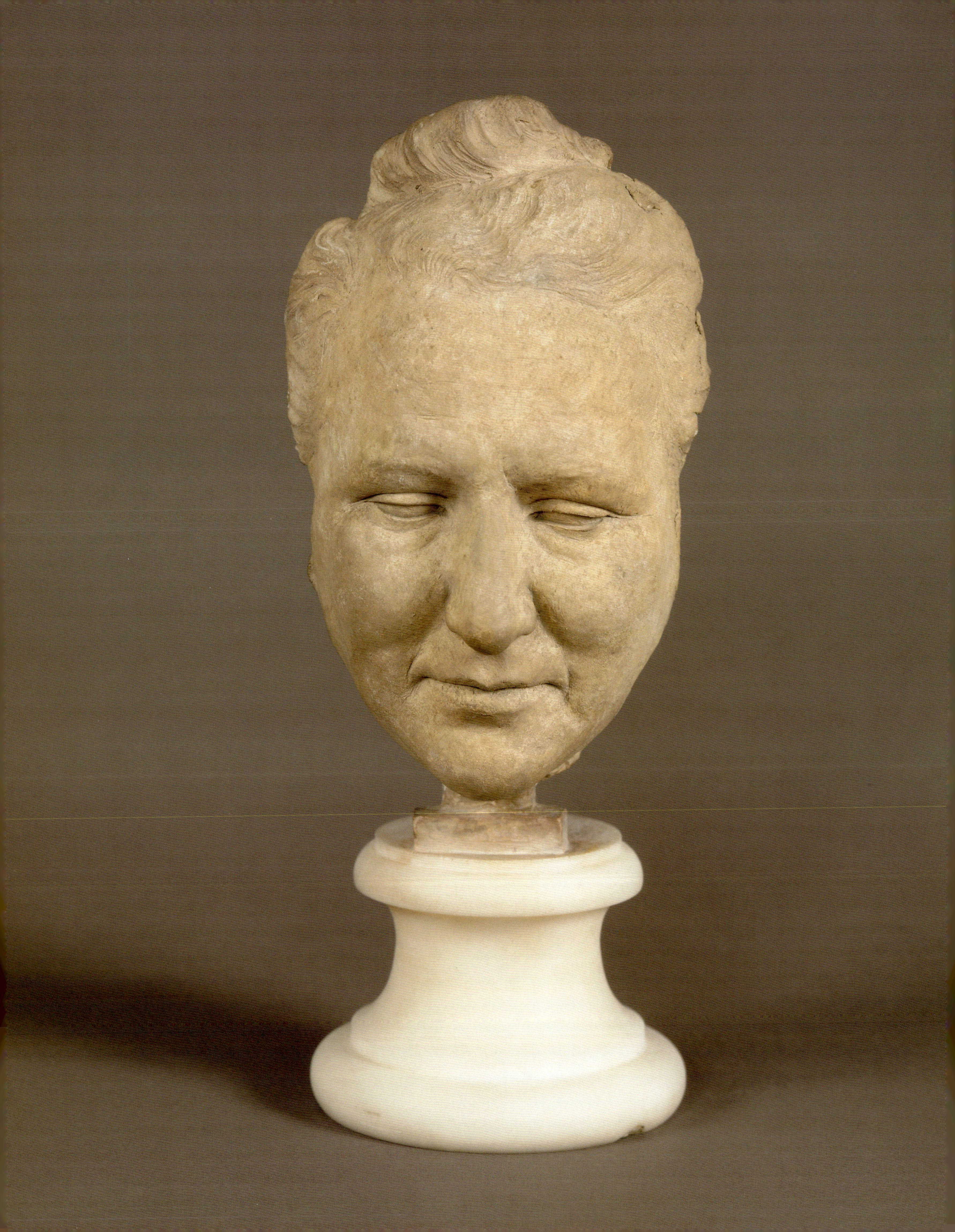

JO DAVIDSON

48 b. 1883, New York City; d. 1952, Tours, France
Portrait Head of Gertrude Stein, 1923
Terra cotta, mounted on original marble base, 15 × 6 × 4
(38.1 × 15.2 × 10.2)
Inscribed [illegible] Davidson
Museum purchase made possible by the Simon Schwob Acquisition Fund 95.24

PROVENANCE: Estate of the artist, until 1988; Conner-Rosenkranz, New York; Hirschl and Adler Galleries, New York; Richard York Gallery, New York.
EXHIBITIONS: *Uncommon Spirit: Sculpture in America 1800–1940,* Hirschl and Adler Galleries, New York, April 22–June 9, 1989.
PUBLICATIONS: *Uncommon Spirit,* 70, pl. 47.

Jo Davidson was born to an immigrant Russian family on New York's Lower East Side. He showed an early talent for drawing, and at age sixteen he won a scholarship to the Art Students League in New York, where he studied painting with George DeForest Brush and sculpture with Hermon McNeill. In 1907 he went to Paris to study at the École des Beaux-Arts but was unhappy with the school's emphasis on classicism. Gertrude Vanderbilt Whitney, a wealthy art patron and sculptor, offered Davidson financial support as he continued to seek his own naturalistic approach. Working in a variety of materials, including terra cotta, marble, and bronze, Davidson sculpted portrait busts that were realistic, strongly modeled, and psychologically perceptive. His engaging personality helped him to gain an understanding of his subjects and win their cooperation. In addition to Gertrude Stein, Davidson's sitters included such contemporary notables as Woodrow Wilson, Franklin D. Roosevelt, Anatole France, Marshal Foch, and Albert Einstein. In his autobiography, *Between Sittings,* Davidson discussed the many people he had encountered over his long career. About Stein, he wrote, "Gertrude would stand . . . watching the crowd like a Cambodian caryatid, wearing a smile of patience, looking as if she knew something that nobody else did. . . . Gertrude's was a very rich personality. Her wit and her laughter were contagious."[1]

Stein, who was born in Allegheny, Pennsylvania, in 1874, spent her youth in Europe and California. At Radcliff College, she studied psychology with the philosopher William James. After further study at Johns Hopkins Medical School, she moved to Paris, where she remained with her lifelong companion Alice B. Toklas and her brother Leo, a noted art critic and collector. Stein, an eccentric, and self-styled genius, was an accomplished writer. Her Paris home became the leading international salon for artists and writers of the first four decades of the twentieth century. She died July 27, 1946, in Paris.

This face mask by Davidson is one of two known to exist (the other is in the National Portrait Gallery, Washington, D.C.). It was made in 1922–23, before Stein's literary fame was firmly established, yet it shows the visage of a strong, sensitive person fully in control of her own destiny.[2] Davidson worked in terra cotta, modeling his famous portrait of Stein, slightly stooped forward, her eyes cast downward like a meditating Buddha. The fully modeled sculpture was cast in bronze after 1923. The two portrait masks were made at the time the artist was working on the full-scale model. The museum's mask effectively suggests the undeniable presence of the sitter, as it confirms the artist's ability to capture her authority and magnetism without any idealization or glorification. Instead, it is her natural countenance that is so striking. CTB

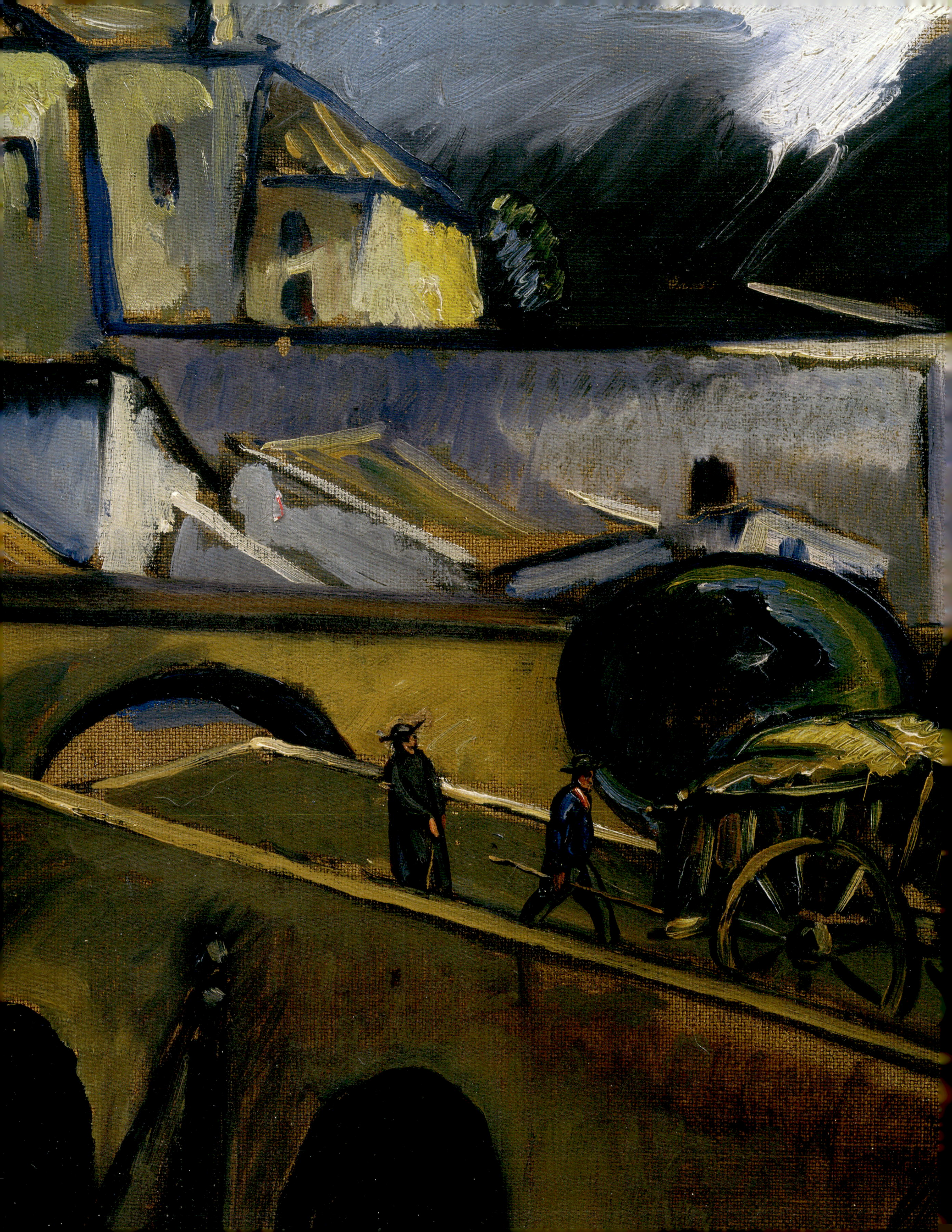

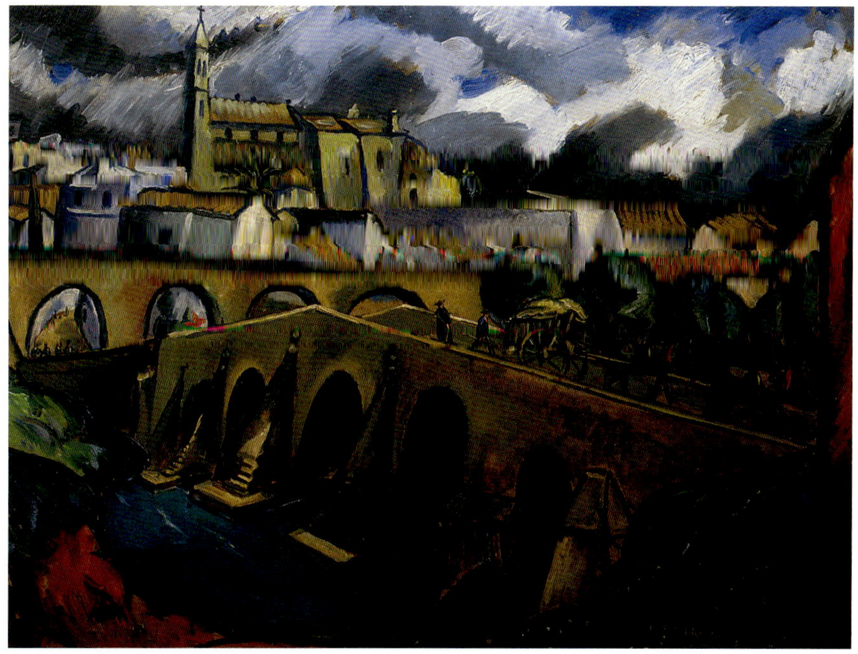

HENRY GLINTENKAMP

49 b. 1887, Augusta, New Jersey; d. 1946, New York City
Spanish Town, Alcalá de Guadaira, 1923
Oil on canvas, 29 × 39 (73.66 × 99.06)
Signed lower right: Glintenkamp
Museum purchase made possible by Norman S. Rothschild in honor of his parents, Aleen and Irwin B. Rothschild 98.55

PROVENANCE: Private collection; Spanierman Gallery, New York.

Hendrik (Henry) J. Glintenkamp, a painter, printmaker, and writer, was part of a generation of early American modernists. He attended classes at the National Academy of Design in New York from 1903 to 1906, and then spent the next two years at the New York School of Art, where his teachers included Robert Henri and John Sloan. In 1908 Glintenkamp began sharing studio space with Stuart Davis and Glenn O. Coleman. The three had met in Henri's classes and shared his philosophy of art.

In 1910 Glintenkamp's work was included in the *Exhibition of Independent Artists,* organized by Henri, Sloan, Arthur B. Davies, and others. His work was also included in the Armory Show, which had a huge influence on him and many other young American modernists.[1] Abandoning his earlier style inspired by the painters of the Ashcan school, Glintenkamp developed a distinctive approach, joining the vibrant colors and bold brushwork of fauvism and expressionism with his own intuitive response to a subject. His paintings dating from the 1920s and 1930s range from modernist views of New York, Mexico, and Europe to the occasional portrait. His finest work is from this period.

Glintenkamp's assimilation of advanced aesthetic strategies is evident in *Spanish Town, Alcalá de Guadaira.* A popular destination for American artists and writers since the early nineteenth century, Spain had attracted such noted painters as Mary Cassatt, John Singer Sargent, Ernest Lawson, and Henri, all of whom gravitated to the bright sunlight and exotic surroundings of Madrid, Granada, Toledo, and Barcelona.[2] A number of other American artists and writers had visited the small, picturesque Spanish village of Alcalá long before Glintenkamp's first visit in 1921. In *The Alhambra,* of 1832, Washington Irving described his journey to Alcalá:

> Our route [to Seville] lay through old Alcalá de Guadaira. . . . The Guadaira winds round the hill, at the foot of these ruins. . . . A picturesque bridge was thrown across the little river. . . . Altogether it was an admirable scene for a landscape painter.[3]

It is very likely that Irving's scene and the one painted by Glintenkamp are the same. A powerful painting, *Spanish Town, Alcalá de Guadaira* is a classic example of Glintenkamp's mature style, which reflects his thorough assimilation of postimpressionism. It is a panoramic view of the old town, looking from its famous Roman bridge toward the church of San Roque, which dominates the skyline. Village residents in varying dress stroll through the streets and over the bridge. A threatening cloudy sky provides the dramatic lighting that contrasts deep shadow and brighter architecture. Glintenkamp used broad, vigorous brushstrokes, eliminating detail and purposefully distorting, simplifying, and exaggerating forms for expressive effect. He also included dark, emphatic contour lines to define the arches of the bridges and the edges of rooftops. This pictorial device, which suggests the influence of Paul Cézanne, heightens the underlying angular structure of the composition, a result of the artist's careful spatial analysis.

Ten years after Glintenkamp's death in 1946, Raphael Soyer, Philip Evergood, and several other artists arranged a memorial exhibition of the artist's work, which was held at the Art of Today Gallery in Manhattan. CTB

GASTON LACHAISE

50 b. 1882, Paris; d. 1935, New York City
Head of a Poet, 1925–26
Cast bronze (one of two lifetime casts), 13½ × 9½ × 5¾ (34.29 × 24.13 × 14.05)
Museum purchase made possible by Norman Rothschild in honor of his parents, Aleen and Irwin B. Rothschild 98.37

PROVENANCE: Kraushaar Galleries, New York; private collection; Kraushaar Galleries, New York.
EXHIBITIONS: *Summer Potpourri.*

Gaston Lachaise was the fourth child of an accomplished wood carver and cabinetmaker.[1] At thirteen, he entered the École Bernard Palissy, where he studied drawing, carving, and art history. Three years later, he began his studies at the École des Beaux-Arts and exhibited his work in four annual Paris Salons. From school, he went to work for the renowned jeweler and glassmaker René Lalique. In 1903 he met Isabel Dutaud Nagle, a married woman ten years his senior; he was smitten, and she became his lifelong inspiration for sculptures of voluptuous females. Using the funds he had saved from his work with Lalique, he followed Nagle back to Boston in 1906.[2] Referring to his obsession with Nagle, Marsden Hartley wrote that he saw "the entire universe in the form of a woman."[3] By 1917 he had become an American citizen, and he married Nagle (by then divorced from her first husband).

In 1912 Lachaise opened a studio in New York. The next year his work was included in the Armory Show. He also apprenticed to the sculptor Paul Manship, and worked with him on many garden sculpture commissions as well as the J. P. Morgan Memorials at the Metropolitan Museum of Art and Rockefeller Center. Stephan Bourgeois Gallery in New York offered him his first solo show in 1917. While much of his mature work features female torsos modeled after Isabel, Lachaise also made portrait studies in the tradition of Jean-Anton Houdon. His sitters included prominent American artists and intellectuals such as John Marin, Georgia O'Keeffe, Alfred Stieglitz, and a number of distinguished writers affiliated with the *Dial,* an early art and literary magazine.[4]

The sensitively modeled *Head of a Poet* is a portrait of an anonymous male, with a strong visage, an unusual pageboy hairstyle, rugged craggy features, and deep furrows that seem to activate the surface overall.[5] The artist's hand is evident throughout the piece, as he added, deleted, gouged, pushed, and pulled the modeling material to achieve his desired result.

Lachaise became associated with Kraushaar Galleries in New York in 1922. During the time he sculpted *Head of a Poet,* he had a solo exhibition at the Art Institute of Chicago. In 1927 he exhibited at Alfred Stieglitz's Intimate Gallery. In early 1935 Lachaise had a retrospective exhibition at the Museum of Modern Art, New York, in which he showed many of his pieces in plaster, since he could not afford to have them cast in bronze. Many were cast later for exhibitions at the Whitney Museum of American Art, Los Angeles County Museum of Art, and again at the Museum of Modern Art. Lachaise died in 1935 of leukemia at the age of fifty-three. EW

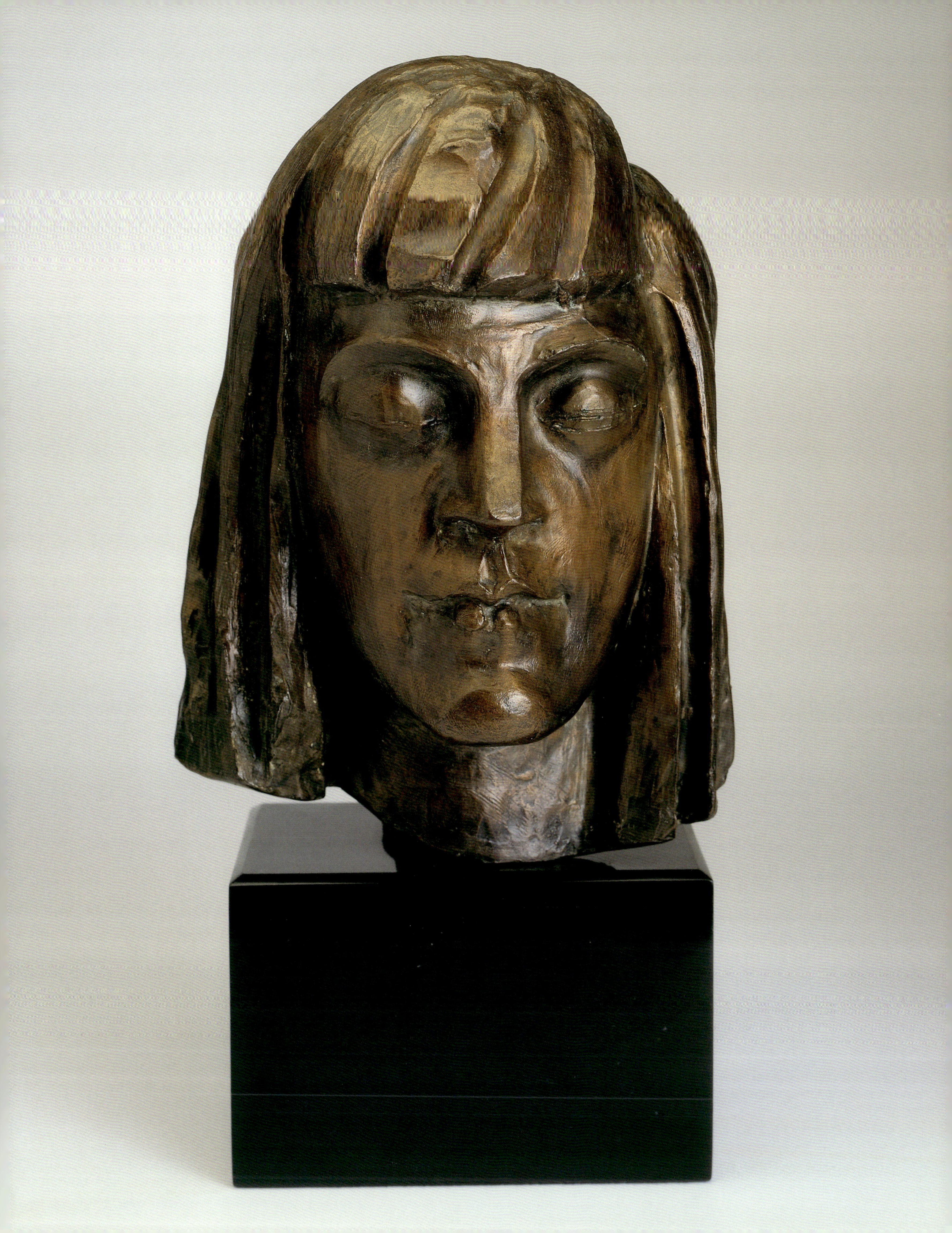

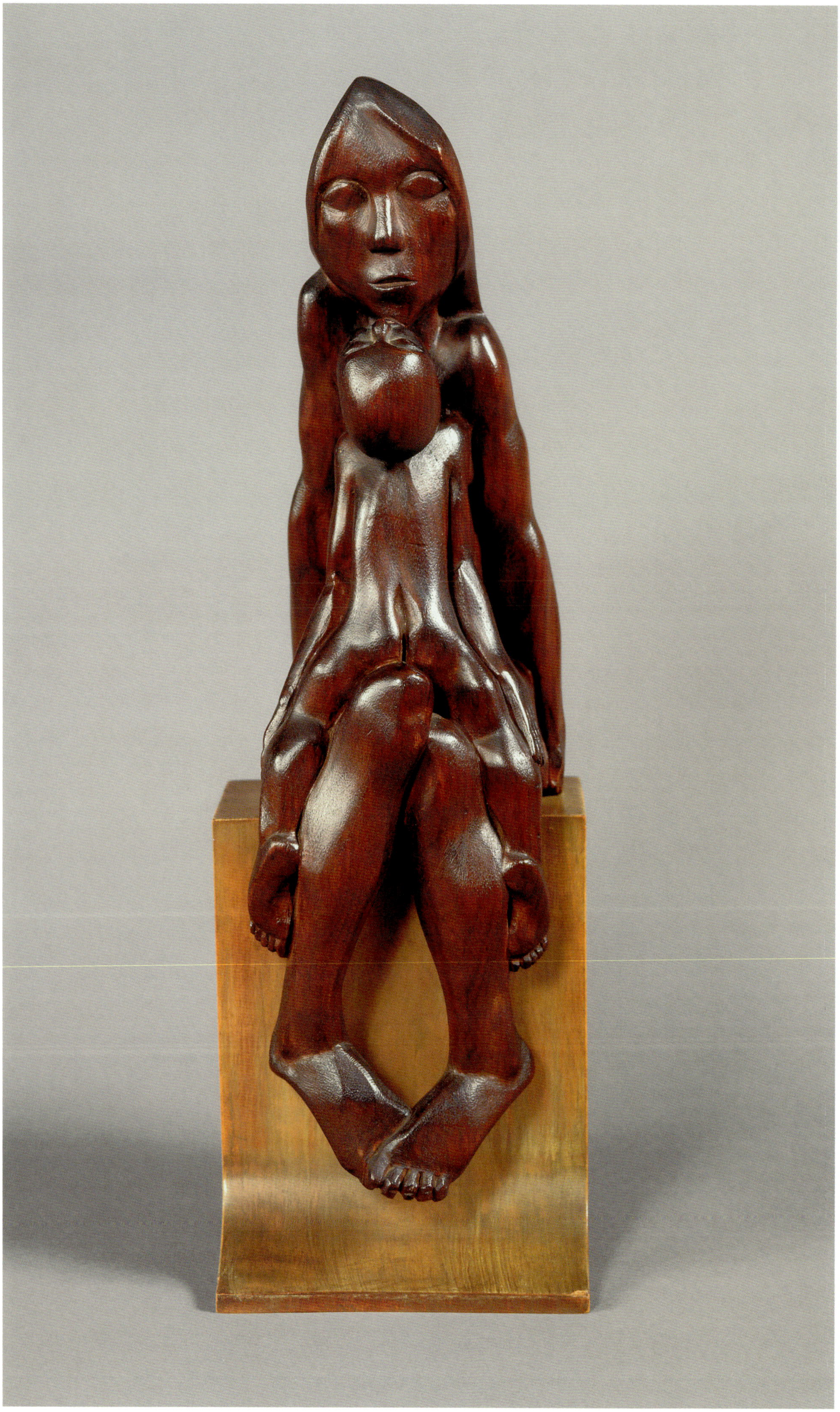

JOHN FLANNAGAN

51 b. 1895, Fargo, North Dakota; d. 1942, New York City

Mother Earth, ca. 1926

Mahogany, on original wood mount, 24 × 7½ × 6½
(61.0 × 19.05 × 16.51)

Museum purchase made possible by the Art Acquisition and Restoration Fund, The Edward Swift Shorter Bequest Fund and the Endowment Fund in Honor of D. A. Turner 96.4

PROVENANCE: Harold B. Smith, New York, Frederick Zimmerman, New York, until 1944; Vladimir and Martha Selinsky, New York, until 1988; private collection, California, until 1993; Conner-Rosenkranz, New York.

EXHIBITIONS: *Sculpture by J. B. Flannagan,* Weyhe Gallery, New York, 1927; *John B. Flannagan,* University of Notre Dame Art Gallery, South Bend, Indiana, 1963.

John Flannagan began his formal art instruction at the Minneapolis Institute of Arts. After a tour of duty in the merchant marines, he moved to New York, hoping to resume his art career, but he was destitute and forced to sleep many nights in the city's subways. In 1922 Arthur B. Davies employed him as an assistant and encouraged an active schedule of painting and sculpting as part of his daily work routine. At this time he started carving wood, and soon after began exhibiting at the Weyhe Gallery, which provided a stipend for the next fourteen years.[1]

Although Flannagan's later stone sculptures gained much favor, it is important to note that he began as a wood carver, preferring the process of direct carving that provided immediate contact with his material. He said, "My aim is to produce sculpture with such ease, freedom, and simplicity that it hardly seems carved but rather to have endured so always."[2] After 1926 he abandoned wood carving and began to work in stone, experiencing that medium's inherent and literal strength and the new challenges it offered. In the 1930s Flannagan traveled to Ireland and became enamored with the carved stone steles and Celtic crosses he saw throughout the countryside.

Flannagan's favorite subjects were animals and the female figure, both of which he viewed as nature in its purest form.[3] The influence of totemic African sculpture is evident in his wood carvings, as exemplified by *Mother Earth,* which depicts a woman with a child on her lap. While there appears to be a symbiotic unity between the two figures, the mother does not embrace the child who leans toward her, hungrily gazing upward for love, as she stares outward, avoiding the plea. During this same period, around 1926, Flannagan produced another mahogany carving entitled *Mother and Son,* depicting a loving and protective mother holding and embracing her young child. These conflicting views of nurturing and intimacy are in all probability a direct response to the artist's childhood experience of abandonment. Because his mother could not afford to care for her children, she left them at an orphanage when Flannagan was only five. In 1914, when he was nineteen and his mother and brother were dependent on him, he deserted them—a decision that plagued his conscience for the rest of his life. About his sculpture, *Mother Earth,* Flannagan said, "As a boy I very rarely saw my mother, and I think that the whole psychological story of what that means to a child is implied in this piece."[4]

Whatever personal catharsis the sculpture may have provided for the artist, it also projects the idea of a human relationship with Mother Earth in which humankind, represented by the smaller figure, is both part of and separate from the larger life-giving figure. *Mother Earth* typifies Flannagan's exploration of universal themes such as birth, life, and death presented in semi-abstract designs of continuous flowing movement. As the artist said, "Pure abstraction is dead. Make it come alive by the use of living form. Warm the cold geometry of abstraction with a naturalism in which the superficial and accidental have been eliminated by their union with pure form."[5] Unlike some of his contemporaries, Flannagan did not produce large-scale sculptures. Nevertheless, *Mother Earth* is monumental in its amalgamation of universal themes, sensitive carving, and concept of abstraction. BF

ROBERT HENRI

52 b. 1865, Cincinnati; d. 1929, New York City
Fergus, Boy in Blue Jacket, 1928
Oil on canvas, 28 × 20 (71.12 × 50.8)
Signed lower right: Robert Henri
Museum purchase 65.214

PROVENANCE: Grand Central Art Galleries, New York.
EXHIBITIONS: *William Merritt Chase and Robert Henri: American Master Painters,* Center for the Arts, Vero Beach, Florida, 1986; *Robert Henri and the Ashcan School,* Telfair Museum of Art, Savannah, Georgia, June 28–August 13, 1989; *Select View*; *My People: The Portraits of Robert Henri,* Orlando Museum of Art (Florida), Museum of Art (Fort Lauderdale, Florida), Columbus Museum, October 22, 1994–January 8, 1995.
PUBLICATIONS: *William Merritt Chase and Robert Henri: American Master Painters* (Vero Beach, Fla.: Center for the Arts, 1986), no. 50; Timpano, pl. 8, no. 17; Winn, et al., 105; Leeds, *My People,* no. 60.

Born Robert Henry Cozad, he changed his name to Robert Henri to avoid association with his father's serious legal problems.[1] He is often credited as a leader of the modernist art revolution in America, yet his early training consisted of a traditional academic preparation. Henri first studied with Thomas Anshutz and Thomas Hovenden at the Pennsylvania Academy of the Fine Arts. Later he traveled and studied in Europe, taking classes with William Adolphe Bouguereau at the Académie Julian and enrolling in the École des Beaux-Arts, both in Paris. He also studied with the painters Jean-Léon Gérôme and Léon Bonnat and the sculptor Augustin-Alexandre Dumont.

On his return to Philadelphia, Henri began teaching and holding weekly meetings of the Charcoal Club, whose members included William Glackens, John Sloan, Everett Shinn, and George Luks. Henri encouraged his students to draw or paint what they knew, not an idealized version of the subject. In 1906 he became a member of the National Academy of Design, although he often assisted in planning exhibitions that challenged the academy's position as an arbiter of traditional taste and artistic discernment.[2] When the academy rejected the work of Luks and other Henri students from their annual exhibition, Henri removed his own work and organized an exhibition of eight like-minded artists at Macbeth Gallery in 1908. The work of the Eight, as they became known, while controversial, reflected the artists' time and place and received much recognition. Henri was also instrumental in organizing the *Exhibition of Independent Artists* in 1910, which dealt another blow to the academic system and had a direct impact on the success of the Armory Show of 1913.

As a portraitist, Henri preferred people he believed to have an unspoiled natural spirit. Referring to them as "my people," he wrote,

> Folk who live in remote places, and especially those who live on islands, are thrown on their own responsibility for amusement, and in the general life each one has to develop the power to entertain others and himself, and so [those who live in remote places] become exceptional people. There is a lot of detail of life in great communities which they do not know, but they become possessed, through the force of necessity, of facts of life which it would be desirable for any city man to know.[3]

Such were the people that he came to love on Ireland's Achill Island. In 1924, after many trips there, he purchased a home, where he spent every remaining summer of his life.

Henri's respect for simple, unassuming people is apparent from his writing, but it is also obvious in his Irish portraits. *Fergus, Boy in Blue Jacket* is one of many portraits of children that Henri made in the last few years of his life. Henri said, "Children are greater than the grown man. . . . In the faces of children I have seen a look of wisdom and of kindness expressed with such ease and such certainty that I knew it was the expression of a whole race."[4]

In this portrait, the artist painted the face without blending hues on the canvas. It is in the clarity and color of the child's wide eyes that we discover the boy's innocence, as he expectantly looks out at the viewer. Henri wrote,

> The mass of the face is the most important and should be considered as principal to the other masses. . . . No feature should be started until you have fully comprehended its character and have established in your mind the manner of its full accomplishment. No feature should be drawn except in its relation to the others. There is a dominating movement . . . a sequence in their relationship. . . . Work with great speed. Have your energies alert, up and active. Finish as quickly as you can.[5]

In this delightful painting, the artist confirms that he followed his own advice. BF

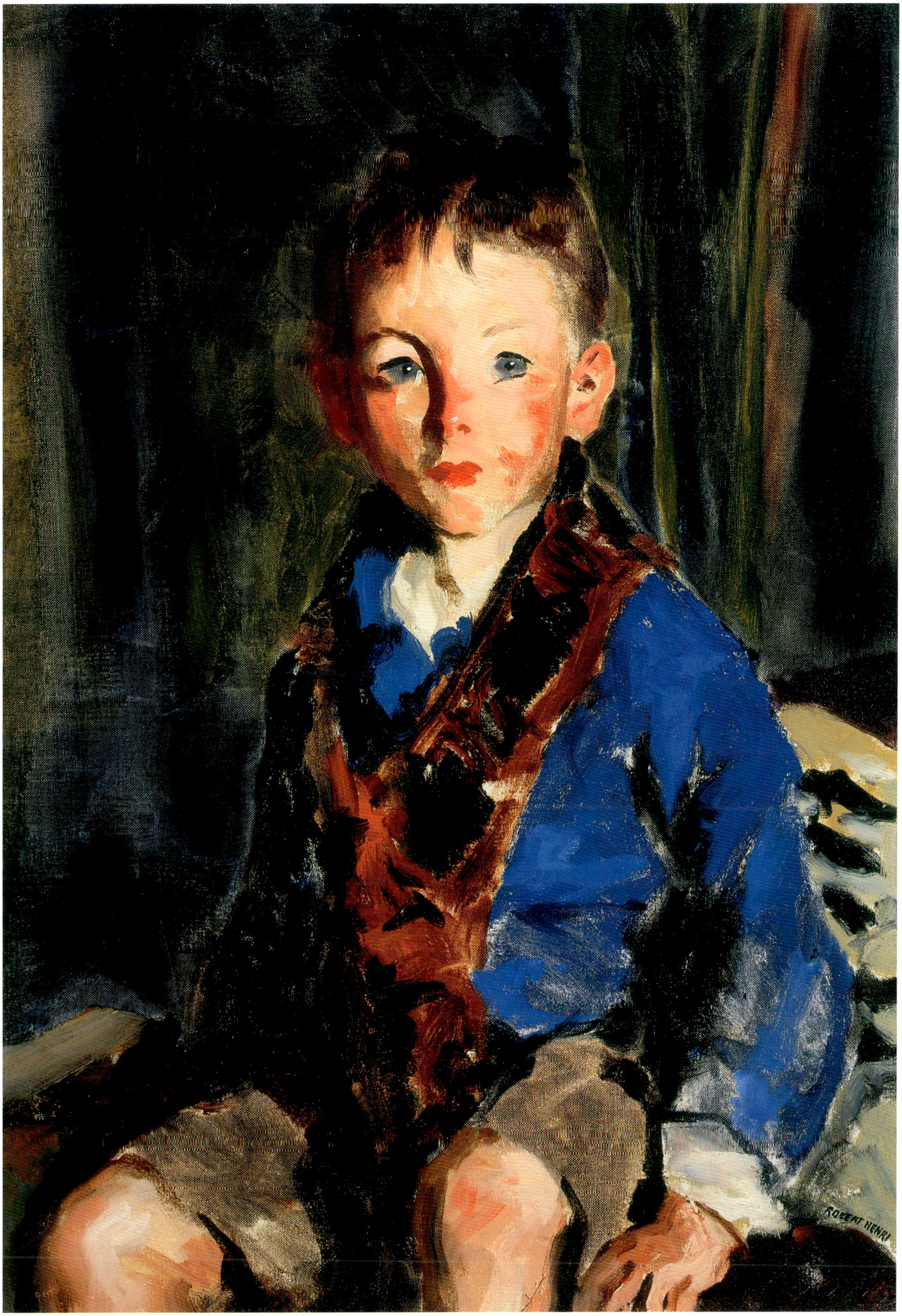
ROBERT HENRI

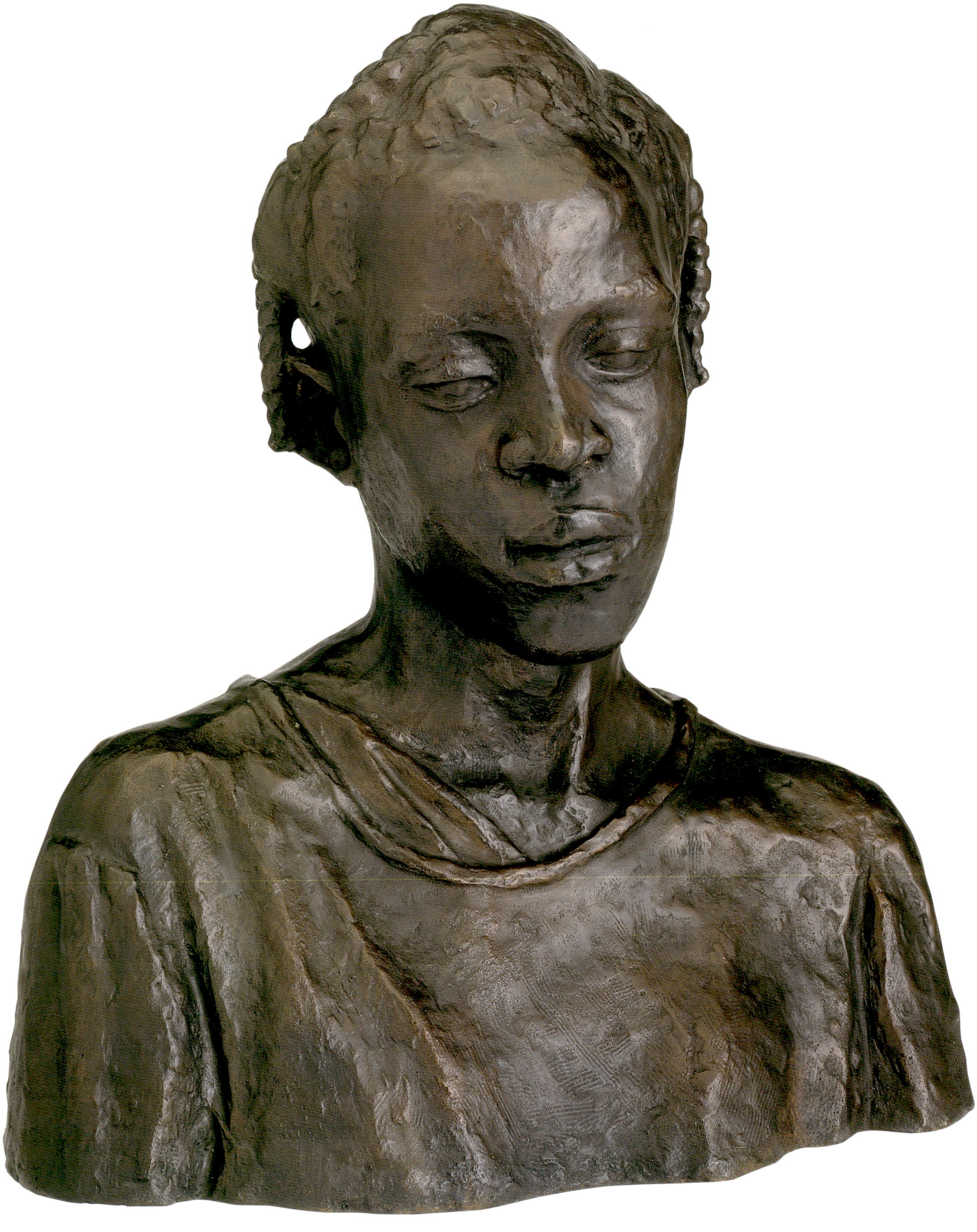

ANGELA GREGORY

53 b. 1903; d. 1990, New Orleans
La Belle Augustine, 1928
Cast bronze, 16 × 14 × 8 (40.64 × 36.83 × 20.32)
Signed and dated in cast: ANGELA/GREGORY/N.O. 1928.
Foundry mark in cast: ©3/B/I/M
Museum purchase made possible by the Art Acquisition and
[illegible]

PROVENANCE: Estate of the artist; Jean Bragg Gallery, New Orleans.
EXHIBITIONS: *A Retrospective Exhibition, Angela Gregory,* Newcomb College, New Orleans, 1925; *Salon d'Automne,* Paris, 1930; *Angela Gregory: A Sculptor's Life,* H. Sophie Newcomb Memorial College, New Orleans, March 8–May 18, 1981; *Newcomb College: Arts and Crafts Sales Exhibition,* Jean Bragg Gallery, New Orleans, October 30–November 30, 1998.
PUBLICATIONS: "Angela Gregory," cover; *Newcomb College: Arts and Crafts Sales Exhibition* (New Orleans: Jean Bragg Gallery, 1998), 44, cat. 37.

Unlike other women of her generation, Angela Gregory was nurtured and encouraged to follow a career in art. Her father was a well-respected professor of engineering at Tulane University, and her mother, a graduate of H. Sophie Newcomb Memorial College School of Art, was an artist and teacher. Gregory attended the private school for young women where her mother taught, and by the age of fourteen, while taking summer classes at Tulane University, she became adept at clay modeling and relief casting. In 1921 she entered Newcomb College, where she received accolades during her three years of study. Her skills as a sculptor developed under the instruction of the German artist Albert Reicker, who taught sculpture at the Arts and Crafts Club in New Orleans.[1]

In 1925 Gregory received a scholarship to the Paris branch of the Parson's School of Fine and Applied Art, which allowed her to study in France and Italy. While in France, she studied with sculptor Émile-Antoine Bourdelle, a former student of the great French master Auguste Rodin. She attended sketching classes during this time, completing her European studies in three years. She returned to New Orleans in 1928, where she established a studio.

Gregory's work soon attracted critical recognition from fellow artists as well as the public. Sculptor Harriet Frishmuth recommended her for membership in the National Sculpture Society. In 1929 General Allison Owen of the New Orleans architecture firm of Diboll and Owen visited Gregory's studio and was so impressed by the works he saw there—among them, *La Belle Augustine*—that he offered her a sculpture commission for the exterior of the Criminal Courthouse in New Orleans. This initial project was followed by numerous other commissions for architectural sculpture, such as those for the Louisiana State Capitol, the Tulane Medical School, St. Gabriel's Catholic Church in Louisiana, First National Bank of Commerce, the Union Passenger Station in New Orleans, and many others. She also continued to cast smaller works such as portrait busts and medallions in bronze and was involved in both the Public Works of Art Program and the Federal Art Project in Louisiana. She taught at Newcomb College and later at St. Mary's Dominican College in New Orleans for fourteen years before retiring in 1976.

La Belle Augustine is perhaps Gregory's most important early work, created soon after she returned from her studies in Europe. Her modeling of the head appears to be unfinished, but its folds, crevices, and bumps give it character and a sense of immediacy. Gregory used the conventional French sand-cast technique in producing this work, but the subject—the head of a young African American girl—was quite unconventional. Gregory approached it with sensitivity. The young girl's head is slightly bent and her gaze is averted, suggesting her apparent diffidence and modesty. Gregory produced only three casts of *La Belle Augustine*.[2] BF

LEON KROLL

54 b. 1884, New York City; d. 1974, Gloucester, Massachusetts
A Cove in Maine, 1929
Oil on canvas, 27 × 36 (64.8 × 91.44)
Signed lower right: Leon Kroll. Inscribed on stretcher: Leon Kroll/ A Cove in Maine/1929 (Ogunquit)/Owner: Kroll no. 133
Museum purchase made possible by Norman S. Rothschild in honor of his parents, Aleen and Irwin B. Rothschild 97.26

PROVENANCE: Estate of the artist; Spanierman Gallery, New York.
PUBLICATIONS: Hale and Bowers, eds., no. 73, as *Rocks at Island House.*

Abraham Leon Kroll began art instruction at the Art Students League as a student of John Henry Twachtman.[1] Later, he attended the National Academy of Design in New York and the Académie Julian in Paris, where he studied with Jean-Paul Laurens. In Paris he absorbed the influence of impressionist and postimpressionist artists such as Claude Monet, Vincent van Gogh, Auguste Renoir, and Paul Cézanne. Returning to New York at the age of eighteen, he was invited to exhibit his work at the National Academy of Design. As a young artist, he formed strong friendships with other American realists, including George Bellows, Robert Henri, and Eugene Speicher. Kroll often met with Henri's circle, and along with fellow artists received critiques of his work upon request. Over the years, he occasionally taught.

Kroll painted landscapes, portraits, and still lifes, but became best known for his figurative work—especially his nudes. His most successful work is the combination of figures in a realistic landscape. The artist noted, "I've never given up landscape painting. I've never limited myself as to subject. I've always been curious for a new kind of motif. I've painted still lifes and landscapes, compositions with figures, nudes, everything."[2]

Kroll first visited Maine as a student. There he found a cove in Ogunquit, with the unique features of rock, sea, and meadow. He returned to paint in this setting many times throughout his life, always varying the combinations and altering the perspectives.[3] "I always use nature as a kind of abstract encyclopedia of fact," he said. "I use parts and compose a picture. And even while I'm creating in this space, I never copy nature."[4] It is therefore unlikely that *A Cove in Maine* describes a specific site.[5]

The painting's subject is a sheltered cove in which a sailboat and a skiff drift lazily. In the foreground, on the shore, is a triangular group of two women and a baby, one woman seated and holding the baby, the other reclining with her back to the viewer. Picturesque white clapboard homes overlook the water, and dark clouds are gathered above. Kroll chose a high horizon line for this composition, moving the focus to the figures in the foreground by means of repeated diagonal lines. The smoothed rock formations with stark contrasts of light and shadow approach near abstraction, energizing the otherwise calm composition. During an early trip to Maine, Kroll met Winslow Homer, who advised him, "Do figures, my boy. Leave rocks to your old age. They're easy."[6] Kroll acknowledged Homer in his many paintings of the Maine coast, but his delineation of these impressive boulders has little to do with the works of the nineteenth-century American master. The painting is a distillation of Kroll's understanding of Cézanne, as exemplified in the planar fracturing of the landscape. Yet, in his narrative of the everyday character of the scene, with its old houses, drifting boats, and restful figures, it also reflects the artist's American roots. BF

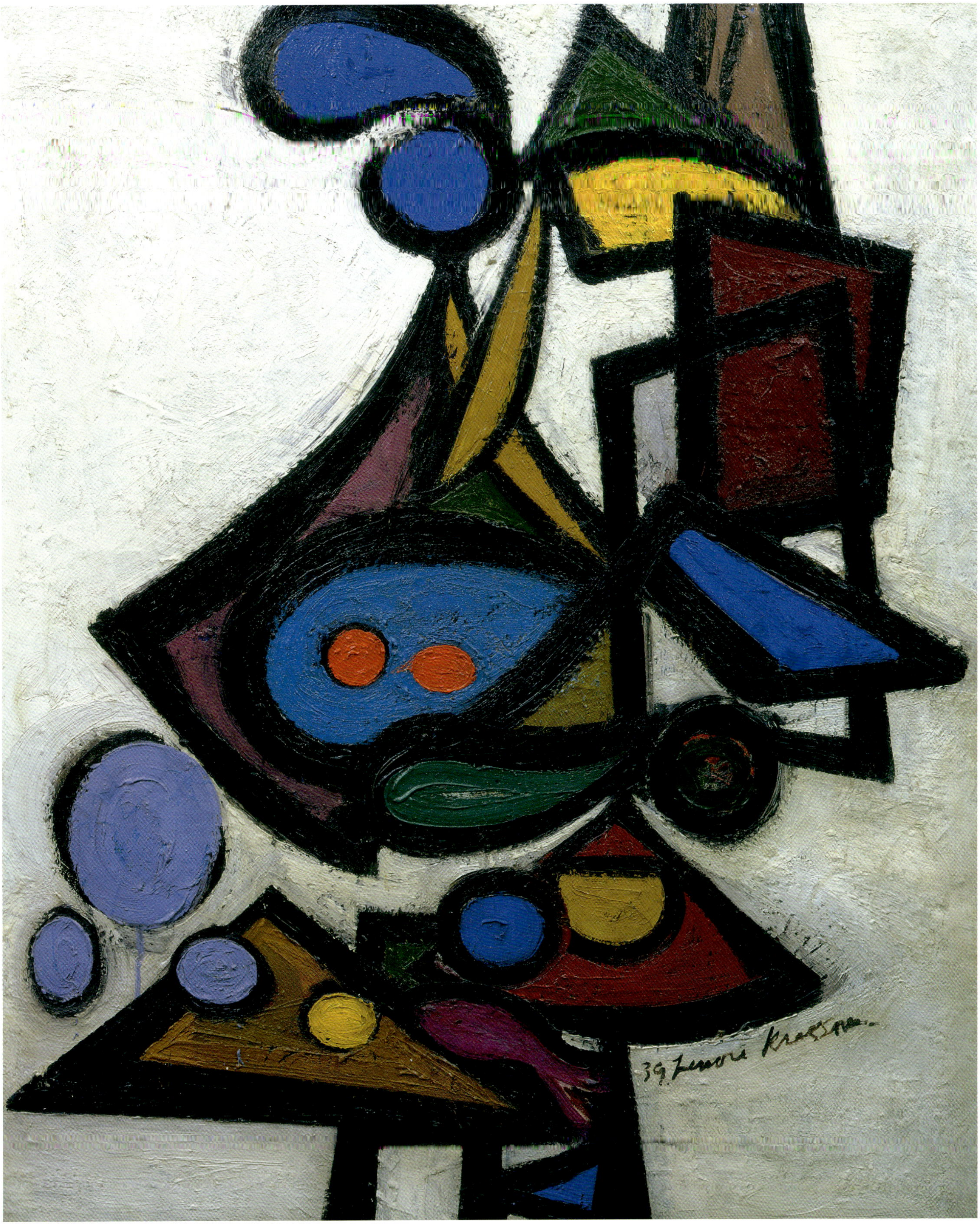

STUART DAVIS

60

b. 1892, Philadelphia; d. 1964, New York City
Shapes of Landscape Space #3, 1940
Oil on canvas, 15½ × 19½ (39.37 × 49.53)
Signed lower right: Stuart Davis
Museum purchase made possible by the Ella E. Kirven Charitable Lead Trust for Acquisitions 97.93

PROVENANCE: Mrs. Ralston Crawford (née Peggy Frank), 1942; Hirschl and Adler Galleries, New York; Linda Hyman Fine Arts, New York, 1996.
EXHIBITIONS: *Stuart Davis and Marsden Hartley,* Cincinnati Art Museum, 1941; *Streamlined: The Precisionist Impulse in American Art,* Hirschl and Adler Galleries, New York, November 22, 1995–January 6, 1996.
PUBLICATIONS: *Streamlined: The Precisionist Impulse in American Art* (New York: Hirschl and Adler Galleries, 1995), 19, cat. 21; *News,* Columbus Museum newsletter, summer, 1997, 5.

Stuart Davis was born in 1892.[1] His father was the art editor of the *Philadelphia Press*—the employer of illustrators such as John Sloan, William Glackens, George Luks, and Edward Shinn. His mother was a sculptor. Davis's early interactions with his parents' friends and colleagues, combined with parental support and commitment to his career in art, paved the way for his unusually rapid development. One of the most important American painters in the first half of the twentieth century, he described the vitality of modern life through his innovative use of form, color, and rhythm.

His professional career began in 1909, when he became a student of Robert Henri. As Davis's mentor, Henri arranged for his work to be included in the 1910 *Exhibition of Independent Artists* in New York. In 1913 Davis submitted his work to the Association of American Painters and Sculptors, who were organizing what has since become known as the Armory Show. Five of his watercolors were accepted into this show, which not only energized an entire generation of artists, including Davis, but also represented a significant turning point in American art.[2]

In her biography of Davis, art historian Patricia Hills wrote, "From the 1920s until his death . . . he developed a personal art theory . . . scorning academic banality, sentimentality, and bourgeois sensibilities."[3] Davis was committed to abstraction, even though he realized that most museums, collectors, and the public preferred an art based in realism. In the 1930s Davis divided his time between painting in Gloucester, Massachusetts, and teaching at the Art Students League. He showed his work in New York at the Downtown Gallery, the Museum of Modern Art, and at the Whitney Biennial exhibition. He created easel paintings as well as a number of large murals in Manhattan and Brooklyn for the Works Progress Administration's Federal Arts Project.[4]

Throughout his life, Davis was an articulate and outspoken art theorist who wrote extensively.[5] He was excited and inspired by the energy of jazz music, which played an increasingly significant role in his approach to art. As Gail Levin noted, "Rhythm is created [in Davis's paintings] by the variety of words and shapes overlapping in transparent layers. This is the rhythm of the city [New York] where Davis first enjoyed the jazz music that he loved."[6] His compositions are the visual equivalent of improvisation in American jazz.

Shapes of Landscape Space #3 was painted in January 1940. In December of that year, Davis provided a most cogent and provocative explanation of his work from this period for the journal *Parnassus.* Curator Lowery Stokes Sims quotes Davis describing his famous *Hot Still-Scape for Six Colors* (Museum of Fine Arts, Boston),[7] in terms that could easily apply to *Shapes of Landscape Space #3:*

> The subject matter of this picture is well within the experience of any modern city dweller. Fruit and flowers; kitchen utensils; fall skies; horizons; taxi cabs; radio; art exhibitions and reproductions; fast travel; Americana; movies; electric signs; dynamics of city sights and sounds; these and a thousand more are common experience and they are the basic subject matter my picture celebrates. The painting is abstract in the sense that it is highly selective, and it is synthetic in that it combines these selections of color and shape into a new unity, which never existed in nature but is a new kind of nature. This picture gives value and formal coherence to the many beauties in the common things in our environment, and is a souvenir of pleasure felt in contemplating them.[8]

The vibrancy of color and the staccato rhythm of this painting take the viewer on a fast-paced joy ride through the urban scene. LR

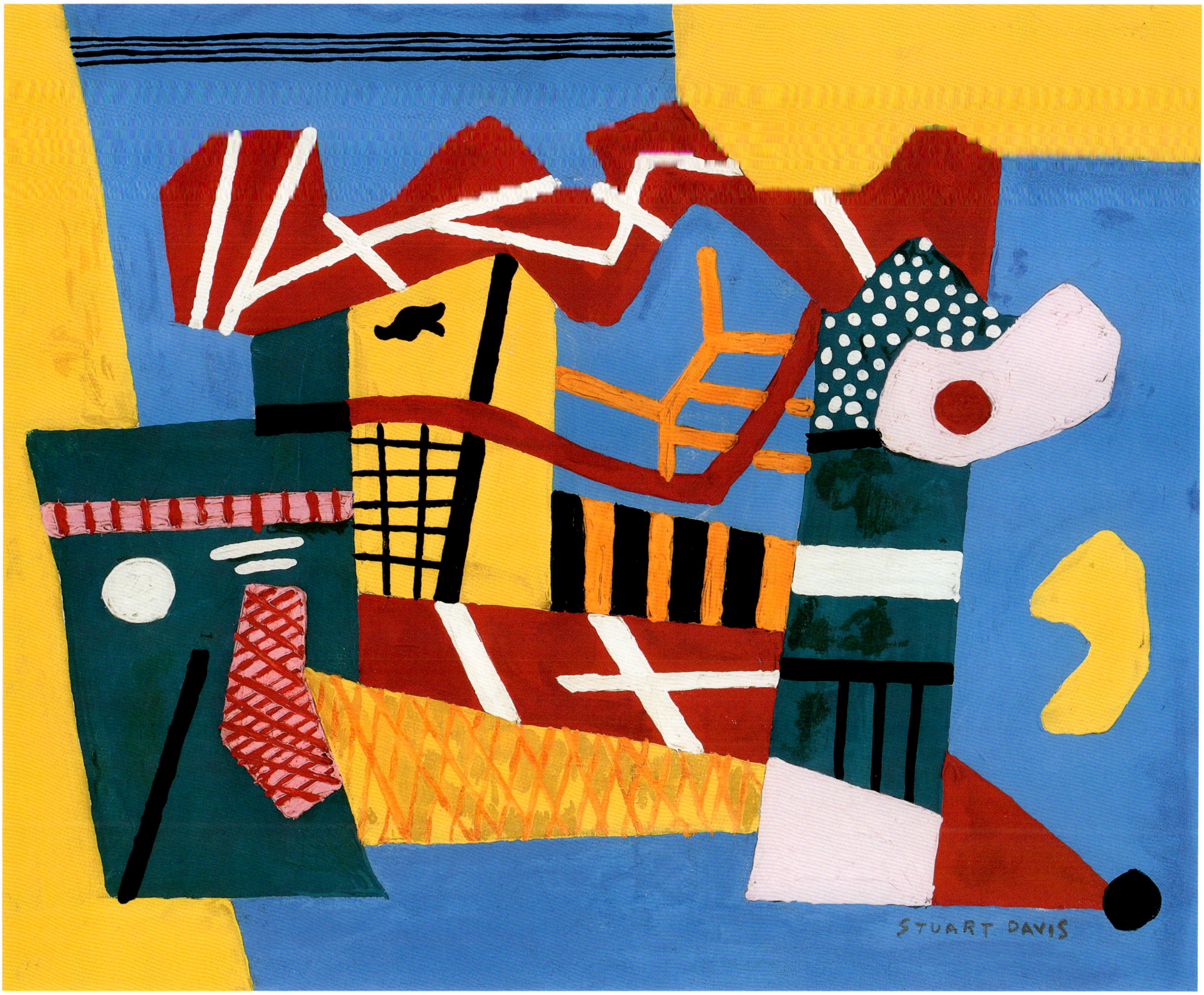
STUART DAVIS

WILLIAM SPRATLING

61 b. 1900, Sonyea, New York; d. 1967, Taxco, Mexico
Coffee Service, ca. 1931–50
Sterling silver with rosewood handles; coffee pot, 8¼ × 9¼ × 4 (20.96 × 23.5 × 10.16); creamer, 3 × 5½ × 4 (7.62 × 13.97 × 10.16); sugar, 3¾ × 6½ × 4 (9.53 × 16.51 × 10.16); waste bowl, 3 × 6 × 3¼ (7.62 × 15.24 × 8.26)
Marked on bottom: Spratling Co./Made in Mexico/Spratling Silver
Museum purchase made possible by the Endowment Fund in Honor of D. A. Turner 2002. 1.1–4

PROVENANCE: Private collection; Marc Navarro Gallery, Santa Fe, New Mexico.
EXHIBITIONS: *Summer Potpourri.*
PUBLICATIONS: Cederwall and Riney, 47.

In 1910 William Spratling's mother and sister Wilhelmina died, and his father sent his two sons and surviving daughter to his family home (Roamer's Roost) in Alabama, where they became wards of their grandfather.[1] By the end of 1912, the children had been separated and sent to live with various relatives. William ended up in Auburn, where he graduated from high school, then went on to attend Auburn University.

As an undergraduate at Auburn, he was asked to teach courses in the architecture department. In 1921 he left Auburn, without completing his degree requirements, to take a position as associate professor of architecture at Tulane University, New Orleans. He shared an apartment with author William Faulkner in the French Quarter. In addition to Faulkner, his circle of acquaintances included artists Caroline Durieux and Ellsworth Woodward; writers Lyle Saxon, Hamilton Basso, and Sherwood Anderson; and contributors to the magazine, *Double Dealer.*

Spratling first visited Mexico in 1926. He returned every summer until he moved there in 1929 and became active in the arts community. At first, he concentrated on promoting the art of Diego Rivera in New York galleries, which led to his participation in the first exhibition of Mexican artists held in the United States. In 1931 Dwight Morrow, ambassador to Mexico, suggested that Spratling start a craft center in Taxco, home of many artisans and the site of centuries-old silver mines. He began his new venture by hiring an experienced goldsmith from Iguala, who moved to Taxco and created silver jewelry from Spratling's designs. Other artisans soon joined the project, producing works in silver, tin, copper, textiles, and wood—all based on Spratling's designs. In 1935 Spratling's success warranted a move to a larger shop. As tourism expanded, Spratling designs in both jewelry and hollowware were greeted with great enthusiasm.

In June 1944 the company—then called Spratling y Artesanos S. A.—expanded again, this time to an abandoned hacienda. At this point, Spratling employed approximately four hundred workers, but his financial problems forced him to resign from the company in 1945. Shortly thereafter the company dissolved. In 1947 Spratling formed a new silver workshop called William Spratling, S.A. This time he limited his output, resulting in simplified designs of greater refinement. Although embittered about his lack of financial success and the loss of his original company, he continued designing silver pieces and pressed for continuing development in Taxco-el-Viejo. William Spratling died from injuries he suffered in an automobile accident just outside his adopted home of Taxco on August 7, 1967.

The museum's service is an early design called *Olavado* (*cafetera,* or coffee maker, #1504), with a nautilus motif where the rosewood handles attach.[2] The set was also made with silver handles. Spratling revolutionized silver design in the twentieth century by introducing pre-Columbian elements to his overall modernist approach, much as Rivera had done in his art. His creative inventiveness was matched only by his determination to establish an ongoing industry that provided worthwhile employment for the Mexican silversmiths he so admired. CTB

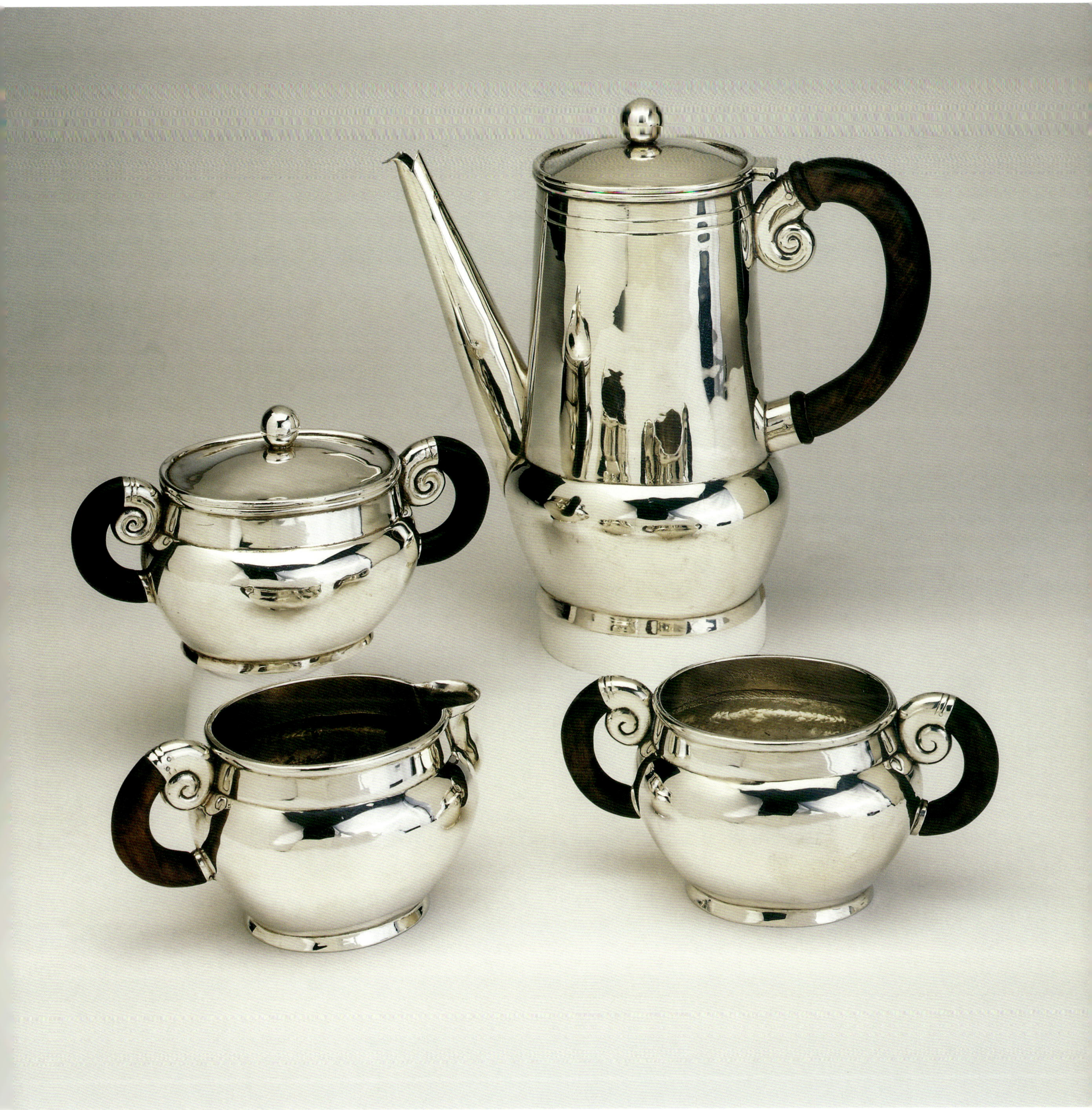

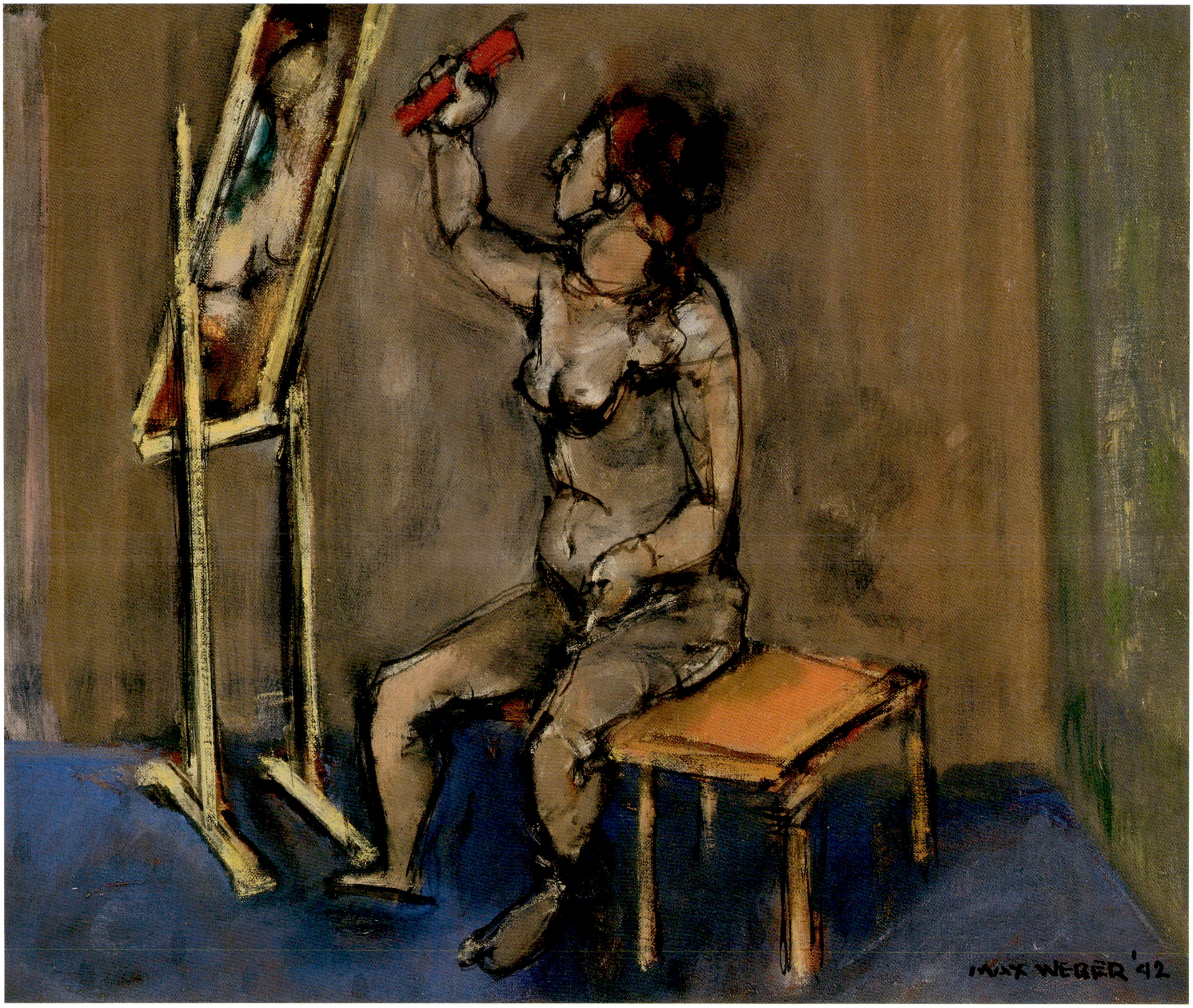
MAX WEBER '42

MAX WEBER

62 b. 1881, Bialystock, Russia; d. 1961, Great Neck, New York

The Red Comb, 1942

Oil on canvas, 13⅛ × 16⅛ (33.40 × 41.02)

Signed and dated: Max Weber '42

Museum purchase 01.22

PROVENANCE: Christie's Auction House, New York.

EXHIBITIONS: *Select View.*

PUBLICATIONS: Timpano, fig. 7; Winn, et al., 110.

Max Weber's artistic vision first developed at the Pratt Institute under Arthur Dow, who introduced his students to non-western aesthetic traditions. After leaving school, Weber began teaching, hoping to raise enough funds to travel abroad. In 1905 he was in Paris, one of the first American artists to be directly influenced by European modernism. He studied at the Académie Julian (where he met Abraham Walkowitz), Académie Colarossi, Académie de la Grande Chaumière, and with Henri Matisse and Jean-Paul Laurens. In his travels through Europe, he not only learned more about western art traditions but also absorbed African and Asian art.[1] His Parisian circle of friends included Pablo Picasso, Robert Delauney, André Donoyer de Segonzac, and Henri Rousseau.

Weber could not have arrived in Paris at a more opportune time. Matisse was exploring the brilliant colors of Persia; Picasso was experimenting with the planar surfaces of African masks and beginning to develop the theories of what became known as cubism. Weber understood and appreciated these new ideas, but was most influenced by Paul Cézanne's unique depiction of space in paintings he saw at the Salon d'Automne in 1906 and 1907.[2]

Although Weber produced a series of cubist-inspired abstract paintings from 1915 to 1918, after 1919 all of his work was representational; his subjects were still life, landscape, and genre scenes of recent immigrants and the working class. From the 1940s on, Weber developed a more emotional, expressionist approach in his work. His attempts to fuse diverse styles into a new modernist aesthetic are evident in *The Red Comb,* which dates to his later period.

When he returned to the United States in 1909, his new style of painting brought hostile reactions. The next year he met Alfred Stieglitz, art dealer and photographer, who understood Weber's modernist vocabulary. Stieglitz provided Weber with moral and financial support and exhibited his work with a handful of contemporary American modernists.[3] Weber assisted Stieglitz by organizing exhibitions. However, the artist's association with Stieglitz would be short-lived, for he continued to develop independent theories of modern art and soon fell out of favor with Stieglitz and his circle.

Weber was invited to participate in the Armory Show in 1913, but he withdrew after learning that only two of his pictures had been accepted, whereas eight or ten images by each of his French counterparts would be exhibited.[4] But the slight was soon forgotten. That same year Weber had a successful solo show at the Newark Museum of Art, the first ever devoted to an American modernist artist. He experimented with sculpture, both figurative and abstract, and wrote poetry and treatises on modernist theories. He exhibited at the Whitney Museum of American Art, the Museum of Modern Art, and the Art Institute of Chicago, among others.

In *The Red Comb* a nude figure looks into a mirror, preparing to comb her hair. Weber delineated the room she occupies by using three colors to identify the two walls and floor. The bench on which the model sits and the tilted mirror help to define the picture's space. The figure is reminiscent of Weber's earlier nudes that date from the beginning of the twentieth century. The fractured image in the mirror recalls his previous interest in cubism. The strong outlines and physical mass of the figure and Weber's use of contrasting colors reveal his ongoing interest and insight into the works of Cézanne and Matisse. Painted later in his career, *The Red Comb* retains much of the vibrancy and assuredness that defined his earlier works, even as it reflects the lessons he learned and made his own. BW and CTB

LAMAR DODD

63 b. 1909, Fairburn, Georgia; d. 1996, Athens, Georgia
Landscape with Haystacks and Hills, ca. 1942
Oil on canvas, 20¼ × 30¼ (51.44 × 76.84)
Signed lower right: Lamar Dodd
Bequest of Edward Swift Shorter 91.7.8

PROVENANCE: Edward Swift Shorter, Columbus, Georgia.
EXHIBITIONS: *A Shared Vision: The Life and Art of Lamar Dodd,* Lamar Dodd Art Center (LaGrange, Georgia), LaGrange College (Georgia), and Chattahoochee Valley Art Museum (LaGrange, Georgia), July 18–September 27, 1996; *Old Friends: Lamar Dodd and Howard Thomas,* Columbus Museum, July 2–September 24, 2000.
PUBLICATIONS: King, no. 9.

Perhaps no one else in the twentieth century had as great an influence and effect on the art produced in Georgia as did artist, advocate, and educator Lamar Dodd. Born and raised in Georgia, Dodd began to study art at the age of twelve at LaGrange Female College. As a young man he continued to pursue his art education in New York City, where he studied at the Art Students League with instructors such as George Luks, Boardman Robinson, and John Steuart Curry. Dodd returned to the South in 1933 and took a daytime job in an art supply store in Birmingham. At night he painted those southern scenes that would bring him national and regional attention and awards. By 1937 Dodd's reputation came to the attention of administrators at the University of Georgia in Athens, who invited him to join their faculty. Dodd built the art department, brought in visiting artists, hired faculty, and raised money for scholarships. By perseverance and devotion he made the program one of the most prominent in the Southeast. He chaired the department until 1973.

Hereward Cooke, in an essay about Dodd's southern regionalism, wrote, "[Dodd] has been the eyewitness and recorder of this critical phase in our history."[1] Dodd was not one to rely on past successes, however. Instead, his stylistic tendencies continued to evolve as he experimented with various new ideas and techniques. He believed that he would always remain a student. Dodd wrote, "Painting, for me, is a constant and never-ending quest for artistic objectivity based indirectly and directly upon my personal observations and reactions to the visual world; but of even more importance is a search for, and an awareness of, the inner structures of matter rather than the surface appearance of things."[2]

Dodd's first artworks entered the permanent collection of the Columbus Museum in 1956, three years after its founding, primarily due to the strong ties between the artist and the museum's first director, Edward Swift Shorter. Both were artists, and both were strong advocates of the visual arts for the people of Georgia. In 1966 Dodd was invited to be the keynote speaker at Shorter's retirement dinner. Dodd's painting, which had been in Shorter's personal collection, was given by bequest to the museum.

Landscape with Haystacks and Hills describes the rural beauty of the American landscape. No human figure animates this scene, though a human presence is clearly evident in the distant building. Rather it is the rich golden color and sensual undulating contours of the hills that bring this image to life. The composition is balanced, yet the curving and diagonal lines create a sense of dynamism. The exact locale of the scene is unknown, but the date of this painting suggests that Dodd was working in northern Georgia, near the Tennessee border, a region to which he returned many times in the late 1930s and early 1940s. Unlike an earlier work that explores the devastating effects of mining in the region, this painting celebrates the pastoral beauty of the American South. BF

CHARLES EAMES

b. 1907, St. Louis, d. 1978, Pacific Palisades, California

RAY KAISER EAMES

b. 1912, Sacramento, d. 1988, Pacific Palisades, California

67 **Dining Chair with Wood Legs** (from a set of four), ca. 1946
Laminated birch plywood, 29 × 19¼ × 20½ (69.6 × 48.9 × 52.07)
Gift of Jim and Marge Krum, Hilton Head, South Carolina 98.24.2

PROVENANCE: Auction, 1981; Jim and Marge Krum, Hilton Head, South Carolina.
EXHIBITIONS: *Towards a New Century.*

Charles and Ray Eames were a husband-and-wife design team whose interests included furniture design, architecture, and filmmaking. Charles Eames studied architecture at Washington University in St. Louis, then worked as a draftsman for several firms in the 1930s during the Great Depression, when employment opportunities were limited. Ray Kaiser studied with Hans Hofmann at the Art Students League and at his school in New York, where she became well versed in the theories and practices of modernism. The two met at Cranbrook Academy of Art in Michigan and married in 1941, thereafter collaborating on unique and innovative design projects, mainly furniture.

This chair design is the result of their desire to create modern, everyday furniture for middle-income American families. They created new forms with new materials, taking advantage of technological breakthroughs in the use of molded plywood. The curving chair form was introduced when Charles Eames worked with Eero Saarinen to create a simplified design for the 1940 *Organic Design in Home Furnishings* competition sponsored by the Museum of Modern Art, New York. Eames and Saarinen won the competition, but their original design proved too complicated for mass production. When the Eameses moved to Los Angeles, they continued to experiment with new plywood molding techniques, various glues, and the use of technologically advanced machinery for the production of military products.[1] Eventually, they modified the chair's original design to include separate pieces for the seat and back.[2]

By 1946 the Herman Miller Furniture Company was making and marketing the Eames plywood chair, and they continued to do so through subsequent variations for the next few years.[3] In its 1952 catalogue, the company advertised, "The Eames molded plywood chair has become a classic. Its clean details and sculptured curves have shown what beauty can come from modern production techniques. The seat and back, molded to the contours of the human body, together with the rubber mounts that permit the chair to flex with any shifting of position, provide comfort rarely found in a non-upholstered chair." The chair was listed as a DCW, a dining chair with wood legs, which is suitable as a desk chair.[4] The museum's collection also includes another Eames classic, the lounge chair with ottoman.

The Herman Miller Company was a pioneer in the field of modern furniture production and marketing at a time when many considered the style too progressive for most American homes. The Eames plywood chair, once a fresh aesthetic, has become a classic, and its considerable influence is seen in furniture design to this day. BF

ROBERT GWATHMEY

68

b. 1903, Richmond, Virginia; d. 1988, South Hampton, New York
Sunday Morning, ca. 1948
Oil on canvas, 60 × 40 (52.4 × 101.6)
Signed upper left: gwathmey
Museum purchase made possible by the Art Acquisition and Restoration Fund 97.2

PROVENANCE: Eric Sternberg, Connecticut, inherited from his father, who acquired the work from the artist, ca. 1950; Michael Rosenfeld Gallery, New York.
EXHIBITIONS: *Robert Gwathmey: Works from Southern Collections,* Columbus Museum, Morris Museum of Art (Augusta, Georgia), October 18–May 9, 1999; *Robert Gwathmey: Master Painter,* Butler Institute of American Art (Youngstown, Ohio), Museum of Fine Arts (St. Petersburg, Florida), Virginia Historical Society (Richmond), Telfair Museum of Art (Savannah, Georgia), Pennsylvania Academy of the Fine Arts (Philadelphia), September 5, 1999–August 13, 2000.
PUBLICATIONS: Kammen, pl. 9; Piehl and Foley, n.p.; Mary Bentz Gilkerson, "Augusta Museum Explores Southern Art," *Columbia, S.C., State,* February 28, 1999, F4.

Robert Gwathmey's paintings are personal expressions of his appreciative understanding of life in the South as he experienced it. He first studied art at the Maryland Institute in Baltimore. Of that experience he wrote,

> When I went to Baltimore to study art, the first thing I saw was Negro policemen and statues of Yankee generals. When I got back home, I was shocked by the poverty. If I had never gone back home, perhaps, I would never have painted the Negro. The Negro seemed to be everywhere, too, omnipresent. But he was a thing apart, so segregated. When people ask me why I paint the Negro, I ask "Don't artists have eyes?"[1]

Gwathmey continued his studies at the Pennsylvania Academy of the Fine Arts, where he won a William Emlen Cresson Traveling Scholarship for study in Europe, which he undertook during the summers of 1929 and 1930. Of the many things he saw and studied while abroad, the Gothic style inspired him the most.[2] Gwathmey taught at several schools in Pennsylvania before settling permanently in New York, where he joined the faculty of the Cooper Union in 1942. In 1944–45, he received a Rosenwald Fellowship, which he used to live and work on a tobacco farm in North Carolina while creating paintings on the theme of life in the rural South. Gwathmey's most effective work seems less about social advocacy and more about the nature of community and the relationships between the races and sexes within his native region.[3]

Dedicated to the figural tradition, Gwathmey painted in a representational style when many other American artists were following the path of abstract expressionism. Because of this, he was called a social realist when that was no longer fashionable or progressive. His work, however, reflects a modernist understanding of shapes, forms, and colors, seen in his fragmentation of the figure and flattening of the picture plane.

Sunday Morning is a powerful image in which the modern formalist vocabulary is used to portray an event in African American culture of the 1940s.[4] Here, three generations of a family walk to church on a Sunday morning. The dominant central figure was modeled after Sarah Wade, a woman who worked for the artist's in-laws in Charlotte, North Carolina.[5] She is clearly the head of this family and an elder in her church, leading the next generation of women and the lone adult male and two children bringing up the rear of the procession. In her mode of dress the older woman reflects an earlier time, while her children and grandchildren dress according to the fashion of the day.

Gwathmey's fragmented figures and even their parasols break into crisply outlined shapes of intense color, recalling the Gothic stained-glass windows the artist had seen almost two decades earlier. This bold patterning unites the figures in a tight, yet rhythmic composition that is set against a field of neutral colors. Gwathmey said,

> I believe that in painting the use of limited imagery is the best method of presentation of your content. I believe that if the symbols are strong enough and simple enough and inventive enough, they can transcend [what is literal] in painting. One technical way of gaining this end is with simplified pattern. I'd also like to say that this is a modern way of painting.[6]

BF

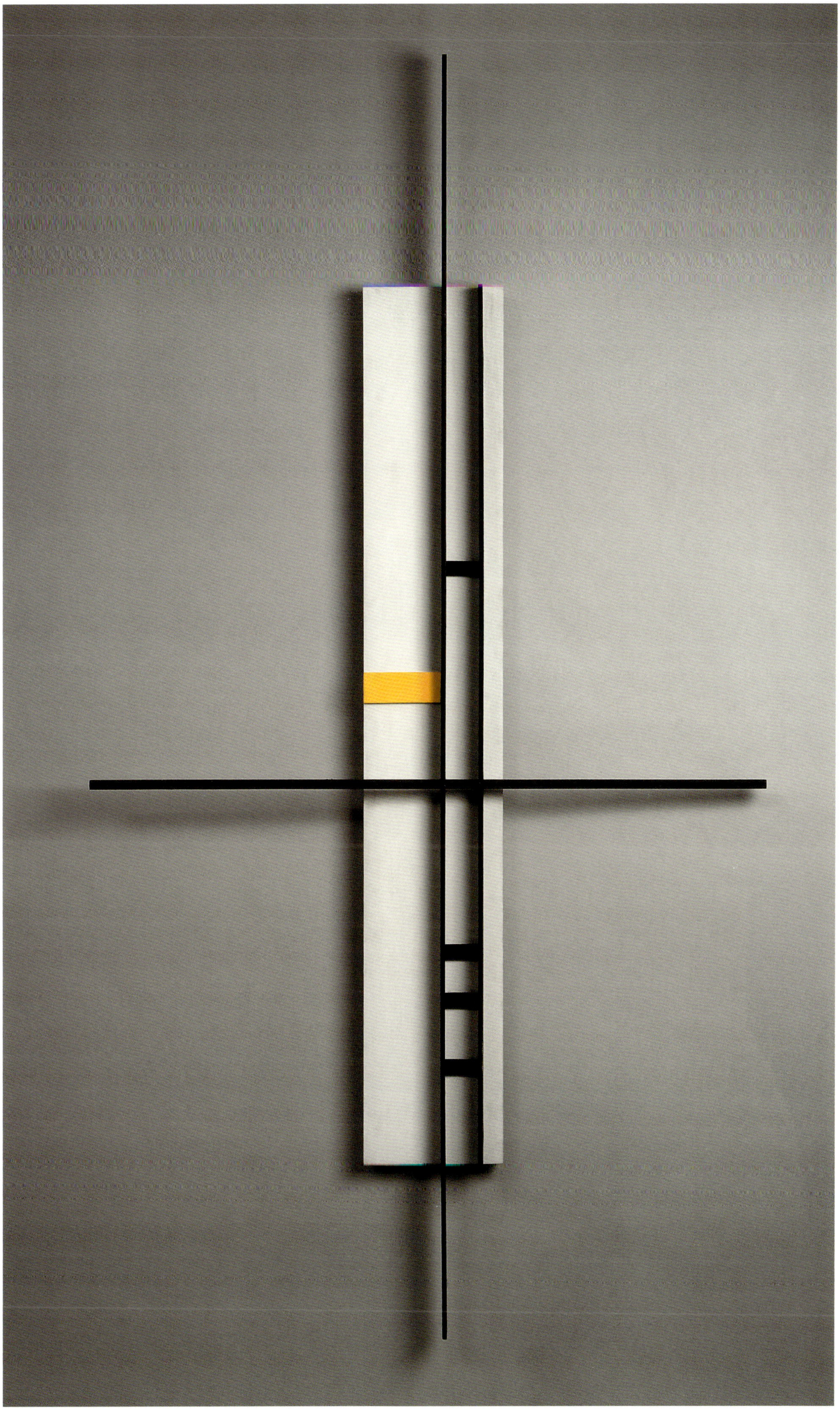

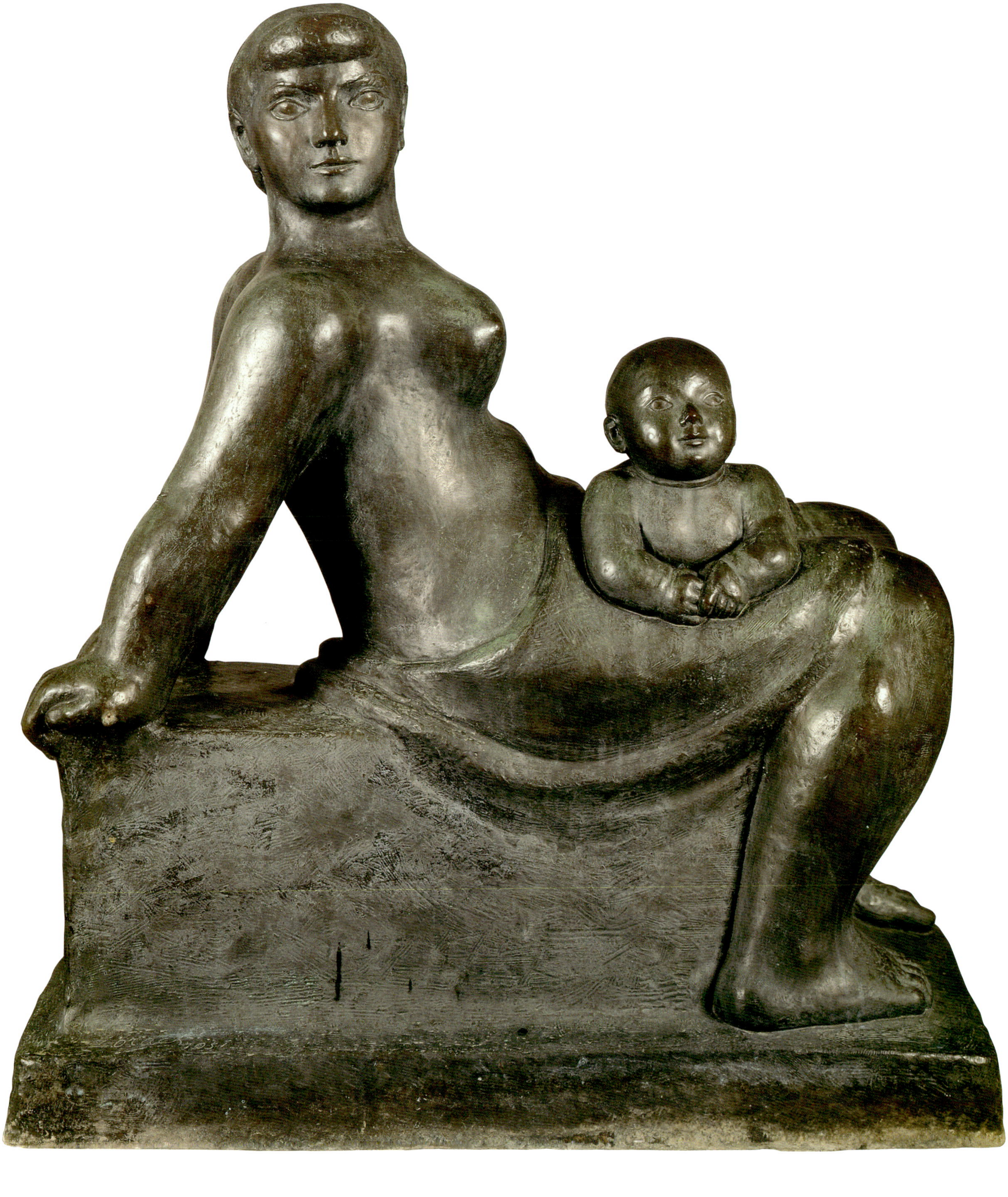

WILLIAM ZORACH

[illegible]

71 **New Horizons**, 1951
Cast bronze (from edition of six), 44 × 38½ × 20
(111.76 × 97.79 × 50.8)
Signed and dated on base at lower left: Zorach–1951
Museum purchase made possible by the Endowment Fund
in Honor of D. A. Turner 91.6

PROVENANCE: Christie's Auction House, New York.
PUBLICATIONS: Winn, et al., 118.

Art historian Wayne Craven described William Zorach as one of the first American modernists to fully understand the aesthetics of the movement and to break completely with academic tradition.[1] Zorach began his studies at the Cleveland School of Art (now the Cleveland Institute of Art) and later attended the National Academy of Design in New York. In 1910, while abroad, he met Marguerite Thompson, whom he married three years later. Returning to New York, they set up a studio and led a frugal but free-spirited, bohemian life as part of the early American avant-garde. At first they worked so closely together that it was difficult to distinguish his oils or watercolors from hers. Both exhibited in the 1913 Armory Show.

Eventually, however, their art took them in different directions. Zorach began to work in direct carving in the summer of 1917. He had been working on a series of wood-block prints, when he found that he was more interested in the butternut wood panel than the print. Using a jack-knife as a gouge, he quickly turned the panel into a carved relief. Although he had no formal training in sculpture, he had a natural instinct for the materials. The grain of wood or the texture of the stone set limits in the shaping process, but the innate beauty and the sensuous tactile character of the raw material compelled him. Direct carving was a slow process. Zorach said that it took him a year to cut a full-sized figure in stone. Yet, in the beginning, he resisted modeling in clay. "He came to believe in the aesthetic necessity of carving directly into a block of wood or stone."[2] While Zorach's emphasis on mass and volume over fine details may explain in part his earlier preference for carving, he soon found that he could also achieve his desired effects through the modeling and casting of figures.

Much of Zorach's art explores nuances of human emotion and universal themes, such as the importance of family, the subject of some of his most moving works.[3] One of his earliest successes was on the theme of mother and child, a topic he would repeat periodically. Between 1927 and 1931, he carved in marble a five-foot sculpture on the subject. He returned to the idea of family in later works, such as *The Future Generation* (1942–47; Whitney Museum of American Art) and *Devotion* (1946; private collection, New York).

New Horizons was cast in 1951. Its monumentality belies the intimacy between the two figures. Zorach had an affinity for primitive sculpture, especially African carvings, but this work resembles the great guardian sculptures of the ancient Mayas at Chichén Itzá. Tessim Zorach, the artist's son, recalled the circumstances surrounding the composition of this piece: "One summer when my youngest son was having his diapers changed on the front lawn my father came out of his studio in Robinwood, Maine, and said 'Hold that pose—I have never done a sculpture like that.'"[4] Zorach made an immediate sketch, which he later modeled in clay, then cast in plaster and finally in bronze. The artist captured the relaxed pose of the figures, who look at the viewer independently yet together. Despite the bulk and weight of the sculpture, Zorach has endowed it with a gentle and lyrical quality appropriate to the subject, the extraordinary bond between a mother and her child. EW

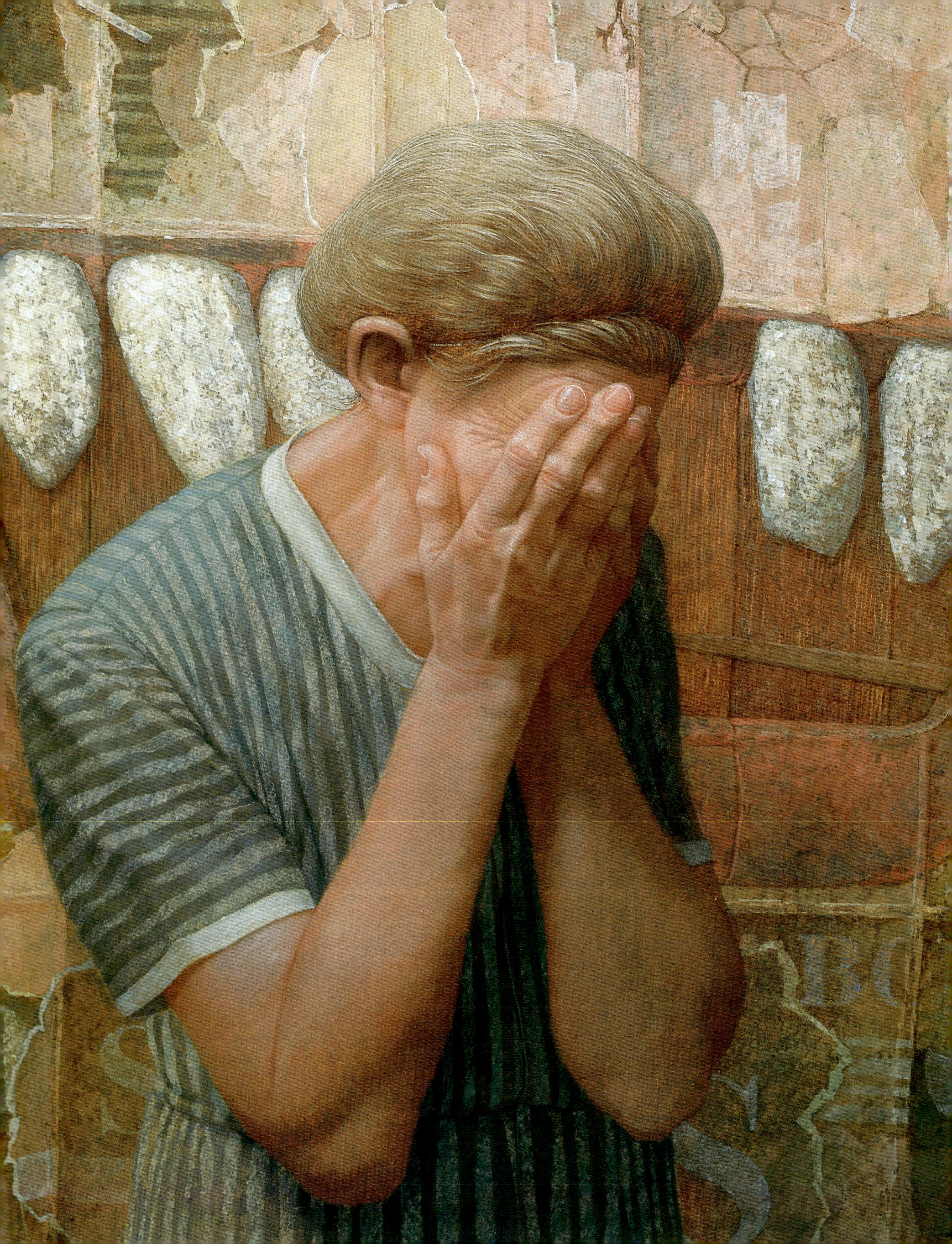

ROBERT VICKREY

72 b. 1926, New York City

Woman Weeping, 1957

Tempera on Masonite, 60 × 42 (152.4 × 106.68)

Signed lower right: Robert Vickrey

Gift of halley k harrisburg and Michael Rosenfeld 97.1

PROVENANCE: Midtown Galleries, New York, 1957; private collection; Colorado Springs Fine Arts Center, until 1965; Sotheby's, New York, 1996; halley k harrisburg and Michael Rosenfeld, New York, 1996.

EXHIBITIONS: *Robert Vickrey: A Retrospective of Paintings, Drawings and Watercolors,* University of Arizona (Tucson), Fine Arts Gallery of San Diego, February 17–July 8, 1973; *American Art Exhibition,* Fine Arts Center, Colorado Springs, May–July 1977; *20th Century Painting from the Fine Arts Collection,* Fine Arts Center, Colorado Springs, 1982.

PUBLICATIONS: *Robert Vickrey,* 13.

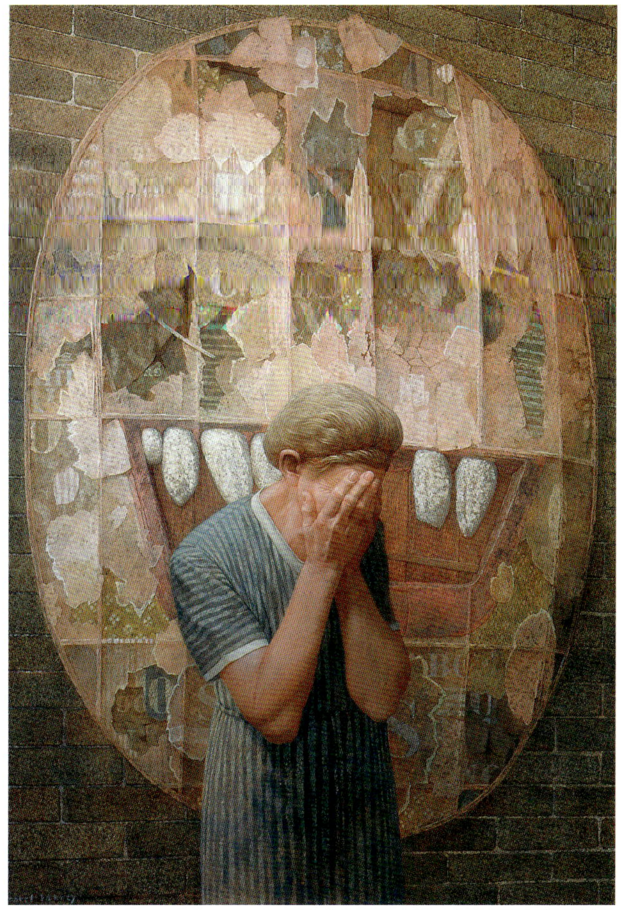

Robert Remsen Vickrey received his bachelor's degrees from Yale University and the Yale School of Fine Arts, where he studied with Louis York and Dean Kellar. He also attended the Art Students League and studied with Kenneth Hayes Miller and Reginald Marsh. In 1952 he was invited to exhibit his paintings at the Whitney Museum of American Art, and he began experimenting with filmmaking. Between 1957 and 1968 *Time* magazine commissioned him to produce more than seventy-five cover images. His family, including his four children, often became models for his paintings.

There is disquiet in much of Vickrey's work, which some have linked to surrealism, though the artist himself did not acknowledge this association. In a reference to dream imagery, he wrote,

> Most of my ideas come with an element of surprise. I never had a dream that gave me an idea for a painting, but I have painted pictures that influenced my dreams. I have seen, in some form, most of the things I have painted, although I have changed or heightened them to make them more visual.[1]

Vickrey's mastery of tempera sets him apart from other artists of his time. He first learned tempera painting as a student, although he initially hesitated to attend a course in the medium. Tempera allowed a kind of substance and detail that heightened the electric effect and emotional content of his work. William Steadman wrote, "His best tempera has an inner illumination, a textural excitement and a sureness of stroke which can only appear in tempera."[2] Of his own work the artist commented,

> I have been told that my work has strong psychological overtones, and I guess it's true. Of course, I feel that daily life has strong psychological overtones, which I simply try to portray. I feel that I exaggerate about ten percent, which is enough to cause my work to be considered occasionally bizarre.[3]

The model for *Woman Weeping* was a member of Vickrey's extended family. She had served as nanny for three generations of Vickreys, first caring for the artist's mother-in-law, then his wife, and then his children. The woman, named Chrissie, was forced to retire due to declining health.[4] The tragic nature of the woman's circumstances is mocked by a grimacing mask on the brick wall behind her, a disturbing backdrop to her expression of grief. The decaying mask contains layers of secondary images—references to the domesticity that has defined and dominated much of her life. Now as those surfaces peel away, she is left with only remnants of her past and the solidity of the brick wall, which further hems her in, suggesting that she has no options outside this confinement. *Woman Weeping* is an unsettling exploration of the realities of illness and old age. BF

HENRY NORDHAUSEN

73

b. 1901, Hoboken, New Jersey; d. 1993, Columbus, Georgia
Tying Her Ballet Slipper, 1958
Oil on canvas, 36 × 30 (91.44 × 76.2)
Signed lower right: A. Henry Nordhausen
Gift of Mrs. Benjamin Hurt Hardaway Jr. in memory of her husband 66.339

PROVENANCE: Mrs. Benjamin Hurt Hardaway Jr., Columbus, Georgia.
EXHIBITIONS: *A. Henry Nordhausen,* Capricorn Galleries, Bethesda, Mississippi, February 5–28, 1971; *Old Friends: Focus on A. Henry Nordhausen,* Columbus Museum, April 4–May 30, 1999; *Summer Potpourri.*
PUBLICATIONS: Schmeckebier, pl. 50.

August Henry Nordhausen was born to a family that immigrated to the United States in the late 1880s from the historic medieval town of Nordhausen in Lower Saxony, Germany. His parents eventually settled in the Catskill Mountains of New York, where they ran a successful boarding house for summer residents.

In the early twentieth century, when modernist theories and abstraction had become the way for many American artists, Nordhausen was one of very few painters who chose to continue in the realist tradition.[1] His early education had been interrupted by his family's need for financial assistance, but at the age of sixteen he resumed study at Stuyvesant Technical High School in New York, where he developed a major interest in art. In 1920 he won a scholarship to the New York School of Fine and Applied Arts (now Parsons School of Design), where he studied with Harry Baker, Howard Giles, Guido Rosa, and Frank Fiore. In 1922 he went to Munich to continue his education at the Royal Academy of Fine Arts, studying with the realist Hugo Freiherr von Habermann and portraitist Wilhelm Heinrich Funk. In the evenings he attended drawing classes led by Hans Hofmann.

Returning to New York in 1925, Nordhausen shared an apartment in Greenwich Village with Alexander Calder. He received favorable critical reviews and was invited to become a member of the Salmagundi Club.[2] In 1928 he received a fellowship from the Louis Comfort Tiffany Foundation and returned to Munich for one year.

Nordhausen's studio in New York was often filled with "colorful characters and bums" whom he encountered in the neighborhood and asked to serve as models.[3] In 1930 he had a major solo exhibition at the High Museum of Art in Atlanta, which included more than fifty of his paintings, watercolors, drawings, and prints. He received a Spencer Trask Foundation (Yaddo) grant in 1932 and Macdowell Colony Fellowships in 1933 and 1934.

The artist's fascination for the circus led him to travel with one for a time, making sketches of colorful performers for later paintings. He also appreciated the elegance and youthful beauty of ballet dancers. In a 1989 interview, he said, "It gives me so much pleasure to paint a ballerina. It is like painting a flower."[4] Primarily a figure painter, Nordhausen always painted from the model.[5] He said, "Nothing is more beautiful than a woman's body."[6] The young dancer depicted in the museum's painting is Durine Dieters, whose father was Dutch and whose mother was Indonesian. She was born in her mother's homeland, studied dance in the Netherlands, and eventually went to New York and joined a ballet troupe of the Metropolitan Opera Company. This painting is one of five that Nordhausen painted of Dieters.

Nordhausen maintained his studio in New York for many years, but finally established a studio in Columbus, Georgia, in 1960. While living in Georgia, he received many commissions and continued his successful career in portrait painting.[7] In 1978 he married Ethel Chandler Williams, then a member of the Columbus Museum's board of directors. Nordhausen died in 1993; he is buried in Columbus, beside his wife. EW

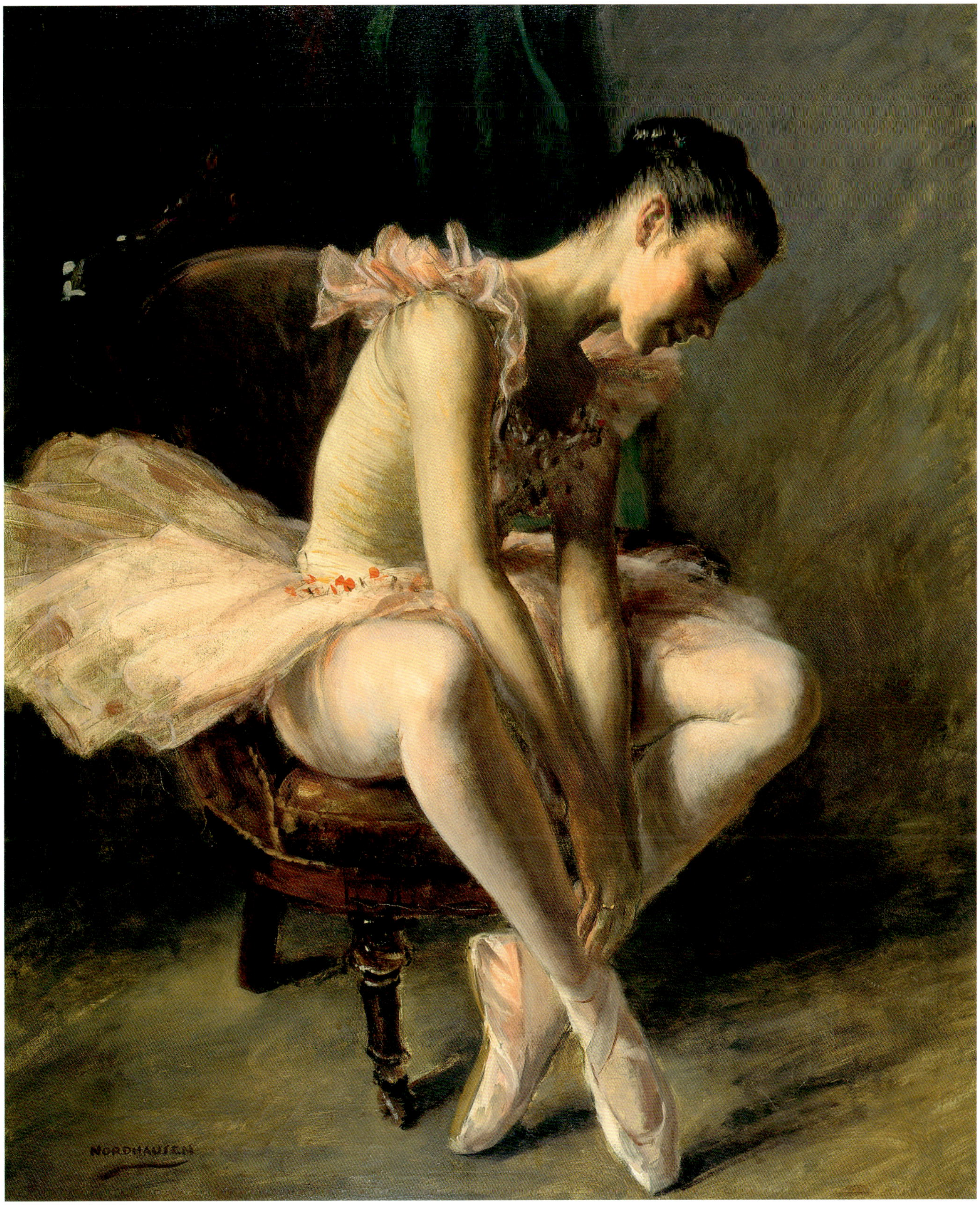
NORDHAUSEN

ROBERT MOTHERWELL

b. 1915, Aberdeen, Washington; d. 1991, Provincetown, Massachusetts

74 ***Caprice #5,*** 1962

Oil on canvas, 72 × 36 (182.88 × 91.44)

Signed and dated: R. Motherwell 62. Inscribed on verso in red marker: "CAPRICE #5 R Motherwell 1962" (on horizontal stretcher), and "R Motherwell 1962" (at lower left on canvas).

Museum purchase made possible by Shannon L. Amos; Ethelyn J. Coleman; Willie Mae Heard; JoAnne J. Hecht; Melinda M. Hinter; Aminta Flournoy Jordan; Susan C. Lawhorne; Helen J. Olnick in honor of Helen Swift Jordan; Claudia Stephenson; Sherry F. Wade; special assistance from the Ella E. Kirven Charitable Lead Trust for Acquisitions; and a gift from the Dedalus Foundation, New York. 2000.13.2

PROVENANCE: Estate of the artist; Dedalus Foundation, New York.

EXHIBITIONS: Sidney Janis Gallery, New York.

Robert Motherwell was a pioneer abstract expressionist, the first art movement to bring international attention to American artists. In 1926 his family moved to California, and the very precocious Motherwell received a scholarship to attend the Otis Art Institute in Los Angeles. He received a B.A. in philosophy from Stanford University in 1936 and headed east to attend graduate school in philosophy at Harvard University. In 1938 he went to France, where he studied French literature and devoted himself to painting. His first solo exhibition was at the Galerie Duncan in Paris.

Back in the United States in 1940, he studied art history at Columbia University, New York. In 1944 Peggy Guggenheim gave him a solo exhibition at Art of this Century Gallery in New York. In addition to painting, Motherwell wrote eloquently about modern art and taught at Hunter College. In 1953 he began to spend summers painting in Provincetown, Massachusetts. He moved to Greenwich, Connecticut, in 1970 but maintained his studio and house in Provincetown.

Along with Jackson Pollock, Mark Rothko, Clifford Still, and William Baziotes, Motherwell developed an expressionist aesthetic that reflected widespread confusion and uncertainty during the years of the Cold War. As critic Dore Ashton remarked, "An impression of emptiness [and] despair prevailed."[1] The American movement known as abstract expressionism emerged from an accumulation of European influences—including surrealism, constructivism, and expressionism—and resulted in something new. In heroic and monumental, large-scale canvases, artists such as Motherwell evoked the immediacy of the moment in bold, gestural manipulations of paint.

Caprice #5 is part of a series of experiments the artist conducted over several years, beginning with a group of small oil sketches collectively called Beside the Sea, and concluding with Lyric Suite, a monumental series of nearly six hundred ink drawings he painted on rice paper in 1965.[2] H. H. Arnason noted that in these series of works the artist had begun his exploration of a spontaneous, intuitively conceived brush gesture.[3] In *Caprice #5,* as in other paintings in the series, the artist recorded his response to seeing the ocean's waves break against the sea wall near his summer home. As the waves crashed violently against the wall, explosive gestures of water seemed to levitate before him and then fall back into the sea. Motherwell's intention was to re-create rather than illustrate what he observed. As Dore Ashton so aptly put it, "All of his paintings are oblique metaphors, and hold fast to the Mallarméan rule that things must be suggested or evoked, and not described."[4] Motherwell's painting demonstrates his awareness of the very core of modernism: that the artist is constantly rediscovering, reinventing, and re-creating the world. LR and ML

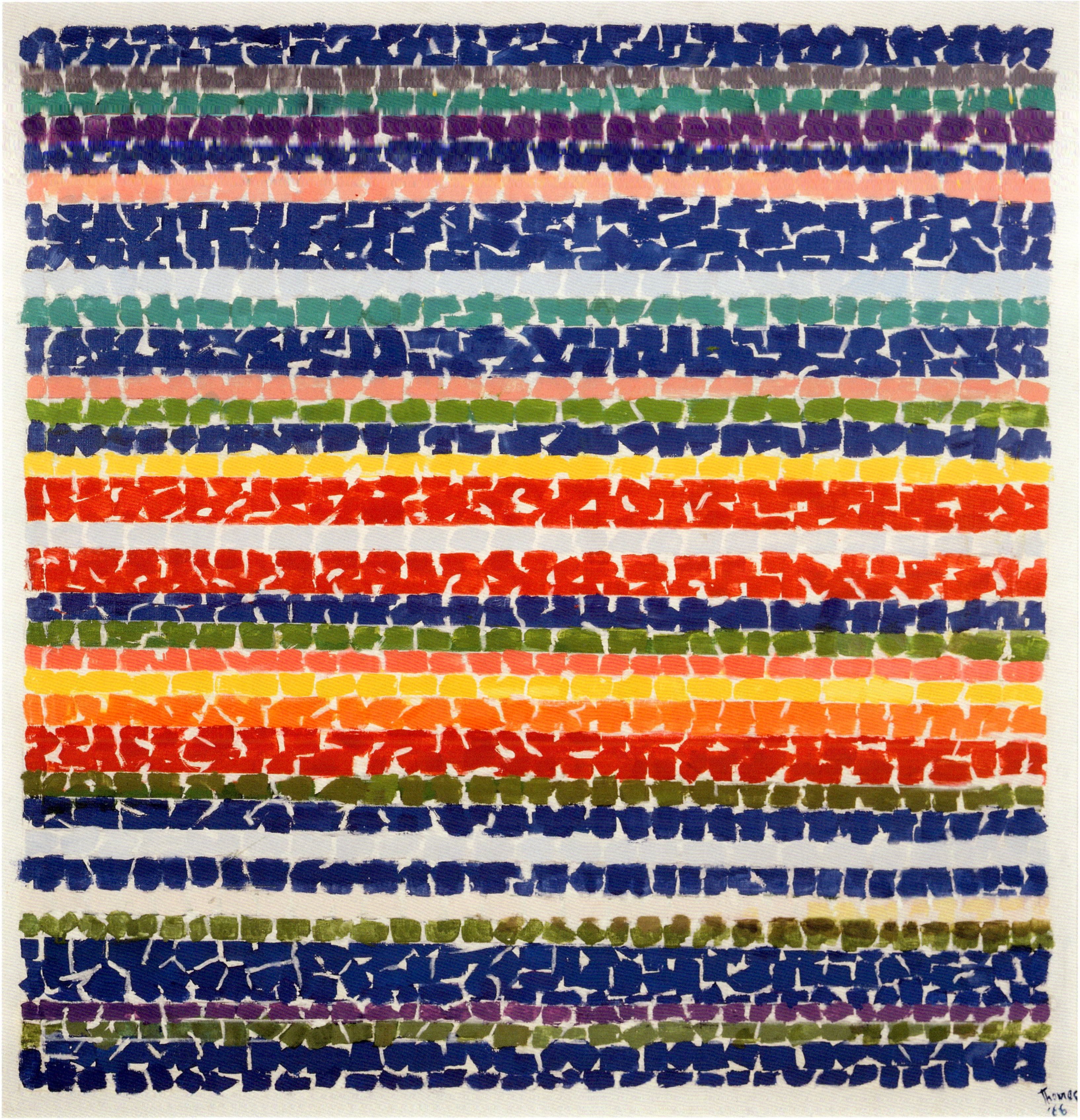

ALICE NEEL

77

b. 1900, Merion Square, Pennsylvania; d. 1984, New York City
Swedish Girls, 1968
Oil on canvas, 50 × 36 (127 × 91.44)
Signed and dated in lower left: Neel/68
Museum purchase made possible by The Ella Kirven Charitable Lead Trust for Acquisitions and partial gift of the Artist's Estate
98.21

PROVENANCE: Estate of the artist; Robert Miller Gallery, New York.
EXHIBITIONS: *Alice Neel: The Woman and Her Work,* Georgia Museum of Art at University of Georgia, Athens, September 7–October 19, 1975.
PUBLICATIONS: Neel and Nesmer, no. 51; Carr, 126, pl. 97.

While supporting herself working as a secretary, Alice Neel attended art classes at night and eventually graduated from the Philadelphia School of Design for Women. Focusing on a career was difficult because her early life seemed defined by many disruptive personal relationships. Her lovers and their circle of friends, however, became the subject matter of her early works, in which she used expressive gesture and somber colors.[1] She married a fellow artist, but they became estranged after the death of her first child. A subsequent lover destroyed more than three hundred of her works in a fit of rage.

Neel survived the 1930s by working for the Works Progress Administration. Her first solo show in 1938 featured portraits of the people she knew and admired: the liberal writers and artists living in Spanish Harlem, family and friends, and members of the New York art scene. Even in her early portraits, Neel was developing her style of direct and psychologically charged portraiture. As one of her critics discovered, "Neel seems to detect a hidden weakness in her sitters which she drags out, yelping, into the clear glare of day."[2]

About her work, Neel said, "I never followed any school. I never imitated any artist. I never did any of that. I believe what I am is a humanist. That's the way I see the world, and that is what I paint."[3] She maintained that life was the theme of her work and that her desire to paint portraits evolved from her belief that contemporary artists were doing portraits without life. For Neel, life was harsh and sometimes barbarous, and survival was difficult.[4] In her later commissioned portraits, she was able to capture the essence of the subject, including any vulnerabilities that she sensed. People reveal themselves in many ways, through posture, body language, clothing, and facial expressions. Neel seized upon those traits rather than relying on mere likeness.

Swedish Girls, a portrait of two cousins, is a wonderful example of Neel at her best. Only the older girl, Linda, age sixteen, was actually from Sweden; she was living with her cousin. Ulrika later recalled that they discussed serious social issues with Neel during the five or six sessions they posed for her. Neel's ability to engage them in interesting conversation made the process enjoyable. Ulrika also said that Neel deliberately posed the two girls to create tension, seating them awkwardly on the corner of a backless couch.[5] Despite their discomfort, they look attentively at the viewer. Their teen and preteen awkwardness is stressed by their clothing, especially the teenager's trendy mini-dress, her shoes and green tights, and her heavy make-up. In contrast, the less self-conscious younger girl is seen in clogs, knee socks, knickers, and a headband that pulls back her hair to reveal a peachy complexion. The two interact warmly with one another, the teenager grasping the arm of the younger girl, who responds by leaning toward her cousin. Neel developed this painting as a coming-of-age image. The younger girl faces the end of her childhood innocence while her older cousin matures toward adulthood. It is an intimate portrayal of two young women on the verge of physical and psychological change. They appear wary but intrigued with what lies before them. BF and ML

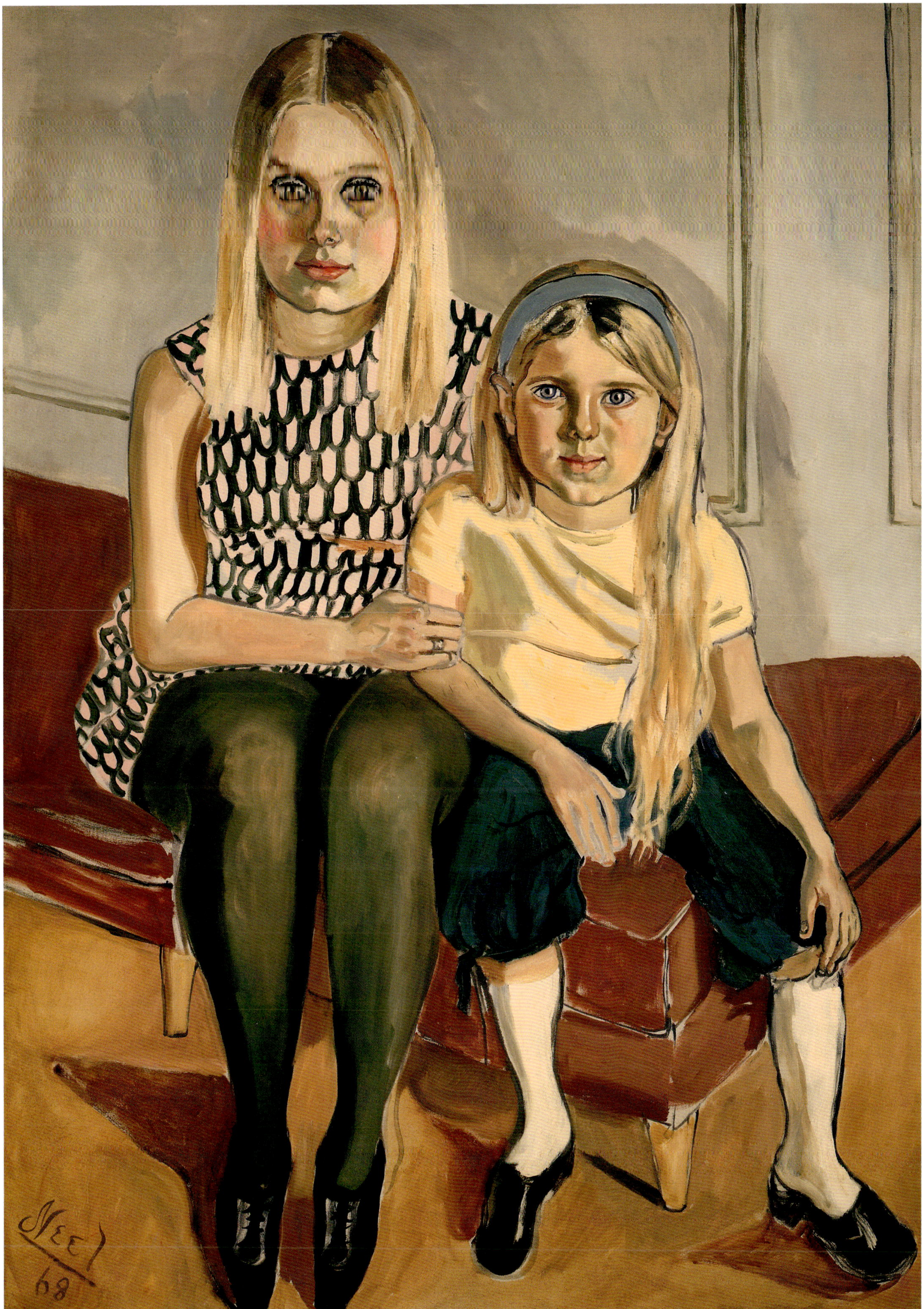
NEEL
68

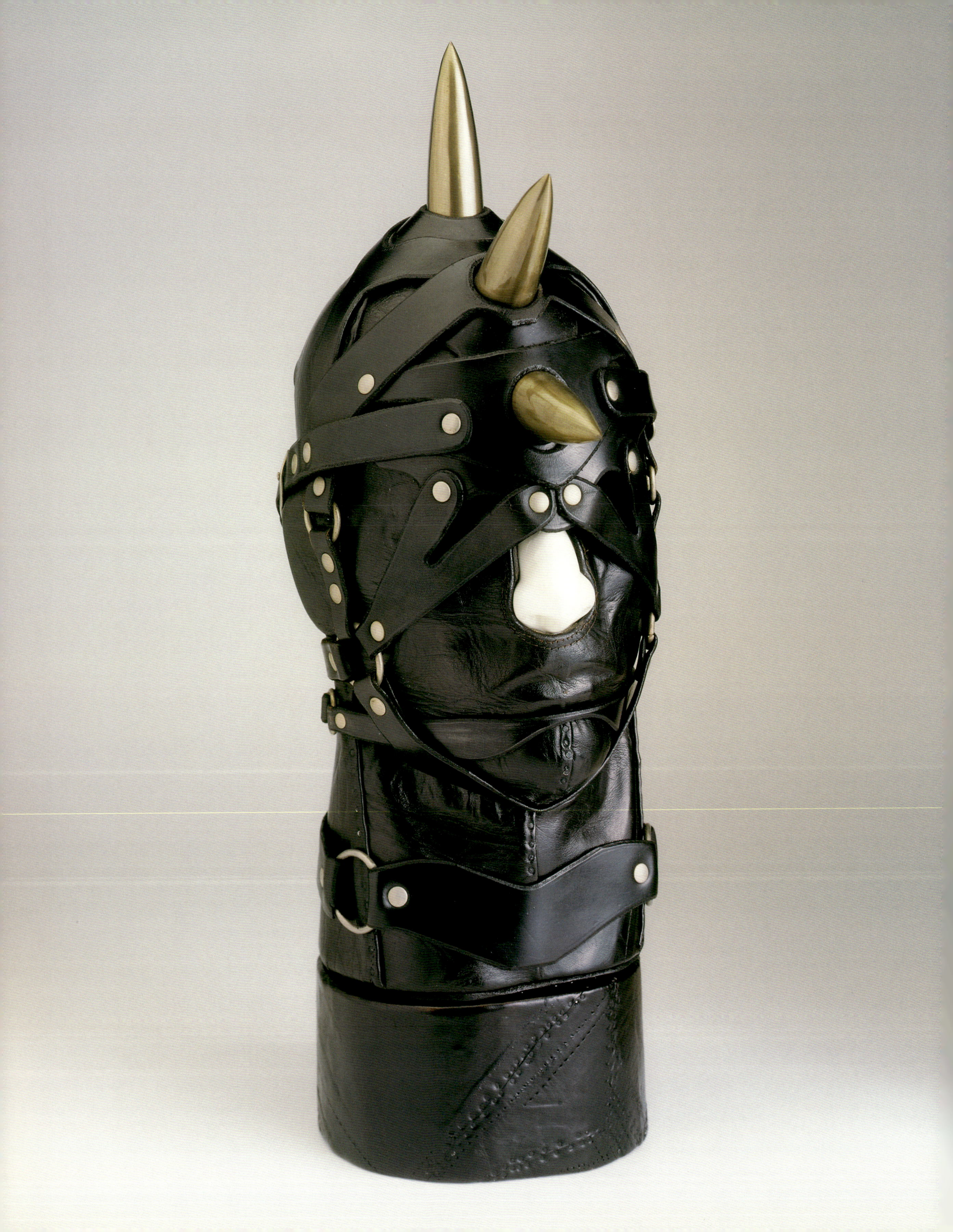

NANCY GROSSMAN

78

b. 1940, New York City

T.U.F., 1969

Wood, leather, and metal, 21 × 10 × 8 (53.34 × 25.4 × 20.32)

Signed on bottom of head: Grossman [illegible]

[illegible]

[illegible]

PROVENANCE: Michael Rosenfeld Gallery, New York.
EXHIBITIONS: *Nancy Grossman,* Hillwood Art Museum (New York), C. W. Post Campus (Brookville, New York), Sculpture Center (New York City), Exit Art Gallery (New York City), Arkansas Art Center (Little Rock), Artemisia Gallery (Chicago), Beacon Street Gallery (Chicago), September 7, 1991–July 5, 1992; *Loud Whispers,* Michael Rosenfeld Gallery, New York, November 2, 2000–January 13, 2001; *Summer Potpourri.*
PUBLICATIONS: Raven, 78, pl. 60; Sims, *Loud Whispers,* 25.

Nancy Grossman was raised on a farm in Oneonta, New York, where she lived with her extended family of eight adults and sixteen children.[1] When she reached the age of sixteen, she began working in her parents' dress factory as a "dart and gusset girl." Her skills in patterning, sewing, and piecing became very important technical aspects of her career as an artist-creator of works such as *T.U.F.*

At eighteen, Grossman entered Pratt Institute in Brooklyn, where she studied with Richard Lindner. Later, on a study grant in Europe, she visited a collection of Samurai armor in Venice. The imaginative body coverings on exhibit intrigued her, and perhaps inspired the leather-covered-head series of sculptures begun in the late sixties after a series of drawings on the subject.[2] These powerful sculptures have mystified, repelled, and fascinated audiences for more than three decades. In her progression as an artist she moved from painting to collage, then between assemblage and relief sculpture, and finally to the earliest examples of her heads, which were first exhibited at the Cordier and Ekstrom Gallery in New York in 1969.[3]

For *T.U.F.,* Grossman carved a head from wood, then sanded and lacquered it to attain a highly polished finish. Then, as if to shroud its exquisiteness or perhaps shield its vulnerability, she meticulously covered the carving in a stitched, harnessed, riveted, and metal-spiked leather covering. With the exception of the bare nose, the head is not seen in the final work. Other heads and torsos from this period have leather coverings adorned with horns, chains, zippers, spikes, or other objects with loaded psychological and sexual meaning.

Her life-size heads bound in leather are provocative objects that at first suggest a violent sado-masochistic suppression and censorship in their forceful binding and resultant obliteration of individual identity. It is only after further consideration that the ideas of armament and defense also come to mind. As sado-masochistic objects, they are both shocking and intriguing references to a subculture of pain and pleasure with which most of Grossman's audience is only fleetingly familiar. Such themes in art may compel viewers to confront notions of acceptable behavior and ultimately to question all human relationships in terms of authority and powerlessness, vulnerability and security, aggression and self-preservation. Grossman, it seems, is engaged in the pursuit of her own inner-directed motif, her own concept of the human condition.[4]

The artist has pointed out that the abuse and destruction people inflict on one another through words and ideas are often the most wounding kind of violence. Armored with steel spikes, *T.U.F.* suggests a certain inward helplessness that begs for a defensive posture. Perhaps *T.U.F.* is a warning that even the most secure and well-guarded person can be susceptible to exploitation and attack. This extremely evocative work, according to the artist, is a metaphor for man's inhumanity toward man.[5]

Grossman taught sculpture at the Boston Fine Arts School in 1985, and drawing at Cooper Union, New York City, in 1989. She was the recipient of a Guggenheim Foundation Fellowship in 1965, the American Academy and Institute of Arts and Letters award in 1985, and a National Endowment for the Arts sculpture award in 1991. A series of illnesses and accidents since 1995 have resulted in physical limitations that have made it nearly impossible for her to continue to carve. Undaunted, she has returned to collage and assemblage in the neo-Dada spirit that had inspired her at the beginning of her successful career.[6] ML

ROGER BROWN

79 b. 1941, Hamilton, Alabama; d. 1997, Chicago
Trailer Park, Truck Stop, 1971
Oil on canvas, 48 × 59¼ (121.92 × 150.5)
Signed and dated on verso, upper left: Roger Brown 1971
Museum purchase made possible by the Edward Swift Shorter Bequest Fund 93.5

PROVENANCE: Collection of the artist; Phyllis Kind Gallery, Chicago; Sotheby's Auction House, New York.
PUBLICATIONS: Winn, et al., 193.

Roger Brown, who grew up in Opelika, Alabama, was most closely associated with Chicago art of the 1960s and 1970s. Had he not discovered the arts and moved to Chicago, he might have pursued a future in the ministry or the family business, so strong was his traditional southern upbringing. He studied at the American Academy of Design and the School of the Art Institute of Chicago, receiving bachelor's and master's degrees from the latter. As a student, he benefited from the instruction of Ray Yoshida and explored the wonders of the Art Institute's permanent collection. He became interested in the work of self-taught artists and the folk traditions of the South, in particular, ceramic vessels from Alabama and Georgia modeled with humorous faces. By the end of his life, he had acquired an enormous collection of artworks and artifacts, ranging from outsider and folk art to countless examples of popular culture.

Brown was a proponent of the art movement known as Chicago imagism. As he explained it,

> Chicago has not exactly taken over as the nation's art capital, but it was the birthplace in the mid-1960s of what I feel has become a significant movement in recent art history. That movement is concerned with the making of art as an individual and very personal endeavor. . . . Inspiration is taken from the raw, direct art of the naïve or folk artist whose work is unencumbered with pretentions [*sic*] to "high art." . . . It might be appropriate to describe this new and uniquely American movement as a loose association of individual artists who briefly came together in group shows, exhibiting their autonomy from all previous artistic traditions, and even from each other.[1]

Brown emphasized the individuality of artists associated with the group, avoiding any attempt to classify them as followers of a certain style or directive. The group was in fact quite diverse.[2] Brown's painting style is distinctive, with its flat patterns and simple outlined forms. His subjects and themes were often aggressive criticisms of contemporary politics, religion, and art. "My work is really about wherever I am, what I'm involved in, whatever I'm experiencing. . . . It's involved with Chicago. . . . Sometimes it goes back and deals with things from my own personal background, from my own family history." More specifically, his deep-set southern ties remained relevant throughout his art: "What I feel is influential, being a southerner, in my work, is just the tendency toward being interested in narrative. . . . I don't feel narrative is something that has to be left out of painting."[3] In a 1990 letter, Brown wrote, "For me art is not about repeating historical mannerisms, it is about inventing a new language of my own which can communicate to people my perception of my own time."[4]

In *Trailer Park, Truck Stop,* Brown includes a suggested narrative but avoids specific detail, leaving the story open-ended. The setting—a trailer park and truck stop—is so generalized that it can be anywhere in the United States. Street lights and the yellow glow of lights in trailers and parked trucks signal the approach of night, as silhouetted figures run, wave, converse, and water the lawn. Their actions are quite ordinary, but these frozen, shadowy figures contribute a sense of foreboding akin to the tone of film noire. A calculated use of light and color—somber grays and heavy tones—set a dark mood, as an eerie yellow band lights up the horizon and day passes into night.[5]

In a 1978 interview, Brown discussed his work within the context of simplification, saying, "There has to be complexity in a painting, but to make things instantly readable is very important."[6] *Trailer Park, Truck Stop* is both complex and simple. The composition is divided into wide horizontal bands of flat color and space, and simple forms—trailers, trucks, and shrubs—are repeated, perhaps to convey the banality of American suburbia or the everyday sameness of a life without roots. To delineate depth, the artist placed objects in the background on a higher plane than those in the foreground, a concept that often appears in folk art to indicate distance. Like the pop artists, Brown has elevated the commonplace to high art with all its implicit complexities. BF

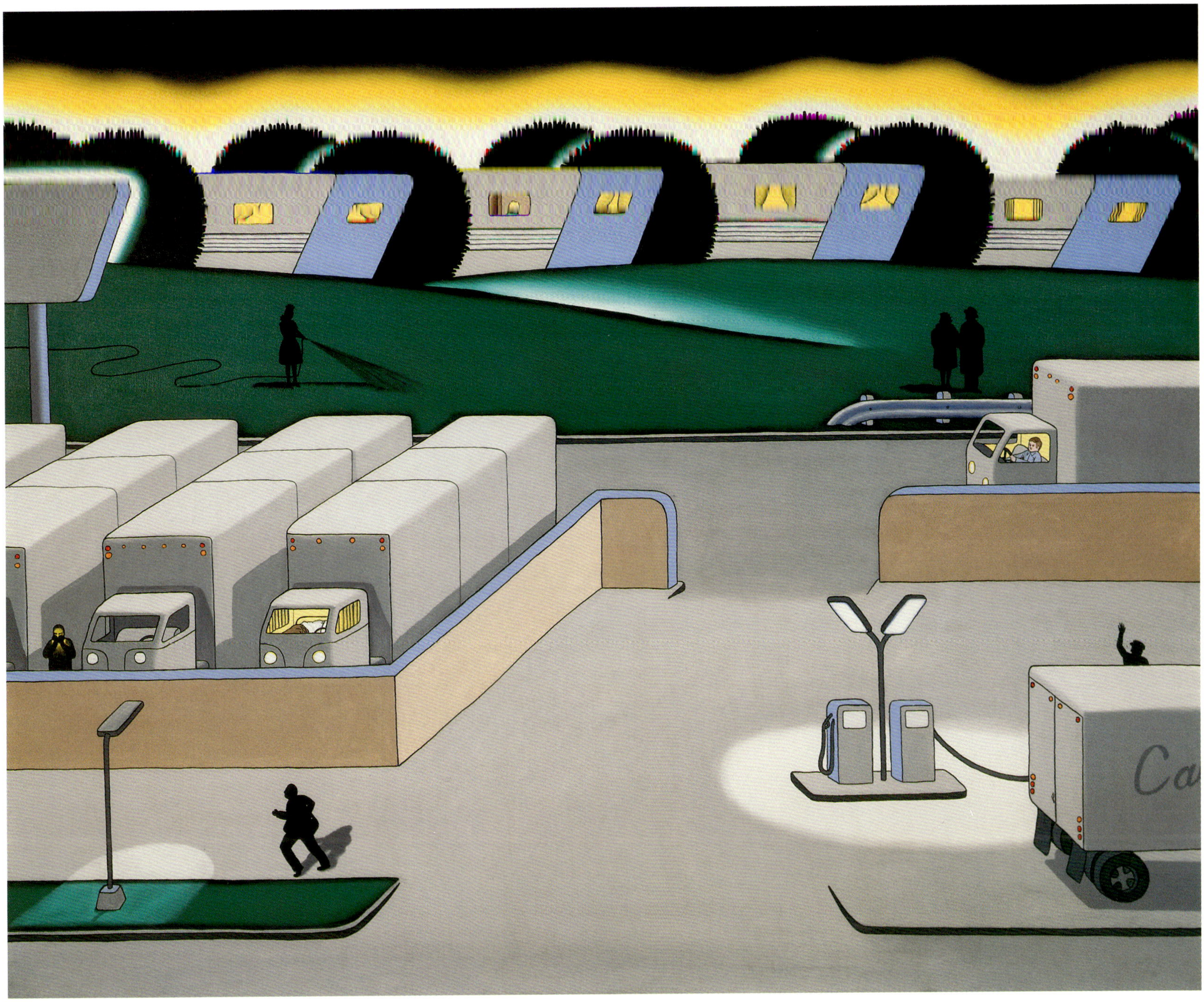

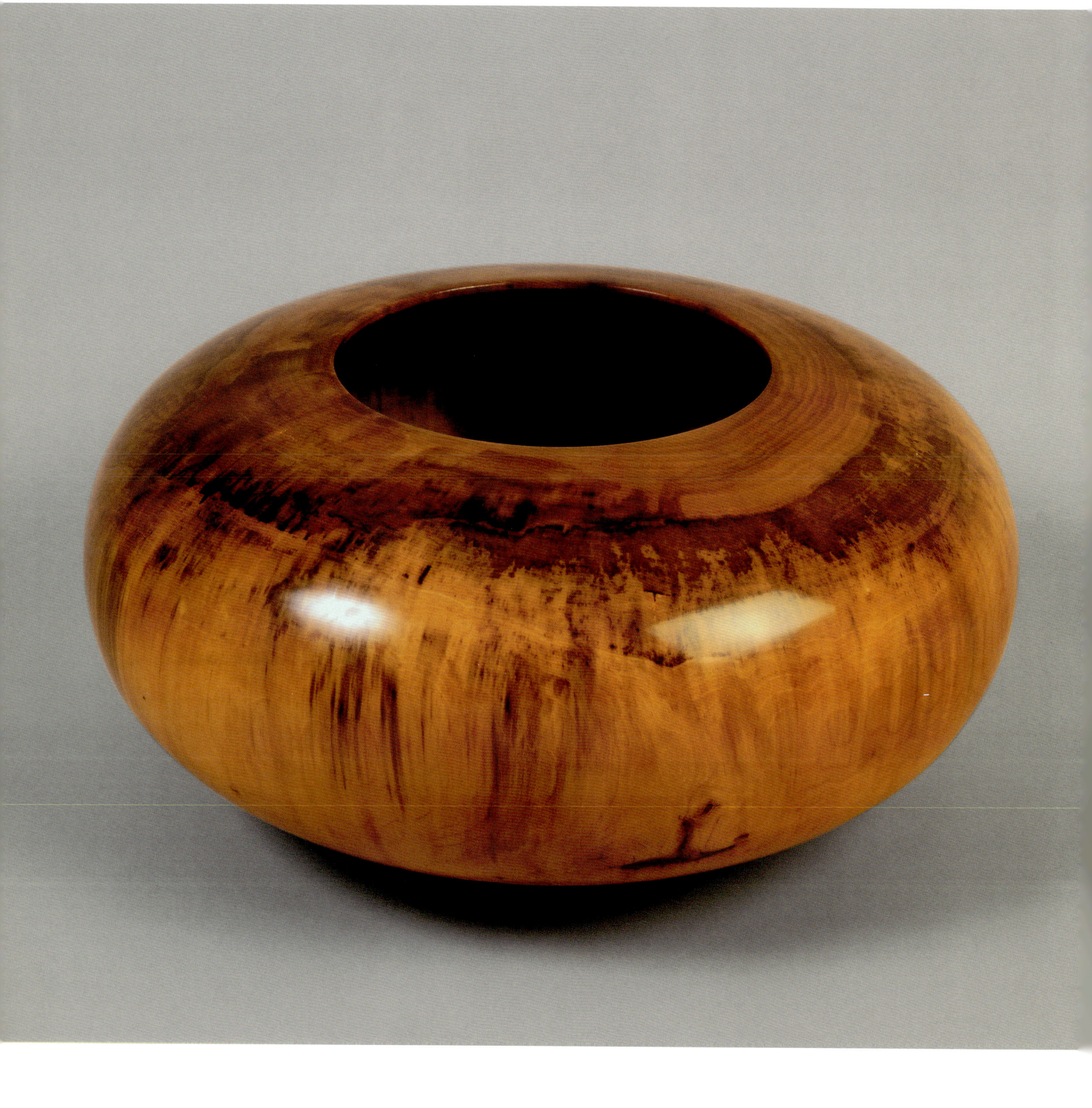

EDWARD MOULTHROP

80 b. 1916, Rochester, New York

Bowl, 1977

Figured tulipwood, H. 10, [illegible]

Inscribed on bottom: M/ Moulthrop/Figured Tulipwood/105990-U

Museum purchase 77.39

PROVENANCE: Collection of the artist; [illegible] Shop, Atlanta

EXHIBITIONS: *Vessels: Contemporary and Traditional Decorative Arts from the Permanent Collection,* Columbus Museum, September 15, 1993–May 1995; *Towards a New Century.*

Edward Moulthrop grew up in Cleveland, Ohio. He received a bachelor's degree in architecture from Western Reserve (now Case Western Reserve) University in 1939 and a master's degree in architecture from Princeton in 1941. He taught at Georgia Institute of Technology until 1949, when he left teaching and joined Robert and Company Associate Architects and Engineers in Atlanta as chief designer. Moulthrop designed such well-known structures as the Atlanta Civic Center and the Hartsfield Atlanta International Airport.[1]

Since childhood, when he began whittling, Moulthrop had been attracted to working with wood. In his teens, he bought a small lathe with money he earned from delivering newspapers and started to turn wood. In the 1960s he began to make large bowls, and in 1962 he won an award for a walnut bowl at the Atlanta Arts Festival. He resigned from the architectural firm in 1974 to focus on woodturning full-time. He has since become what many consider one of the finest woodturners in the country.

Moulthrop is especially skilled at shaping a block of wood as it revolves rapidly on a lathe. During his active career, he worked with large equipment that he designed and built himself. With this machinery, he could turn a 1,600-pound block into an 80-pound bowl. His rare woods are from the forests of Georgia, South Carolina, and Florida. Before forming a block of wood, he would try to predict how the natural colors and unseen inner patterns of grain would affect the finished piece. First, he cut the block into a rough shape to expose the grain, then he soaked it in polyethylene glycol for four to six months to keep the surface from shrinking, cracking, or splitting in the forming process. Next, he turned the rough-shaped block into its final form on the lathe, and afterward sanded and polished it to a high luster.

Moulthrop prefers simple shapes so that the inherent colors and patterns of the wood become the defining characteristics of the piece. He has said, "I really don't like to do designs or creations that are complicated or esoteric. . . . I like to do things where the aesthetic impact is direct, as in a nonobjective painting, sunsets, or instrumental music."[2]

The Columbus Museum's tulipwood bowl is an ellipsoid shape, with varied hues, from light honey to dark brown. The opening of the bowl, which is surrounded by the concentric growth rings of the tree from which it is made, is relatively small compared to the width of the piece. Here, as in other works, Moulthrop's artistry is in the exquisite forms he designs to celebrate the hidden beauty of natural wood. KMZ

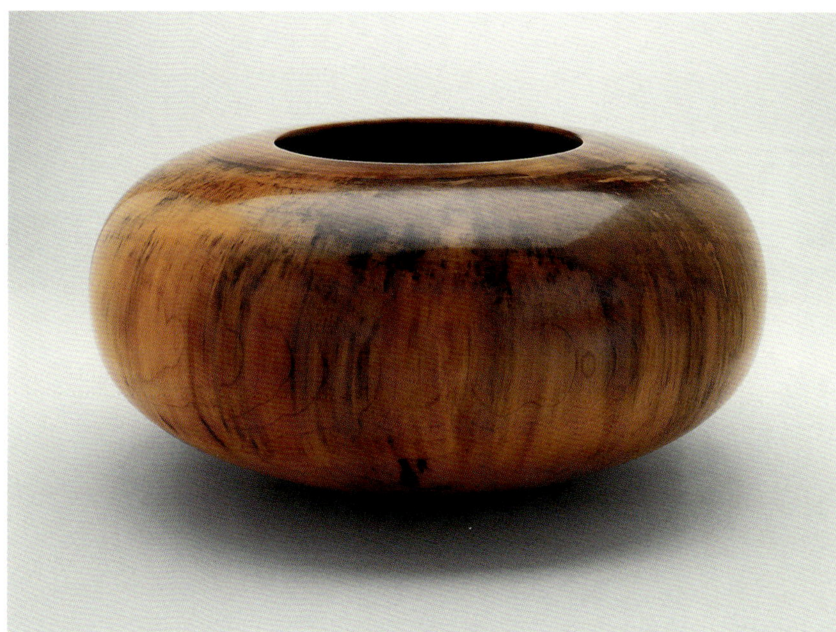

LEONARD BASKIN

b. 1922, New Brunswick, New Jersey; d. 2000, Northampton, Massachusetts

81 ***Sibyl with Crows,*** 1980

Cast bronze (edition of three), 33 × 21½ × 18 (79.2 × 51.6 × 45.76)

Signed and dated on base at rear right: L. B. 1980. Marked: Kennedy Galleries, Inc. 1/3. Foundry mark: BEDI-MAKKY NY

Museum purchase made possible by the Edward Swift Shorter Bequest Fund 93.2

PROVENANCE: Kennedy Galleries, New York.
PUBLICATIONS: Winn, et al., 1995.

Leonard Baskin began his study of sculpture with Maurice Glickman at the Educational Alliance in New York when he was fifteen years old.[1] He attended Yale University from 1941 to 1943, and later graduated from the New School for Social Research. After living and working in Florence and Paris for a few years, he returned to the United States and taught printmaking and sculpture at Smith College. He remained on the Smith faculty for twenty-one years, during which time he also founded Gehenna Press and published more than one hundred illustrated books on the fine arts. He received numerous honors, among them the Jewish Cultural Achievement Award, the Gold Medal of the National Academy of Arts and Letters, and a Guggenheim Fellowship.

His fine reputation as a printmaker notwithstanding, Baskin's principal focus throughout his life was sculpture. A large portion of his work is figurative and includes wood and stone carving and clay modeling in preparation for bronze casting. The iconic, monolithic imagery of ancient Egypt and Sumeria influenced the formal aspects of his work. He questioned the limitations of naturalism, which he argued was concerned only with physical truths, and he avoided abstraction, which he saw as abandoning the figure. Instead, he invented forms and figures that deal with the dichotomy of man's imperfections and the idea that man is made in God's image. He also used avian or animal images, such as the raven and dog, to illustrate other human traits and frailties.

Baskin, the son of a rabbi, drew much of his inspiration from Judaic imagery, the Bible, ancient Greek philosophers, and modern Western poetry. A recurring image in his art is that of the sibyl, or prophetess, of Greek mythology, as exemplified by the museum's bronze.

Sibyl with Crows refers to the ancient myth of a woman endowed with the gift of prophecy, who often is asked to intercede with the gods on behalf of mortals. Here the bald sibyl is clothed in a loosely draped garment. She sits astride a plinth, with a larger-than-life crow standing between her legs and a fledgling at her right foot. She embraces the powerful bird, which has a complex iconography symbolizing such diverse ideas as truth, death, and solitude. In response, the bird leans back into her grasp to show an equal affinity. Baskin noted that crows have often been understood as bad omens and therefore ostracized and avoided. As a Jew, he understood what it was to feel marginalized and treated as an outsider, and perhaps he identified with the crow.[2] An outcast can find acceptance and understanding only from a source with an exceptional ability to see beyond the surface of things to the truth. In that sense, the crow and the sibyl are kindred souls.

Baskin first modeled the figure in plaster (now lost or destroyed), using an aggressive and physical technique that lends a sense of urgency to the finished sculpture. He cast the sculpture at Bedi-Makky Foundry in Brooklyn, which used the French sand-casting method he preferred.[3] Its enigmatic and mysterious qualities are enhanced by the dark patina of the bronze. KMZ

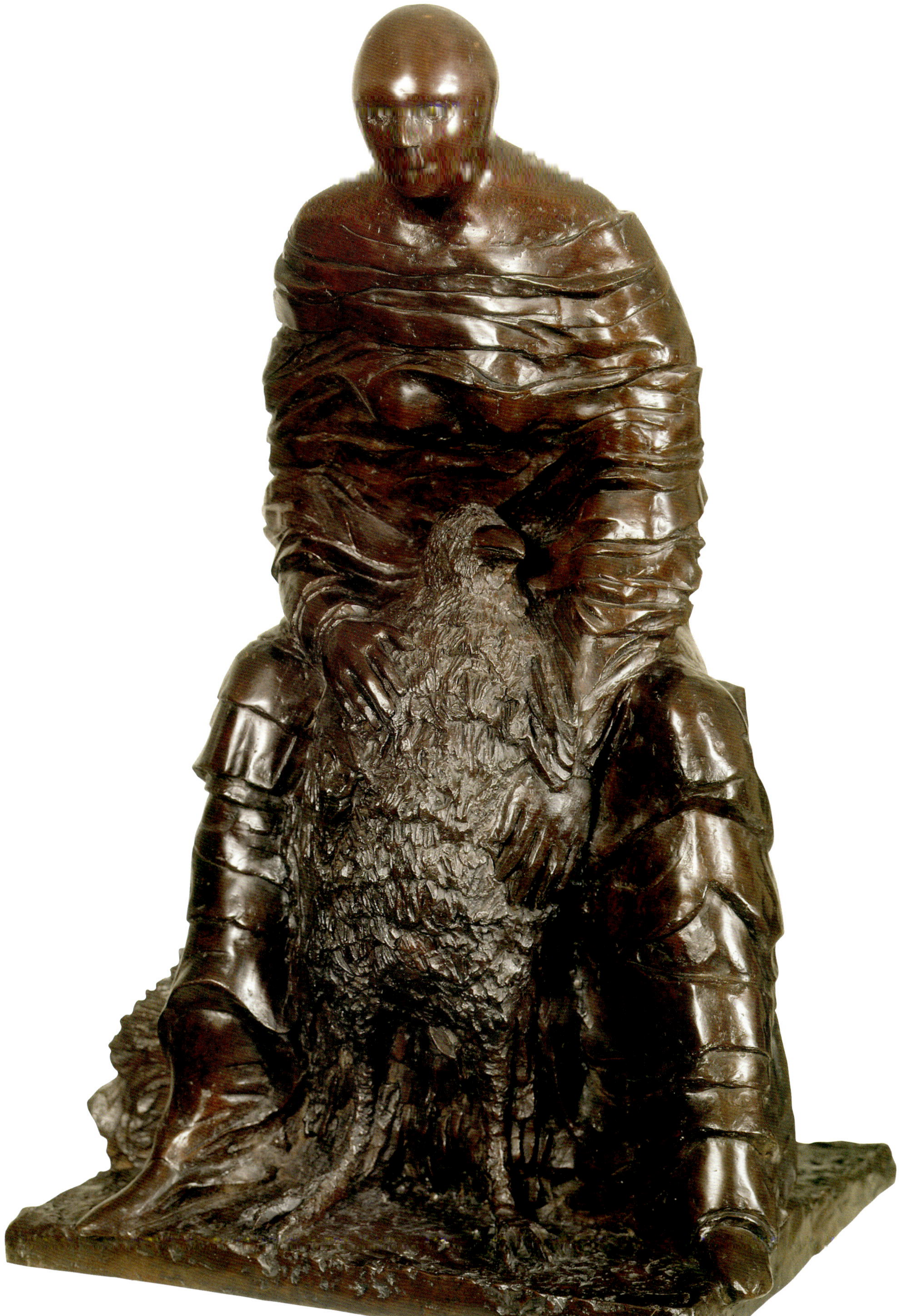

JOYCE TREIMAN

82

b. 1922, Evanston, Illinois; d. 1991, Los Angeles
The Torso, The Ram, Self-Portrait with Skull, The Smoker No. 21 (Mortality series), 1983
Oil on canvas, each 70 × 24 (177.8 × 60.96)
Signed either lower left or lower right: Treiman
Museum purchase made possible by Norman S. Rothschild in honor of his parents, Aleen and Irwin B. Rothschild 98.49.1–4

PROVENANCE: Estate of the artist; Schmidt-Bingham Gallery, New York.
EXHIBITIONS: *Painting in a Lonely Arena: Joyce Treiman and the Old Masters,* National Museum of Women in the Arts, Washington, D.C., December 14, 1998–July 5, 1999.
PUBLICATIONS: Duncan and Wolff, 118–19, pls. 70–73.

Joyce Wahl Treiman has said that her frequent visits to the Art Institute of Chicago as a young girl were influential in shaping her development as an artist. She attended Iowa State University, where she studied painting and drawing with Philip Guston, and graduated in 1943.[1] Returning to Chicago, she worked as a commercial artist, but after successful exhibitions at the Art Institute of Chicago and in New York, she devoted herself full-time to painting. In 1960 Treiman and her husband moved to Pacific Palisades, California. Over the next three decades, she attracted a loyal group of collectors and devoted students. In 1990 she was elected a member of the National Academy of Design.

Joyce Treiman adhered to the figurative tradition of the old masters, developing a technical virtuosity and thematic approach that resulted in a body of autobiographical work, which considered the transient nature of life, the wry comedy of human existence, the creative process, and what she considers to be her rightful place in art history. Treiman consistently worked in what she termed the lonely arena of figurative painting. Reflecting her knowledge and admiration of the artistic past, Treiman's paintings often include her self-portrait in conjunction with portraits of artists she admired, such as Giambattista Tiepolo, Thomas Eakins, and Claude Monet.

Confronted with physical illness, Treiman shifted her focus from paintings submerged in art history to themes of mortality laced with her own dry humor. She had decided to make a series of "paintings that nobody [would] want . . . in terms of making them so personal . . . that [they] couldn't be turned into wallpaper."[2] Theodore Wolff stated that nothing in her previous work had even hinted at the anger and brooding imagery that suddenly appeared.[3] Of these four canvases, Wolff describes *The Torso* as the best example of that pivotal year.[4] Collectively known as the Mortality series, the four columnar-shaped canvases are complete as separate images but are equally effective when seen as a group. While extremely personal images, these paintings also present a modern-day *vanitas,* replete with symbols of death such as a candle and skulls. Treiman's self-portrait is included in each canvas, floating above the image as a specter or serving as the central focus.[5] The intense color and heavy impasto add to the emotional and expressive power of these pieces. The physical surfaces of the paintings suggest a kind of battlefield where the artist metaphorically confronted her demons. Treiman was diagnosed with lung cancer later in 1983 after these four paintings were completed. Her dramatic change of style and theme suggests that she had a premonition of her own mortality, and in choosing to explore this question produced these very vivid and meaningful images. Theodore Wolff noted that these and other paintings produced in 1983 were the best of her career.[6] Joyce Treiman died in 1991 of a heart attack. She was sixty-nine years old. CTB

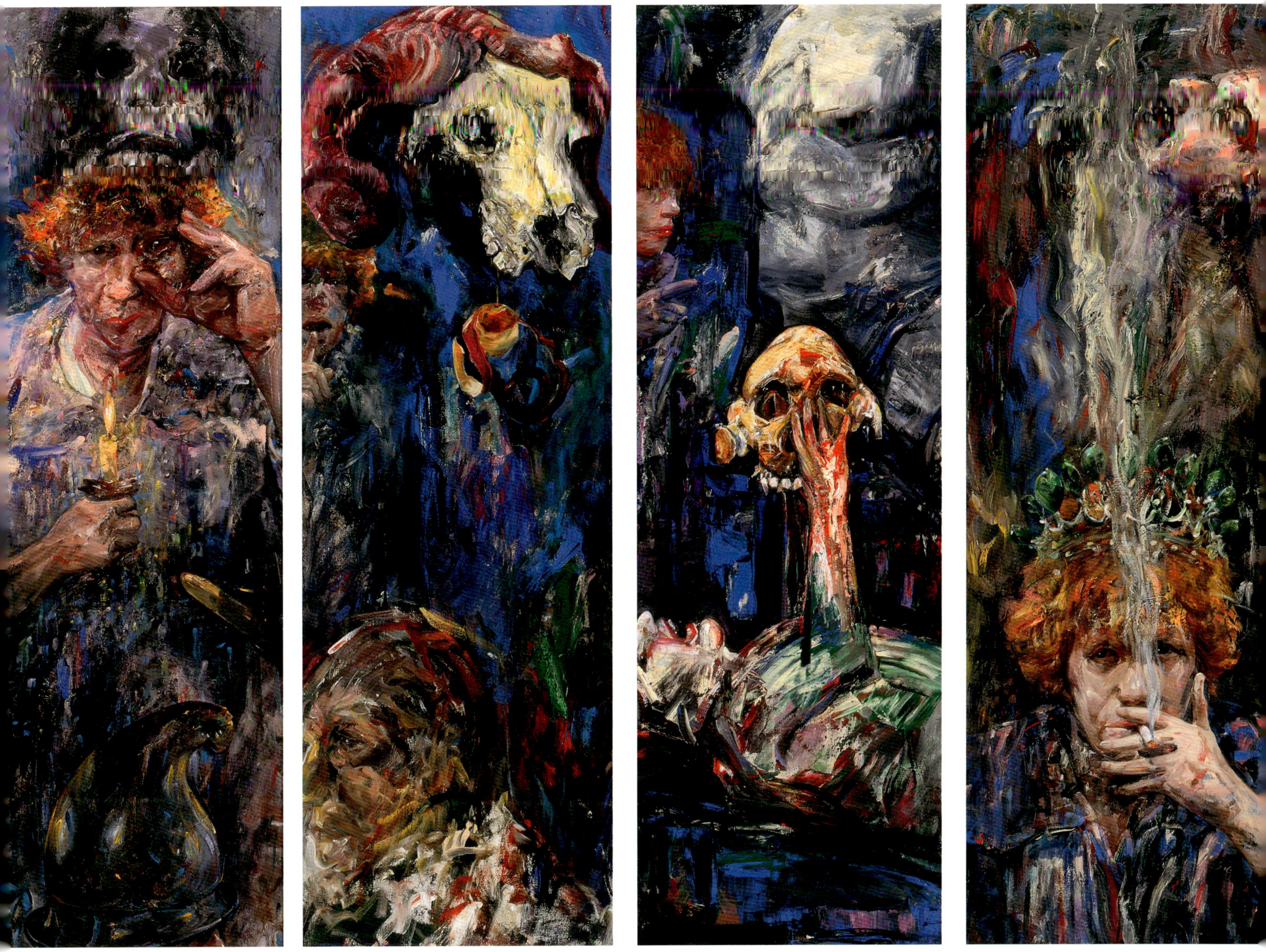

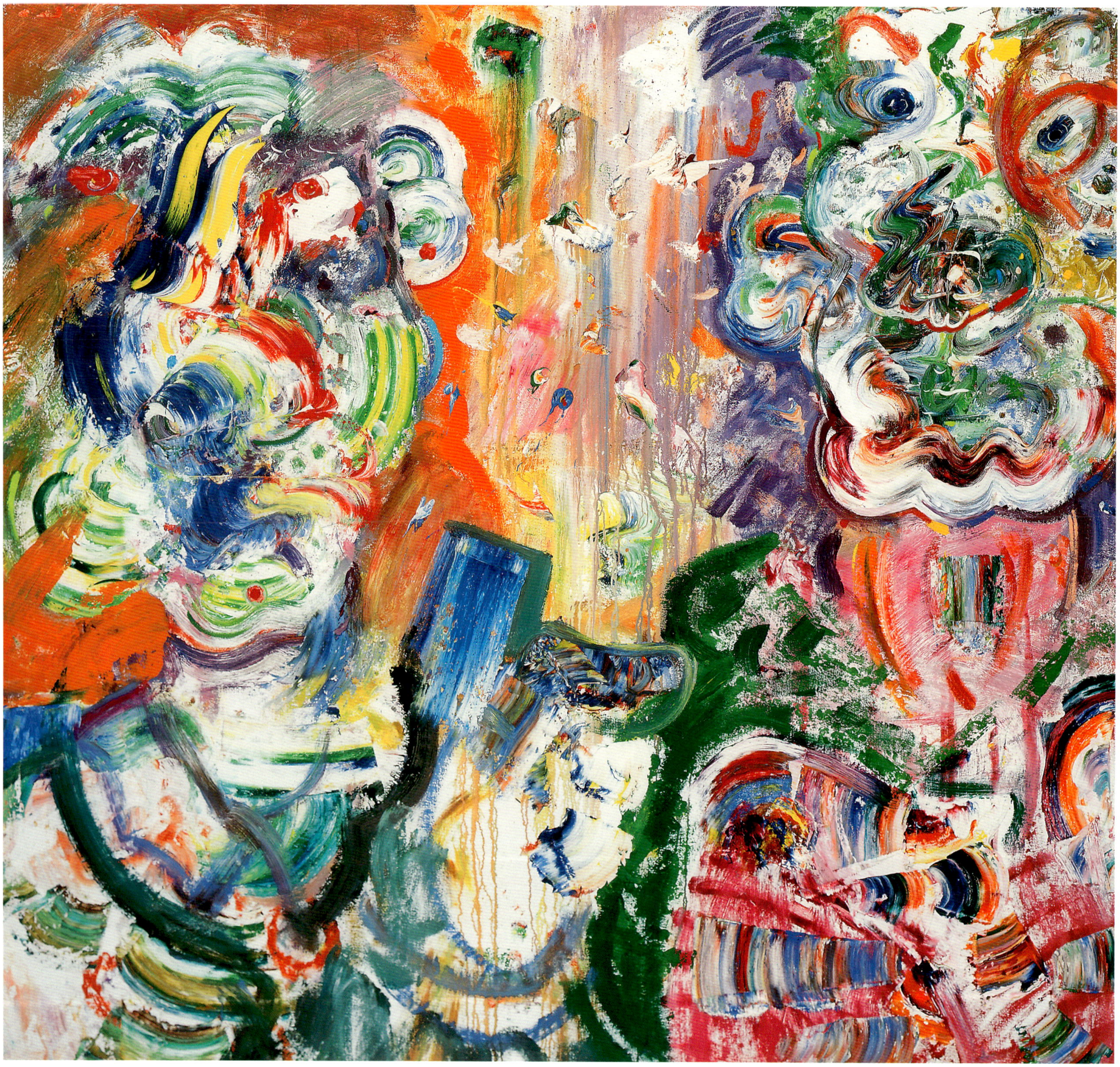

ROBERT BEAUCHAMP

83 b. 1923, Denver; d. 1995, New York City

34–83, 1983

Oil on canvas, 71¼ × 77 (180.[illegible] × 194.[illegible])

Signed in pencil on back of canvas: 34–83 Robert Beauchamp

Gift to the Museum from the Fay Gold Gallery, Atlanta, Georgia

2001.1

PROVENANCE: Max Schmallinger, London; Fay Gold Gallery, Atlanta.

Robert Beauchamp's early art education began when he won a scholarship to the Colorado Springs Fine Arts Center, where he studied with Boardman Robinson. After serving in the navy during World War II, he returned to complete his studies at the Colorado Springs Fine Arts Center. In 1947 Beauchamp went on to study painting and sculpture at the Cranbrook Art Academy in Michigan.

Intrigued by a show of abstract expressionist art, Beauchamp became a student of Hans Hofmann and eventually settled in New York. There he met other abstract expressionist painters who gathered in the early 1950s at the famed Cedar Bar and the Club to engage in discussions on art and to celebrate their camaraderie as avant-garde artists, writers, and critics of the time. He also exhibited regularly with members of the New York school of painters.

Hofmann instilled in Beauchamp the concept that painting is a process of revelation through the expressive manipulation of color on a canvas. For Beauchamp, this painting technique provided the means to explore emotional and psychological emancipation. In this manner, he was able to develop his own, idiosyncratic approach to abstract expressionism, in which he used loose brushwork to describe human and animal forms in strange and vibrant painterly manifestations. Of his teacher, Beauchamp noted, "Hofmann helped me see that through purely plastic means, pictorial elements could transform themselves into a spiritual experience. Sounds grand, and so it is, but it's what makes a masterpiece. I studied with Hofmann for another three years—an intense schooling."[1]

In *34–83* Beauchamp explored form and color to produce a dreamlike reality. He applied his paint in layers of thick impasto—often squeezed straight from the tube—lending the work an element of sculptural relief. The presence of figures is unmistakable. In 1984, a year after this work was produced, Beauchamp wrote, "The Abstract Expressionist way of painting has given me a kind of freedom and flexibility—such as throwing colors on a canvas and making them into a butterfly, or a horse, or leaving it a color that articulates the space—keeping the possibilities open ended."[2] The figures inhabiting the densely painted surface are possibly references to himself and his brother, a victim of polio, confined to a wheelchair. This familial relationship preoccupied Beauchamp for nearly ten years. During that time he also served three years (1980–83) as the Lamar Dodd Chair of the art department at the University of Georgia.[3] LR

RICHARD ANUSZKIEWICZ

84 b. 1930, Erie, Pennsylvania
Temple of Electric Turquoise, 1984
Acrylic on canvas, 60 × 48 (152.4 × 121.92)
Signed on reverse: Anuszkiewicz
Museum purchase made possible by the Endowment Fund in Honor of D. A. Turner and the Art Acquisition and Restoration Fund 85.7

PROVENANCE: Graham Modern Gallery, New York.
PUBLICATIONS: Winn, et al., 187.

American painter, printmaker, and sculptor Richard Joseph Anuszkiewicz credits his high school teacher for introducing him to the Ostwald system of complementary colors and the spectrum prism and setting the course for his artistic career.[1] While attending the Cleveland Institute of Art from 1948 until 1953 on scholarship, Anuszkiewicz began to include elements of design and abstraction in works whose subjects were rooted in American scene painting. In 1953 he was awarded a Pulitzer scholarship, which allowed him to study briefly at the National Academy of Design. His particular interests soon brought him under the tutelage of Josef Albers at the Yale University School of Art and Architecture, where he received a master's degree in 1955. While a student at Yale, he made his earliest studies that clearly revealed his future interests in color and line. He also became interested in the psychology of perception, developing his own theories on how the eye organizes visual material according to psychological laws.[2]

In 1957 he moved to New York, where he worked as a conservator at the Metropolitan Museum of Art and later as a silver designer for Tiffany and Company. During this period, he began to produce abstract paintings, using repetition of either organic or geometric forms. In the early 1960s these led to asymmetrical geometric compositions, and later to more rigidly structured arrangements.

Anuszkiewicz's work was part of a group show held at the Contemporaries Gallery in New York in 1960. The Museum of Modern Art purchased one of his op art paintings from this show and in 1963 invited him to participate in an exhibition. The Whitney Museum of American Art also exhibited his work at this time, and *Time* magazine featured him in a complimentary article that resulted in the sale of seventeen paintings in one month.

In 1965 the Sidney Janis Gallery gave the artist his first solo show. That same year, having become a noted leader of the op art movement, he participated in the landmark exhibition *The Responsive Eye* at the Museum of Modern Art. A pioneer in this style of nonrepresentational art, Anuszkiewicz applied pigments directly to the canvas, not blending them on his palette beforehand but intending them to mix optically, in the viewer's eye. The artist's intense colors seen under warm light result in visually vibrant compositions, which create the effect of an afterimage.[3] The strong internal structure of each work is the result of much trial and error. In his later works, he remains faithful to the approach he established in the 1960s while developing increasingly sophisticated investigations of spatial sensation using intense color modulations and geometry.

Temple of Electric Turquoise exemplifies the artist's ability to create these optical illusions. On a trip to Egypt, Anuszkiewicz noted how the architectural forms appeared to vibrate in the strong noonday light of the Valley of the Kings.[4] He tried to recreate that experience in this painting using contrasting colors and radiating lines. The result is the illusion of projecting and receding tunnels of color that shimmer and vibrate before the viewer, contradicting the idea of a flat two-dimensional surface. BW and CTB

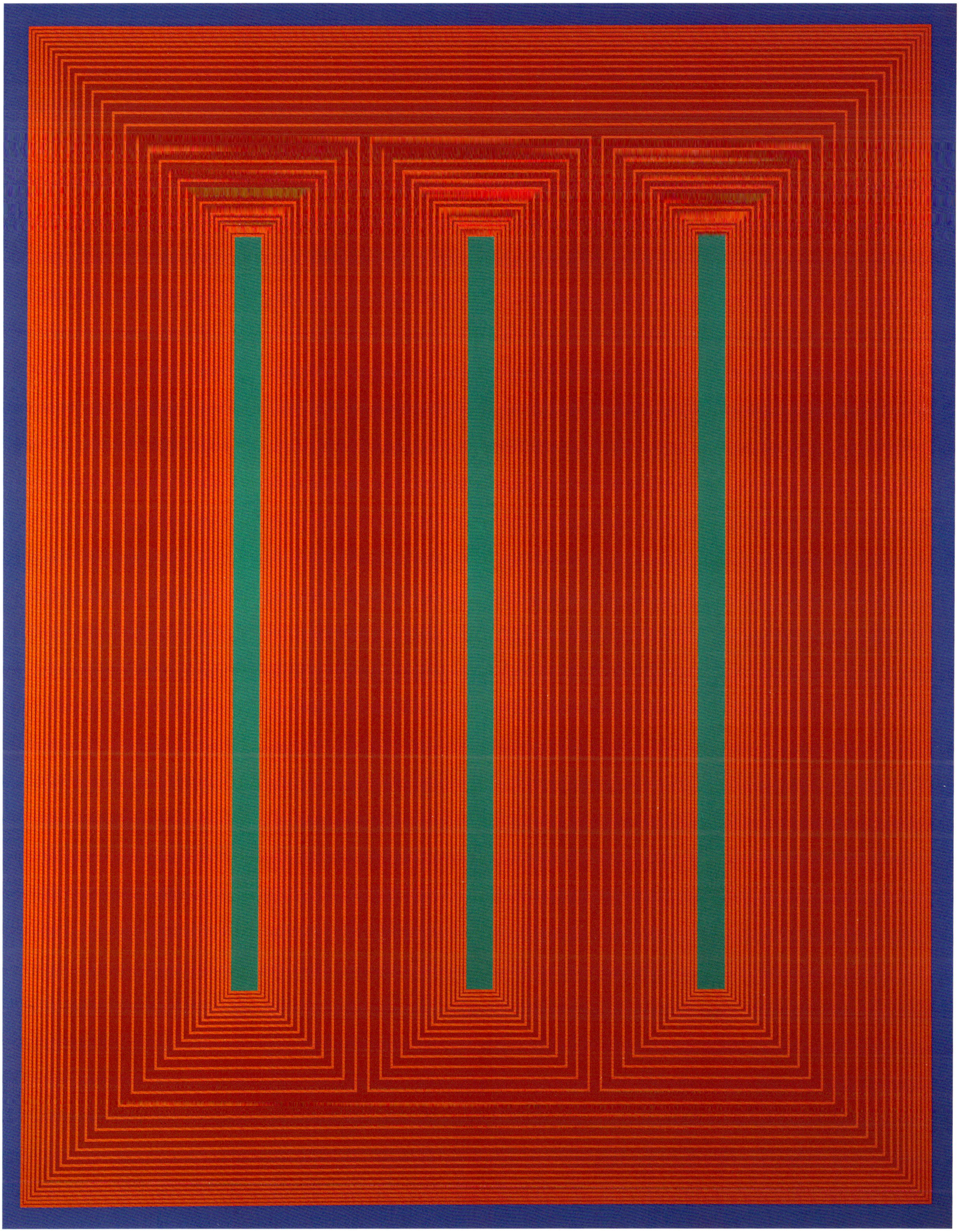

DANIEL GREENE

85 b. 1934, Cincinnati
The Watchman, 1986–87
Oil on canvas, 72 × 50 (180 × 124)
Signed lower right: Daniel Greene
Gift to the Museum by Mr. and Mrs. Daniel P. Amos 2001.9

PROVENANCE: Mr. and Mrs. Daniel P. Amos, Columbus, Georgia.
EXHIBITIONS: Hammond Museum, North Salem, New York, May 24–September 30, 1987; Gallery Henoch, New York, 1988; *Artist of America Exhibition,* Colorado Historical Museum, Denver, 1989.
PUBLICATIONS: Hammond Museum, North Salem, New York, exh. bro. and poster, May 1987; *Denver Post,* September 15, 1989, H, 1.

At the age of ten, Daniel Greene began his formal studies at the Art Academy of Cincinnati. He moved to New York City in 1953 and became immersed in traditional figure painting at the Art Students League under the instruction of Robert Brackman, a student of George Bellows and Robert Henri. Greene taught painting and drawing at the Art Students League and the National Academy of Design from the 1960s through the 1980s.

One aspect of Greene's art is his focus on narrative figure painting. In the 1980s he began a series of "environmental portraits" based on New York City subways. These evolved from flat, abstract motifs to large, figural compositions. Later he produced a series of works on art auction houses, in which he explored the relationship between the artist and the marketplace through metaphor.

Greene's technical virtuosity allows him enormous versatility in describing and selecting subject matter. Stephen Doherty wrote that Greene's work transcends mere descriptive painting: "But going beyond the technical achievement, Greene's figure and still-life paintings are compositions of provocative images. The viewer knows that each shape and color holds a fascination for the artist because they are presented in a way that provokes a similar response from us."[1]

Greene maintains an interest in realistic still-life painting, in which he uses found objects in compositions that are often jarring. As critic Judd Tully noted, Green's "shamanistic bouts with painted space agitate the traditional notions of still life."[2] Greene has achieved his greatest distinction, however, as a painter of contemporary portraits. His sitters have included authors, astronauts, politicians, entertainers, educators, and business leaders.

The Watchman resulted from several drawings he made of ninety-six-year-old Berendt "Opa" Snit. Green painted Snit with his back to the viewer, seated in front of the barn door of his studio. The feeling of solitude and isolation in this image suggests an affinity with the work of twentieth-century American artists such as Andrew Wyeth and Edward Hopper. Greene included certain visual elements, such as the empty coat hangers, the exit sign, the open fuse box, and the figure averting his face from the viewer.

Daniel Greene enjoys an international reputation as a pastel artist. He is the author of two books: *The Art of Pastel* (1972) and *Pastel* (1985), which have been published in eight languages. LR

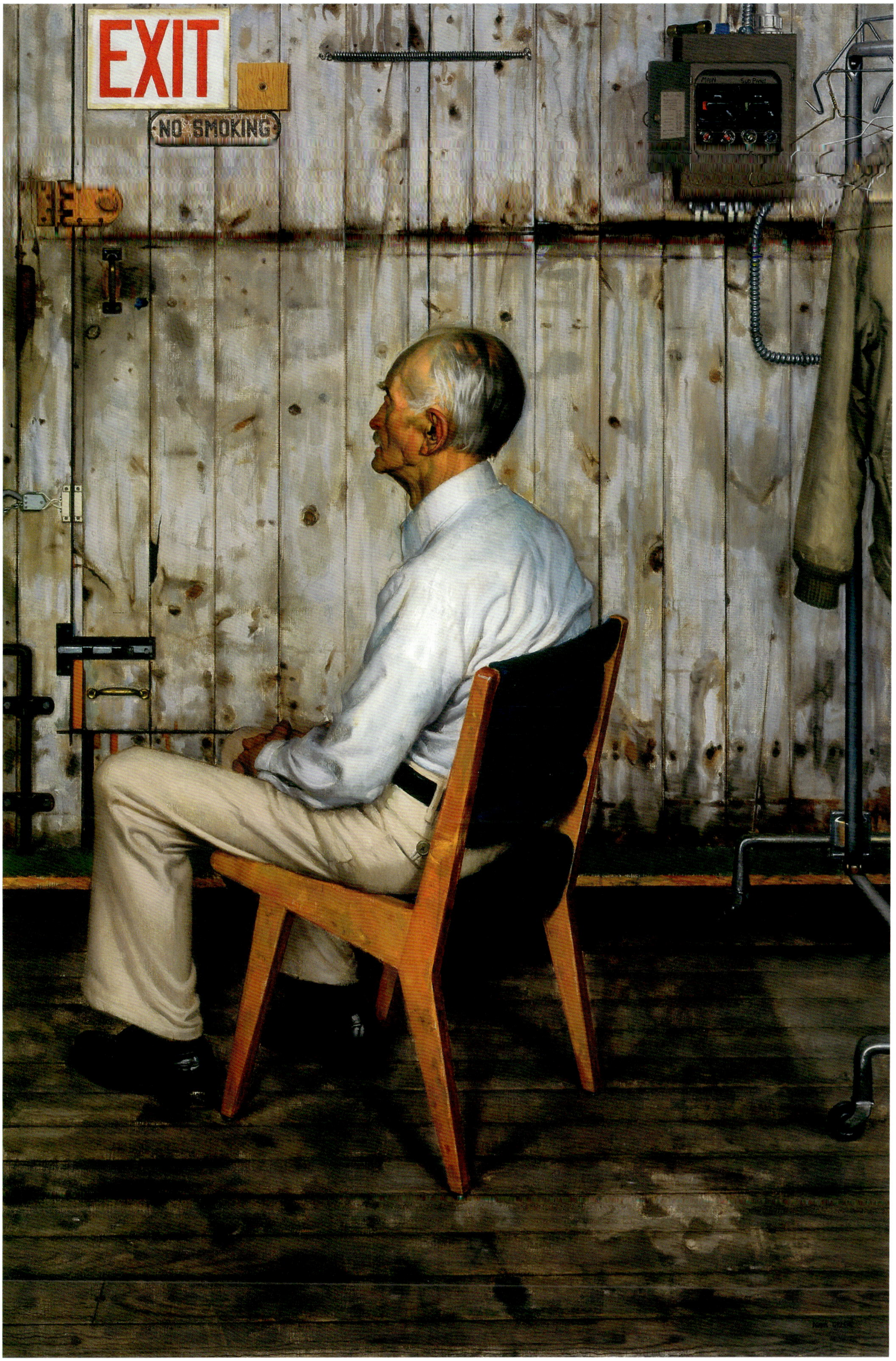
EXIT
NO SMOKING

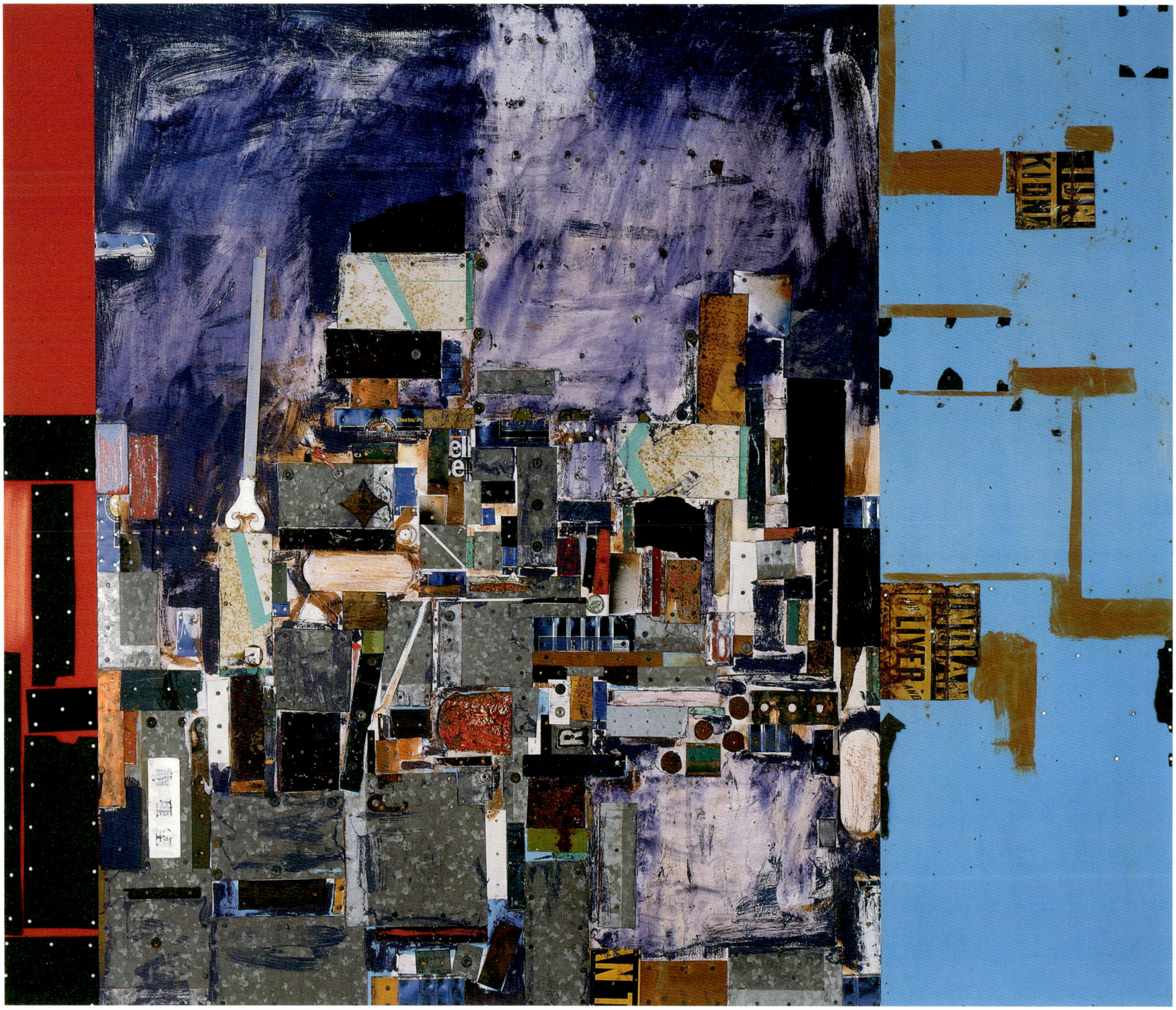
LIVER

WILLIAM CHRISTENBERRY

86 b. 1936, Tuscaloosa, Alabama
Columbus Wall, 1989
Mixed media construction, 60 × 72 (152.1 × 102.00)
Signed and noted on reverse: Christenberry/Columbus Wall/1989
Museum purchase made possible by the Crowley Foundation Inc.
[illegible] National Endowment for the Arts [illegible]

PROVENANCE: Collection of the artist.
PUBLICATIONS: Winn, et al., 192.

William Christenberry's paintings, sculptures, prints, and photographs have evolved out of his spiritual link to the South, particularly Hale County, Alabama, which his family has called home for generations. He has returned there for many summers from Washington, D.C., where he lives and teaches at the Corcoran School of Art.

His artistic inspiration comes from the sights, sounds, smells, and textures of the Alabama landscape. In 1960, after receiving both his undergraduate and graduate degrees in painting from the University of Alabama, Christenberry purchased a reissued copy of the 1941 book *Let Us Now Praise Famous Men,* with text by James Agee and photographs by Walker Evans. The book featured images and thoughts inspired by the authors' stay in Hale County during the summer of 1936, the year Christenberry was born. Much of what Agee and Evans examined was second nature to this artist who had already begun to use regional architectural references in his expressionist paintings.[1] He now returns to that landscape for further inspiration. Christenberry has explored a variety of media through which he mined the imagery of memory, time, and place that were an essential part of his experience and identity as a southern artist. The resulting works often reflect upon vernacular architecture, the signage of southern material culture, and red clay farmland.

Christenberry's training as an artist is rooted in abstract expressionism. In his large tenant house paintings of the early 1960s, structures are suggested through broad gestural applications of paint. By the mid-1960s, he was adding collage elements to his canvases, suggesting the actual surfaces of buildings that were layered with years of advertisements, graffiti, repair patches, and paint. These works also reflect his interest in the combines and collages of Robert Rauschenberg.[2] In time, the paintings became three-dimensional collages of found objects from the South, including actual pieces of wood, tin, and discarded signs. In 1978 he was commissioned by the Arts-in-Architecture Program of the United States General Services Administration to produce a wall construction for a new federal building in Jackson, Mississippi. With the success of this construction, he continued to create others, exercising his fascination and love for found objects.

Each time he returned to Alabama, he photographed the land and the aging structures that have become an essential part of the scene. He also collected the rusting and peeling outdoor advertising signs he remembered from his childhood.[3] He treasures the signs and admires their intrinsic beauty, all the while noting how they were once an important part of the visual landscape and now are vanishing.

> His continuous interest in vernacular culture stems from his own fascination with what he calls the "aesthetics of aging" that he has been witnessing in the rural South and to which his work pays homage. The declining structure and weathered signage he incorporates in his work are not just cultural properties to be consumed. It is their passage through time and their related histories with the people and landscape that surround them that resonate here.[4]

Columbus Wall resulted from the artist's visit to Columbus during his 1987 Columbus Museum exhibition.[5] He photographed various walls and signs in the city, and these images inspired him to produce a mixed media construction that includes fragments of tin roofing tiles, aluminum cans, wood, and other materials in deliberate patterns. Certain objects, such as a license plate, a bottle cap, and a Coca-Cola can, are easily recognized by their shape or logo. His found objects are not only the useless refuse of a materialist society, they are also the cultural accumulation of a specific time and place.

The painted areas of blue, purple, and red contrast with Christenberry's intricate alignment of selected detritus. In his hands, found objects are not only personal references to the past but intriguing abstract elements of shape, color, and texture. As Christenberry said, "*Columbus Wall* is not meant to be literal, it does not represent things that I saw in my visit there."[6] Christenberry's wall has as many layers of intended meanings and ideas about the nature of art, history, time, place, and impermanence as it has literal layers of physical elements. It is in the complex intersection of these ideas that we find the simple grace and intelligence of the artist. DF and ML

ROBERT MOTHERWELL

b. 1915, Aberdeen, Washington; d. 1991, Provincetown, Massachusetts

87 ***Massive Image,*** 1991

Acrylic on canvas, 60 × 120 (152.4 × 304.8)

Signed upper left: RM

Museum purchase made possible by Doris E. Black; Donald F. Broda Jr. in honor of Kathleen L. Broda; Natalie Harris; Sally Foley Hughston; Pat Hurst Jordan in memory of her parents, Dr. A. E. and Ruth Hurst; Jan J. Miller; Babette M. Rothschild; Sandy Bartlett Scarborough; Marge Tilley in memory of Mr. and Mrs. L. A. Platt; Rebecca K. Yarbrough in honor of Dr. Sidney H. Yarbrough III; special assistance from the Ella E. Kirven Charitable Lead Trust for Acquisitions; and a gift of the Dedalus Foundation, New York 2000.13.5

PROVENANCE: Estate of the artist; Dedalus Foundation, New York.

EXHIBITIONS: *Robert Motherwell: La Puerta,* Museo Rufino Tamayo (Mexico), Museo de Monterrey (Mexico), Modern Art Museum of Fort Worth (Texas), September 9, 1991–April 10, 1992.

Robert Motherwell was among the most literate and articulate of the abstract expressionists. His work is often monumental in scale, while communicating an intimate, personal expression. His style, which was influenced by the biomorpohic and automatic expression of the surrealists, revolutionized painting in the second half of the twentieth century. As the artist noted, "The subject does not pre-exist. It emerges out of the interaction between the artist and the medium. That is why, and only how [my work] can be created, and why its conclusion cannot be predetermined."[1]

Massive Image was completed during the last year of the artist's life. The painting recalls his experimentation with large areas of flat color in the Spanish Elegies series that he created in reaction to the Spanish Civil War and its aftermath. In this 1991 painting, the artist covered, scraped, and re-covered large areas of the canvas with black paint, allowing only a few areas of raw canvas or patches of white or ochre paint to counterbalance the immense weight of black. The evidence of the artist's hand is also seen in the upper right corner where he painted over a darker section with white paint, allowing the color to bleed through. The sporadic use of the warm ochre lends a visual rhythmic quality to the composition, but it is the large scale dominated by black that commands the viewer's attention.

Jack Flam, Motherwell's biographer, points out that the Renaissance notion of pictorial space, in which the canvas is seen as a window, is gradually filled in by the impressionists and early modernists. Paintings came to function as "a wall on which marks have been made. . . . Motherwell's painting, right from the beginning of his career, was conceived of in this way, as a kind of wall."[2] While *Massive Image* is indeed a kind of wall in its shallow pictorial space and two-dimensionality, the painting, like others by Motherwell, is almost overwhelming in its visual impact. LR

BENNY ANDREWS

88

b. 1930, Plainview, Georgia
The Oath, 1992
Oil and collage on canvas, 35 × 25 (88.9 × 63.5)
Signed on reverse: Benny Andrews 1992
Gift of the American Academy of Arts and Letters; Hassam, Speicher, Betts and Symons 93.3

PROVENANCE: American Academy of Arts and Letters, New York.
EXHIBITIONS: *Annual Purchase Show,* American Academy of Arts and Letters, New York, 1993.
PUBLICATIONS: Winn, et al., 194.

Benny Andrews, the son of a sharecropper, was raised on a tenant farm in rural Georgia along with nine siblings. In spite of humble beginnings and many roadblocks, he has become a successful artist.[1] His roots are in the South, and his imagery often is culled from memory and the experience of southern culture. Andrews's father, George, was an imaginative folk artist, and his mother, Viola, and brother Raymond were writers. Andrews credits his mother with first encouraging his art. She supplied him and the rest of her children with pencils, crayons, and paper whenever she had extra money.[2]

In 1948 Andrews received a $400 scholarship to attend Valley State College in Georgia. In 1950, when the scholarship money ran out, he joined the air force and served in the Korean War. He graduated from the Art Institute of Chicago in 1958, then relocated to New York City—"The place I'd always set out to come to."[3]

Andrews's artistic endeavors include collage, painting, printmaking, book illustration, writing, and criticism. A professor of painting and drawing at Queens College, New York, he has lectured and taught in a variety of settings. He has been active in outreach programs across the country, and has been an effective advocate for the inclusion of African American artists in museum and gallery exhibitions. Andrews served as Director of the Visual Art Program at the National Endowment for the Arts from 1982 to 1984. He has received numerous awards and fellowships, including the John Jay Whitney and Rockefeller Foundation fellowships.

The Oath is part of a series of collage images based on immigration as an American experience. In this work, collage elements and paint are seamlessly combined. Andrews uses found objects and fabrics to add a physical reality to his work, selecting materials that reflect the personality, social status, and occupation of the subject. Here, all three subjects are dressed appropriately for the solemn swearing in of a new citizen. The oath taker, right hand raised, expresses the solemnity of the ritual through his gesture and dignified appearance in a suit and tie. The woman who stands close to him—dressed in high heels, a broad-brimmed hat, and dress trimmed in real lace—reaches for his left hand in a sign of support. The red, white, and blue colors of the American flag above their heads are repeated in the man's clothing. "I tried to capture the moment. It is 'dream-like.' To people like these, coming to America is like coming to Paradise."[4] EW

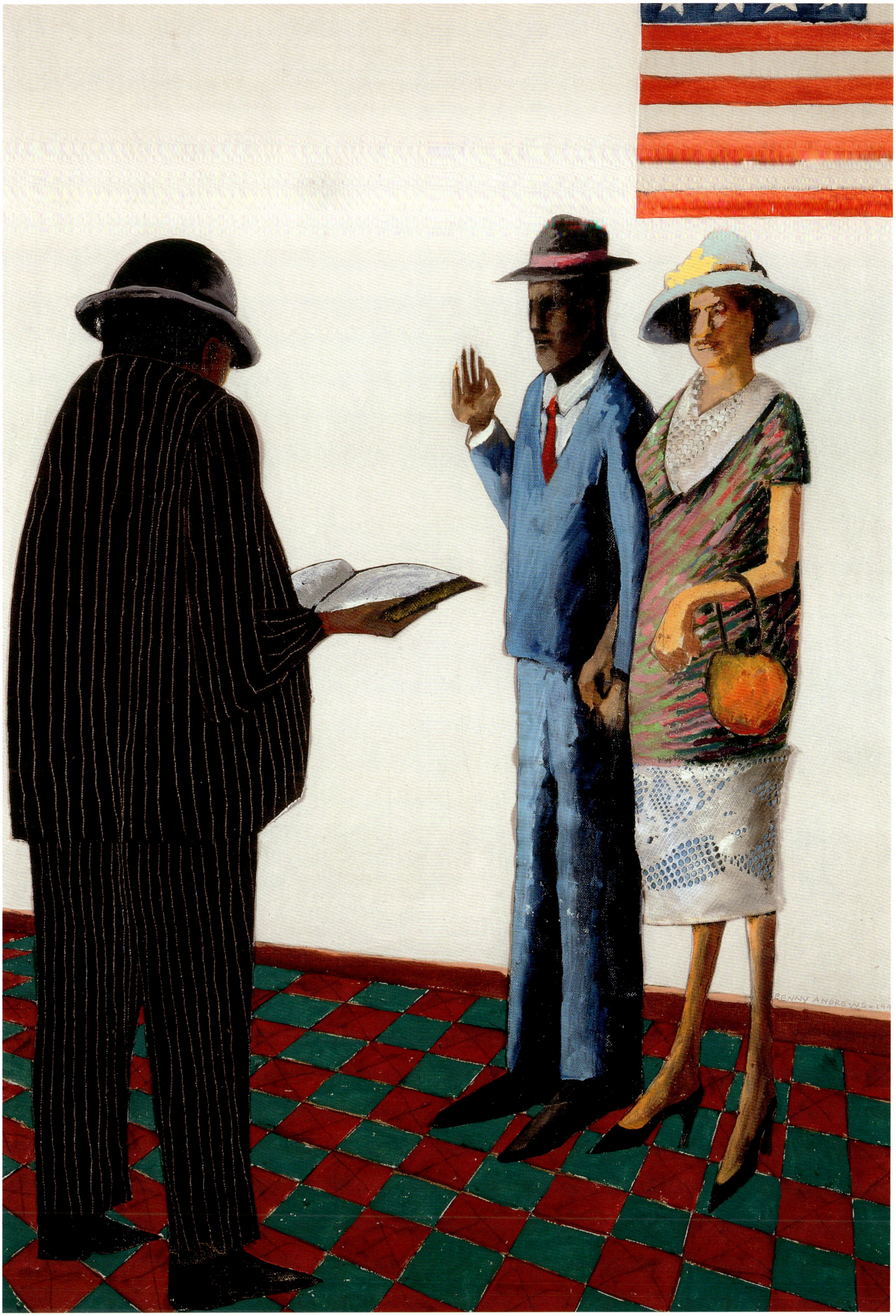
BENNY ANDREWS

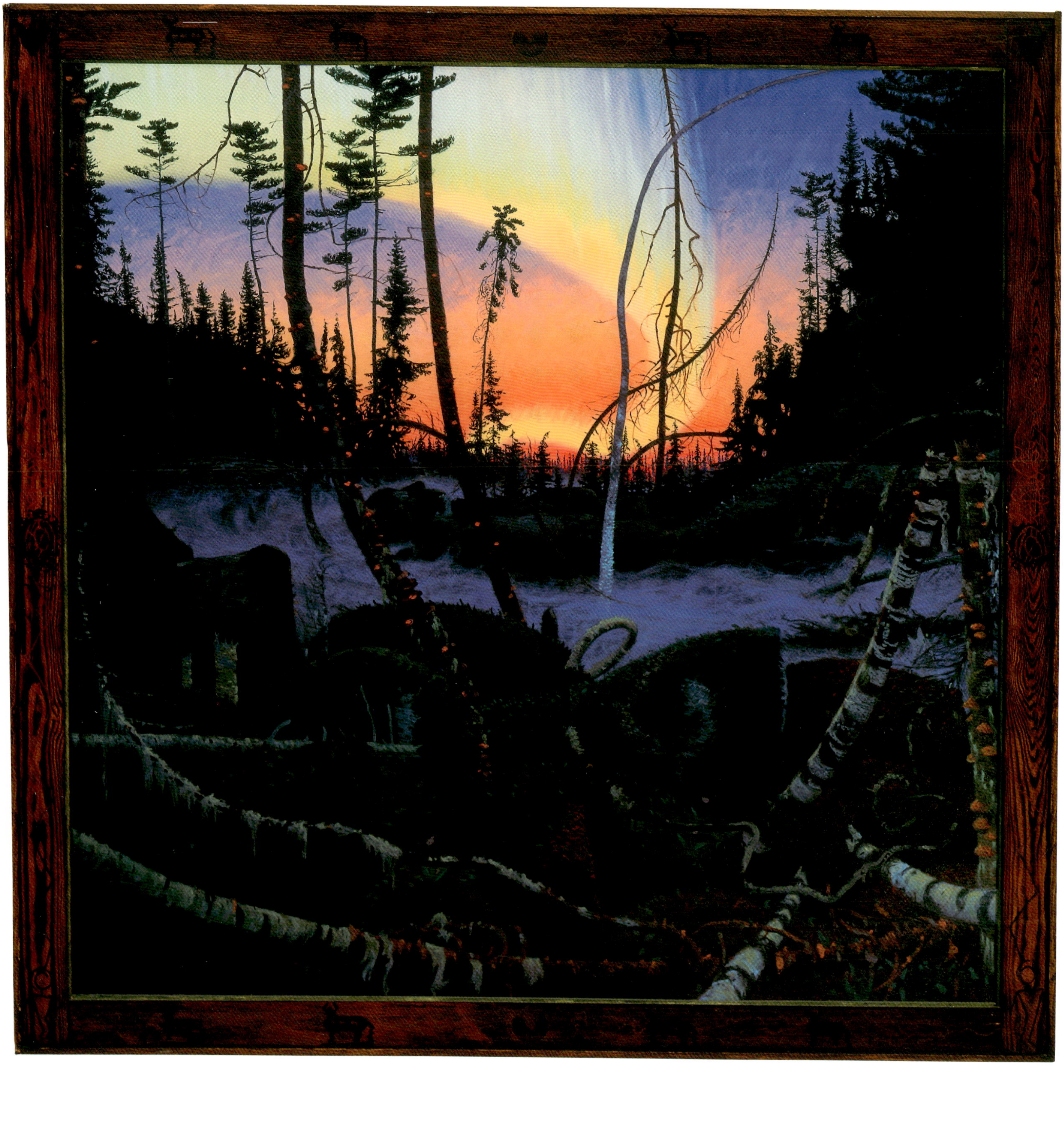

TOM UTTECH

89 b. 1942, Merrill, Wisconsin
Wegimind Akaii, 1993
Oil on canvas, 78 x 79¼ (198.12 x 201.3)
Signed, dated, and inscribed on verso: #521/Wegimind Akaii/oil Jan. 1993/Tom Uttech
Museum purchase made possible by Norman S. Rothschild in honor of his parents, Aleen and Irwin B. Rothschild 98.50

PROVENANCE: Schmidt-Bingham Gallery, New York.
EXHIBITIONS: *Tom Uttech,* Schmidt-Bingham Gallery, New York, February 5–March 1, 1997; *The Waking Dream: Psychological Realism in Contemporary Art,* Castle Gallery, College of New Rochelle, New York, September 1–October 25, 1998; *Towards a New Century.*
PUBLICATIONS: *Towards a New Century,* n.p.

Tom Uttech has spent most of his life in Wisconsin, where he studied at the Layton School of Art in Milwaukee. He also attended the University of Cincinnati, then returned to Wisconsin to accept a teaching position and to paint.[1] Among the state's unspoiled natural habitats, the artist finds abundant inspiration. He explores the wilderness on foot, hiking and camping but not sketching. Instead, he relies on memory and imagination to translate his experience to canvas when he returns to the studio. According to the artist, "The best response to my paintings, would be for you to march right out of the gallery and go straight to the wildest piece of land you can find and sit down and let it wash over you and tell you secrets."[2]

Uttech paints images that touch upon primordial rhythms. His large-scale paintings, which have been described as mystical, have an intrinsic power that transcends the idea of a simple, painted landscape. He selects titles for his works from a copy of an eighteenth-century Ojibwa dictionary. According to the artist, the title of this painting, *Wegimind Akaii,* translates to "Mother Earth," the source of life, a subject that artists have explored in concept and symbol since prehistoric times.

In *Wegimind Akaii,* Uttech includes four aspects of the natural landscape: sky, earth, creatures, and water. As the artist said, "The context has to be there, the sweep of landscape. But the details have to be persuasive."[3] At first observation, the context is a light-filled sky and shadowy woods. Birches, vines, moss-covered rocks, and undergrowth are delineated in the dim foreground. The trees become increasingly indistinct the further they recede into the background, and ultimately they become a line of dark silhouettes against the sunset. Uttech's pensive image of a natural landscape becomes a symbolic reference to Mother Earth in the mysterious cloud that swoops from the heavens to earth and in the swirling blue mist surrounding a land form shaped like the figure of a reclining woman. Much about this painting persuades the viewer that a far more meaningful context has been presented than first impressions might indicate—that of life on earth and a spiritual world beyond.

Uttech makes the frames for his paintings, as much to complement—or even extend—the image as to protect it. The frame for *Wegimind Akaii* includes images of several hand-carved horned animals in profile, a small circular landscape scene, two animal heads, and two human stick figures that evoke immediate associations with prehistoric cave paintings. BF

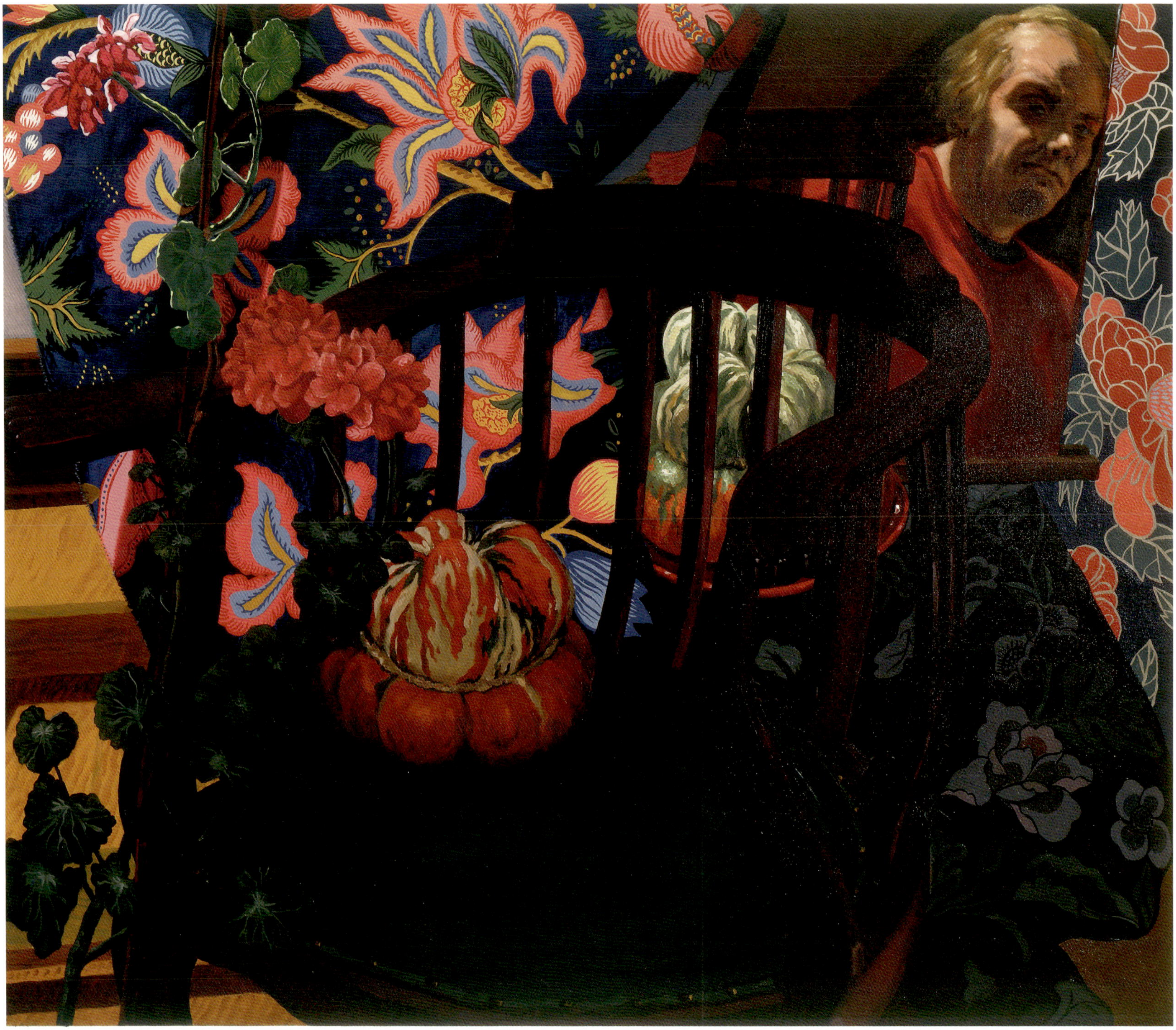

JACK BEAL

90 b. 1931, Richmond, Virginia

Still Life with Chair and Self-Portrait, 1994

[illegible]

Signed upper right: Jack Beal

Museum purchase made possible by the Hardaway Foundation Endowment 2001.10.1

PROVENANCE: George Adams Gallery, New York; Glenn Janss, Sun Valley, Idaho; private collection, Roseland, New Jersey; George Adams Gallery, New York.

EXHIBITIONS: *It Figures,* Steven Austin State University, Nacogdoches, Texas, October 1–November 15, 1996; *Jack Beal: A Survey, 1963–1994,* Art Gallery, Oglethorpe University, Atlanta, September 13–December 20, 1998; *Realism Today,* John Pence Gallery, San Francisco, October 10–November 20, 2000; *Abstract Expressionism and the New American Realism: Paintings by Jack Beal and Philip Pearlstein,* Columbus Museum, Yeager Museum at Hartwick College (Oneonta, New York), April 1, 2001–April 21, 2002; *Summer Potpourri.*

PUBLICATIONS: Adams and Reker, 18.

Jack Beal attended the School of the Art Institute of Chicago in the mid-1950s with fellow students Red Grooms, Richard Estes, John Chamberlain, and Claes Oldenburg. His painting instructor was Isobel Steele MacKinnon, a student of Hans Hofmann in the 1920s, who urged her students to embrace abstract expressionism. Beal became acquainted with artists who were exploring this new style when he married fellow student and sculptor Sondra Freckelton and moved to Lower Manhattan in 1955. Eventually he concluded that he wanted to make art that went further than the current trends in abstraction. "I didn't want to be a second- or third-generation anything," he said in an interview.[1] He had seen and studied the work of the old masters at the Art Institute of Chicago and had developed a special affinity for the work of Diego Velásquez. He said,

> I asked myself: "If you love Velásquez so much, why don't you try to paint like him, with all the complexity and passion of the masters?" I wanted to paint like Velásquez—not de Kooning-does-Velásquez—but Velásquez. . . . Alfred Leslie once said that he wanted to put back into art everything that modernism had taken out. That was how I felt, too.[2]

Beal made realist drawings and paintings from direct observation, using the fluid brushstrokes he had developed as an abstract expressionist. He became increasingly realistic in his description of objects, eventually shunning "the somewhat expressionistic depiction of forms and subjective emotional intensity of his earlier painting."[3] In time, the edges of his painted objects became more tightly defined, and eventually he abandoned the flattened spatial relationships of abstraction.

Beal approached *Still Life with Chair and Self-Portrait* by balancing the quantity and quality of color and shape. His inclusion of a self-portrait in the background of this interior is a pictorial device that dates to the fifteenth century. The painting, for all of its realism, retains much of the spatial ambiguity of his abstract expressionist work. Beal recalled that 1994, the year he painted the museum's still life, was the first year that he and his wife remained at their country farm for the winter instead of returning to New York City.

> The Winter of 1994 was particularly brutal, dropping nearly twenty feet of snow all told. I hunkered down in the studio (which I shared with Sondra) and painted as densely and compactly as I have ever done. This picture, which I privately call *The Winter of My Discontent,* is busy throughout, with the only resting-place occurring appropriately on the seat of the chair. Otherwise I feel the painting is about to explode, and the self-portrait image expresses a similar intensity. I am very proud of this picture, but it almost did me in.[4]

LR

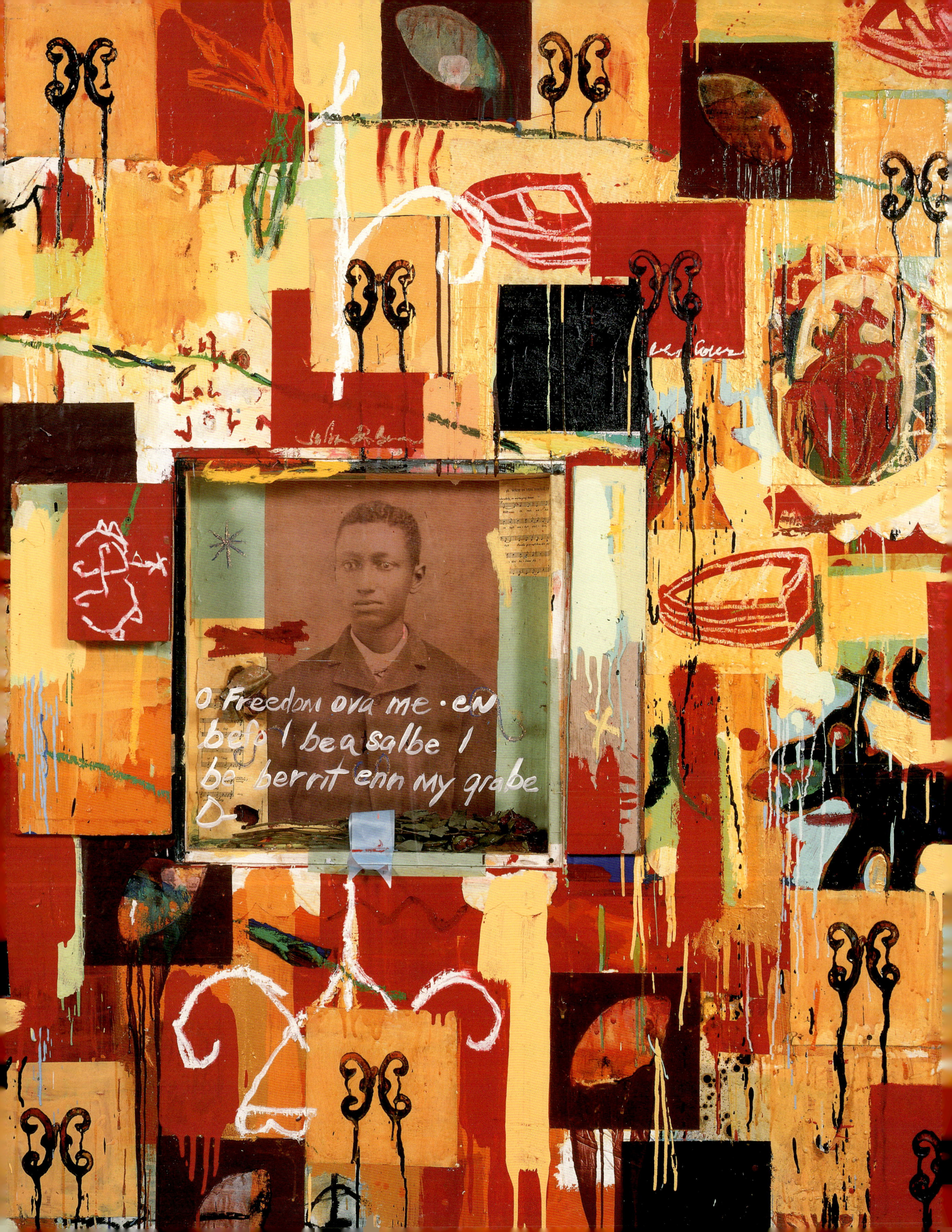
O Freedom ova me · en
befo I bea salbe I
be berrit enn my grabe

RADCLIFFE BAILEY

91 b. 1968, Bridgeton, New Jersey
O Freedom Ova Me, 1995
[illegible]
(203.2 × 203.2 × 10.16)
Museum purchase made possible by the
Edward Swift Shorter Bequest Fund 96.5

PROVENANCE: Fay Gold Gallery, Atlanta.
EXHIBITIONS: *Out of Bounds: New Work by Eight Southeast Artists,* Nexus Contemporary Art Center, Atlanta, summer 1996.
PUBLICATIONS: Carlozzi, et al., 28; *News,* Columbus Museum newsletter, fall 1996, cover.

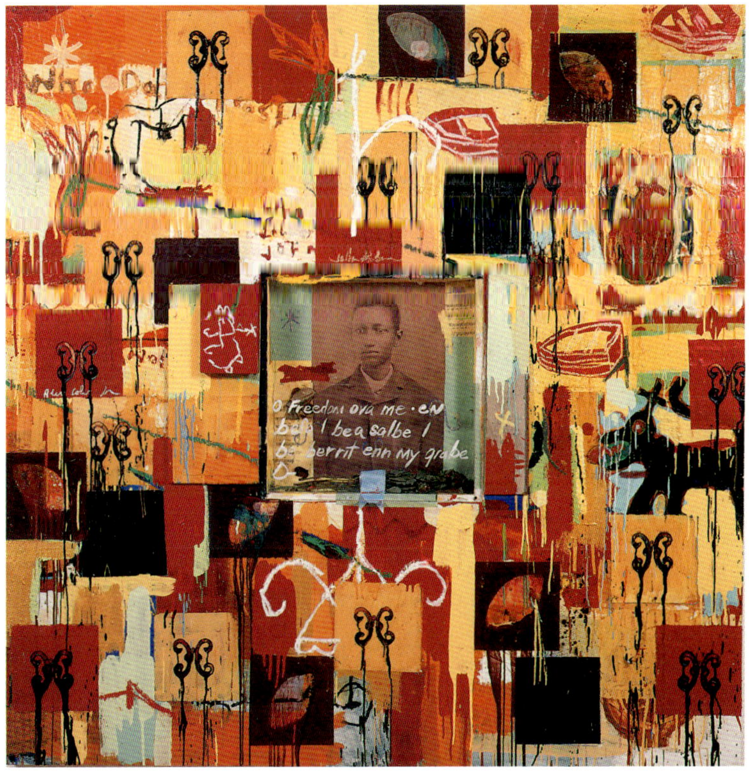

Radcliffe Bailey was raised and educated in Atlanta. He received a bachelor's degree from Atlanta College of Art in 1991. He usually constructs works from found objects, drawing on a variety of sources, including historical events, popular culture, family memories, and African traditions that have been adapted and preserved in African American culture.[1] His work has been exhibited at the Birmingham (Alabama) Museum of Art, the Whitney Museum of American Art in New York, the Studio Museum in Harlem, and the High Museum of Art in Atlanta.

O Freedom Ova Me is an assemblage of painted symbols that surround a constructed portal or window through which are seen relics of another time—a copy of an old photograph, sheet music, words of a spiritual, and a dried bouquet of roses. The title of the work is from an African American hymn. Bailey has phonetically adapted some of the lyrics from the song and written them in the window: "O Freedom ova me, en/befo I bea salbe I/be berrit enn my grabe/O."[2] Bailey produced this work in response to the death of his grandmother and his aunt, both of whom died from cancer in the same week. He chose to reference "O Freedom Ova Me" because the words were appropriate to their fight for life, and their death came as freedom from pain. Bailey often combines historical references with personal experience in order to find meaning in tragedy and to discover the wonder of survival and life. In this composition, he included some favorite things of each woman, such as the bouquet reminiscent of his grandmother's rose garden and the bird of paradise, his aunt's favorite flower. The words above the flowers were written in Georgia clay with the artist's fingers. The bleeding hearts signify the sorrow associated with the loss of loved ones.[3]

The windowlike space in the middle of the composition, where the mementos are clustered, is like the cavity in the belly of a West African *nkisi* sculpture, in which ritual substances are placed. The canvas that surrounds the portal is brightly painted in a quiltlike pattern, with areas of citrus orange, bright yellow, and mint green, and details and overlays in black, brown, and red. An overlay pattern of boats or boatlike symbols in black is repeated throughout the composition and refers to the forced migration and enslavement of Africans. Another repeated pattern consists of two arabesque shapes that recall the filigree work in wrought-iron balconies made largely by African American blacksmiths all over the South. The shape also relates to a symbol found on *adinkra* cloths made in West Africa.[4] Bailey said that the correlation between his art and African ritual is both direct and diverse.

> I take the basic tenets of many African and African inspired belief systems and transmute them into a personal code. This piecing together also has precedents in the textile works of Africans and African Americans. . . . By using a symbolic language that invokes African and African American influences, I wish to show a [cultural] continuum that leads directly to the modes of expression that we use to link ourselves to the past and steady our steps toward the future.[5]

KMZ

DALE KENNINGTON

92

b. 1935, Savannah, Georgia
Cocktail Party, 1995
Oil on canvas, 48 × 96 (121.92 × 243.84)
Signed lower right: Kennington
Gift of Mr. and Mrs. Robert Lindstrom 99.3

PROVENANCE: Mr. and Mrs. Robert Lindstrom.
EXHIBITIONS: Wiregrass Museum of Art, Dothan, Alabama, 1995; *Body and Soul: Contemporary Southern Figures,* Columbus Museum, Mississippi Museum of Art (Jackson), Mobile Museum of Art (Alabama), Cummer Museum of Art and Gardens (Jacksonville, Florida), May 30–September 1998; *Always and Never,* Cheekwood Museum of Art, Nashville, 1999; *Towards a New Century; The Human Condition: Recent Work by Gary Chapman, Dale Kennington and Art Rosenbaum,* Columbus Museum, May 6–August 12, 2001.
PUBLICATIONS: Butler, *Body and Soul,* 35.

Dale Kennington has spent most of her life in Dothan, Alabama. Reminiscing about her earliest art experiences, she wrote, "When I was in the fifth and sixth grades, my teachers would allow me to skip other subjects to draw and work with pastels. These were then put up in the classroom."[1] Attending both Huntingdon College and the University of Alabama, she acquired strong skills in drawing, but her subsquent painting and teaching career was interrupted by the demands and necessities of raising a family. In 1974, while painting a portrait of her children, she became intrigued with the exploration of the human figure. Eventually she moved from individual portraits to large-scale vignettes of people interacting. As curator Peter Baldaia noted,

> Kennington paints the world in which she lives with great observational skill, employing a straightforward and confident realist style that is closely allied in spirit to the Ash Can painters and Edward Hopper. However, unlike Hopper, to whom she superficially is compared, Kennington avoids starkness and provocation in her paintings, favoring engaging compositions that evoke a viewer response and reveal layered meanings with quiet subtlety. She is a master at capturing the essence of a narrative by focusing on a moment that is revealing, but not necessarily charged with drama.[2]

Since the mid-1990s Kennington has often used an open-ended narrative to examine relationships and interactions among different social groups in what appear to be actual encounters in real time. In these works, the viewer may become aware of larger social and cultural issues surrounding race, age, gender, and class. The settings and subjects are drawn from the artist's innate grasp of the human condition, including frailties, emotional balance, relationships, and the precarious roles that each person plays in society.[3]

In describing her working process for *Cocktail Party,* Kennington wrote,

> My paintings begin with an idea. This one obviously was to capture the feeling of a contemporary cocktail party. I obtained permission to attend four large cocktail parties and to wander around with a camera. Nothing was posed (until much later when I persuaded a few friends to model for me to fill in areas for which I needed specific things). Some one hundred fifty candid shots later I began putting the painting together.[4]

Kennington captures fleeting gestures, postures, and expressions to project the atmosphere and experience of this particular type of social gathering while also carefully balancing the formal aspects of color, shape, and line throughout the composition. By these means she represents a seemingly spontaneous interweaving of figures engaged in a universally understood ritual. She explained:

> Each of my paintings comes forth in a similar manner. I take bits and pieces and put them together to form a whole that never really existed. If the painting is successful it has such familiarity to it that viewers often insist that they know what city it's located in, that they have been there and just can't recall the name of the place.[5]

What the viewer distinguishes as familiar or recognizable is in fact a shared perception of memory and experience. Although the portrayals are not always flattering, Kennington is not directly critical of anyone. Certainly, issues of wealth, self-indulgence, and self-importance are apparent, but what becomes primary is the recognition of this place and the implications that result from being observers rather than participants in the time-honored revelry. At once humorous, provocative, and compelling, *Cocktail Party* describes a common social situation experienced by most American adults by the end of the twentieth century. BF and ML

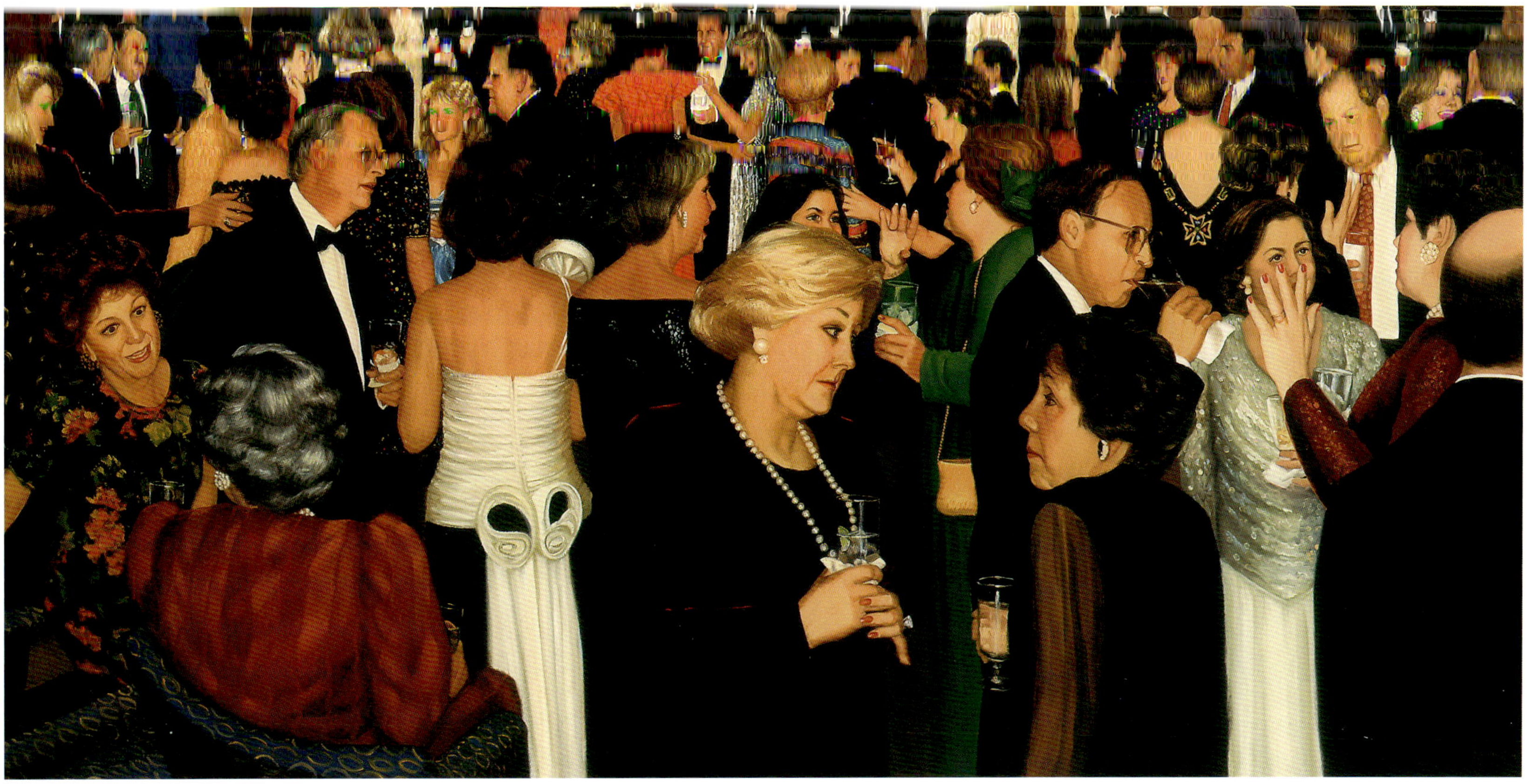

PHILIP PEARLSTEIN

93 b. 1924, Pittsburgh
Zeppelin and Horses #1, 1995
Oil on canvas, 60¼ × 72 (153 × 182.9)
Signed lower right: Pearlstein 95
Museum purchase made possible by the Ella E. Kirven Charitable Lead Trust for Acquisitions 2001.12

PROVENANCE: Robert Miller Gallery, New York.
EXHIBITIONS: *Philip Pearlstein: Recent Work,* Robert Miller Gallery, New York, February 11–March 8, 1997; *American Abstraction/American Realism: The Great Debate,* Susquehanna Art Museum, Harrisburg, Pennsylvania, June 9–August 21, 1999; *Abstract Expressionism and the New American Realism: Paintings by Jack Beal and Philip Pearlstein,* Columbus Museum, Yeager Museum at Hartwick College (Oneonta, New York), April 1–June 17, 2001.
PUBLICATIONS: Bourdon, 94–97, pl. 96; Adams and Reker, 12.

Philip Pearlstein graduated from the Carnegie Institute in Pittsburgh with a degree in graphic design in 1949. Following graduation, he and fellow Carnegie graduate Andy Warhol moved to New York, where they shared an apartment. Pearlstein continued his formal education at the Institute of Fine Arts, New York University. Having first visited Europe's greatest museums as a soldier during World War II, he returned to the Continent to study Italian art under a Fulbright travel grant in 1958. He then taught painting and drawing at Brooklyn College. Pearlstein has been recognized with numerous awards including grants from the National Endowment for the Arts and the Guggenheim Memorial Foundation.

As a second-generation abstract expressionist, Pearlstein achieved critical acclaim for his work when that movement was dominating the New York art scene. In spite of the attention he received as a member of that prestigious group of artists, and in the face of genuine hostility from his peers, he decided to become a realist painter.[1] Today he is regarded as one of the leading figurative painters of the second half of the twentieth century.

Pearlstein developed his own personal style, combining his understanding of classical painting and abstract expressionism in an approach that came to be known as new realism. He intended that formal structural elements would be the subject of his painting, and figures and settings would be the means to delineate these elements. As a result, portions of the figures would often be cropped for the sake of the overall composition. The artist said, "I had [the notion] . . . that large forms deployed across the canvas produce axial movements that clash and define fields of energy. . . . In relation to one another in nature, [they] are as capable of creating these axial movements and fields of energy as abstract forces are."[2] He noted further, "Technically, the main new problem I wished to impose upon myself was to apply all I knew about abstract painting to recording that which met my eyes."[3]

Pearlstein always works directly from posed models, which he renders in a factual and unemotional manner. This straightforward style, in which the figure becomes simply another object in a still life, so to speak, has been perceived by some critics as dehumanizing. Art historian John Ward, for example, commented that "the intersection of bodies with the edge of the picture seems to represent a kind of perverse and inhuman indifference to his subjects."[4] On the other hand, Pearlstein's biographer, Russell Bowman, contends that "the deep space in his pictures calls to mind Renaissance illusionism. . . . Pearlstein's people are visually 'rounded,' but in every other way they are 'flat.'"[5]

In *Zeppelin and Horses #1* the figures are static, while the zeppelin and toy horses appear to be active, even dynamic by comparison. In another intentional contradiction the figures and toys exist within the space defined by the intricate pattern of the Navajo rug on the floor, which creates the perception that the space is both flat, as on the left, and illusionistic, as on the right. Curiously, the carefully rendered figures and toys on both sides of the room seem to exist within three-dimensional space. In an interview, the artist said that the toys and the rug have more visual texture than do the figures, whose surfaces and colors are less vivid.[6] LR

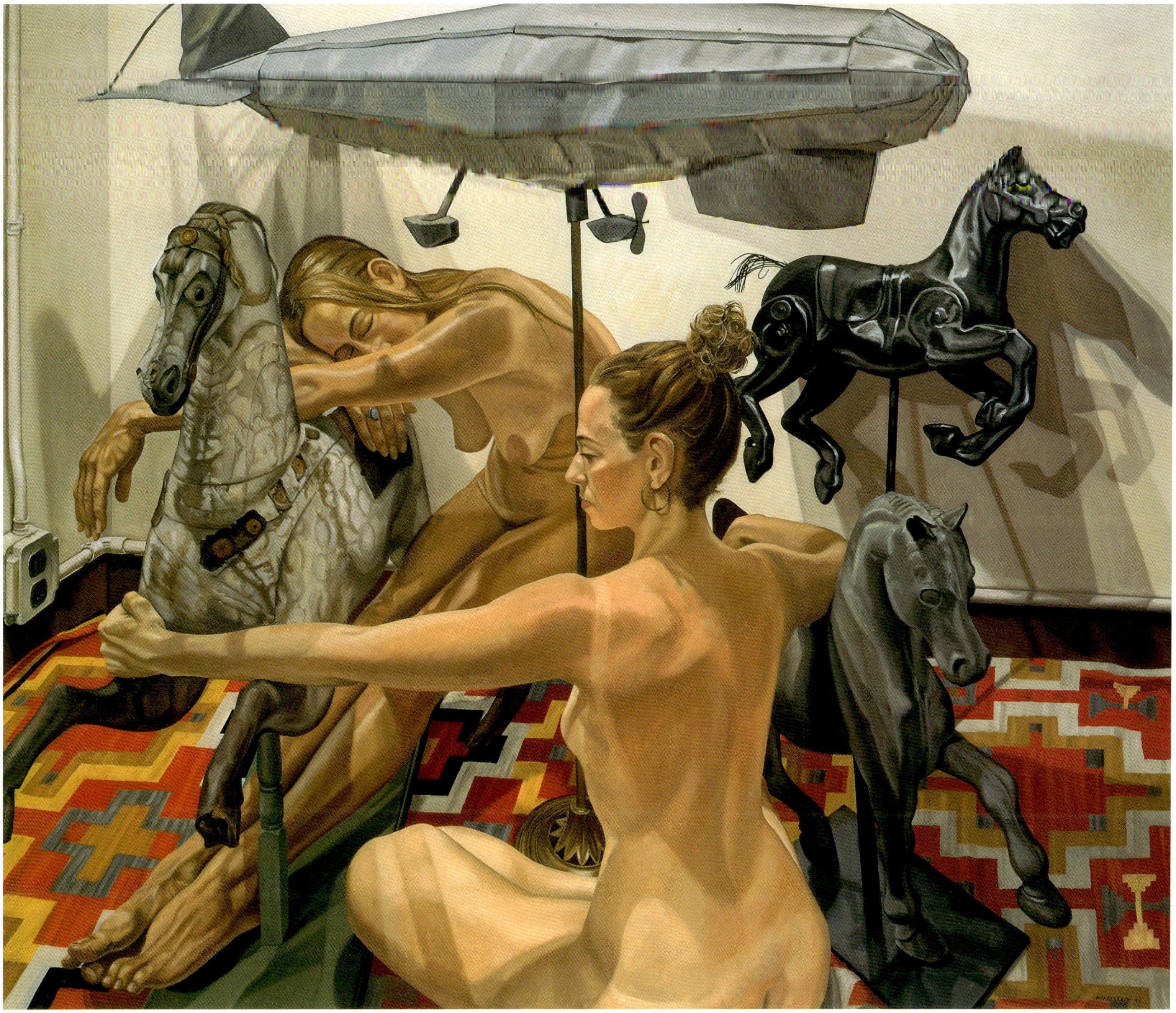

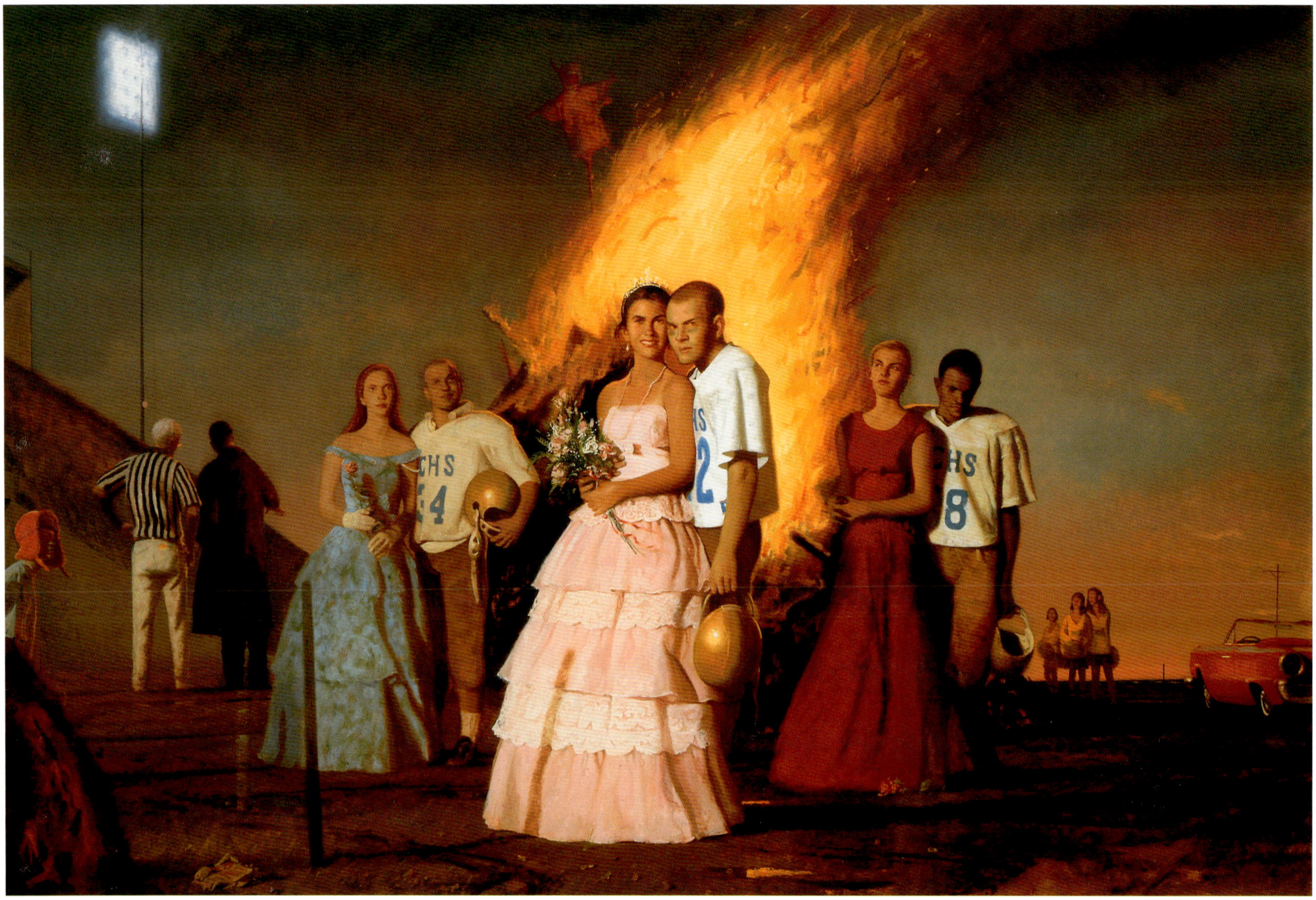
CHS
CHS

b. 1955, Columbus, Georgia

94 ***Homecoming,*** 1995

Oil on linen, [illegible] (... [illegible])

Signed with monogram lower right: IGN

Museum purchase made possible by [illegible]

honor of his parents, Alvan and Irwin B. Rothschild 98.32

PROVENANCE: P•P•O•W Gallery, New York; Kristy Stubbs Gallery, Dallas, Texas.

EXHIBITIONS: *Heroic Painting*, Southeastern Center for Contemporary Art (Winston-Salem, North Carolina), Queens Museum of Art (New York), April–June 1996; *Bo Bartlett,* Kemper Museum of Contemporary Art, Kansas City, Missouri, 1996; *Bo Bartlett: Homecoming,* Edwin A. Ulrich Museum of Art, Wichita, Kansas, September–October 1996; *Bo Bartlett,* P•P•O•W Gallery, New York, March 19–April 18, 1998; *Heartland: Paintings by Bo Bartlett, 1978–2002,* Columbus Museum, Greenville County Museum of Art (Greenville, South Carolina), Frye Art Museum (Seattle), Santa Barbara Museum of Art (California), Pennsylvania Academy of the Fine Arts (Philadelphia), January 29, 2003–November 30, 2004.

PUBLICATIONS: Gablik, n.p.; Butler, et al., pl. 18.

As a child, James W. "Bo" Bartlett III was fascinated by drawing and art in general. Recognizing that his future was in art, he decided to study with artists who could guide him toward his artistic vision. He went to Florence in 1974 to study with Ben Long, then with Ives Gammel in Boston, and with Aaron Shikler and Harvey Dinnerstein in New York. In 1975 Bartlett and his wife Melonie moved to Philadelphia so that he could attend the University of the Arts and the Pennsylvania Academy of the Fine Arts, where his instructors were Ben Kamihira, Morris Blackburn, and Sidney Goodman. He also worked with Nelson Shanks in Philadelphia. Like Thomas Eakins, Bartlett studied anatomy at the Philadelphia College of Osteopathic Medicine and Thomas Jefferson University. In 1993 he received a Pew Fellowship in the Arts.

Bartlett lives and works in Pennsylvania and Maine, but his work is rooted in a southern gothic tradition in which characters sometimes suffer desperation and frustration, much as do those in the novels of William Faulkner and the plays of Tennessee Williams.[1] His paintings are usually large-scale, figurative, and charged with spiritual, psychological, and art historical meaning, all of which are evinced in *Homecoming.*[2] His family regularly appears in his work; here, his sons and wife are included. As T. S. Eliot, Bartlett's favorite author, wrote, "Here is a place of disaffection . . . filled with fancies and empty of meaning. . . . Men and bits of paper, whirled by the cold wind that blows before and after time . . . wind in and out of unwholesome lungs."[3]

The scene is a homecoming ceremony, a ritual associated with American high school football. The queen and her escort are flanked by her court, while in the background a roaring bonfire consumes an effigy of an opposing team member. The passion and heat of the fire pale in comparison to the strong and visible emotions evident in the barely masked faces of the young participants. The couple on the right reflects the artist's thoughts on the then-current national drama surrounding O. J. Simpson and his wife, Nicole. The artist himself appears in his father's long trench coat in the left background, while his son, Emmanuel, in a red cap, enters the scene, also on the left. The girl wearing the crown is a distant memory of his sister Sandy, who was homecoming queen in 1964. His son, Will, modeled for the football star standing beside her. Although the scene is deliberately non-specific in its intent, it is close to reality. Bartlett grew up in the shadow of Columbus High School, whose football arch-rivals were the Jordan High School Red Jackets. The protagonists are accompanied by characters seemingly intent on malevolent acts, and the atmosphere is charged with dramas of jealousy and betrayal. CTB

CRAIG NUTT

95 b. 1950, Belmond, Iowa

Tomato Table, 1996

Tulip poplar inlaid with bloodwood and curly maple, and black gum woods, with oil-based paint and stains, 25¾ × 23¼ × 23¼ (65.41 × 59.01 × 59.01)

Inscribed on bottom: Nutt 96

Museum purchase made possible by Dr. and Mrs. Sidney Yarbrough III and the Edward Swift Shorter Bequest Fund 97.12

PROVENANCE: Connell Gallery, Atlanta.

EXHIBITIONS: *Beyond Function: Contemporary Southern Crafts,* Columbus Museum, December 4, 1996–July 6, 1997; *Southeastern Craft Innovations,* Knoxville Museum of Art, Tennessee, February 1–May 19, 2002.

PUBLICATIONS: *1997 Annual Report,* Columbus Museum (winter 1998), n.p.

Craig Nutt grew up in Huntsville, Alabama. He received a bachelor's degree in religious studies with a minor in fine art in 1972 from the University of Alabama. He was first employed as a furniture restorer, but he soon began to design original pieces as well as kinetic wooden sculptures. His furniture, a blend of humor and exquisite artistry, is based on an irreverent interpretation of traditional antique designs and inspired by a delight in bizarre juxtapositions.[1]

Nutt's childhood fascination with vegetables has become an adult obsession. He explains the progression in this way:

> When I made my first piece employing a vegetable motif, *Amazing Three Foot Long Flying Wonder Bean,* in 1982, I never imagined it would lead me to love vegetable furniture or that it would develop into a body of work spanning more than a decade and a half. That first piece, an impulsive reaction to seed catalogs by a gardener with no place to grow vegetables, appealed to me as much for its absurdity as for any other quality. I soon found myself fascinated with the forms and colors of the vegetables themselves, and with the associations, images, and emotions they could conjure.[2]

Nutt's vegetable-inspired furniture is in numerous public collections. A major commission, *Concorde* (a giant flying ear of corn), is in Hartsfield International Airport, Atlanta. His work has been featured in *Fine Woodworking, American Craft* and *Southern Living* magazines. He has received residency fellowships from the state art councils of Alabama and Tennessee, and the National Endowment for the Arts/Southern Arts Federation, and has been honored with the Alabama Governor's Arts Award (1985) and the University of Alabama's Alumnus Arts Award (1997). According to the artist,

> Having two-foot-long vegetables from earlier works flying around the studio inevitably led me back to furniture. The vegetable motif gave me a chance to poke fun at period furniture styles while being respectful of the designers and craftsmen who made them. If you bend an asparagus stalk just right it becomes a corbel leg. Plant forms have been used traditionally as applied ornament on furniture. In these works the ornament and structure are one and the same.[3]

For *Tomato Table,* Nutt formed the top as half of a tomato and carved a tripod stalk for the legs and base. He uses bright paint and stains as well as colors that are indigenous to exotic woods to create his fanciful fruit. Here, inlaid woods define the interior sections of the sliced tomato. The overall effect is at once humorous in concept and elegant in design. BW

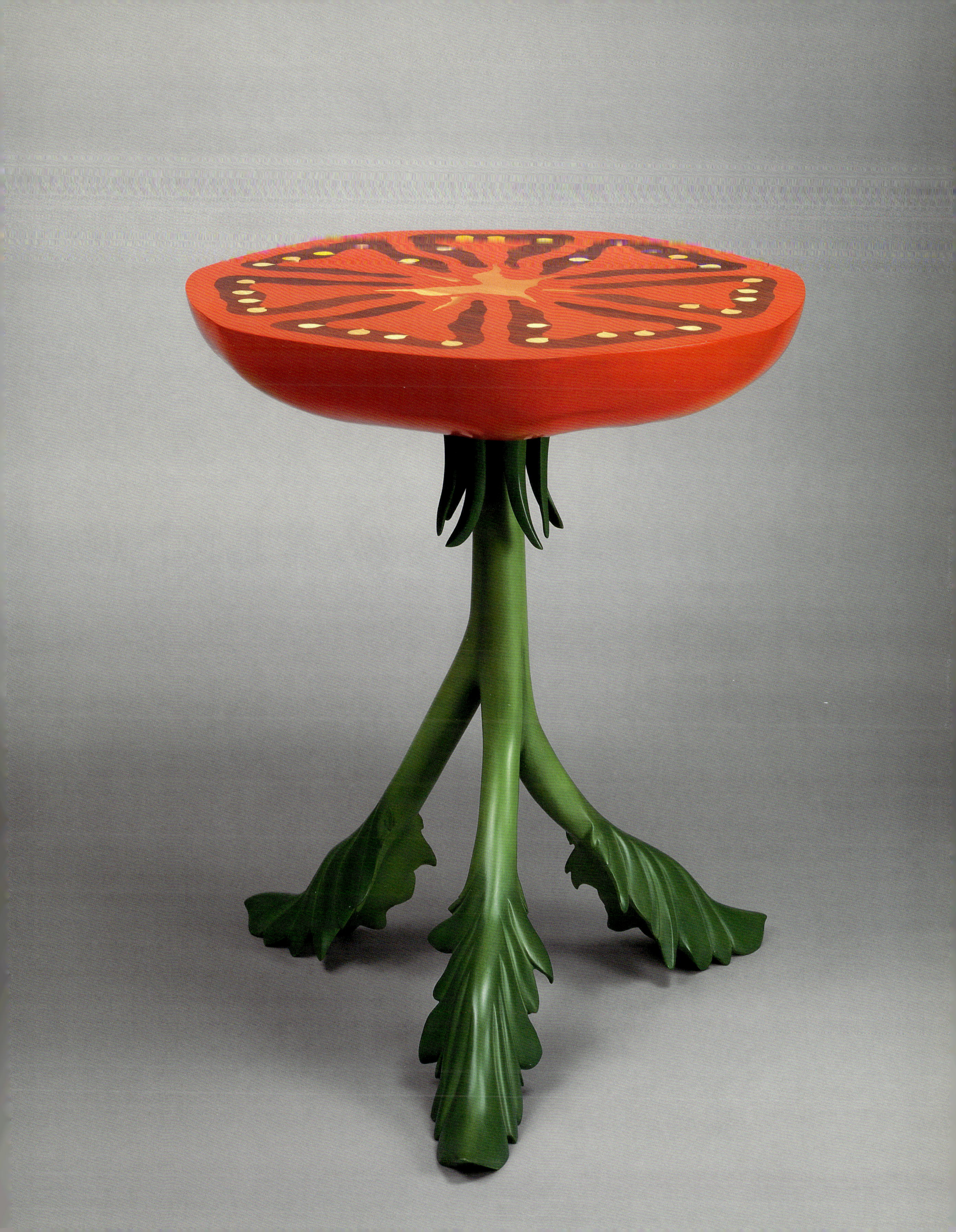

IDA KOHLMEYER

96

b. 1912; d. 1997, New Orleans, Louisiana
Composition 96-31A, 1996
Oil on canvas, with charcoal stick, 60 × 60 (152.4 × 152.4)
Signed and dated on reverse of canvas, lower left: Kohlmeyer/JKC 1997
Museum purchase made possible by Norman S. Rothschild in honor of his parents, Aleen and Irwin B. Rothschild 97.20

PROVENANCE: Estate of the artist; Arthur Roger Gallery, New Orleans.
EXHIBITIONS: *Ida Kohlmeyer: 1912–1997,* Arthur Roger Gallery, New Orleans, November 1997–January 1998.

Ida Rittenberg Kohlmeyer graduated from Isadore Newman Manual Training School in New Orleans and entered H. Sophie Newcomb Memorial College of Tulane University to study English literature. She graduated in 1933, having excelled in sports but apparently showing no interest in the visual arts. On a trip to Mexico in 1934, Kohlmeyer began what was to become a lifelong interest in the ceramic folk art and masks of Central and South America. She attended John McCrady's Art School in the French Quarter, New Orleans, in 1947. Much later in an interview, she described her first studio painting class: "I was so new at this that just putting pink next to green was a moment of ecstasy and I let out an exclamation so that the whole class turned around."[1] She then pursued her master's degree at Tulane with Pat Trivigno, who was a major influence on her work and in her life. Her works in the early 1950s were mostly figural compositions and portraits of children.

A profound change occurred during the summer of 1956, when she spent time at Hans Hofmann's Provincetown workshop and became exposed to abstract expressionist theories and colors.[2] Then, in 1957 Mark Rothko, as a visiting artist at Newcomb College, set up his studio in the garage at Kohlmeyer's family home and created paintings that he considered a major breakthrough in his career. Kohlmeyer's response to the paintings was intense, and her work for the next seven years reflected Rothko's influence. She had learned that a painting should be an "invention and not an imitation," and she moved from figurative painting toward her own idiom of abstract expressionism.[3] From the time of Hofmann's and Rothko's influence until the beginning of her geometric style in the late 1960s, Kohlmeyer explored the freedom of the automatic method in works that ranged from anthropomorphic imagery to nonrepresentational abstraction.[4]

The Columbus Museum first showed Kohlmeyer's work in a solo exhibition in 1963, the year that her *Passage No. 2* entered the collection.[5] By the mid-1970s, inspired by the work of Joan Miró and with an avid interest in South American art, she developed her distinctive vocabulary of shapes and symbols originally organized in grid format and later in loose flowing patterns. That style, which she continued to explore for the rest of her life and eventually translated into sculpture, expresses her strengths of draftsmanship and individual sense of color.

Kohlmeyer taught art fundamentals and drawing at Newcomb College from 1956 until 1965. In 1957 she had her first solo exhibition at the New Orleans Museum of Art. She also was a faculty member at the University of New Orleans from 1973 until 1975. Henri Ehrsam, of the Henri Gallery in Washington, D.C., the first dealer to take a serious interest in her work, was successful in placing her paintings in many private and corporate collections. At the 28th Biennial of Contemporary American Painting at the Corcoran Gallery, Kohlmeyer received a purchase award through a grant from the Ford Foundation. Among her many honors, the city of New Orleans pronounced March 1985 as Ida Kohlmeyer Month.

Composition 96-31A is one of her last major paintings. Although an estate agent dated it 1997 on the reverse, it was finished in the last weeks of December 1996. This evocative and seductive work reflects the artist's profound interests in vibrant color and grid as well as pictographic figures. A charcoal border frames the composition, adding a suggestion of fragility due to the transitory nature of the medium as opposed to pigments. The final image, much of which seems deceptively simple and delightfully spontaneous, is nonetheless the result of diligent intellectual appraisal, stern and unrelenting self-criticism, and a tenacious search for better, or at least fresher and more distinctly challenging, solutions. GBG

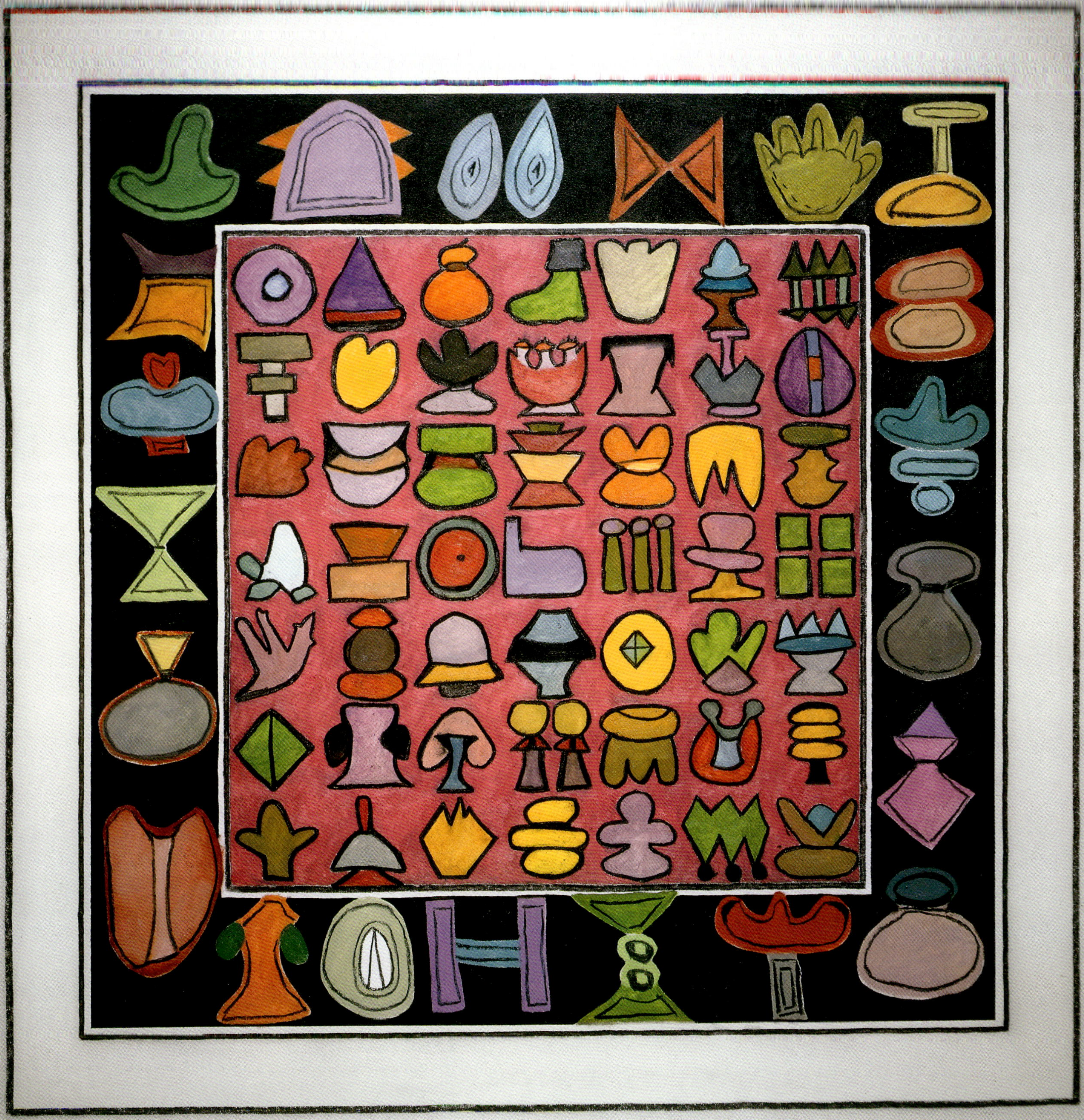

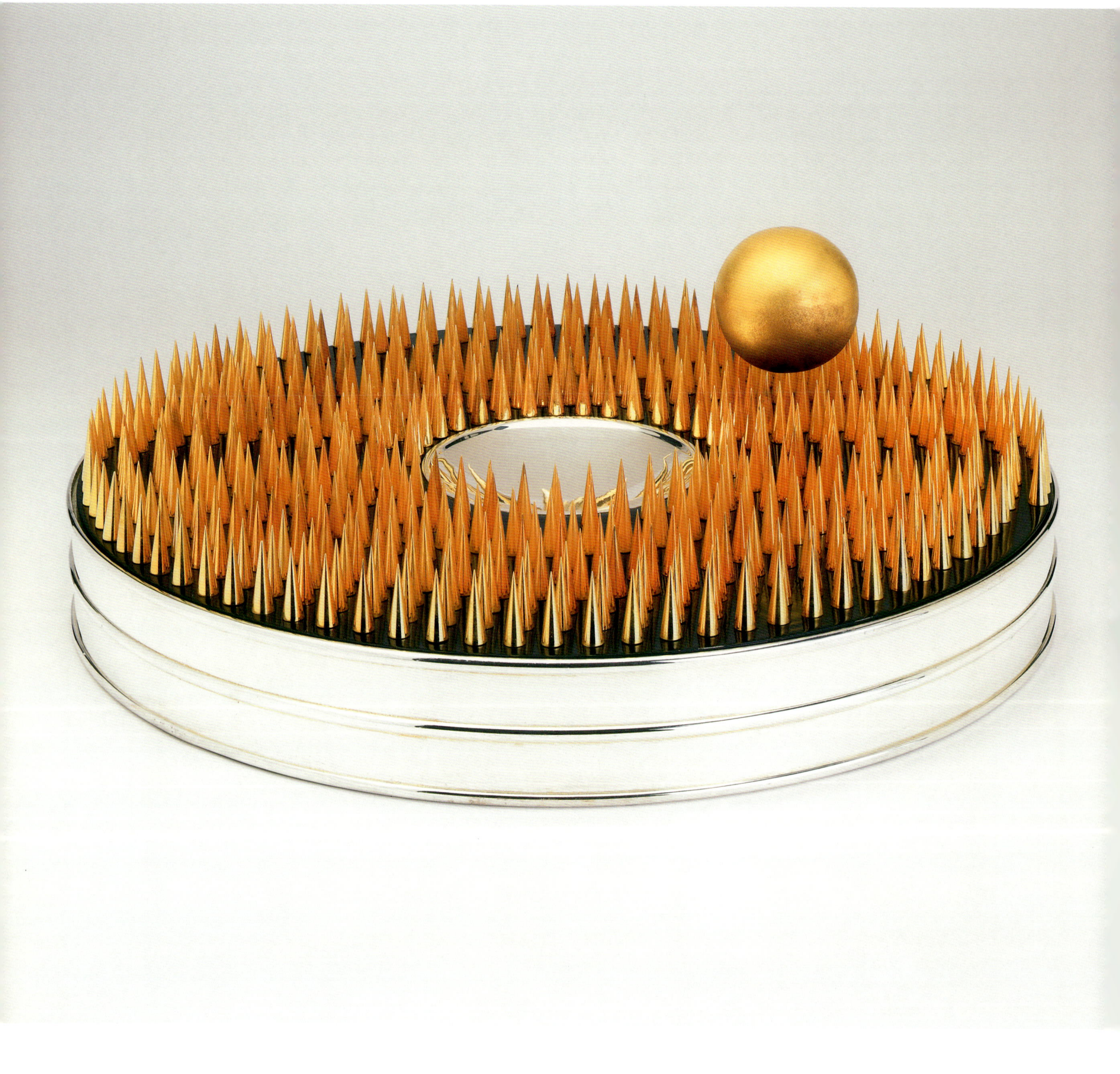

RICHARD MAFONG

97 [illegible]
[illegible]
Gold- and silver-plated brasses, sterling silver, and steel,
h. 4, diam. 19 (h. 10.16, diam. 49.53)
Museum purchase made possible by Norman S. Rothschild in honor of Helen Olnick, president of The Columbus Museum board 1996–1998 98.42

PROVENANCE: Collection of the artist.
EXHIBITIONS: *The Art of Teaching: Regional Faculty Invitational,* Columbus Museum, May 24–August 2, 1998.
PUBLICATIONS: *The Art of Teaching: Regional Faculty Invitational* (Columbus, Ga.: Columbus Museum, 1998), 19.

Richard Mafong grew up in Mexico, Asia, and the United States. As a young child, he became interested in building things and working with his hands. His first art instruction was in high school, then at San Diego State College, where he majored in painting and drawing and took several courses in jewelry. An instructor, Arlene Fisch, introduced him to the possibility of working in metal. He entered graduate study at Indiana University, with a concentration in metals, studying under Alma Eikerman. Upon graduation, Georgia State University employed him to establish a metals program and head the department upon its inception in 1968.

Mafong retired from teaching in 2002 to dedicate more time to his own design work. On his years at the university, he reflected, "I think that teaching has given me the time to pursue my career as an artist and at the same time has kept me stimulated in many ways. Some of these are the daily interaction with my students, where ideas and design concepts are discussed. Another is guiding my students on their projects, and teaching them the necessary skills."[1]

Mafong continues to hone his craft as he travels widely—to Italy, Spain, Peru, Bolivia, China, Russia, India, Nepal, and Thailand—to learn new techniques. In addition, he often serves as a consultant and guest lecturer. He has received commissions for medallions, awards, maces, jewelry, and relief panels from universities, hotels, community organizations, and corporations. He is one of the founding members of the Atlanta International Museum of Art and Design.

Mafong's art is not just jewelry making or metalsmithing. He also creates sculptures, combining diverse materials such as precious and nonprecious metals. The museum's *Pi* is one example in which he showcases the media's intrinsic qualities in a design based on symbolic imagery. As the artist stated, "I have an affinity and admiration toward art works that are well crafted, detailed, and inventive in concept, and that show the mastering of a particular skill and technique. This is inclusive of all the areas with no distinction between the fine arts and crafts."[2] Mafong fabricated *Pi*'s silver-plated brass base from sheet metal and attached gold-plated brass spikes to the patinated steel plate. The central silver bowl was die-formed, and the gold-plated brass ball was cast.

Pi evolved as part of a body of works in which spikes are a recurring theme. Circular Chinese ritual forms made of jade and perforated in the middle with a circular hole inspired this piece. Dating from the eleventh century B.C., the flat disks traditionally symbolize heaven and power. In his modern interpretation of the ancient Chinese form, Mafong strikes a balance between innovative shapes, surface beauty, and symbolism. BF

JANET FISH

98

b. 1938, Boston
Yellow Pad, 1997
Oil on linen, 36 × 50 (91.44 × 127)
Signed lower right: Janet Fish/97
Museum purchase made possible by Norman S. Rothschild in honor of his parents, Aleen and Irwin B. Rothschild 98.10

PROVENANCE: D. C. Moore Gallery, New York.
EXHIBITIONS: *Janet Fish: Recent Paintings,* D. C. Moore Gallery, New York, February 10–March 7, 1998.
PUBLICATIONS: Stein, 33, cover; Katz, 129.

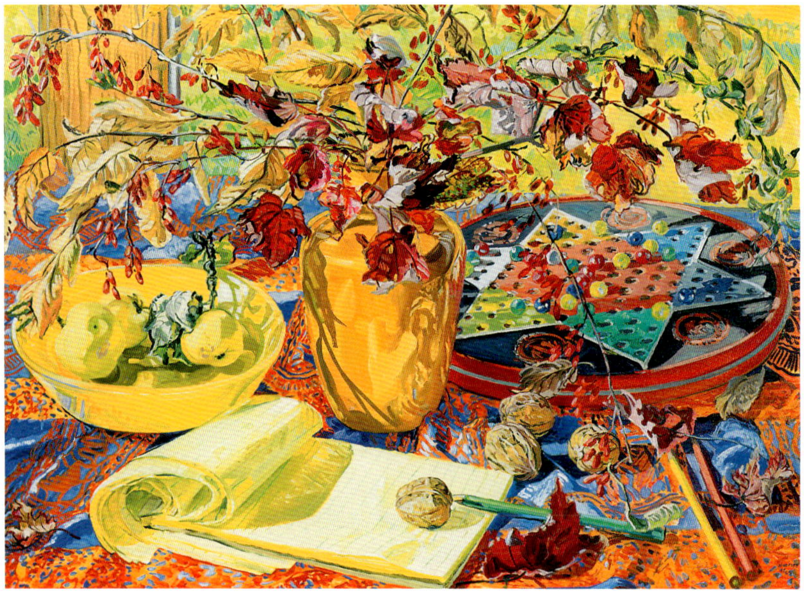

Janet Fish received a degree from Smith College in Northampton, Massachusetts, in 1960. The following year she studied painting at the Skowhegan Art School in Maine, where she met visiting painter and art critic Alex Katz. Katz became a lifelong mentor, encouraging her to expand her horizons beyond the heavy influence of abstract expressionism she encountered in graduate school.[1] Nonetheless, the fluid brushstrokes, brilliant colors, and organic approach of the abstract expressionists continued to influence her landscapes and still-life paintings. She received her master's degree in painting from Yale in 1963. Among her Yale classmates was a new generation of artists whose work also rose from abstract expressionism—Chuck Close, Nancy Graves, Richard Serra, Brice Marden, and Rackstraw Downs.

Fish's reputation comes from her large, colorful still-life paintings of glasses and other reflective objects placed on cloth-covered tabletops. While her work is obviously influenced by the seventeenth-century Dutch still-life tradition that celebrates the bounty of the harvest and the beauty of nature, it also speaks of French impressionist influence in the intertwining strokes of vibrant color. Smooth yet lively gestures of paint move across the canvas, drawing the viewer's eye from object to object. Fish's interest in exploring the concept of a lively canvas can be traced in part to growing up in Bermuda, which she describes as "a small, crowded island . . . [where] there's a profusion, a density, of vegetation which might have led me toward the very active surfaces I paint."[2]

Janet Fish is a new realist painter, one who is less concerned with copying superficial likeness than expressing light, colors, and textures. She builds on her experience with the active canvas of abstract expressionism while painting real objects. *Yellow Pad* is an excellent example of her work. Here is an assemblage of everyday objects articulated through a tangle of sinuous brushstrokes of contrasting colors. The back edge of the tabletop appears to be tipped forward in a manner reminiscent of Paul Cézanne. This pictorial device compresses the space, thereby emphasizing the flatness of the picture plane and effectively countering the illusion of depth developed through overlapping shapes.

In 1997, forty years after the introduction of the new American realism, Fish's *Raspberries and Goldfish* was included in *Still Life: The Object in American Art 1915–1995* at the Metropolitan Museum of Art in New York. Curator Lowery Sims noted the skepticism then surrounding the new realism:

> We may be a little suspicious these days of the pictorialism in realist painting. Right now, there's a greater interest in the objective gaze that captures the more gritty aspects of life. There's a tendency to favor theory over the formal aspects of painting. When I was putting together this show, I noticed how Janet hadn't just randomly arranged these flowers. . . . The painting was deliberate in its compositional and lighting choices. There was a lot more going on than met the eye. It was more than skillfully capturing visual effects.[3]

Sims's observations are equally appropriate to *Yellow Pad*.
LR

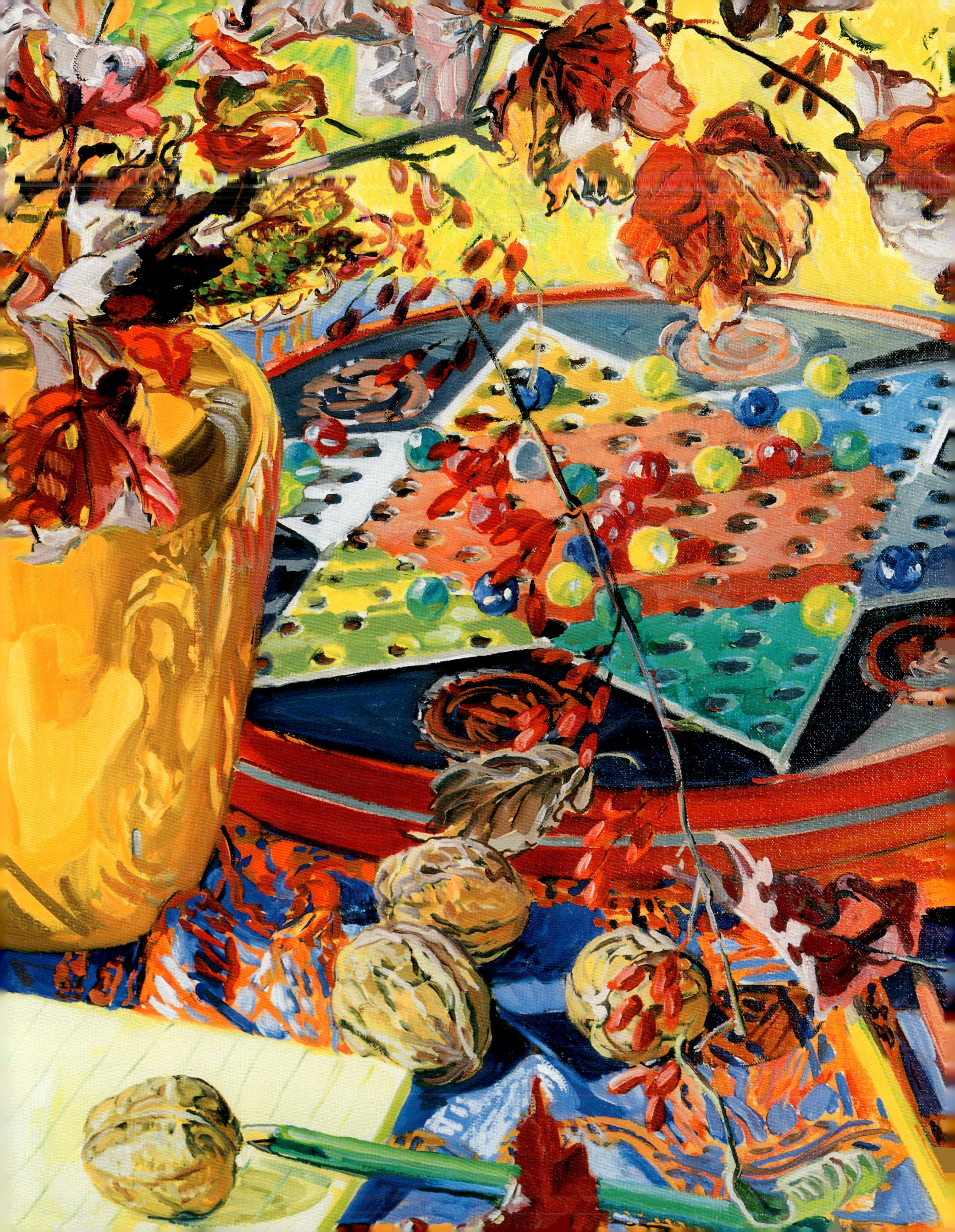

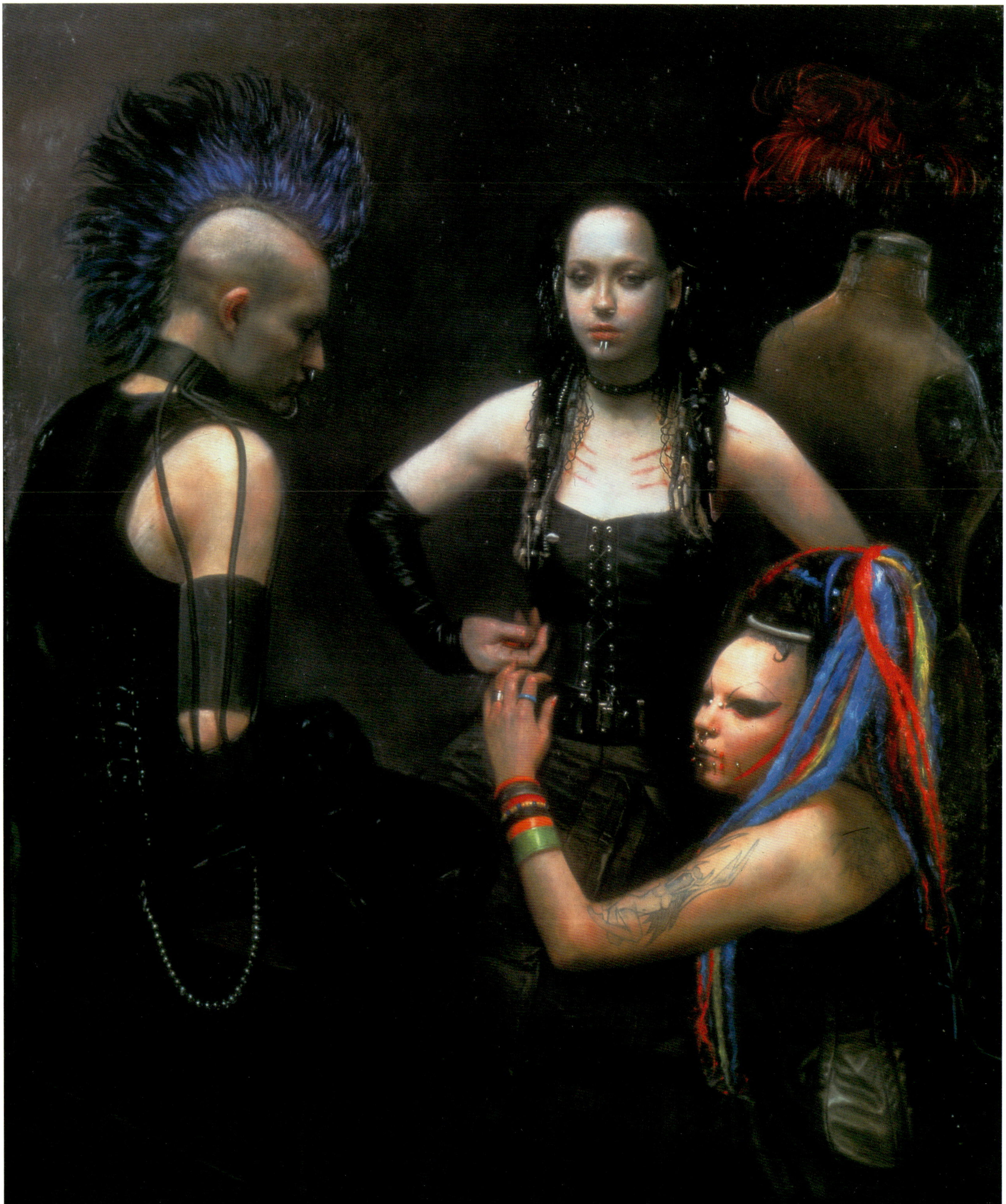

STEVEN ASSAEL

99 b. 1957, New York City
***Club Kids*,** 2001
Oil on canvas, 73 × 60 (185.4 × 152.4)
Signed and dated lower left: Assael 01
Museum purchase made possible by the [illegible]
Lead Trust for Acquisitions 2002.62

PROVENANCE: Forum Gallery, New York.
EXHIBITIONS: Forum Gallery, New York, November 1–December 7, 2002.
PUBLICATIONS: Maxwell, cat. 1.

As a child, Steven Assael showed an interest and skill in drawing. He attended the Pratt Institute in the 1970s, when figural art was less in favor than minimalist painting and sculpture, process art, and word art. Despite this proclivity toward abstraction, Assael and a group of like-minded artists pursued their interest in figurative painting.

Assael portrays the heroic image in his contemporary compositions,[1] much in the manner of Caravaggio, Velásquez, or Goya. With consummate skill, the artist builds surfaces to accurately reflect textures and to suggest complex psychological scenarios. In a 1995 statement, Assael wrote:

> From a conscious abandonment of modernist tenets grew a yearning for reconciliation and redemption for the figure in painting. . . . The play between the historical and the contemporary . . . can fill the work with internal oppositions. These opposing forces, by the way of unpredictable juxtapositions and narrative contradictions, challenge the viewer to find balance and equilibrium.[2]

In his latest work, Assael explores the club culture of New York and the people who participate in it. *Club Kids* is a part of a series begun in 1999, the subjects of which are drawn from an after-hours club called Mother. Three individuals are shown in full club regalia: leathers, feathers, body piercing, and tattoos. The figures, who appear to be indifferent to the stares and reactions of a nonclub viewer, are masterful representations of alienated youths. They may at first seem to be impenetrable, but under Assael's painterly brush they become much more than mere representatives of an urban subculture. The artist wrote about his attraction to this group:

> I think it has less to do with the specifics of who these kids are than the adoption of a persona and how that persona is manufactured by an individual. In some ways, that is what we all do, we each create on some level a theatrical persona, and that objectification becomes like body armor or protection. . . . What these people are doing exaggerates that very basic human characteristic.[3]

Assael does not use photographs to compose his paintings; instead, he relies on observation and drawings. From the start, drawing has been both a support for and a release from painting. His skilled draftsmanship is evident in minute details such as tattoos and in larger concerns such as defining human forms and clothing.

Assael's portrayal of these three youths with physical markings and costumes (costuming is implied by the tailor's dress form at the right, complete with pins) reflects a much older tradition in body art and dress; that is, the use of scarification, body piercing, and ceremonial wear among African tribes, Native American groups, and many others. Often an individual's importance in the group is directly linked to the extent of that person's physical adornments. Assael presents these club kids as proud and uncompromising. CTB

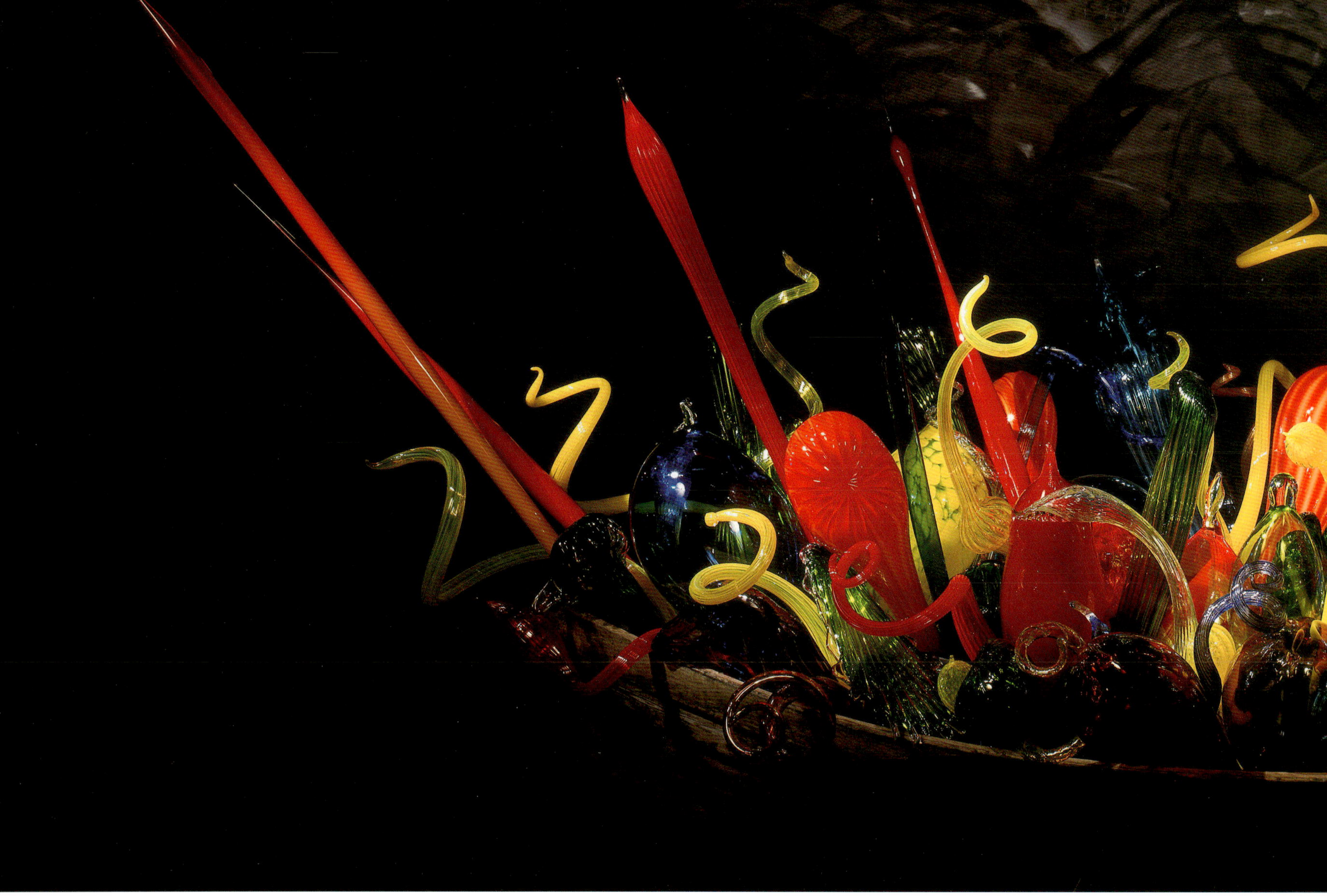

DALE CHIHULY

100 b. 1942, Tacoma, Washington
Boat Installation, 2001
Blown glass and wood, approximately 120 × 240 × 72 (304.8 × 609.6 × 182.88)
Museum purchase made possible by Thornton and Sue Jordan with Miles, and C. Dexter Jordan Jr. and Pat Jordan, with Mint, Ruth, and Zach, in Memory of C. Dexter Jordan Sr., Chairman of the Board of Trustees, 1956–1963, of the Columbus Museum and one of the five original Life Trustees.

PROVENANCE: Lowe Gallery, Atlanta.
EXHIBITIONS: *Dale Chihuly: Recent Work*, Lowe Gallery, January–February 2002.

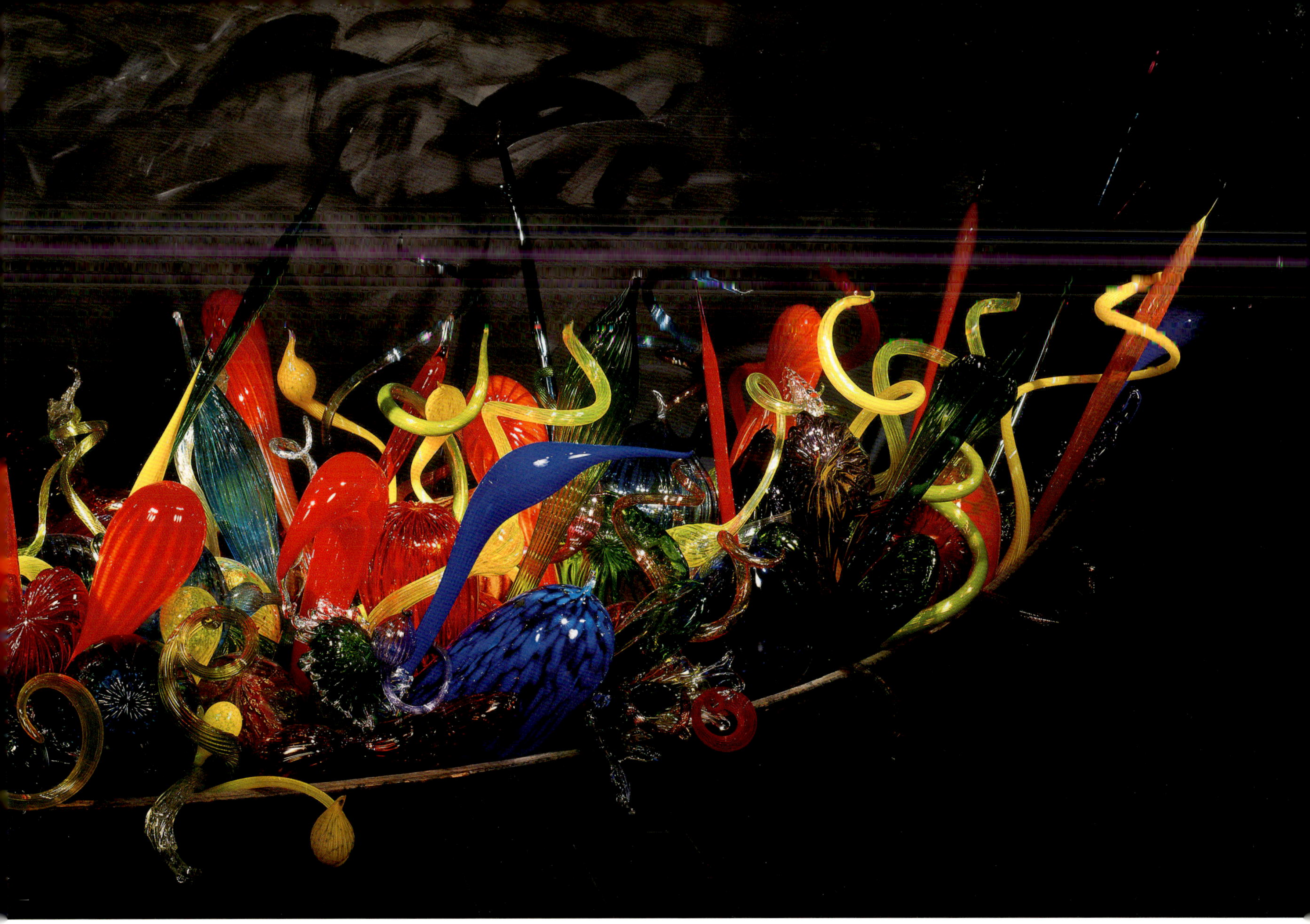

Born in Tacoma, Washington, Dale Chihuly was introduced to glass making while studying interior design at the University of Washington in Seattle.[1] After graduating in 1965, he enrolled at the University of Wisconsin in Madison to study glass blowing under Harvey Littleton, who inaugurated the first glasswork program in the country. He continued his studies at the Rhode Island School of Design, where he later established a glass program and taught for more than a decade.

In 1968 Chihuly was awarded a Fulbright Fellowship to work at the prestigious Venini Fabrica on the island of Murano, near Venice. There he observed the team approach to glassblowing, which is critical to the way his workshop functions today. In 1971 he founded, along with Anne and John Hauberg, the Pilchuck Glass School in Stanwood, Washington (fifty miles north of Seattle), now acknowledged as an important international glass center. Through Pilchuck, he has led the avant-garde in the development of glasswork as a fine art.

Chihuly has received many awards, including seven honorary doctorates and two fellowships from the National Endowment for the Arts. He has created a number of series in glass, such as Baskets, Chandeliers, Persians, Seaforms, and Seal Pups, and he is also known for large architectural installations. His art glass is included in more than two hundred museum collections worldwide.

Boat Installation introduces a new and fairly unusual form that incorporates Chihuly's two major loves: glass and water. He first made glass boats in Finland during the Chihuly Over Finland project in June 1995. After several days of glassblowing in the "hotshop," his team made temporary installations along the Nuutajärvi River, hanging several of his celebrated chandeliers from trees and small bridges, piling examples of his seal pups on rocks, and planting tall glass reeds in shallow water. At one point Chihuly began tossing the bulbous seal pups and belugas into the river and letting them float downstream. Local children in small wooden rowboats gathered them up. It was then that Chihuly saw the opportunity for a new kind of installation. Much to the delight of townspeople along the river, he began filling locally owned rowboats to overflowing with chandelier parts, seal pups, belugas, reeds, and other glass forms that were blown during the Finland trip. The museum's wooden boat from Finland is overflowing with glass in a re-creation of the artist's 1995 experience along the Nuutajarvi River. CTB

WOLF KAHN

101 b. 1927, Stuttgart, Germany
Barns near a Pond, 2001
Oil on canvas, 52 × 66 (132.08 × 167.64)
Signed lower right center: W Kahn
Museum purchase with funds provided by the Swift Family Foundation in honor of Mrs. Gunby Jordan 2001.23.1

PROVENANCE: Reynolds Gallery, Richmond, Virginia.
EXHIBITIONS: *Wolf Kahn: New Work,* Reynolds Gallery, Richmond, Virginia, November 9–December 22, 2001; *Summer Potpourri.*

Wolf Kahn, the youngest of four siblings, was born into a well-to-do artistic family. His father was the conductor of the Stuttgart Philharmonic Symphony, and his mother came from a family of art collectors.[1] Kahn took his first art lessons in 1938, drawing mostly military or historical events. The next year, following Hitler's rise to power, he left Germany and went to England. In 1940 he immigrated to the United States, and in 1942 entered New York's High School of Music and Art. When not in school, he made illustrations for a commercial art firm. After a stint in the navy, Kahn entered Hans Hofmann's school, where he met Neil Blaine, Jane Freilicher, Allan Kaprow, and Larry Rivers. Initially he painted abstracted forms in a dark palette.

Kahn's first exhibition was a 1951 group show in a loft in lower Manhattan. From this impromptu show evolved a group effort called the Hansa Gallery Cooperative.[2] In 1953 Kahn had a solo show at the Hansa gallery, which was favorably reviewed by the painter Fairfield Porter. At this time Kahn was painting with bolder, more vivid colors, but by the mid-1950s, on a summer trip to Provincetown, Massachusetts, he began to soften his palette, using warm colors in the manner of Bonnard. He was included in Meyer Shapiro's seminal exhibition, *The New York School: The Second Generation,* at the Jewish Museum, and by the end of the 1950s he had developed the abstracted landscape style for which he is best known. In 1966, on Martha's Vineyard, he made his first barn painting, in which he reduced the complexities of architectural detail to more basic forms, as in the museum's painting. Here the gradual buildup of colors resembles the beauty and translucent nature of pastels. Kahn has since commented frequently on his use of color as a unique and specific component of each work.[3]

Kahn's reputation as one of the country's foremost landscape artists is now firmly established. Over the past fifty years, he has gone from student to teacher, and has given numerous workshops in many southern communities, such as Charleston, South Carolina; Lexington, Kentucky; Syria, Virginia; Laurel, Mississippi; and Columbus.[4] He has demonstrated a technical virtuosity in monotypes and pastels, as well as in his primary medium of oil painting. His compositions seem to range from extreme close-ups to broad vistas, and his subjects from streams, estuaries, and open water to fields, trees, and man-made structures, such as barns.

Barns near a Pond, a large painting, comes from a body of his latest work and represents a return to the barnlike structures of earlier years.[5] In the synthetic architectural forms that span the middleground, Kahn used hot vibrant colors, placing them next to cool, intense, shaded areas. The sun-drenched foreground and the expansive sky above enhance each other by their contrasts. A shallow, reflective pond breaks up the wide sweep of grass in the foreground. This is a mature work in which the artist completely controls the colors and forms that he knows so well from years of close observation. CTB

CAT. 19

1. Aspects of William Frerichs's life and career are drawn principally from Williams and Safford. See also Chambers, *Art and Artists*; and Pennington, *Subdued Hues*.

CAT. 20

1. Miscellaneous journal, Smith Family Papers, Archives of American Art, Smithsonian Institution, reel 2040, frame 9. Also Fisher, n. 32.

2. Jonathan Smith to Russell Smith, February 10, 1869, in Xanthus Russell Smith Family Papers, Archives of American Art, Smithsonian Institution, reel [illegible], frame 504.

3. Dr. Robert W. Torchia, art historian and noted Smith scholar, in a letter to the museum, May 20, 1999, collections files, Columbus Museum. Of the three panel paintings, *Group of Contraband Huts, Hilton Head, S.C* seems to conform most closely to the dimensions listed as 9 × 13 (the museum's panel painting measures 9 × 12¾).

CAT. 21

1. For additional biographical information, see Weiss.

2. Novak, *American Painting*, 97–98. The term "luminism" was coined by John I. H. Baur in 1954. Baur did not include Sanford Gifford in his discussion of luminism. However, Gifford's place in this movement was acknowledged later in Novak's essays and subsequent publications. See Novak, *Nature and Culture;* and Wilmerding, *American Light*.

3. Discussions of this painting between the author and Dr. John Driscoll, director of Babcock Galleries, suggest that the identity of the mountain in the composition is Chocorua in New Hampshire. Weiss, 255, suggests it is Moat Mountain. However, Albert Bierstadt's painting of *Moat Mountain* (Currier Gallery) and the fact that a large body of water does not exist near Moat Mountain, are the reasons that Dr. Driscoll and the author remain confident that the mountain is Chocorua.

4. There is at least one other painting of the same scene, *Home in the Woods*, ca. 1866, oil on canvas, 10½ × 20 inches (collection of Mr. and Mrs. Charles Shoemaker). These pictures have no obvious reference to economic plight or tensions from the Civil War despite their close dating to the conflict.

CAT. 22

1. Much of this material is from obituary notices in New York newspapers. The museum is indebted to Professor William H. Gerdts for his help in researching Marshall.

2. Information on the Cropsey painting is from the Minneapolis Institute of Arts.

CAT. 23

1. Biographical information is from Shaw; Robert Hughes, 258; and Sears, 176–78.

CAT. 24

1. Driscoll, 2.

2. Howat, n.p.

3. Driscoll and Howat, 141. This body of work was done in three different locations: Lake George, New York; Newport, Rhode Island; and around Contentment Island near Darien, Connecticut. This area on the Long Island Sound was largely unexplored by artists until Kensett's body of work. There is some uncertainty about the exact number of works executed by Kensett during the summer of 1872. Oswaldo R. Roque, in Driscoll and Howat, 141, wrote that the number of works ranged between thirty and forty. Thomas Kensett, the artist's brother, offered thirty-eight works to the Metropolitan Museum of Art in a letter dated March 19, 1874, to John Taylor Johnston, president of the museum. "The Last Summer's Work" (New York: Metropolitan Museum of Art, 1874).

CAT. 25

1. Webster, 11.

2. Landgren, 90.

3. Knowlton, 106.

4. A larger version of this oil painting and at least one charcoal drawing are in the Museum of Fine Arts, Boston. The Columbus Museum also has on long-term loan, Hunt's *Child at Water's Edge*, a charcoal drawing on paper (Promised Gift, Dr. and Mrs. Philip L. Brewer Collection).

CAT. 26

1. Zellman, comp., 455. The author is also indebted to the Smithsonian American Art Museum for research assistance.

2. Winn, et al., 13. Naegele also exhibited works by Robert Henri, Guy Wiggins, and Frederick Waugh, as well as displays of Egyptian scarabs and brasses and bronzes from Asia. A fire in 1969 at the Christian Fellowship Association destroyed all of the Penny Art Fund pictures remaining in the community except the Jones landscape.

CAT. 27

1. For additional biographical information, see Lee M. Edwards, "Noble Domesticity"; see also Terhune, Yount, and Woods.

2. Lee M. Edwards, *Domestic Bliss*, 14.

3. Ann Terhune believes that the title is not original. She also believes the male model was one Hovenden used in other paintings after 1885, therefore calling the date into question as well. Letter to Karol Lawson, June 1994, following Terhune's visit to the museum; accession files, Columbus Museum.

CAT. 28

1. The authors are indebted to Johnson scholar Patricia Hills and the Ira Spanierman Gallery for the research they have shared on Eastman Johnson. Hills's catalogue raisonné on the artist is forthcoming.

2. The painting was once called *Old Kentucky Home*, after Stephen Foster's song.

3. Zellman, comp., 378.

4. Baur, *An American Genre Painter*, 23.

5. Patricia Hills, letter, 1996, Spanierman Gallery archives, New York.

6. Ibid.

7. Ibid.

CAT. 29

1. Baur, *Theodore Robinson*, 20. For additional biographical information, see Baltimore Museum of Art.

2. Young, 45.

3. Sona Johnson, in Baltimore Museum of Art, xxiv.

CAT. 30

1. Biographical information is from Lee M. Edwards, *Domestic Bliss*, 108; and Zellman, comp., 583. The museum's painting is included in a forthcoming catalogue raisonné by Kaycee Benton.

2. Edward Lamson Henry established an artists' colony in Cragsmoor in 1879.

3. Kaycee Benton to Kristen Miller Zohn, July 29, 2002.

CAT. 31

1. See Conner and Rosenkranz, 123–31.

2. Though the piece could have been cast in Paris or in the United States, it was most likely created in Paris. Given its post-1894 dating, it was probably sold through Theodore B. Starr Gallery in New York, the artist's most active gallery. MacMonnies also sold his work through Tiffany and Co. and Durand-Ruel Galleries in New York.

3. Craven, *Sculpture in America*, 421.

4. Apparently, this piece was modeled after a well-known entertainer in Paris, and was viewed with disfavor by temperance groups. Charles F. McKim donated it to the Metropolitan Museum of Art.

5. Robert Hughes, 212.

CAT. 32

1. For more information on George Ohr, see Clark, et al. Meyer taught Ohr the secrets of Old World glaze formulas.

2. See the autobiographical essay, George Ohr, "Some Facts in the History of a Unique Personality," *Crockery and Glass Journal* 54 (December 1901). Ohr's son Leo destroyed much of his personal notes and journals after his father's death, and scholars are only now starting to piece together a more complete account of Ohr's life and career.

3. A photograph from *Harper's Magazine* in 1895 shows Ohr's Biloxi Pottery already in full production. Illustrated in Clark, et al., 13.

4. Their first child, Ella Louise, died after just a few months, and their son, Asa Eugene, died before he reached the age of five. At some point, George became interested in the fact that his abbreviated name, Geo. was spelled with his initials G.E.O. When his third child was born, he named him Leo Ernest to correspond with his initials. This eccentric practice continued with all of his children thereafter—Clo, Lio, Oto, Flo, Zio, Ojo, and Geo.

5. Ellsworth Woodward had established a crafts program that provided training and income for women through Newcomb College at Tulane University.

6. Clark, et al., 17. As early as May 1890, Ohr had referred to himself as an art potter in the *Biloxi Herald*.

7. According to Jean Bragg, gallery owner and Ohr connoisseur, Ohr's pottery can be dated by the mark on the bottom, as follows: those created 1888–94 (prior to the fire of 1894) are stamped GEO.E. OHR, BILOXI, MISS or GEO.E.OHR BILOXI; those from 1895–1900 are stamped G.E.OHR, Biloxi, Miss; those from 1898–1910 have handwritten signatures; and those from 1888–1910 are marked Biloxi.

8. The museum's teapot retains its original price tag of $20. This would have been very expensive for a clay vessel in the late nineteenth century.

9. Patti Carr Black, "George E. Ohr, America's First Art Potter," http: //mshistory.k12.ms.us/features/feature27/ohr.html. Also see, Black, ed.

10. A new museum, the Ohr-O'Keefe Museum of Art, designed by architect Frank Gehry, will open in Biloxi in 2004. Civic leader and civil rights activist Jeremiah O'Keefe raised $7 million toward a $16 million capital campaign.

CAT. 33

1. Pisano, 149.

CAT. 34

1. Frankenstein, 99.

2. Ibid., xv.

3. Ibid.

CAT. 35

1. See Havens, "F. J. Waugh," 30–37, for more about Waugh's marine paintings.

2. See Gary A. Hood, n.p.

3. The museum also owns Waugh's *Seascape* (Gift of Mr. Jefferson D. Box, 71.22).

4. Nelson, 47. Nelson suggests that this close-up of the water gives the impression that the artist is standing in the surf as he paints.

CAT. 36

1. See Peters, 18.

2. Ibid., 24. Leibl was a student of Gustave Courbet, who came from the realist tradition and advocated painting subjects from everyday life.

3. For additional biographical information see John Douglass Hale. See also Boyle, *John Henry Twachtman* and *John Twachtman*.

4. Hale, quoted in Boyle, *John Twachtman*, 16.

5. Peters, 131, 135.

CAT. 37

1. Young, 123.

2. For additional biographical information, see Burke.

3. Previous titles of this painting include *The Hilltop Road* and *Weir's Farm*. The museum is grateful to Hildegard Cummings, Curator of Education (retired), the William Benton Museum of Art, Storrs, Connecticut, for this information. April 1, 2002, letter to Brigitte Foley, Columbus Museum files; attached to this letter is a copy of a November 15, 1920, letter from previous owner Henry Smith, New York, to Dorothy Weir, Windham, Connecticut, which states that the painting's title was *Pelham Lane*. Columbus Museum accession records.

4. Wood, a friend, lived in Portland, Oregon. He acted as an informal dealer and sold many of Weir's paintings.

5. Young, 217.

CAT. 38

1. The Newcomb College design program had its genesis at the 1876 Philadelphia Centennial Exposition, where William and Ellsworth Woodward became enamored with the William Morris Arts and Crafts aesthetic. They enrolled at the Rhode Island School of Design. In the mid-1880s they went to New Orleans, and in 1888 William founded the New Orleans Art Pottery. Six years later, Ellsworth began the pottery program at Newcomb. See Kemp.

2. Bragg and Saward, 89–90.

3. The determination to base decorative motifs on flora and fauna from the southern environment reflects the philosophy of the Arts and Crafts movement, which sought an art appropriate for the modern age but was not imitative of historical forms. For more on Newcomb pottery, see Poesch, 21.

4. Ibid., 49.

CAT. 39

1. Hiesinger, 14.

2. Bye, 213–14.

3. Ibid., 30. Carlsen, 6–8.

4. Hiesinger, 15.

CAT. 40

1. Biographical information is from Gerdts, *Pride in Place;* Karpiscak; and Milroy.

2. The Lawsons moved to Columbus, Georgia, in 1896, but he soon realized that he had no real teaching skills and left his job. This caused a serious rift in his marriage; his wife left him, and he moved to Toronto. This was the first of a number of long separations in their marriage.

3. Lawson exhibited three paintings in the Armory Show, including *Harlem River—Winter*, which the Metropolitan Museum of Art purchased two years later as their first acquisition of Lawson's work.

4. Dennis Anderson wrote, "For the first time evidence has come to light that there were at this time, a series of robberies and assaults made upon Miami beachgoers by bands of young hooligans. It is suspected, because of police and medical evidence, that Ernest Lawson was one of their victims, and subsequently died of a heart attack." Quoted in Karpiscak, 17.

5. According to Karpiscak, he learned this method during his early studies with Ella Holman.

6. Keyes, *American Impressionism in Georgia Collections*, 68. The Columbus Museum has two other works by Lawson: *View of Garden in Paris Suburb* (oil on canvas, 78.9) and *Landscape* (monotype in oil on paper, Gift of Dr. and Mrs. Philip L. Brewer 2001.16.2).

CAT. 41

1. For additional biographical information, see Elzea; St. Johns, ed.; and Scott.

2. Sloan, 107.

3. According to Elzea, the artist's file card indicates that he painted the canvas in December 1913.

4. Elzea, 23. The quotation is from Sloan's notes on file at the Delaware Art Museum.

5. Sloan, 109.

6. Ibid., 105.

CAT. 42

1. For additional biographical information, see Gerdts, *William Glackens;* and Glackens.

2. See Kern and Dawson, 84.

CAT. 43

1. For more on Garber's works, see Foster. See also Folk; Gerdts, et al.; and the forthcoming catalogue raisonné by Lane Humphries and others, published by Hollis Taggert Gallery, New York.

2. Gerdts, *American Impressionism*, 237.

3. Gerdts, "The Square Format," 70–75.

4. Gerdts, *American Impressionism*, 188.

CAT. 44

1. Biographical information is from Hoopes; and Zellman, comp.

2. Charles Hawthorne was the founder of the Provincetown, Massachusetts, art colony and one of the principal instructors at the New York School of Art.

3. Hoopes, n.p. Hoopes states that Davey combined the influences of both Henri and Hawthorne in realizing a perfect balance between a formal, abstract concern for paint on canvas and the meaning and emotions that lie under the surface.

4. This system required precise measurements in color mixing. Hoopes noted that Davey painted almost solely in his studio, where the lighting was invariable and he could use color in a consistent manner.

CAT. 45

1. Kane, 9.

2. Zellman, comp., 764.

3. Kane, 26, 30.

4. MacChesney, xxiv. Albright Art Gallery (now Albright-Knox Museum of Art) purchased *La Toilette* in 1914 and exhibited it in May. Other museums purchasing his work at this time include Syracuse Museum of Fine Art, the Corcoran Gallery of Art, and the Saint Louis Art Museum.

CAT. 46

1. Biographical information is from De Veer and Boyle; MacAdam, *Winter's Promise;* Pierce; and Zellman, comp., 543. The dates in this entry conform to those in De Veer and Boyle.

2. The other members were Frank W. Benson, Joseph R. De Camp, Thomas Dewing, Childe Hassam, Robert Reid, Edward E. Simmons, Edmund C. Tarbell, John Henry Twachtman, and J. Alden Weir. William Merritt Chase was asked to join the group after the death of Twachtman.

3. The sculptor Augustus Saint-Gaudens founded the art colony at Cornish. Metcalf often painted there, as did other artists such as Maxfield Parrish, Kenyon Cox, and Thomas Dewing.

4. Bruce Chambers, in a telephone conversation with Kristen Miller Zohn. Chambers, who is completing the catalogue raisonné on Willard Metcalf, said that the painting has been known as *Thawing Brook* and *The Thawing Brook*. He is not sure which was the original title. Elizabeth de Veer, who also worked on Metcalf's catalogue raisonné, created the previous title used by the museum, *Thawing Brook Number 2*. Her designation was based on the identification of two additional Metcalf paintings titled *Thawing Brook*, and was an attempt to place all three paintings in chronological order. Note in museum accession file from Brigitte Foley, associate curator.

5. Painting outdoors was a basic tenet of the impressionists. The 1917 photograph shows Metcalf painting with a gloveless hand. De Veer and Boyle, pl. 152. Apparently he did not generally work from preliminary sketches, as there are no existing sketchbooks from his stays in Cornish. Barbara J. MacAdam, *Winter's Promise*, 16–17.

6. The museum owns Edward Redfield's *Road to Lambertville* (cat. 56), which is also a winter scene. Twachtman, Hassam, and others frequently painted snow scenes as well.

7. Cortissoz acknowledged that the painting's traditional style was currently out of critical favor: "The picture spells 'conservative,' if you like. It discloses no new, recondite method. . . . But it happens to interpret nature with freshness and truth, it happens to be . . . very beautiful." Originally published in *New York Herald Tribune* (April 18, 1918), 15 (roll N70/13, Archives of American Art). Quoted in MacAdam, *Winter's Promise*, 64.

CAT. 47

1. For additional biographical information, see Oresman; and Lesko and Persson, eds.

2. Dreiss, xvi.

3. The Dutch people were Melchers's primary inspiration. He was influenced by the Hague school of artists, which included Josef Israels, Anton Mauve, and Johan Neuhuijs, who all favored sentimental depictions of mother and child.

4. Reid, 163. Besides his home in Virginia, Melchers had a strong connection to Savannah, Georgia, the home of his in-laws. He had considerable influence in building the early-twentieth-century painting collection of their beloved Telfair museum by convincing his artist friends to sell their works to the museum at affordable prices. Pivotal works by Bellows, Cassatt, and others entered the Telfair's collection because of Melchers's expertise and guidance.

5. The museum also owns Melchers's *Mother and Child*, ca. 1885–95 (Gift of Jack Passailaigue, 98.38.2), which dates from the years of his European residence.

6. The 1899 date of Kate Kendall's only exhibition in Paris coincides with the date of an earlier or first version of a Melchers portrait of Kendall, a ca. 1900 study in the Columbus Museum's collection (Gift of George Dudley, 80.19). This pastel on canvas was for many years thought to be a study for the 1919 version of the head of Kate Kendall.

7. An earlier version of the museum's painting, called *Portrait of a Lady*, was completed around 1900. It was exhibited in 1901 at the Art Institute of Chicago as *Portrait of Miss Kendall* and possibly again in Düsseldorf in 1904.

8. The authors are grateful for information provided by Joanna D. Catron, curator, Belmont, the Gari Melchers Estate and Memorial Gallery, October 1, 1998.

CAT. 48

1. Jo Davidson, 174–75.

2. The museum is grateful to Branden Fortune, curator, National Portrait Gallery, for providing valuable information on Davidson and this mask. Additional thanks go to Joel Rosenkranz and Janis Conner, co-directors, Conner-Rosenkranz Gallery, for reading the entry for accuracy.

CAT. 49

1. The museum is grateful to Lisa Peters and Carol Lowrey of Spanierman Gallery for sharing valuable information on Glintenkamp.

2. Glintenkamp enjoyed a lengthy visit to Spain in 1921. He probably returned there again during 1922–23, when he resided in England. See Chronology in Leff, 14. He returned to Europe during 1930–31, accumulating visual material for his book, *A Wanderer in Woodcuts* (1932), which includes a chapter on Spain.

3. Washington Irving, *The Alhambra* (New York: Macmillan, 1926).

CAT. 50

1. Information on the artist's life is from Nordland.

2. Rose, *Gaston Lachaise Sculpture,* 12.

3. Hartley, "Twice a Year," in Kramer, ed., 27.

4. Rose, *Gaston Lachaise Sculpture,* 87. Among these were Scofield Thayer, James S. Watson Jr., Henry McBride, M. R. Werner, and the poet e.e. cummings.

5. In a 1997 telephone conversation with Charles T. Butler, modern art collector Roy Neuberger, who owns the only other cast of this piece, described his search for the poet's identity and suggested that it might be Ezra Pound, who was given an award of excellence by the *Dial* in 1927. However, he concluded that it really didn't matter who it was, since it was such a wonderful cast. This sculpture is similar to other portrait heads by the artist, such as *Henry McBride* (1928; Museum of Modern Art) and *John Marin* (1928; Phillips Collection).

CAT. 51

1. Valentiner. See also Dorothy C. Miller.

2. Quoted in Cheney, 156.

3. Bernard and Miller, eds., n.p.

4. Dorothy C. Miller, 12. Despite his success in art, he remained troubled for most of his life, enduring mental illnesses, divorce, and serious injuries from automobile accidents. He took his own life in 1942.

5. Quoted by Carl Zigrosser, in Dorothy C. Miller, 11.

CAT. 52

1. Homer, 17.

2. Ibid., 120.

3. Ibid., 206.

4. Ibid., 238.

5. Henri, 22–26.

CAT. 53

1. For the most complete biographical information to date, see the exhibition brochure, "Angela Gregory," n.p.; and Rubenstein, 293–96.

2. James Lamantia in a telephone conversation with Brigitte Foley; Lamantia, of New Orleans, represents the estate of Angela Gregory. The IBM Corporation currently owns the first cast. The other cast is in a private collection.

CAT. 54

1. Lisa Peters of Spanierman Gallery, in notes that accompanied the painting, cites 1899 as the year that Kroll began working with Twachtman at the Art Students League. Valerie Ann Leeds, in *Leon Kroll Revisited,* 123, places him with Twachtman in 1901, the year of Twachtman's death.

2. Hale and Bowers, eds., 46.

3. *Blanche Reading* (1932; Dayton Art Institute) appears to have been painted in the same cove but viewed from the top of the hill, beyond the buildings. Another painting, *Landscape, St. Jean* (1926; location unknown) is similar to the museum's painting and the others mentioned in its construction, with figures and buildings placed throughout a landscape.

4. Hale and Bowers, eds., 106.

5. Although the title *A Cove in Maine* is inscribed on the painting's stretcher, the image was published with the title *Rocks at Island House* in Hale and Bowers, eds., while the painting was still part of the artist's estate.

6. Hale and Bowers, eds., 13.

CAT. 55

1. Tchelitchew had displayed a noticeable talent for drawing as a child. An early influence was the art of Gustave Doré, whose penchant for fantasy and romanticism he had seen in illustrated books in his father's library. Another important instructor was Issac Rabinovitch, whom he met at the Kiev Academy.

2. In addition to *Spahi,* the museum has a 1929 ink drawing by the artist, *Study for Blue Clown* (2003.1.51). Tchelitchew had a solo exhibition at Galerie Vignon in Paris in 1931; at the Esther Surrey Gallery, The Hague, Netherlands, the following year; and at Arthur Tooth and Sons in London in 1935. Because the provenance records include a London-based ownership, it is possible that *Spahi* was in at least one of these shows. We are indebted to halley k harrisburg and Michael Rosenfeld of Michael Rosenfeld Gallery for assistance in preparing this entry.

3. Tchelitchew began to use blue as a predominant color as early as 1925, but by the end of 1931 red had become his key hue.

4. Soby, 22.

CAT. 56

1. Fletcher, 5.

2. Gerdts, *American Impressionism,* 231.

3. This date is based upon a careful comparison to other known works by Redfield. For example, the technique observed in *Christmas Morning* (Montclair Art Museum, New Jersey), dated 1932, is similar to that in *Road to Lambertville.*

4. Gerdts, *American Impressionism,* 235.

CAT. 57

1. Much of the information in this entry is from gallery notes developed by Kraushaar Gallery. The authors are indebted to Carole M. Pesner and Katherine Kaplan for their assistance.

2. Goodrich, 13.

3. Kraushaar Gallery.

4. Ibid. Many of these artworks were later donated to museums.

5. Goodrich and Baur, 79.

6. The copper-domed buildings still stand near this subway stop, but the ornate entrance has been replaced.

CAT. 58

1. Kornhauser, , cat. 252

2. Fort, "James Guy: A Surreal Commentator," 147.

3. Ibid., 131.

4. Ibid., 148.

CAT. 59

1. Cannell, 88.

2. Barbara Rose interview with Krasner, March 1972; quoted in Landau and Grove, 75. Landau cites the title as *Untitled;* Spanierman Gallery listed it as *Still Life* in 1998.

3. Ibid.

4. For full documentation about Krasner's signature, see Landau and Grove, 73.

CAT. 60

1. Hills, *Stuart Davis,* 10. Hills's research in the archival records of the East Orange, New Jersey, High School, which Davis attended, states that his birth date was actually 1892 instead of 1894, as has long been thought. For later information, see Salander.

2. Brown, *Story of the Armory Show,* 66.

3. Hills, *Stuart Davis,* 9.

4. Zellman, comp., 3: 902.

5. Kachur, in Wilkins and Kachur, 30.

6. Levin, 82.

7. Sims, *Stuart Davis,* 252.

8. Davis, 6.

CAT. 61

1. For additional biographical information, see Littleton; Mark; and Merrill.

2. According to Cederwall and Riney, 171, the hallmarks on this set indicate that it was made between 1931 and 1945. Marc Navarro Gallery estimated that they were made between 1945 and 1950. The phrase "Spratling Silver" engraved in a lozenge apparently was not used after 1945, but it appears on the coffee set.

CAT. 62

1. Bolin, 119.

2. Abraham A. Davidson, 29.

3. Stieglitz's Little Galleries of the Photo-Secession, or 291, as it was more commonly known, was an important factor in the rise of modern art in America. Few individuals have exerted as strong an influence on twentieth-century American art and culture as photographer and art dealer Alfred Stieglitz. He brought modern European art to the United States, organizing the first exhibitions in this country of works by Pablo Picasso, Henri Matisse, Georges Braque, and Paul Cézanne, among others. He was one of the first to champion and support American modernist artists such as Georgia O'Keeffe, Arthur Dove, John Marin, Marsden Hartley, Charles Demuth, and photographer Paul Strand.

4. Brown, *Story of the Armory Show,* 121.

CAT. 63

1. Cooke, n.p. A comprehensive survey of Dodd's career and art is found in Eiland and Dodd.

2. *Lamar Dodd,* n.p.

CAT. 64

1. Larkin, 454.

2. Wechsler, 16.

CAT. 65

1. Quoted in Lawson, "Nobody Knows," n.p. Other sources consulted for this entry are Archives of American Art, Smithsonian Institution. microfilm reel N 76, frames 829–37; and Rosenwald Fund papers, Fisk University Library Special Collections, Fisk University, Nashville.

2. Julius Rosenwald, president of Sears, Roebuck and Company, established the Rosenwald Fund in 1917 in Chicago. The fund had several goals, including the improvement of rural education, especially in the South. Money also was given to white and black southerners through fellowships. Other artists who benefited from the fund were Hale Woodruff and Jacob Lawrence.

3. In addition to this series, the museum owns a master set of Baker's graphics, plus numerous other paintings and drawings. The museum was the recipient of the artist's personal collection at the time of his death.

4. Lawson, "Nobody Knows," n.p.

5. Baker, 142.

6. Stephen E. Henderson, "On 'Memphis Blues'" *Modern American Poetry,* January 1, 2000; see www.english.uiuc.edu/maps/poets/a_f/brown/memphis.htm (1/6/2003).

7. Ibid.

CAT. 66

1. Kuspit, in Perkins and Kuspit, 8.

2. Phagan, 174, quoted from *Sketchbook no. 14, 1955–1957* (Georgia Museum of Art, University of Georgia, Athens, 94.20).

CAT. 67

1. Albrecht, et al., 74.

2. Kirkham, 107–14.

3. Charles and Ray Eames introduced the final design to the public at the Museum of Modern Art's 1946 exhibition, *New Furniture Designed by Charles Eames,* which notably failed to include Ray Kaiser's name. In fact, their lifelong collaboration and the cross-hybrid nature of their ideas are fundamental to understanding their designs and their work.

4. Caplan, 92.

CAT. 68

1. Quoted in McCausland, 149.

2. Kammen, 18–19.

3. Piehl, 130.

4. The New Orleans Museum of Art owns a smaller version of this painting with the same title and dating from 1957. It has four figures, and measures 12 × 9 inches.

5. Information about Sarah Wade is from Kammen, 61. Gwathmey often repeated single figures in other paintings. Wade has a secondary role in the painting *Saturday Afternoon* (1949; private collection).

6. Quoted in McCausland, 151.

CAT. 69

1. Biographical material is from Keyes, *Andrée Ruellan,* and Polly Kline, *Andrée Ruellan: A Retrospective* (see www.woodstockart.org/perm_coll/ruellen/).

2. Keyes, *Andrée Ruellan,* 30 and 35.

3. Ibid., 35. After sketching the architecture of the town and the people in the streets, Ruellan took the drawings back to her studio and used them to compose paintings. Later, she used the figures of the dancing couple on the left as the basis for a print, *Masques* (1951; aquatint on paper, collection of the artist).

4. Henkes, 91.

CAT. 70

1. Parts of this entry come from Daphne Deeds, "Burgoyne Diller," in *The American Painting Collection of Sheldon Memorial Art Gallery,* 48; also Larson; and O'Connor.

2. Although the Mondrian influence is clear and documented, Diller went to great pains to deny it, always claiming to be original. For Reinhardt, see Rosenfeld, 4.

3. Deeds, in *American Painting Collection of Sheldon Memorial Art Gallery,* 48. In addition, Diller said, "The Whitney Museum was the center. . . . Now at that time there were very few abstract painters. I happened to be one of the abstract painters that were in that group, the original group. I think Gorky and Stuart Davis and I am not sure who else, but there were not very many at the time. Then that of course went out of existence." Harlan Phillips, Oral History Interview with Burgoyne Diller, Atlantic Highlands, New Jersey, October 2, 1964, Archives of American Art.

4. Greenberg, "The New Sculpture," 641.

5. The museum owns the preliminary charcoal drawing for this sculpture, *Study for Wall Construction,* 1950 (98.8) and an untitled tempera, pencil, and ink drawing by Diller, a promised gift on long-term loan from Dr. and Mrs. Philip L. Brewer.

6. Larsen, 4.

7. Larson, 15.

CAT. 71

1. Craven, *Sculpture in America,* 576.

2. Penelope Curtis, 95.

3. Kloss and Mecklenburg, 145.

4. Tessim Zorach letter to Karol Lawson, March 5, 1993.

CAT. 72

1. Vickrey, 29.

2. William E. Steadman, in *Robert Vickrey,* foreword, n.p.

3. Ibid.

4. Letter from Midtown Galleries, collections files, Columbus Museum.

CAT. 73

1. See Schmeckebier. Additional information has come from interviews with Sally Foley, the artist's stepdaughter and longtime museum trustee. The museum owns a number of Nordhausen's paintings, drawings, and monotypes.

2. Nordhausen presided over the prestigious Salmagundi Club, the oldest arts club in America, from 1959 until 1963. Its members have included John la Farge, Albert Pinkham Ryder, George Inness, William Merritt Chase, Louis C. Tiffany, Stanford White, and Thomas Moran, among others.

3. Interview with Sally Foley, January 16, 2002.

4. Notes from videotape of Nordhausen's gallery walk at Columbus Museum, September 10, 1989.

5. Schmeckebier, vii.

6. Videotape of gallery walk.

7. Interview with Sally Foley, January 16, 2002.

CAT. 74

1. Dore Ashton, in Pleynet, 11. We are grateful to the staff and trustees of the Dedalus Foundation in New York for their support and assistance.

2. Thanks to a generous gift from the Dedalus Foundation, there were eight ink drawings from Motherwell's 1965 Lyric Suite series donated to the museum in honor of museum director Charles T. Butler. Other works by Motherwell acquired by the museum include an early painting on paper, *Untitled,* 1961 (2000.13.1), a collage, *Edgar Allen Poe Series, #1,* 1973 (2000.13.4), and a large oil painting, *Open #14,* 1967 (2000.13.3).

3. Arnason, 64.

4. Dore Ashton, in Arnason, 8.

CAT. 75

1. Charles T. Butler interview with Zupan, spring 1999.

2. Gail Greenblatt interview with Zupan, January 24, 2002. Additional paintings by Zupan in the museum are *Bagley's Store* (74.40), *Natasha in Calle Rectoria* (80.52), *Bird Cage and Tile, Valldemossa* (81.52), *Andrew Shepherd Home* (83.20), *Boats on the Shore at Majorca* (84.10), and *Golden Sea* (88.12). Works on paper include *Ulysses* (77.14) and *The Columbus Museum* (89.4), which commemorated the museum's expansion in 1989.

CAT. 76

1. Alma Woodsey Thomas was the eldest of four daughters born to John Harris Thomas and Amelia Cantey Thomas. The museum is fortunate that Maurice Thomas, the artist's sister, donated in 1994 numerous paintings, watercolors, ceramics, and related Thomas family memorabilia to the collections.

2. Munro, 193.

3. For the most complete publication on the artist's life to date, see Fort Wayne Museum of Art.

4. "Alma W. Thomas," n.p.

5. Artists Kenneth Noland, Sam Gilliam, and Morris Louis formed the core known as the Washington color field school, the group with which Thomas frequently is compared.

6. Wilson, 90.

7. Ibid.

CAT. 77

1. For biographical information, see Hills, *Alice Neel;* Allara.

2. Lawrence Campbell, 24. Quoted in Temkin, ed., 172.

3. Munro, 128.

4. Ibid., 130.

5. Information about the sitters was obtained during a telephone interview by Brigitte Foley with Ulrika Brand, the younger girl in *Swedish Girls,* on August 12, 1998. Ulrika Brand was born at Fort Benning, Georgia, in Muscogee County.

CAT. 78

1. Thomas Styron, comments on Nancy Grossman, in Sims, *Loud Whispers.*

2. An excellent example of Grossman's early drawing is seen in the museum's masterful pencil drawing from 1973, *Gunhead #2* (2003.1.38). Also in the collection is a large pencil drawing (60 × 90 inches) made a decade later in 1984, *Untitled* (98.27).

3. Morgan, 37. Morgan stated that although the gallery was hesitant about handling the work at the beginning—perhaps because it was transported to the owner in two large shopping bags—he eventually agreed to show it.

4. Ibid.

5. Grossman discussed this idea with Philip Brewer in her studio in November 1999, and with Les Reker in a telephone interview in January 2001.

6. Morgan, 36.

CAT. 79

1. Roger Brown, in *Who Chicago?,* 29.

2. The other artists in this group include Jim Nutt, Ed Paschke, Ray Yoshida, Karl Wirsum, Barbara Rossi, and Gladys Nilsson.

3. Ellen Edwards, C1.

4. Roger Brown to Fred Fussell, November 1990, museum accession files.

5. In a statement that Brown provided for the 1990 Columbus Museum exhibition *Home Again,* Brown said that his use of eerie light comes from his memories of Saturday afternoons at the Martin Theatre in Opelika, Alabama, where he became acquainted with film noire, a source of his anxious themes.

6. Interview in *Art in America* (January–February 1978): 107; quoted in Yau, 13.

CAT. 80

1. Biographical material was developed from the following sources: Fox, 1-H; [illegible], 163–66.

2. Helen S. Smith, 1-B.

CAT. 81

1. Biographical information is from Jaffe and [illegible].

2. Jaffe, [illegible]

3. Baskin fabricated a mold from French sand, chosen for its binding qualities. The mold was divided into a number of pieces so the plaster model could be removed easily. Once the sculpture was cast, the pieces were joined together. Rough spots and seams were removed in the finishing process. To color the bronze, special acids were used in a process referred to as patination.

CAT. 82

1. Parts of this entry are drawn from Pomeroy.

2. Pomeroy, 5–6.

3. Wolff, 21–22.

4. Ibid.

5. Pomeroy, 5–6; see also Duncan and Wolff, 37–47.

6. Wolff, 21.

CAT. 83

1. Beauchamp, in *Robert Beauchamp,* 19.

2. Ibid., 20.

3. Severens, 228.

CAT. 84

1. Wilhelm Ostwald's career was marked by a deeply rooted pursuit of unity and harmony, ranging from his earlier attempts at unifying chemistry and physics to his final theoretical and experimental work on color theory and aesthetics. Ostwald developed his color theory in 1914. He selected four evenly spaced primaries to develop a color wheel. Ostwald's primaries were lemon yellow, scarlet, ultramarine, and turquoise green. He divided his original color wheel into one hundred equally spaced hues. Finding this to be impractical, since it was difficult to distinguish one color step from another, he finally decided to divide the color wheel into four primary colors with five intermediates between each pair of primaries to form a color wheel of twenty-four distinct hues.

2. Lunde, 23. James Gibson and Rudolf Arnheim were the faculty members who made an impression upon Anuszkiewicz.

3. The visual effect of afterimage occurs when the eye focuses on a bright surface. Light-sensitive photoreceptors (whose job it is to convert light into electrical activity) in the retina respond to the incoming light. Other neurons that receive input from these photoreceptors respond as well. As one continues to stare at the object, the photoreceptors become desensitized (or fatigued). Most afterimages last only a few seconds to a minute, since in the absence of strong stimulation, most nerve cells quickly readjust.

4. Russell, in a review of Graham Gallery's exhibition that included *Temple of Electric Turquoise.*

CAT. 85

1. Doherty, 52–57.

2. Tully, "Daniel Greene: Still Lifes," 2.

CAT. 86

1. Christenberry made a series of paintings on the subject of tenant farmers' shacks. These works are very much rooted in the abstract expressionist teachings of his time but are also fully charged with his emotional response to the southern landscape.

2. Gruber, *William Christenberry,* 70.

3. See Kahan, n.p., for a more detailed discussion of Christenberry's use of found signage.

4. Kalinovska, 6.

5. *William Christenberry: A Southern Perspective,* Columbus Museum, April 12–May 24, 1987. The museum also owns a number of other works by Christenberry, including the preparatory drawing for *Columbus Wall* (*Drawing Related to Columbus Wall,* 1989, 89.6) and five lithographs from Rolling Stone Press (*Pointed Female,* 1990, 94.18.35; *Pointed Male,* 1990, 94.18.36; *Brute,* 1990, 94.18.37; *Dream of Fear,* 1990, 94.18.38; and *Ghost Image,* 1990, 94.18.39), which deal with Klan members.

6. Brigitte Foley telephone interview with the artist, April 5, 2002.

CAT. 87

1. Terenzio, 9.

2. Flam, 26.

CAT. 88

1. In a review, Brenson references Andrews's first collage in 1957, titled *Janitors at Rest.*

2. For a detailed review of Andrews's early life, see Gruber, *American Icons,* 1–41.

3. Gail Greenblatt telephone interview with Andrews, January 10, 2002.

4. Ibid.

CAT. 89

1. For biographical information, see Joosse, 4–17.

2. Arthur, 23.

3. Ibid., 13.

CAT. 90

1. George [illegible] interview with Jack Beal, [illegible]

2. Adams and Reker, 19.

3. Shanes, 22.

4. Beal letter to Les Reker, Columbus Museum collections archive.

CAT. 91

1. Bailey's work has been discussed in numerous publications, including those by the following authors: Carlozzi; Carlozzi, Fenton, and Maschke; Rifkin; and Leach.

2. The song "Before I'd Be a Slave (Oh, Freedom)" is from Barton. The full lyrics are: "Before I'd be a slave / I'd be buried in my grave / And go home to my Lord / And be saved / O, what preachin'! / O, what preachin'! / O, what preachin' over me, over me / O, what mourning . . . / O, what singing . . . / O, what shouting . . . / O, weeping Mary . . . / Doubting Thomas . . . / O, what sighing / O, Freedom. . . ."

3. Bailey, in telephone interview with Kristen Miller Zohn, June 18, 2002.

4. *Adinkra* is a kind of cloth made by the Ashanti people of Ghana. The dyers draw a grid on the cloth and then print a different stamp in each square. The stamp patterns have names and refer to household objects, historic people, or proverbs. The shape found in this work is similar to the *adinkra* symbol known as the ram's horn, a reference to a proverb saying that when two rams fight, one must admit defeat to the other. It is a symbol of strength.

5. Quoted in Carlozzi, Fenton, and Maschke, 17–19.

CAT. 92

1. Kennington, in interview by Brigitte Foley, March 2002. Columbus Museum accession files. Also see Gluhman; and Baldaia, *Dale Kennington.*

2. Baldaia, "A Conversation with Dale Kennington," n.p.

3. Kennington, in interview by Foley.

4. Kennington's statement about the painting, Columbus Museum accession files.

5. Ibid.

CAT. 93

1. Adams and Reker, 11.

2. Pearlstein, 39.

3. "Realism vs. Existentialism," Alan Frumkin Gallery Newsletter, no. 5 (spring 1978), 4.

4. John L. Ward, 146.

5. Bowman, 20.

6. Pearlstein, in interview with Les Reker, August 7, 2001.

CAT. 94

1. More, n.p. Also see Butler, et al.

2. Variants of the title are inscribed on the rear left edge of the canvas: "F&L 425"; "American Dream"; "Home Coming Queen"; "Fire and the Rose"; "Glory"; "Deals with bod"; "The Crowned Knot of Fire"; "Royalty"; and "Sovereignty." Other paintings by Bartlett in the museum's collection are *Youth and Adolescence from a Distance,* n.d. (1979.81); *A Moment in Dinglewood,* 1979 (1979.86); *Untitled (Landscape),* n.d. (1980.58); *G.I.'s in Columbus Airport,* n.d. (1981.2); *Assignation,* 1981 (1984.43), and *Untitled,* n.d (1991.3).

3. T. S. Eliot, "Burnt Norton," *Four Quartets* (New York and London: Harcourt Brace Jovanovich, 1971), 17.

CAT. 95

1. Connell, 10.

2. Ibid., 38.

3. The artist's web site, between December 12, 2001, and January 5, 2002. http://www.bobartlettart.com.

CAT. 96

1. Berman.

2. Heller and Heller, 312.

3. Kessler, 12.

4. William J. Ergeran Jr., "Reflections on Lyrical Power: A Kohlmeyer Study," in Kessler, 27.

5. Besides Kohlmeyer's *Composition 96-31A* and *Passage No. 2* (ca. 1962), the museum owns a polychrome welded aluminum sculpture, *Slanted No. 3* (1993). Another painting, *Untitled* (ca. 1975–80), is a promised gift from Mr. and Mrs. Clarke Prather, Atlanta.

CAT. 97

1. Artist's statement to Brigitte Foley, collection files, Columbus Museum.

2. Ibid.

CAT. 98

1. Stein, 6. For additional biographical information, see Katz.

2. Ratcliff, n.p.

3. Nadelman, 175.

CAT. 99

1. Mann, 26

2. Ibid.

3. Dannatt and Assael, 36.

CAT. 100

1. Much of the biographical materials have been supplied by Chihuly Studios. Also see Chihuly Studios; Rose and Lanzone, *Chihuly*; Rose and Lanzone, *Chihuly Projects;* and Rose, Roberts, and McDonnell.

CAT. 101

1. Much of the biographical information is drawn from Spring.

2. This group included Jane Wilson, Allan Kaprow, Richard Stankiewicz, John Chamberlain, Lucas Samaras, George Segal, and Robert Whitman. The group's name paid homage to Hans Hofmann.

3. Wolf Kahn, "Notes 1990–1991," in *Wolf Kahn: New Landscape Paintings,* n.p. In *Wolf Kahn, New Paintings,* n.p., Kahn states that the "use of color, especially bright color, requires the strict exercise of tact and decorum. . . . Art must not be allowed to degenerate into stroking."

4. Gruber, *Wolf Kahn,* 4.

5. The museum also owns the 2001 pastel study for this painting, titled *Three Barns in a Row* (2001.23.2), and two 1991 monotypes, *Last Glow II* (95.15.1) and *Looking East of Dusk* (95.15.2).

BIBLIOGRAPHY

Adams, George, and Les Reker. *Abstract Expressionism and the New American Realism: Paintings by Jack Beal and Philip Pearlstein*. Columbus, Ga.: Columbus Museum, 2001.

Albrecht, Donald, Beatriz Colomina, Joseph Giovannini, Alan Lightman, Helene Lipstadt, Philip Morrison, Phylis Morrison. *The Work of Charles and Ray Eames: A Legacy of Invention*. New York: Harry N. Abrams in association with the [illegible] Vitra Design Mu[illegible], 1997.

Allara, Pamela. *Pictures of People: Alice Neel's American Portrait Gallery*. Hanover, N.H.: University Press of New England, 1998.

"Alma W. Thomas." exh. bro. New York: Whitney Museum of American Art, 1972.

American Painting: Philadelphia Collection III. Philadelphia: Frank Schwarz & Son, 1989.

American Painting Collection of Sheldon Memorial Art Gallery. Lincoln: University of Nebraska Press, 1988.

Andrus, Lisa Fellows. "Design and Measurement in Luminist Art." In *American Light: The Luminist Movement, 1850–1875*. Washington, D.C.: National Gallery of Art and Princeton University Press, 1989.

"Angela Gregory: A Sculptor's Life." Exh. bro. New Orleans: Newcomb College, 1981.

Arnason, H. H. *Robert Motherwell*. New York: Harry N. Abrams, 1982.

Aronson, Joseph. *The Encyclopedia of Furniture*. New York: Crown, 1965.

Arthur, John. "Visionary Landscapes." American Artist 62, no. 672 (July 1998): 18–23.

Baigell, Matthew. *Oil Sketches by Albert Bierstadt, 1830–1902*. New York: Davis & Langdale, 1982.

Baker, Lamar. *Recollections of an Art Student*. New York: Vantage Press, 1990.

Baldaia, Peter J. "A Conversation with Dale Kennington." In *Encounters: Dale Kennington*, Huntsville, Ala.: Huntsville Museum of Art, 1997.

———. *Dale Kennington: The Realm of the Everyday*. Philadelphia: Claire Oliver Fine Art, 1998.

Baltimore Museum of Art. *Theodore Robinson, 1852–1896*. With an introduction by Sona Johnston. Baltimore: Baltimore Museum of Art, 1973.

Banks, William Nathaniel. "George Cooke, Painter of the American Scene," *Antiques* 102, no. 3 (September 1972): 448–54.

Barol, Bill. "Tucker Porcelain." *American Heritage* 40, no. 4 (1989).

Barquist, David L., and Charles Uht. *American Tables and Looking Glasses: In the Mabel Brady Garvan and Other Collections at Yale University*. New Haven, Conn.: Yale University Press, 1992.

Barratt, Carrie Rebora. *Queen Victoria and Thomas Sully*. Princeton, N.J.: Princeton University Press in association with Metropolitan Museum of Art, 2001.

Barton, William E. *Old Plantation Hymns*. Boston: Lamson and Wolff, 1899.

Baskin: Sculpture, Drawings, & Prints. New York: G. Braziller, 1970.

Baur, John I. H. *An American Genre Painter: Eastman Johnson, 1824–1906*. Brooklyn, N.Y.: Brooklyn Museum, 1940.

———. *Theodore Robinson, 1852–1896*. New York: Brooklyn Museum, 1946.

Baur, John I. H., and Lloyd Goodrich. *American Art of Our Century*. New York: Whitney Museum of American Art, 1961.

Beckerdite, Luke, ed. *American Furniture*. Milwaukee: The Chipstone Foundation, 2000.

Berardi, Marianne, and Henry Adams. *Under the Influence: The Students of Thomas Hart Benton*. St. Joseph, Mo.: Albrecht-Kemper Museum of Art, 1993.

Berman, Avis. "Interview with Ida Kohlmeyer." Archives of American Art, 1989.

Bernard, John, and Dorothy C. Miller, eds. *John B. Flannagan: Sculpture and Drawings, 1924–1938*. St. Paul: Minnesota Museum of Art, 1973.

Biddle, Edward, and Mantle Fielding. *The Life and Works of Thomas Sully*. New York: Kennedy Graphics, 1970.

Bjerkoe, Ethel Hall, and John Arthur Bjerkoe. *The Cabinetmakers of America*. Garden City, N.Y.: Doubleday, 1957; reprint. Exton, Penn.: Schiffer Ltd., 1978.

Black, Patti Carr. *Art in Mississippi*. Oxford, Miss.: Mississippi Historical Society, the Mississippi Department of Archives and History, and the University Press of Mississippi, 2002.

———, ed. *The Biloxi Art Pottery of George Ohr*. Jackson, Miss.: Department of Archives and History, 1978.

Bolin, Anne M. *The American Collection: Selected Works from the Norton Museum of Art Collection*. West Palm Beach, Fla.: Norton Museum of Art, 1995.

Bourdon, David. "Up Close and Impersonal." *Art in America* (May 1997).

Bowman, Russell. *Philip Pearlstein: The Complete Paintings*. New York: Alpine Fine Arts Collection, 1983.

Boyle, Richard J. *John Henry Twachtman: 1853–1902, an Exhibition of Paintings and Pastels*. New York: Spanierman Gallery, 1968.

———. *John Twachtman*. New York: Watson Guptill, 1979.

Bragg, Jean Moore, and Susan Saward. *The Newcomb Style: Newcomb College Arts & Crafts and Art Pottery Collector's Guide*. New Orleans: Jean Bragg Gallery, 2002.

Breeskin, Adelyn D. *Baltimore Furniture: The Work of Baltimore and Annapolis Cabinetmakers from 1760 to 1810*. Baltimore: Baltimore Museum of Art, 1947.

Brenson, Michael. "The Collages of Benny Andrews," *The New York Times*, November 4, 1988.

Brix, Maurice. *List of Philadelphia Silversmiths and Allied Artificers, 1682–1850*. Philadelphia: privately printed, 1920.

Brown, Milton W. *American Art*. New York: Harry N. Abrams, 1970.

———. *The Story of the Armory Show*. New York: Joseph Hirshhorn Foundation, 1963.

Browne, Pat, ed. *Heroines of Popular Culture*. Bowling Green, Ohio: Bowling Green University Popular Press, 1987.

Bundy, David, ed. *Painting in the South: 1564–1980*. Richmond: Virginia Museum, 1983.

Burke, Doreen Bolger. *J. Alden Weir: An American Impressionist*. Newark: University of Delaware Press, 1983.

Burlingham, Michael J. *Daniel E. Greene, N.A.: Auctions, Subways, and Still Lifes*. New York: Hollis Taggart Galleries, 2000.

Burroughs, Paul H. *Southern Antiques*. New York: Bonanza Books, 1967.

Butler, Charles T. *Body and Soul: Contemporary Southern Figures*. Columbus, Ga.: Columbus Museum, 1997.

———. *Thirty five Years Later: Bruno Zupan and the Columbus Museum*. Columbus, Ga.: Columbus Museum, 2000.

Butler, Charles T., Al Harris-Fernandez, Sylvia Yount, and Suzi Gablik. *Bo Bartlett*. Columbus, Ga.: Columbus Museum of Art, 2002.

Butler, Joseph, and Kathleen Eagen Johnson. *Field Guide to American Antique Furniture*. New York: Roundtable Press, Henry Holt, 1985.

Bye, Arthur Edwin. *Pots and Pans or Studies in Still Life Painting*. Princeton: Princeton University Press, 1921.

Campbell, Catherine. *The White Mountains: Place and Perceptions*. Hanover, N.H.: University Press of New England, 1980.

Campbell, Lawrence. "Reviews and Previews: Alice Neel." *ARTnews* 69 (November 1970): 24.

Cannell, Michael. "An Interview with Lee Krasner," *Art Magazine* 59, no. 1 (September 1984): 87–89.

Caplan, Ralph. *The Herman Miller Collection 1952*. New York: Acanthus Press, 1995.

Carlozzi, Annette, *Radcliffe Bailey*. Atlanta: Hammonds House Gallery, 1997.

Carlozzi, Annette, Julia Fenton, and Kathy Maschke. *Out of Bounds: New Work by Eight Southeast Artists*. Atlanta: Nexus Press, 1996.

Carlsen, Emil. "On Still-Life Painting." *Palette and Bench* 1 (October 1908): 6–8.

Carr, Carolyn Kinder, and George Gurney. *Revisiting the White City: American Art at the 1893 World's Fair*. Washington, D.C.: National Museum of American Art and National Portrait Gallery, Smithsonian Institution, 1993.

Catalogue of the 110th Annual Exhibition. Philadelphia: Pennsylvania Academy of the Fine Arts, 1915.

Cederwall, Sandraline, and Hal Riney. *Spratling Silver*. San Francisco: Chronicle Books, 2000.

Chambers, Bruce W. *Art and Artists of the South: The Robert P. Coggins Collection*. Columbia, S.C.: University of South Carolina Press, 1984.

———. *The World of David Gilmour Blythe (1815–1865)*. Washington, DC: Smithsonian Institution Press for the National Collection of Fine Arts, 1980.

Cheney, Martha Candler. *Modern Art in America*. New York: Whittlesey House, 1939.

Chihuly Studios. *Chihuly over Venice, Nuutajärvi, Finland: Part I, June 1995: Portfolio*. Seattle: Portland Press, 1995.

Chotner, Deborah, Lisa N. Peters, and Kathleen A. Pyne. *John Twachtman: Connecticut Landscapes*. Washington, D.C.: National Gallery of Art, 1989.

The City as a Source for Artists. New York: D. Wigmore Fine Art Inc., 2001.

Clark, Garth, Robert A. Ellison, Jr., Eugene Hecht. *The Mad Potter of Biloxi: The Art and Life of George E. Ohr*. New York: Abbeville Press, 1989.

Close, Timothy. *French and American Impressionism*. Albany, Ga.: Albany Museum of Art, 1996.

Comstock, Helen. *American Furniture: Seventeenth, Eighteenth, and Nineteenth Century Styles*. New York: Viking Press, 1962.

Conger, Clement E., and Alexandra W. Rollins. *Treasures of State: Fine and Decorative Arts in the Diplomatic Reception Rooms of the U.S. State Department*. New York: Harry N. Abrams, 1991.

A Connecticut Place: Weir Farm, An American Painter's Rural Retreat. Wilton, Conn.: Weir Farm Trust, 2000.

Connell, Martha Stamm. *Celebrating the Creative Spirit: Contemporary Southeastern Furniture*. Mobile, Ala.: Mobile Museum of Art, 1998.

Conner, Janis, and Joel Rosenkrantz. *Rediscoveries in American Sculpture, Studio Works, 1893–1939*. Austin: University of Texas Press, 1989.

Conrads, Margaret. *American Painting and Sculpture at the Sterling and Francine Clark Art Institute*. New York: Hudson Hills, 1990.

Cooke, Charles. "Descriptive Catalogue of Paintings in the Gallery of Daniel Pratt, Prattville, Alabama, Together with a Memoir of George Cooke, Artist." Pamphlet. Prattville, Ala. Self-published, 1853.

Cooke, Hereward Lester. *Lamar Dodd*. New York: Frank Rehn Gallery, 1973.

Counterpoints, American Art: 1930–1945. New York: Michael Rosenfeld Gallery, 1994.

Craven, Wayne. *American Art: History and Culture*. Madison, Wis.: Brown & Benchmark Publishers, 1994.

———. *Sculpture in America*. Rev. ed. New York: Cornwall Books, 1984.

Cummings, Abbott Lowell, ed. *Rural Household Inventories: Establishing the Names, Uses and Furnishings of Rooms in the Colonial New England Home 1675–1775*. Boston: Society for the Preservation of New England Antiquities, 1964.

Curtis, Penelope. *Sculpture 1900–1945: After Rodin*. Oxford History of Art. Oxford, New York: Oxford University Press, 1999.

Curtis, Phillip H. "Tucker Porcelain 1826–1838: A Reappraisal." Master's thesis, University of Delaware, Newark, 1972.

Dannatt, Adrian, and Steven Assael. "Painting the Fullness of Experience." *The Art Newspaper.Com* 13, no. 130 (November 2002): 36.

Davidson, Abraham A. *Early American Modernist Paintings, 1910–1935*. New York: De Capo Press, 1994.

Davidson, Jo. *Between Sittings*. New York: Dial Press, 1951.

Davis, Stuart. "Stuart Davis." *Parnassus* 12 (December 1940): 6.

De Jonge, Eric. "Tucker China, America's Porcelain." *Early American Life* 5, no. 6 (December 1974): 50–53, 83.

De Veer, Elizabeth, and Richard J. Boyle. *Sunlight and Shadow: The Life and Art of Willard L. Metcalf*. New York: Abbeville Press, 1988.

Deák, Gloria-Gilda. *Kennedy Galleries Profiles of American Artists*. 2d ed. New York: Kennedy Galleries, 1984.

Doherty, M. Stephen. "An Emphasis on Values: The Art and Teaching of Daniel Greene." *American Artist* 49 (October 1985): 52–57.

Dreishpoon, Douglas. *New York Realism: Past and Present*. Tampa: Tampa Museum of Art, 1995.

Dreiss, Joseph G. *Gari Melchers: His Works at Belmont*. Charlottesville: University of Virginia Press, 1984.

Driscoll, John Paul. *John Frederick Kensett: Drawings*. University Park: Pennsylvania State University, 1978.

Driscoll, John Paul, and John K. Howat. *John Frederick Kensett: An American Master*. New York: Norton & Company in association with the Worcester Art Museum, 1985.

Ducoff-Barone, Deborah. "Philadelphia Furniture Makers, 1800–1815." *Magazine Antiques* 145, no. 5 (May 1991).

Duncan, Michael, and Theodore F. Wolff. *Joyce Treiman*. New York: Hudson Hills Press, 1997.

Edwards, Ellen. "Roger Brown's Places in the Art." *Washington Post*, August 12, 1987, C1, C4.

Edwards, Lee M. *Domestic Bliss: Family Life in American Painting, 1840–1910*. Yonkers, N.Y.: Hudson River Museum, 1986.

———. "Noble Domesticity: The Paintings of Thomas Hovenden." *American Art Journal* 19, no. 1 (1987): 14–15.

Efird, Callie Huger, and Katherine Gross Farnham. *Georgia Collects American Silver, 1780–1870*. Atlanta: High Museum of Art, 1970.

Eiland, William U., and Lamar Dodd. *The Truth in Things: The Life and Career of Lamar Dodd*. Athens, Ga.: Georgia Museum of Art and University of Georgia Press, 1996.

Eldredge, Charles, William U. Eiland, and Charles T. Butler. *Tales from the Easel: Paintings from Southern Art Museums*. Athens, Ga.: University of Georgia Press, 2003.

Elzea, Rowland. *John Sloan's Oil Paintings: A Catalogue Raisonné*. Newark, Del.: University of Delaware Press, 1991.

Ensko, Stephen Guernsey Cook. *American Silversmiths and Their Marks IV*. Rev. ed. Boston: David R. Godine, 1989.

Exhibition of Americana. New York: Macbeth Galleries, 1939.

Fabian, Monroe H. *Mr. Sully: Portrait Painter*. Washington, D.C.: Smithsonian Institution Press, 1983.

Fales, Dean A., Jr. *The Furniture of Historic Deerfield*. New York: E. P. Dutton, 1976.

Fales, Martha Grandy. *Early American Silver*. New York: Excalibur Books, 1970.

Falk, Peter Hastings. *The Annual Exhibition Record of the Pennsylvania Academy of the Fine Arts, 1876–1913*. Madison, Conn.: Sound View Press, 1989.

Feld, Elizabeth, and Stuart P. Feld. *Of the Newest Fashion: Masterpieces of American Neoclassical Decorative Arts*. New York: Hirschl and Adler, 2001.

Fennimore, Donald L., and Richard T. Trump. "Joseph B. Barry, Philadelphia Cabinetmaker." *Magazine Antiques* 135, no. 5 (May 1989).

Fink, Lois Marie. *American Art in the Nineteenth-Century Paris Salons*. Cambridge and Washington, D.C.: National Museum of American Art, Smithsonian Institution; Cambridge and New York: Cambridge University Press, 1990.

Fisher, James Louis. "Xanthus Smith: Civil War Painter." Master's thesis, University of Delaware, Newark, 1982.

Flam, Jack *Motherwell*. Oxford: Phaidon Press, 1991.

Flanigan, J. Michael. *American Furniture from the Kaufman Collection*. Washington, D.C.: National Gallery of Art, 1986.

Fletcher, J. M. W. *Edward Willis Redfield, 1869–1965: An American Impressionist: His Paintings and the Man behind the Palette*. Lahaska, Pa.: JMWF Publishing, 1996.

Foley, Brigitte. *The Human Condition: Recent Work by Gary Chapman, Dale Kennington and Art Rosenbaum*. Columbus, Ga.: Columbus Museum, 2001.

Folk, Thomas. *The Pennsylvania Impressionists*. Cranbury, N.J.: Associated University Press, 1997.

Foreman, Benno. "Furniture for Dressing in Early America, 1650–1730." *Winterthur Portfolio* 22, nos. 2/3 (summer–autumn 1987): 149–64.

Fort, Ilene Susan. "American Social Surrealism." *Archives of American Art Journal* 22, no. 3 (1982): 8–20.

———. "James Guy: A Surreal Commentator." *Prospects* 12 (1987): 125–48.

Fort Wayne Museum of Art. *Alma W. Thomas: A Retrospective of the Paintings*. San Francisco: Pomegranate Press, 1998.

Foster, Kathleen. *Daniel Garber, 1880–1958*. Philadelphia: Pennsylvania Academy of the Fine Arts, 1980.

The Four Seasons: American Landscape Paintings. Columbus, Ga.: Columbus Museum, 1984.

Fox, Catherine. "Moulthrop's Bowls Get to Root of Nature's Beauty." *Atlanta Journal*, May 6, 1984.

Frankenstein, Alfred. *After the Hunt: William Harnett and Other American Still Life Painters, 1870–1900*. Rev. ed. Berkeley: University of California Press, 1969.

Frelinghuysen, Alice Cooney. *American Porcelain, 1770–1920*. New York: Harry N. Abrams for the Metropolitan Museum of Art, 1989.

French Impressionists Influence American Artists. Coral Gables, Fla.: Lowe Art Museum, University of Miami, 1971.

Gablik, Suzy. *Bo Bartlett*. New York: PPOW Gallery, 1998.

A Gallery Collects Peale. Philadelphia: Frank S. Schwarz & Son, 1987.

Gerdts, William H. *American Impressionism*. New York: Artabras, 1984.

———. *Pride in Place: Landscapes by The Eight in Southern Collections*. Albany, Ga.: Albany Museum of Art, 1999.

———. "The Square Format and Proto-Modernism in American Painting." *Arts* 50, no. 70 (June 1976): 70–75.

———. *William Glackens*. Fort Lauderdale, Fla.: Museum of Art; New York: Abbeville Press, 1996.

Gerdts, William H., Brian H. Peterson, and Sylvia Yount, *Pennsylvania Impressionism*. Bucks County, Pa., and Philadelphia: James A. Michener Art Museum, with University of Pennsylvania Press, 2002.

Gilkerson, Mary Bentz. "Augusta Museum Explores Southern Art." *(Columbia, South Carolina) State*, February 28, 1999, F4.

Glackens, Ira. *William Glackens and The Eight: The Artists Who Freed American Art*. Rev. ed. New York: Horizon House, 1984; Writers and Readers Publishing, 1990.

Glintenkamp, Hendrik. *A Wanderer in Woodcuts*. Self-published, 1932.

Gluhman, Joseph W. *Dale Kennington: Time and Place*. Dothan, Ala.: Wiregrass Museum of Art, 1994.

Goodrich, Lloyd. *H. E. Schnakenberg*. The American Artists Series. New York: Whitney Museum of American Art and the Macmillan Co., 1931.

Goodrich, Lloyd, and John I. H. Baur, *American Art of Our Century*. New York: Praeger and Whitney Museum of American Art, 1961.

Greenberg, Clement. "The New Sculpture." *Partisan Review* 6 (June 1949).

Greene, Jeffrey P. *American Furniture of the 18th Century*. Newtown, Conn.: Taunton Press, 1996.

Groce, George C., and David H. Wallace. *The New York Historical Society's Dictionary of Artists in America*. New Haven: Yale University Press, 1957.

Gruber, J. Richard. *American Icons: From Madison to Manhattan, the Art of Benny Andrews, 1948–1997*. Augusta, Ga.: Morris Museum of Art, 1997.

———. *William Christenberry: The Early Years, 1954–1968*. Tuscaloosa: University of Alabama Press in association with Morris Museum of Art, Augusta, Ga., 1996.

———. *Wolf Kahn: Painting the South*. Augusta, Ga.: Morris Museum of Art, 1999.

Gustafson, Eleanor H. "Museum Accessions." *Magazine Antiques* (March 1999).

Hale, John Douglass. *The Life and Creative Development of John H. Twachtman*. 2 vols., Ph.D. diss., Ohio State University, 1957; Ann Arbor: University Microfilms International, 1958.

Hale, John Douglass, Richard J. Boyle, and William H. Gerdts. *Twachtman in Gloucester: His Last Years, 1900–1902*. New York: Spanierman Gallery, 1987.

Hale, Nancy, and Fredson Bowers, eds. *Leon Kroll: A Spoken Memoir*. Charlottesville: University of Virginia Art Museum, 1983.

Harrisburg, Halley K. *Burgoyne Diller: The Third Dimension, Sculpture and Drawings, 1930–1965*. New York: Michael Rosenfeld Gallery, 1997.

———. *Pavel Tchelitchew: Nature Transformed*. New York: Michael Rosenfeld Gallery, 1993.

Hart, Charles Henry. "Thomas Sully's Register of Portraits, 1801–1871." *The Pennsylvania Magazine of History and Biography* 32, no. 4 (1908).

Havens, George R. "F. J. Waugh, America's Most Popular Marine Painter." *American Artist* (January 1967): 30–37.

———. *Frederick J. Waugh: American Marine Painter*. Orono, Maine: University of Maine Press, 1969.

Haverstock, Mary Sayre. *An American Bestiary*. New York: Harry N. Abrams, 1979.

Hecht, Eugene. *After the Fire, George Ohr: An American Genius*. Lambertville, N.J.: Arts and Crafts Quarterly Press, 1994.

Heller, Jules, and Nancy G. Heller. *North American Women Artists of the Twentieth Century*. New York: Garland Publishing, 1995.

Heller, Nancy. *Women Artists: Works from the National Museum of Women in the Arts*. New York: Rizzoli International Publications, 2000.

Hendricks, Gordon. *Albert Bierstadt: Painter of the American West*. New York: Harrison House, 1988.

Henkes, Robert. *American Women Painters of the 1930s and 1940s: The Lives and Work of Ten Artists*. Jefferson, N.C.: McFarland and Company, 1991.

Henri, Robert. *The Art Spirit*. New York: Harper and Row, 1923.

Hepplewhite, George. *The Cabinet-maker and Upholsterer's Guide and Repository of Designs for Every Article of Household Furniture*. London: 1788–90.

Hewitt, Benjamin A., Patricia E. Kane, and Gerald W. R. Ward. *The Work of Many Hands: Card Tables in Federal America, 1790–1820*. New Haven, Conn.: Yale University, 1982.

Hiesinger, Ulrich W. *Quiet Magic: The Still-Life Paintings of Emil Carlsen*. New York: Vance Jordan Fine Art, 1999.

Hills, Patricia. *Alice Neel*. New York: Harry N. Abrams, 1983.

———. *Stuart Davis*. New York: Harry N. Abrams, 1996.

Hirshorn, Anne Sue. "Anna Claypoole, Mary, and Sarah Miriam Peale: Modes of Accomplishment and Fortune." In Lillian B. Miller, ed., *The Peale Family: Creation of a Legacy*. New York: Abbeville Press, 1996.

Hoeber, Arthur. "Gari Melchers." *International Studio* 31 (March 1907).

Homer, William Innes. *Robert Henri and His Circle*. New York: Hacker Art Books, 1988.

Hood, Gary A. "Majesty in Motion." Exh. bro. Kansas City, Mo.: Smith-Kramer, n.d.

Hood, Graham. *American Silver: A History of Style, 1650–1900*. New York: Praeger, 1971.

Hoopes, Donelson F. *Randall Davey, Artist/Bon Vivant, A Retrospective Exhibition*. Santa Fe: Museum of Fine Arts, 1984.

Howat, John K. *John Frederick Kensett, 1816–1872*. New York: American Federation of the Arts, 1968.

Hughes, Edan Milton. *Artists in California, 1786–1940*. San Francisco: Hughes Publishing Company, 1989.

Hughes, Robert. *American Visions*. New York: Alfred A. Knopf, 1997.

Hunter, Wilbur H., and John Mahey. *Miss Sarah Miriam Peale, 1800–1885: Portraits and Still Life*. Baltimore: Peale Museum, 1967.

Irving, Washington. *The Alhambra*. 1832. Reprint. New York: The Macmillan Company, 1926.

Jaffe, Irma B. *The Sculpture of Leonard Baskin*. New York: Viking Press, 1980.

Jo Davidson Portrait Sculptor. Washington, D.C.: National Portrait Gallery, 1978.

John B. Flannagan: Sculpture and Drawings, 1924–1938. St. Paul: Minnesota Museum of Art, 1973.

Johnson, Ellen. "Kensett Revisited." *Art Quarterly* 20, no. 2, 1967.

Johnston, Phillip M. *Catalogue of American Silver: Cleveland Museum of Art*. Bloomington: Indiana University Press, 1994.

Joosse, Barbara. "Tom Uttech: Retreat to Reality." *Porcupine Literary Arts Magazine* 5, no. 2 (May 2001).

Kahan, Mitchell. "William Christenberry's Southern Wall." Montgomery Museum of Fine Arts newsletter, May 1989.

Kahn, Wolf. *Wolf Kahn: New Landscape Paintings and Pastels*. Charlotte, N.C.: Gerald Melberg Gallery, 1991.

Kalinovska, Milena. *William Christenberry: Changing Landscape—The Source Revisited*. Washington, D.C.: Kreeger Museum, 2001.

Kammen, Michael. *Robert Gwathmey: The Life and Art of a Passionate Observer.* Chapel Hill, N.C.: University of North Carolina Press, 1999.
Kane, Marie Louise. *A Bright Oasis: The Paintings of Richard E. Miller.* New York: Jordan-Volpe Gallery, 1997.
Karpiscak, Adeline Lee. *Ernest Lawson 1873–1939.* Tucson: University of Arizona Museum of Art, 1979.
Katz, Vincent. *Janet Fish: Paintings.* New York: Harry N. Abrams, 2002.
Kemp, John R. "Belles of the Bayou." *Art & Antiques* 25, no. 5 (May 2002): 52–55.
Kent, Norman. *Drawings by American Artists.* New York: Bonanza Books, 1968.
Keown, Ian. "Turner Classics." *Worth Magazine*, December/January 2001.
Kern, Steven, and Anne E. Dawson. "'The Renoir Americans Loved." *Magazine Antiques* 162, no. 2 (August 2002).
Kessler, Jane Q. *Ida Kohlmeyer: Thirty Years.* Charlotte, N.C.: Mint Museum of Art, 1983.
Keyes, Donald D. *American Impressionism in Georgia Collections.* Athens, Ga.: Georgia Museum of Art, University of Georgia, 1993.
———. "American Paintings in Georgia Collections." *American Art Review* 11, no. 1 (January/February 1999): 178–89.
———. *Andrée Ruellan.* Athens, Ga.: Georgia Museum of Art, University of Georgia, 1993.
———. *George Cooke: 1793–1849.* Athens, Ga.: Georgia Museum of Art, University of Georgia, 1991.
Keyes, Donald D., and Heidi Domescik. *Before 1948: American Paintings in Georgia Collections.* Athens, Ga.: Georgia Museum of Art, University of Georgia, 1998.
Kinder, Carolyn, and Margaret Christman. *Gaston Lachaise Portrait Sculpture.* Washington, D.C.: National Portrait Gallery, Smithsonian Institution, 1985.
King, Anne. *A Shared Vision: The Life and Art of Lamar Dodd.* LaGrange, Ga.: Lamar Dodd Art Center, LaGrange College, and Chattahoochee Valley Art Museum, 1996.
Kingman, Lee, Joanna Foster, and Ruth Giles Lontoft, comps. *Illustrators of Children's Books, 1957–1966.* Boston: Horn Book, 1968.
Kirkham, Pat. *Charles and Ray Eames: Designers of the Twentieth Century.* Cambridge, Mass.: MIT Press, 1995.
Kloss, William, and Virginia Mecklenburg. *Modern American Realism: The Sara Roby Foundation Collection.* Washington, D.C.: National Museum of American Art, Smithsonian Institution, 1988.
Knowlton, Helen M. *Art-Life of William Morris Hunt.* 1899. Reprint. New York: Benjamin Blom, 1971.
Kornhauser, Elizabeth Mankin. *American Paintings before 1945 in the Wadsworth Atheneum.* vol. 2. New Haven, Conn.: Yale University Press, 1996.
Kramer, Hilton, ed. *The Sculpture of Gaston Lachaise.* New York: Eakins Press, 1967.
Kraushaar Galleries. *John Sloan: The Gloucester Years.* New York: Kraushaar Galleries, 1994.
Kraushaar Galleries and Columbus Museum. *Making Faces: A Selection of Portraits by John Sloan.* New York: Kraushaar Galleries, 2001.
Krumm, Jane. "Nancy Grossman and Ida Kohlmeyer: Artist to Artist," *Art Papers* 5, no. 3 (May/June 1981): 18.
Kushner, Robert. *Janet Fish.* New York: D. C. Moore Gallery, 2000.
"Lamar Dodd." Exh. bro. New York: Grand Central Moderns, 1965.
Landau, Ellen G., and Jeffrey D. Grove. *Lee Krasner: A Catalogue Raisonné.* New York: Harry N. Abrams, 1995.
Landgren, Marchal E., *The Late Landscapes of William Morris Hunt.* College Park: University of Maryland Art Gallery, 1976.
Larkin, Oliver W. *Art and Life in America.* Rev. ed. New York: Holt, Rinehart and Winston, 1960.
Larsen, Susan. *Burgoyne Diller: Collages.* New York: Michael Rosenfeld Gallery, 1999.
Larson, Philip. *Burgoyne Diller: Paintings, Sculptures, Drawings.* Minneapolis: Walker Art Center, 1972.
Laufer, Marilyn. "David Gilmour Blythe's *Land of Liberty:* Speculations on Immigration and the Body Politic of Mid-19th Century Urban America." Columbus Museum files, Columbus, Ga., 1988.
Lawson, Karol. *Local Wonders: Treasures of American Art in Columbus Collections.* Columbus, Ga.: Columbus Museum, 1994.
———. "Nobody Knows the Trouble I've Seen: The Prints and Paintings of Lamar Baker." Columbus, Ga.: Columbus Museum, 1996.
Leach, Mark Richard. "Radcliffe Bailey. ARTCurrents 2." Exh. bro. Charlotte, N.C.: Mint Museum, 1991.
Leeds, Valerie Ann. *My People: The Portraits of Robert Henri.* Orlando: Orlando Museum of Art, 1994.
———. *Leon Kroll Revisited.* New York: Gerald Peters Gallery, 1998.
———. *William Glackens: American Impressionist.* New York: Gerald Peters Gallery, 2003.
Leff, Sandra. *Henry Glintenkamp, 1887–1946: Ash Can Years to Expressionism, Paintings and Drawings, 1908–1939.* New York: Graham and Sons Gallery, 1981.
Lesko, Diane, and Esther Persson, eds. *Gari Melchers: A Retrospective Exhibition.* St. Petersburg, Fla.: Museum of Fine Arts, 1990.
Levin, Gail. *The Thyssen-Bornemisza Collection of Twentieth Century American Painting.* London: Sotheby's Publications by Philip Wilson Publishers, 1987.
Lewis-Hind, Henriette. *Gari Melchers: Painter.* New York: William Edwin Rudge, 1928.
Libin, Laurence. *American Musical Instruments in the Metropolitan Museum of Art.* New York: Norton & Company, 1985.
Littleton, Taylor D. *The Color of Silver: William Spratling, His Life and Art.* Baton Rouge: Louisiana State University Press, 2000.
Lunde, Karl. *Anuszkiewicz.* New York: Harry N. Abrams, 1977.
MacAdam, Barbara J. *Winter's Promise: Willard Metcalf in Cornish, New Hampshire, 1909–1920.* Hanover, N.H.: Hood Museum of Art, Dartmouth College, 1999.
———. "Willard Metcalf in Cornish, New Hampshire." *American Art Review* 6, no. 1 (1999).
MacCash, Douglas. *Ida Kohlmeyer, 1912–1997.* New Orleans: Arthur Rogers Gallery, 1997.
MacChesney, Clara T. "American Artists in Paris." *International Studio* 54 (November 1914).
Magic Realism: An American Response to Surrealism. Loretto, Pa.: Southern Alleghenies Museum of Art, 1999.
Mann, James. "Steven Assael: The Challenge of Realism." *American Arts Quarterly* 13, no. 1 (winter 1996): 22–30.
Mark, Joan. *The Silver Gringo: William Spratling and Taxco.* Albuquerque: University of New Mexico Press, 2000.
Martin, John H., ed. *The Making of a Modern City: Columbus, Georgia, 1827–1865.* Columbus, Ga.: Thos. Gilbert, 1874.
Maxwell, Douglass. *Steven Assael Paintings.* New York: Forum Gallery, 2003.
McCausland, Elizabeth. "Robert Gwathmey." *Magazine of Art* 39 (April 1946).
Merrill, Penny C. *William Spratling and the Mexican Silver Renaissance: Maestros de Plata.* San Antonio, Tex., and New York: San Antonio Art Museum with Harry N. Abrams, 2002.
Metropolitan Museum of Art. *The Last Summer's Work: Descriptive Catalogue of 38 Paintings Given to the MMA by Thomas Kensett.* New York: Metropolitan Museum of Art, 1874.
Miles, Ellen G. *American Paintings of the Eighteenth Century.* Washington, D.C.: National Gallery of Art, 1995.
Miller, Dorothy C. *The Sculpture of John B. Flannagan.* New York: Museum of Modern Art, 1942.
———, ed. *The Life and Work of David G. Blythe.* Pittsburgh: University of Pittsburgh Press, 1950.
Miller, Lillian B., ed. *The Peale Family: Creation of a Legacy.* New York: Abbeville Press, 1996.
Milroy, Elizabeth. *Painters of a New Century: The Eight and American Art.* Milwaukee: Milwaukee Art Museum, 1991.
Moffat, Frederick. *The James M. Cowan Collection: A Catalogue.* Nashville: Parthenon, 1982.
Monkhouse, Christopher P., and Thomas S. Michie. *American Furniture in Pendleton House.* Providence, R.I.: Museum of Art, Rhode Island School of Design, 1986.
Montgomery, Charles F. *American Furniture: The Federal Period.* New York: Viking Press, 1966.
Moos, David. *Radcliffe Bailey: The Magic City.* Birmingham, Ala.: Birmingham Museum of Art, 2000.
More, Charles. *Bo Bartlett: Paintings and Drawings, 1983–1985.* Philadelphia: More Gallery, 1985.
Morgan, Robert. "Nancy Grossman: Opus Volcanus." *Sculpture Magazine* 17, no. 6 (July/August 1998): 36–41.
Munro, Eleanor. *Originals: American Women Artists.* New York: Simon and Schuster, 1979.
Nadelman, Cynthia. "Forbidden Fruit." *ARTnews* 98, no. 9 (October 1999): 174–77.
Neel, Alice, and Cindy Nesmer. *Alice Neel: The Woman and Her Work.* Athens, Ga.: Georgia Museum of Art, University of Georgia, 1975.
Nelson, Harold. *Sounding the Depths: 150 Years of American Seascape.* New York: American Federation of Arts, 1991.
Neubert, George, Norman Geske, and Daphne Deeds. *The American Painting Collection of Sheldon Memorial Art Gallery.* Lincoln, Neb.: University of Nebraska Press, 1988.
Newbold, William Romaine. *Newbold Family and Connections.* Philadelphia: Genealogical Society of Pennsylvania, 1928.
Nordland, Gerald. *Gaston Lachaise: The Man and His Work.* New York: George Braziller, 1974.
Novak, Barbara. *American Painting of the Nineteenth Century: Realism, Idealism, and the American Experience.* 2d ed. New York: Harper and Row, 1979.
———. *Nature and Culture: American Landscape and Painting, 1825–1875.* Rev. ed. New York: Oxford University Press, 1995.
Nutting, Wallace. *Furniture Treasury.* New York: Macmillan Company, 1948.
O'Connor, Francis V. *Diller: The 1930s, Cubism to Abstraction.* New York: Michael Rosenfeld Gallery, 2000.
Ohr, George. "Some Facts in the History of a Unique Personality." *Crockery and Glass Journal* 54 (December 1901).
Oresman, Janice C. *Gari Melchers, 1860–1932: American Painter.* New York: Graham Gallery, 1978.
Park, Lawrence. *Gilbert Stuart: An Illustrated Descriptive List of His Works.* New York, 1926.
Payson, John Whitney. *Leonard Baskin: Angels to the Jews.* New York: Midtown Payson Galleries, 1991.
Pearlstein, Philip. *Real, Really Real, Super Real.* San Antonio: San Antonio Museum Association, 1981.
Pennington, Estill Curtis. *A Southern Collection.* Augusta, Ga.: Morris Museum of Art, 1992.
———. *Subdued Hues: Mood and Scene in Southern Landscape Painting, 1865–1925.* Augusta, Ga.: Morris Museum of Art, 1999.
Perkins, Larry, and Donald Kuspit. *Red Rising: The Transcendent Paintings of Howard Thomas.* Gainesville, Fla.: Samuel P. Harn Museum, University of Florida, 1995.
Permanent Collection: Illustrated Checklist. Washington, D.C.: National Portrait Gallery, 1980.
Permanent Collection of Paintings Checklist. Pittsburgh: Department of Fine Arts Carnegie Institute, 1936.
Peters, Lisa N. *In the Sunlight: The Floral and Figurative Art of J. H. Twachtman.* New York: Spanierman Gallery, 1989.
Peters, Lisa N., and Carol Lowrey. *Hendrik Glintenkamp.* Spanierman Gallery Archives, New York.
Peters, Lisa N., and Judy Larson. *John Henry Twachtman: An American Impressionist.* Atlanta: High Museum of Art, 1999.

Phagan, Patricia, ed. *The American Scene and the South: Paintings and Works on Paper 1930–1946.* Athens, Ga.: Georgia Museum of Art, University of Georgia, 1996.
Piehl, Charles K. "Anonymous Heroines: Black Women as Heroic Types in Robert Gwathmey's Art." *Heroines of Popular Culture.* Ed. Pat Browne. Bowling Green, Ohio: Bowling Green State University Popular Press: 1987.
Piehl, Charles K., and Brigitte Foley. *Robert Gwathmey: Works from Southern Collections.* Columbus, Ga.: Columbus Museum, 1998.
Philadelphia: Three Centuries of American Art. Philadelphia: Philadelphia Museum of Art, 1976.
Phillips, Harlan. *Oral History Interview with Burgoyne Diller, Atlantic Highlands, New Jersey,* Archives of American Art, October 2, 1964.
Pierce, Patricia Jobe. *The Ten.* Concord, N.H.: Rumford Press, 1976.
Pisano, Ronald G. *A Leading Spirit in American Art: William Merritt Chase, 1849–1916.* Seattle: Henry Art Gallery, University of Washington, 1984.
Pisano, Ronald G., and Alice Grant Longwell. *Photographs from the William Merritt Chase Archives.* Southampton, N.Y.: Parrish Art Museum, 1992.
Platt, Charles, Jr. *Newbold Genealogy in America.* New Hope, Pa.: n.p., 1964.
Pleynet, Marcelin. *Robert Motherwell.* Trans. Mary Ann Caws. Paris: Edition Daniel Papierski, 1989.
Poesch, Jessie. *Newcomb Pottery: An Enterprise for Southern Women, 1895–1940.* Atglen, Pa.: Schiffer Publishing, 1984.
Pomeroy, Jordana. *Painting in a Lonely Arena: Joyce Treiman and the Old Masters.* Washington, D.C.: National Museum of Women in the Arts, 1998.
Priddy, Sumpter, III, J. Michael Flanigan, and Gregory R. Weidman. "The Genesis of Neoclassical Style in Baltimore Furniture." *American Furniture* 2000. Ed. Luke Beckerdite. Milwaukee: Chipstone Foundation, 2000.
Prime, Alfred Coxe. *The Arts & Crafts in Philadelphia, Maryland, and South Carolina.* 2 vols. 1929. Reprint. New York: Da Capo Press, 1969.
Private Realisms: American Painting, 1934–1949. New Haven, Conn.: Yale University, 2000.
Prokopoff, Stephen S., James K. Kettleworth, and Joan C. Siegfriend. *John Frederick Kensett: A Retrospective.* Saratoga Springs, N.Y.: Hathorn Gallery, Skidmore College, 1967.
Quick, Michael. *American Expatriate Painters of the Late Nineteenth Century.* Dayton, Ohio: Dayton Art Institute, 1976.
Quimby, Ian M. G. *American Silver at Winterthur.* Charlottesville, Va.: University Press of Virginia, 1995.
Ratcliff, Carter. *Janet Fish.* New York: Robert Miller Gallery, 1985.
Raven, Arlene. *Nancy Grossman.* New York: Hillwood Art Museum, C. W. Post Campus, Long Island University, 1991.
Reid, Richard. "Gari Melchers: An American Artist in Virginia." *Virginia Cavalcade* 28, no. 4 (spring 1979): 154–67.
Richardson, Edgar. *Charles Willson Peale and His World.* New York: Crowell, 1956.
Rifkin, Ned. *Equal Rights and Justice: Thirty Years and Beyond. Issues of Race and Ethnicity in American Art.* Atlanta: High Museum of Art, 1994.
Robert Beauchamp: An American Expressionist. Syracuse, N.Y.: Everson Museum of Art, 1984.
Robert Gwathmey: Works from Southern Collections. Essay by Charles K. Piehl. Columbus, Ga.: Columbus Museum, 1998.
Robert Vickrey. Tucson, Ariz.: Walker Lithograph, 1973.
Rockwell, Charles, ed. *The Catskill Mountains and the Regions Around.* New York: Taintor Brothers & Co., 1869.
Rose, Barbara. *Gaston Lachaise Sculpture.* New York: Salander–O'Reilly Galleries, 1991.
Rose, Barbara, and Dale M. Lanzone. *Chihuly.* Seattle: Portland Press, 2000.
———. *Chihuly Projects.* Seattle: Portland Press, 2000.
Rose, Barbara, Lisa C. Roberts, and Mark McDonnell. *Chihuly Gardens and Glass,* Seattle: Portland Press, 2002.
Rosenfeld, Michael. *Burgoyne Diller: The Third Dimension, Sculpture and Drawings, 1930–1965.* New York: Michael Rosenfeld Gallery, 1997.
Rubenstein, Charlotte Streifer. *American Women Artists.* New York: Avon, 1982.
———. *American Women Sculptors: A History of Women Working in Three Dimensions.* Boston: G. K. Hall, 1990.
Rudolph, Marilou A. "George Cooke and His Paintings." *Georgia Historical Society Quarterly* 44, no. 2 (June 1960): 117–53.
Russell, John. "Critic's Choice: Art." Review, *New York Times,* April 29, 1984.
Sacks, Israel. *The New Points of Early American Furniture.* New York: Crown Press, 1993.
Safford, Hildegard J. "William C. A. Frerichs, Artist, 1829–1905." *The Staten Island Historian* 31, no. 4, October–December 1970.
Safford, Hildegard J., and Williams, Benjamin F. *William C. A. Frerichs, 1829–1905.* Raleigh: North Carolina Museum of Art, 1974.
St. Johns, Bruce, ed. *John Sloan's New York Scene.* New York: Harper & Row, 1965.
Salander, Lawrence. *Stuart Davis: Major Late Paintings.* New York: Salander–O'Reilly Galleries, 2002.
Schmeckebier, Laurence E. *The Art of Henry A. Nordhausen.* Canaan, N.H.: Phoenix Publishing, 1980.
Scott, David. *John Sloan.* New York: Watson-Guptill Publications, 1975.
Sears, Clara Endicott. *Highlights Among the Hudson River Artists.* Port Washington, N.Y.: Kennikat Press, 1968.
Severens, Martha. *Greenville County Museum of Art: The Southern Collection.* New York: Hudson Hills Press in association with the Greenville County Museum of Art, 1995.
Shanes, Eric. *Jack Beal.* New York: Hudson Hills Press, 1993.
Shaw, Marjorie. *Thomas Hewes Hinckley: Artist to a Generation.* Milton, Mass.: Milton Historical Society, 1985.
Shearer, Thomas. *Designs for Household Furniture.* London: n.p., 1788.
Shearer, Thomas, and George Hepplewhite. *The Cabinet Makers' London Book of Prices.* London: n.p., 1788.
Sheraton, Thomas. *The Cabinet Maker and Upholsterer's Drawing Book.* London: 1802.
Simon, Janice. *Images of Contentment: John Frederick Kensett and the Connecticut Shore.* Waterbury, Vt.: Mattatuck Museum, 2001.
Sims, Lowery Stokes. *Stuart Davis: American Painter.* New York: Metropolitan Museum of Art, 1991.
———. *Loud Whispers.* New York: Michael Rosenfeld Gallery, 2000.
Sloan, John. *Gist of Art.* New York: Dover Publications, 1939.
Smith, George. *A Collection of Designs for Household Furniture and Interior Decoration.* 1808. Reprint. New York: Praeger, 1970.
Smith, Gregory W., and Steven W. Naifeh. *Jackson Pollack: An American Saga.* New York: Woodward/White, 1989.
Smith, Helen S. "Finding an Inner Beauty." *Atlanta Constitution.* September 4, 1979.
Smith, Xanthus, to Russell Smith (February 12, 1863). Xanthus Russell Smith Family Papers, Archives of American Art, Smithsonian Institution, reel 2035, frame 504.
Smith Family Papers, Archives of American Art, Smithsonian Institution, reel 2040, frame 9.
Soby, James Thrall. *Tchelitchew: Paintings and Drawings.* New York: Museum of Modern Art, 1942.
Spring, Justin. *Wolf Kahn.* New York: Harry N. Abrams, 1996.
Stein, Judith, *Janet Fish: Recent Paintings.* New York: D. C. Moore Gallery, 1998.
Stoneman, Vernon C. *John and Thomas Seymour: Cabinetmakers in Boston, 1794–1816.* Boston: Special Publications, 1959.
Surrealism Embodied: The Figure in American Art, 1933–1953. New York: Michael Rosenfeld Gallery, 1992.
Swan, M. "John Seymour & Son Cabinetmakers." *Magazine Antiques* 82 (1937).
Temkin, Ann, ed. *Alice Neel.* New York: Harry N. Abrams, 2000.
Tenth Annual Exhibition of Selected Paintings by American Artists. New York: Albright College, 1915.
Terenzio, Stephanie. *The Prints of Robert Motherwell.* New York: Hudson Hills Press, 1984.
Terhune, Anne Gregory, Sylvia Yount, and Maurice Frank Woods Jr. *Thomas Hovenden (1840–1895): American Painter of Hearth and Homeland.* Philadelphia: Woodmere Art Museum, 1995.
Thomas, Howard. "Sketchbook No. 14, 1955–1957." Georgia Museum of Art, University of Georgia, Athens.
Timpano, Anne. *A Select View: American Paintings from the Columbus Museum.* Columbus, Ga.: Columbus Museum, 1989.
Torchia, Robert. Correspondence for Xanthus Smith, May 20, 1999, Columbus Museum collection files.
Towards a New Century: Contemporary Art from the Permanent Collection. Columbus, Ga.: Columbus Museum, 1999.
Tracy, Berry B. *Federal Furniture and Decorative Arts at Boscobel.* New York: Harry N. Abrams, 1981.
Trump, Robert T. "Joseph B. Barry, Philadelphia Cabinetmaker." *Magazine Antiques* 107 (January 1975).
Trump, Robert T., and Donald L. Fennimore, "Joseph B. Barry, Philadelphia Cabinet Maker." *Magazine Antiques* 145 (May 1989).
Tucker China, 1825–1838. Philadelphia: Philadelphia Museum of Art, 1957.
Tully, Judd. "Benny Andrews." *American Artist* 52, no. 549 (April 1988).
———. *Daniel Greene: Pastels and Paintings.* New York: Gallery Henoch, 1985.
———. "Daniel Greene: Still Lifes That Don't Sit Still." In *Daniel Greene, Pastels and Paintings.* New York: Gallery Henoch, 1985.
Twenty-eighth Annual Exhibition of American Oil Paintings and Sculpture. Chicago: Art Institute of Chicago, 1915.
Tyler, Parker. *The Divine Comedy of Pavel Tchelitchew: A Biography.* New York: Fleet Publishing, 1967.
Uncommon Spirit: Sculpture in America, 1800–1940. New York: Hirschl and Adler, 1989.
Valentiner, W. R., ed. *Letters of John B. Flannagan.* New York: Curt Valentiner, 1942.
Vickrey, Robert. *Robert Vickrey: Artist at Work.* New York: Watson–Guptill, 1979.
Vigtel, Gudmund, ed. *Georgia Collects.* Atlanta: High Museum of Art, 1989.
Vigtel, Gudmund, William D. Paul Jr., and Lloyd Goodrich. *Lamar Dodd: A Retrospective Exhibition.* Athens, Ga.: University of Georgia Press, 1970.
Wallach, Alan. "Thomas Cole's River in the Catskills as Antipastoral." *Art Bulletin* 84, no. 2 (June 2002): 334–50.
Waltman, William. "Eastman Johnson, Painter." *Scribner's Magazine* 40 (1906).
Ward, Gerald W. R. *American Case Furniture in the Mabel Garvan and Other Collections at Yale University.* New Haven, Conn.: Yale University Art Museum, 1988.
———, ed. *American Furniture with Related Decorative Arts, 1660–1830: The Milwaukee Art Museum and the Layton Art Collection.* New York: Hudson Hills Press, 1992.
Ward, John L. *American Realist Painting, 1945–1980.* Ann Arbor, Mich.: UMI Press, 1989.
Webster, Sally. *William Morris Hunt.* Cambridge: Cambridge University Press, 1991.
Wechsler, Jeffrey. *Surrealism and American Art.* Boca Raton, Fla.: Boca Raton Museum of Art, 1997.
Weiss, Ila. *Poetic Landscape: The Art and Experience of Sanford R. Gifford.* Newark, Del.: University of Delaware Press, 1987.
Wessels, Glenn. "Surrealism." *Art Digest* (October 15, 1934).
Who Chicago? An Exhibition of Contemporary Imagists. Sunderland, U.K.: Ceolfrith Gallery, Sunderland Arts Centre, 1980.
Wightman, William M. *Life of William Capers, D.D. One of the Bishops of the Methodist Episcopal Church, South; Including an Autobiography.* Nashville: Southern Methodist Publishing House, 1859.
Wilkins, Karen, and Lewis Kachur. *The Drawings of Stuart Davis: The Amazing Continuity.* New York: American Federation of Arts and Harry N. Abrams, 1992.
William Morris Hunt on Painting and Drawing. New York: Dover Publications, 1976.
Williams, Benjamin F., and Hildegarde J. Safford. *William C. A. Frerichs, 1829–1905.* Raleigh, N.C.: North Carolina Museum of Art, 1974.

Wilmerding, John. *American Light: The Luminist Movement, 1850–1875.* Washington, D.C.: National Gallery of Art and Princeton University Press, 1989.

———. *The Art of John F. Peto and the Idea of Still life Painting in Nineteenth Century America.* New York: Harper & Row, 1983.

Wilson, Judith. "Alma Thomas: A One-Woman Art Movement." *Ms.* 7, no. 8 (September 1979): 59–61.

Winn, William, Frank Schnell, and Karol Lawson. *Building on a Legacy.* Ed. Charles T. Butler and Betsy Covington. Columbus, Ga.: Columbus Museum, 1996.

Wolff, Theodore. *Joyce Treiman.* New York: Hudson Hills Press, 1997.

Wolf Kahn: New Landscape Paintings and Pastels. Charlotte, N.C.: Gerald Melberg Gallery, 1991.

Wolf Kahn: New Paintings—Celebrating Color. New York: Grace Borgenicht Gallery, 1995.

Yanari, Sachi. *Alma W. Thomas: A Retrospective of the Paintings.* San Francisco: Pomegranate in association with Fort Wayne Museum of Art, 1998.

Yau, John. *Roger Brown.* New York: George Braziller in association with the Hirshhorn Museum and Sculpture Garden, Smithsonian Institution, 1987.

Young, Dorothy Weir. *The Life and Letters of J. Alden Weir.* New York: Kennedy Graphics, 1971.

Zellman, Michael David. "Realism vs. Existentialism." *Alan Frumkin Gallery Newsletter* 5 (spring 1978).

———, comp. *American Art Analogue.* 3 vols. New York: Chelsea House Publishers, 1986.

Zimmerman, Philip D., William H. Gerdts, Jennifer Faulds Goldsborough, and Roxanne M. Stanulis. *The Sewell C. Biggs Collection of American Art: A Catalogue.* Dover, Del.: Sewell C. Biggs Museum of American Art, 2002.

Zupan, Jane, and Bruno Zupan. *Bruno Zupan: One Artist.* Florence, Italy: Giorgi and Gambi, 2000.

INDEX OF ARTISTS

Alexander, Samuel: Sugar Urn, 24–25, cat. 6
Andrews, Benny: *The Oath*, 188–89, cat. 88
Anuszkiewicz, Richard: *Temple of Electric Turquoise*, 180–81, cat. 84
Assael, Steven: *Club Kids*, 210–11, cat. 99

Bailey, Radcliffe: *O Freedom Ova Me*, 194–95, cat. 91
Baker, Lamar: *Sinner, What You Gonna Do When the World's on Fire?* 142–43, cat. 65
Barry, Joseph B. (attributed to shop): Sideboard, 32–33, cat. 10
Bartlett, Bo: *Homecoming*, 200–201, cat. 94
Baskin, Leonard: *Sibyl with Crows*, 174–75, cat. 81
Beal, Jack: *Still-life with Chair and Self-Portrait*, 192–93, cat. 90
Beauchamp, Robert: 34–83, 178–79, cat. 83
Bierstadt, Albert: *Hunting in the White Mountains, New Hampshire*, 46–47, cat. 17
Blythe, David Gilmour: *Land of Liberty*, 48–49, cat. 18
Brown, Roger: *Trailer Park, Truck Stop*, 170–71, cat. 79

Carlsen, Emil: *Still Life*, 90–91, cat. 39
Chase, William Merritt: *My Daughter, Alice*, 78–79, cat. 33
Christenberry, William: *Columbus Wall*, 184–85, cat. 86
Chihuly, Dale: *Boat Installation*, 212–13, cat. 100
Cooke, George: *Mrs. Philip A. Clayton*, 44–45, cat. 16
Curran, Charles C.: *Self-Portrait*, 72–73, cat. 30

Davey, Randall: *Lady Wearing a Hat*, 100–101, cat. 44
Davidson, Jo: *Portrait Head of Gertrude Stein*, 108–9, cat. 48
Davis, Stuart: *Shapes of Landscape Space #3*, 132–33, cat. 60
Diller, Burgoyne: *Untitled (Wall Construction)*, 152–53, cat. 70
Dodd, Lamar: *Landscape with Haystacks and Hills*, 138–39, cat. 63

Eames, Charles, and Ray Kaiser Eames: Dining Chair with Wood Legs, 146–47, cat. 67

Fish, Janet: *Yellow Pad*, 208–9, cat. 98
Flannagan, John: *Mother Earth*, 114–15, cat. 51
Frerichs, William: *Mt. Toxaway from Lodge at High Hampton, N.C.*, 50–51, cat. 19

Garber, Daniel: *Gray Day, March*, 98–99, cat. 43
Gifford, Sanford: *A Home in the Woods*, 54–55, cat. 21
Glackens, William: *Nude with Red Hair*, 96–97, cat. 42
Glintenkamp, Hendrik: *Spanish Town, Alcalá de Guadaira*, 110–11, cat. 49
Greene, Daniel: *The Watchman*, 182–83, cat. 85
Gregory, Angela: *La Belle Augustine*, 118–19, cat. 53
Grossman, Nancy: *T.U.F.*, 168–69, cat. 78
Guy, James: *Venus on Sixth Avenue*, 128–29, cat. 58
Gwathmey, Robert: *Sunday Morning*, 148–49, cat. 68

Henri, Robert: *Fergus, Boy in Blue Jacket*, 116–17, cat. 52
Hinckley, Thomas Hewes: *Hanging Jack Snipe*, 58–59, cat. 23
Hovenden Thomas: *Contentment*, 66–67, cat. 27
Hunt, William Morris: *Governor's Creek, Florida*, 62–63, cat. 25

Johnson, Eastman: *The Earnest Pupil (The Fifers)*, 68–69, cat. 28
Jones, Hugh Bolton: *Berkshire Mountains (South Egremont, Massachusetts)*, 64–65, cat. 26

Kahn, Wolf: *Barns near a Pond*, 214–15, cat. 101
Kennington, Dale: *Cocktail Party*, 196–97, cat. 92
Kensett, John Frederick: *The Sea, Long Island Sound from Fish Island*, 60–61, cat. 24
Kohlmeyer, Ida: *Composition 96-31A*, 204–5, cat. 96
Krasner, Lee: *Still life*, 130–31, cat. 59
Kroll, Leon: *A Cove in Maine*, 120–21, cat. 54

Lachaise, Gaston: *Head of a Poet*, 112–13, cat. 50
Lawson, Ernest: *Trolleys in the Snow, New York*, 92–93, cat. 40
Lewis, Harvey: Six-piece Coffee and Tea Service, 34–35, cat. 11

MacMonnies, Frederick: *Diana*, 74–75, cat. 31
Mafong, Richard: Pi, 206–7, cat. 97
Marshall, Thomas W.: *Catskill Mountain House, Twin Lakes, Autumn*, 56–57, cat. 22
Melchers, Gari: *Kate Kendall (The Scarlet Jacket)*, 106–7, cat. 47
Metcalf, Willard: *The Thawing Brook*, 104–5, cat. 46
Miller, Richard: *La Toilette*, 102–3, cat. 45
Moore, William: Square Piano, 38–39, cat. 13
Motherwell, Robert: *Caprice #5*, 160–61, cat. 74; *Massive Image*, 186–87, cat. 87
Moulthrop, Edward: Bowl, 172–73, cat. 80

Neel, Alice: *Swedish Girls*, 166–67, cat. 77
Nordhausen, Henry: *Tying Her Ballet Slipper*, 158–59, cat. 73
Nutt, Craig: *Tomato Table*, 202–3, cat. 95

Ohr, George: Teapot, 76–77, cat. 32

Peale, Charles Willson: *Elizabeth Michael Snyder*, 18–19, cat. 3
Peale, Sarah Miriam: *Bishop William Capers*, 40–41, cat. 14
Pearlstein, Philip: *Zeppelin and Horses #1*, 198–99, cat. 93
Peto, John: *Table with a Whale Oil Lamp*, 80–81, cat. 34
Powers, Hiram: *Proserpine*, 42–43, cat. 15

Quirt, Walter: *Untitled (Surrealist Composition)*, 140–41, cat. 64

Redfield, Edward: *Road to Lambertville*, 124–25, cat. 56
Robinson, Theodore: *Nantucket*, 70–71, cat. 29
Ruellan, Andrée: *Children's Mardi Gras*, 150–51, cat. 69

Schnakenberg, Henry: *West Side*, 126–27, cat. 57
Seymour, John and Thomas (attributed to shop): Secretary and Bookcase, 22–23, cat. 5
Sloan, John: *Dorothy Hart, Green Dress*, 94–95, cat. 41
Smith, Xanthus: *Soldiers' Quarters at Hilton Head, South Carolina*, 52–53, cat. 20
Spratling, William: Coffee Service, 134–35, cat. 61
Stuart, Gilbert: *Mrs. Edward Stow*, 26–27, cat. 7
Sully, Thomas: *Mrs. Caleb Newbold and Her Son Thomas*, 30–31, cat. 9

Tchelitchew, Pavel: *Spahi*, 122–23, cat. 55
Thomas, Alma: *Air View of a Spring Nursery*, 164–65, cat. 76
Thomas, Howard: *White Mule*, 144–45, cat. 66
Treiman, Joyce: *The Torso, The Ram, Self-Portrait with Skull, The Smoker No. 21*, 176–77, cat. 82
Tucker, William Ellis, and Company: Vase-shaped Pitcher, 36–37, cat. 12
Twachtman, John Henry: *Horseneck Falls*, 84–85, cat. 36

Unknown Maker: Card Table, 20–21, cat. 4
Unknown Maker: Chest of Drawers, 14–15, cat. 1
Unknown Maker: Desk, 16–17, cat. 2
Unknown Maker: Pair of Card Tables, 28–29, cat. 8
Uttech, Tom: *Wegimind Akaii*, 190–91, cat. 89

Vickrey, Robert: *Woman Weeping*, 156–57, cat. 72

Waugh, Frederick Judd: *The Silver Sea*, 82–83, cat. 35
Weber, Max: *The Red Comb*, 136–37, cat. 62
Weir, J. Alden: *Pelham Lane*, 86–87, cat. 37
Wells, Sabina, with Joseph Meyer: Vase, 88–89, cat. 38

Zorach, William: *New Horizons*, 154–55, cat. 71
Zupan, Bruno: *Trees in Winter*, 162–63, cat. 75

The Columbus Museum
1251 Wynnton Road
Columbus, GA 31906
www.columbusmuseum.com

This publication is made possible by a generous grant from The John P. and Dorothy S. Illges Foundation.

Library of Congress Control Number: 2003110796
ISBN: 1-882650-16-6

Pages 2–3: Pavel Tchelitchew, *Spahi*, detail, 1931 (cat. 55)
Page 4: Benny Andrews, *The Oath*, detail, 1992 (cat. 88)
Page 7: Alice Neel, *Swedish Girls*, detail, 1968 (cat. 77)
Pages 12–13: Sanford Gifford, *A Home in the Woods*, detail, 1868 (cat. 21)

Edited by Norma Roberts
Proofread by Barbara R. McGill
Designed by Jeff Wincapaw
Typeset by Jennifer Sugden
Color separations by iocolor, Seattle
Produced by Marquand Books, Inc., Seattle
www.marquand.com
Printed and bound by CS Graphics Pte., Ltd., Singapore